MCAT®

GENERAL CHEMISTRY

2009–2010 EDITION

Related Titles

Kaplan MCAT Biology 2009-2010
Kaplan MCAT Organic Chemistry 2009-2010
Kaplan MCAT Physics 2009-2010
Kaplan MCAT Verbal Reasoning and Writing 2009-2010

MCAT

GENERAL CHEMISTRY

2009–2010 EDITION

The Staff of Kaplan

KAPLAN PUBLISHING

New York

Published by Kaplan Publishing, a division of Kaplan, Inc.
1 Liberty Plaza, 24th Floor
New York, NY 10006

Printed in the United States of America

10 9 8 7 6 5 4 3 2 1

ISBN: 978-1-4277-9873-2

Kaplan Publishing books are available at special quantity discounts to use for sales promotions, employee premiums, or educational purposes. Please email our Special Sales Department to order or for more information at kaplanpublishing@kaplan.com, or write to Kaplan Publishing, 1 Liberty Plaza, 24th Floor, New York, NY 10006.

Planet Friendly Publishing
✔ Made in the United States
✔ Printed on Recycled Paper
Learn more at www.greenedition.org
GREEN EDITION

- Manufacturing books in the United States ensures compliance with strict environmental laws and eliminates the need for international freight shipping, a major contributor to global air pollution. Printing on recycled paper helps minimize our consumption of trees, water and fossil fuels.
- Trees Saved: 31 • Air Emissions Eliminated: 2,697 pounds
- Water Saved: 11,138 gallons • Solid Waste Eliminated: 1,438 pounds

Contents

How to Use this Book

Kaplan MCAT General Chemistry, along with the other four books in our MCAT subject review series, brings the Kaplan classroom experience right into your home!

Kaplan has been preparing premeds for the MCAT for more than 40 years in our comprehensive courses. In the past 15 years alone, we've helped over 400,000 students prepare for this important exam and improve their chances of medical school admission.

TEACHER TIPS

Think of Kaplan's five MCAT subject books as having a private Kaplan teacher right by your side! We've created a team of the **top MCAT teachers in the country,** who have read through these comprehensive guides. In the sidebars of every page, they offer the same tips, advice, and test day insight that they offer in their Kaplan classroom.

Pay close attention to **Teacher Tip** sidebars like this:

> **TEACHER TIP**
> Know the shorthand notation for cells; it might not be spelled on out on the exam.

When you see them, you know what you're getting the same insight and knowledge that students in Kaplan MCAT classrooms across the country receive.

HIGH-YIELD MCAT REVIEW

At the end of several chapters, you'll find a special **High-Yield Questions** spread. These questions tackle the most frequently tested topics found on the MCAT. For each type of problem, you will be provided with a step-wise technique for solving the question and key directional points on how to solve for the MCAT specifically.

Included on each spread are two icons: the first, a sideways hand pointing toward equations, notes equations that you should memorize for the MCAT. The second, an open hand, indicates where in a problem you can stop without doing further calculation.

At the end of each topic you will find a "Takeaways" box, which gives a concise summary of the problem-solving approach, and a "Things to watch out for" box, which points out any caveats to the approach discussed above that usually lead to wrong answer choices. Finally, there is a "Similar Questions" box at the end so you can test your ability to apply the stepwise technique to analogous questions. You can find the answers in the Answers and Explanations section of this book.

We're confident that this guide, and our award-wining Kaplan teachers, can help you achieve your goals of MCAT success and admission into medical school!

Good luck!

EXPERT KAPLAN MCAT TEAM

Marilyn Engle

MCAT Master Teacher; Teacher Trainer; Kaplan National Teacher of the Year, 2006; Westwood Teacher of the Year, 2007; Westwood Trainer of the Year, 2007; Encino Trainer of the Tear, 2005

John Michael Linick

MCAT Teacher; Boulder Teacher of the Year, 2007; Summer Intensive Program Faculty Member

Dr. Glen Pearlstein

MCAT Master Teacher; Teacher Trainer; Westwood Teacher of the Year, 2006

Matthew B. Wilkinson

MCAT Teacher; Teacher Trainer; Lone Star Trainer of the Year, 2007

Introduction to the MCAT

THE MCAT

The Medical College Admission Test, affectionately known as the MCAT, is different from any other test you've encountered in your academic career. It's not like the knowledge-based exams from high school and college, whose emphasis was on memorizing and regurgitating information. Medical schools can assess your academic prowess by looking at your transcript. The MCAT isn't even like other standardized tests you may have taken, where the focus was on proving your general skills.

Medical schools use MCAT scores to assess whether you possess the foundation upon which to build a successful medical career. Though you certainly need to know the content to do well, the stress is on thought process, because the MCAT is above all else a thinking test. That's why it emphasizes reasoning, critical and analytical thinking, reading comprehension, data analysis, writing, and problem-solving skills.

The MCAT's power comes from its use as an indicator of your abilities. Good scores can open doors. Your power comes from preparation and mindset, because the key to MCAT success is knowing what you're up against. That's where this section of this book comes in. We'll explain the philosophy behind the test, review the sections one by one, show you sample questions, share some of Kaplan's proven methods, and clue you in to what the test makers are really after. You'll get a handle on the process, find a confident new perspective, and achieve your highest possible scores.

TEST TIP

The MCAT places more weight on your thought process. However you must have a strong hold of the required core knowledge. The MCAT may not be a perfect gauge of your abilities, but it is a relatively objective way to compare you with students from different backgrounds and undergraduate institutions.

ABOUT THE MCAT

Information about the MCAT CBT is included below. For the latest information about the MCAT, visit www.kaptest.com/mcat.

MCAT CBT

Format	U.S.—All administrations on computer
	International—Most on computer with limited paper and pencil in a few isolated areas
Essay Grading	One human and one computer grader
Breaks	Optional break between each section
Length of MCAT Day	Approximately 5.5 hours
Test Dates	Multiple dates in January, April, May, June, July, August, and September
	Total of 24 administrations each year.
Delivery of Results	Within 30 days. If scores are delayed notification will be posted online at www.aamc.org/mcat
	Electronic and paper
Security	Government-issued ID
	Electronic thumbprint
	Electronic signature verification
Testing Centers	Small computer testing sites

PLANNING FOR THE TEST

As you look toward your preparation for the MCAT consider the following advice:

Complete your core course requirements as soon as possible. Take a strategic eye to your schedule and get core requirements out of the way now.

Take the MCAT once. The MCAT is a notoriously grueling standardized exam that requires extensive preparation. It is longer than the graduate admissions exams for business school (GMAT, 3½ hours), law school (LSAT, 3¼ hours) and graduate school (GRE, 2½ hours). You do not want to take it twice. Plan and prepare accordingly.

KAPLAN EXCLUSIVE

Go online and sign up for a local Kaplan Pre-Med Edge event to get the latest information on the test.

THE ROLE OF THE MCAT IN ADMISSIONS

More and more people are applying to medical school and more and more people are taking the MCAT. It's important for you to recognize that while a high MCAT score is a critical component in getting admitted to top med schools, it's not the only factor. Medical school admissions officers weigh grades, interviews, MCAT scores, level of involvement in extracurricular activities, as well as personal essays.

In a Kaplan survey of 130 pre-med advisors, 84 percent called the interview a "very important" part of the admissions process, followed closely by college grades (83%) and MCAT scores (76%). Kaplan's college admissions consulting practice works with students on all these issues so they can position themselves as strongly as possible. In addition, the AAMC has made it clear that scores will continue to be valid for three years, and that the scoring of the computer-based MCAT will not differ from that of the paper and pencil version.

REGISTRATION

The only way to register for the MCAT is online. The registration site is: www.aamc.org/mcat.

You will be able to access the site approximately six months before your test date. Payment must be made by MasterCard or Visa.

Go to www.aamc.org/mcat/registration.htm and download *MCAT Essentials* for information about registration, fees, test administration, and preparation. For other questions, contact:

MCAT Care Team
Association of American Medical Colleges
Section for Applicant Assessment Services
2450 N. St., NW
Washington, DC 20037
www.aamc.org/mcat
Email: mcat@aamc.org

You will want to take the MCAT in the year prior to your planned start date. For example, if you want to start medical school in Fall 2010, you will need to take the MCAT and apply in 2009. Don't drag your feet gathering information. You'll need time not only to prepare and practice for the test, but also to get all your registration work done.

ANATOMY OF THE MCAT

Before mastering strategies, you need to know exactly what you're dealing with on the MCAT. Let's start with the basics: The MCAT is, among other things, an endurance test.

If you can't approach it with confidence and stamina, you'll quickly lose your composure. That's why it's so important that you take control of the test.

The MCAT consists of four timed sections: Physical Sciences, Verbal Reasoning, Writing Sample, and Biological Sciences. Later in this section we'll take an in-depth look at each MCAT section, including sample question types and specific test-smart hints, but here's a general overview, reflecting the order of the test sections and number of questions in each.

TEST TIP

The MCAT should be viewed just like any other part of your application: as an opportunity to show the medical schools who you are and what you can do. Take control of your MCAT experience.

Physical Sciences

Time	70 minutes
Format	• 52 multiple-choice questions: approximately 7–9 passages with 4–8 questions each • approximately 10 stand-alone questions (not passage-based)
What it tests	basic general chemistry concepts, basic physics concepts, analytical reasoning, data interpretation

Verbal Reasoning

Time	60 minutes
Format	• 40 multiple-choice questions: approximately 7 passages with 5–7 questions each
What it tests	critical reading

Writing Sample

Time	60 minutes
Format	• 2 essay questions (30 minutes per essay)
What it tests	critical thinking, intellectual organization, written communication skills

Biological Sciences

Time	70 minutes
Format	• 52 multiple-choice questions: approximately 7–9 passages with 4–8 questions each • approximately 10 stand-alone questions (not passage-based)
What it tests	basic biology concepts, basic organic chemistry concepts, analytical reasoning, data interpretation

The sections of the test always appear in the same order:

Physical Sciences

[optional 10-minute break]

Verbal Reasoning

[optional 10-minute break]

Writing Sample

[optional 10-minute break]

Biological Sciences

SCORING

Each MCAT section receives its own score. Physical Sciences, Verbal Reasoning, and Biological Sciences are each scored on a scale ranging from 1–15, with 15 as the highest. The Writing Sample essays are scored alphabetically on a scale ranging from J to T, with T as the highest. The two essays are each evaluated by two official readers, so four critiques combine to make the alphabetical score.

The number of multiple-choice questions that you answer correctly per section is your "raw score." Your raw score will then be converted to yield the "scaled score"—the one that will fall somewhere in that 1–15 range. These scaled scores are what are reported to medical schools as your MCAT scores. All multiple-choice questions are worth the same amount—one raw point—and *there's no penalty for guessing*. That means that *you should always select an answer for every question, whether you get to that question or not!* This is an important piece of advice, so pay it heed. Never let time run out on any section without selecting an answer for every question.

Your score report will tell you—and your potential medical schools—not only your scaled scores, but also the national mean score for each section, standard deviation, national scoring profile for each section, and your percentile ranking.

WHAT'S A GOOD SCORE?

There's no such thing as a cut-and-dry "good score." Much depends on the strength of the rest of your application (if your transcript is first rate, the pressure to strut your stuff on the MCAT isn't as intense) and on where you want to go to school (different schools have different score expectations). Here are a few interesting statistics:

TEST TIP

There's no penalty for a wrong answer on the MCAT, so NEVER LEAVE ANY QUESTION BLANK, even if you only have time for a wild guess.

TEST TIP

The percentile figure tells you how many other test takers scored at or below your level. In other words, a percentile figure of 80 means that 80 percent did as well or worse than you did, and that only 20 percent did better.

For each MCAT administration, the average scaled scores are approximately 8s for Physical Sciences, Verbal Reasoning, and Biological Sciences, and N for the Writing Sample. You need scores of at least 10–11s to be considered competitive by most medical schools, and if you're aiming for the top you've got to do even better, and score 12s and above.

You don't have to be perfect to do well. For instance, on the AAMC's Practice Test 5R, you could get as many as 10 questions wrong in Verbal Reasoning, 17 in Physical Sciences, and 16 in Biological Sciences and still score in the 80th percentile. To score in the 90th percentile, you could get as many as 7 wrong in Verbal Reasoning, 12 in Physical Sciences, and 12 in Biological Sciences. Even students who receive perfect scaled scores usually get a handful of questions wrong.

It's important to maximize your performance on every question. Just a few questions one way or the other can make a big difference in your scaled score. Here's a look at recent score profiles so you can get an idea of the shape of a typical score distribution.

Physical Sciences		
Scaled Score	Percent Achieving Score	Percentile Rank Range
15	0.1	99.9–99.9
14	1.2	98.7–99.8
13	2.5	96.2–98.6
12	5.1	91.1–96.1
11	7.2	83.9–91.0
10	12.1	71.8–83.8
9	12.9	58.9–71.1
8	16.5	42.4–58.5
7	16.7	25.7–42.3
6	13.0	12.7–25.6
5	7.9	04.8–12.6
4	3.3	01.5–04.7
3	1.3	00.2–01.4
2	0.1	00.1–00.1
1	0.0	00.0–00.0
Scaled Score Mean = 8.1 Standard Deviation = 2.32		

Verbal Reasoning		
Scaled Score	Percent Achieving Score	Percentile Rank Range
15	0.1	99.9–99.9
14	0.2	99.7–99.8
13	1.8	97.9–99.6
12	3.6	94.3–97.8
11	10.5	83.8–94.2
10	15.6	68.2–83.7
9	17.2	51.0–68.1
8	15.4	35.6–50.9
7	10.3	25.3–35.5
6	10.9	14.4–25.2
5	6.9	07.5–14.3
4	3.9	03.6–07.4
3	2.0	01.6–03.5
2	0.5	00.1–01.5
1	0.0	00.0–00.0
Scaled Score Mean = 8.0 Standard Deviation = 2.43		

TEST TIP

The raw score of each administration is converted to a scaled score. The conversion varies with administrations. Hence, the same raw score will not always give you the same scaled score.

Writing Sample		
Scaled Score	Percent Achieving Score	Percentile Rank Range
T	0.5	99.9–99.9
S	2.8	94.7–99.8
R	7.2	96.0–99.3
Q	14.2	91.0–95.9
P	9.7	81.2–90.9
O	17.9	64.0–81.1
N	14.7	47.1–63.9
M	18.8	30.4–47.0
L	9.5	21.2–30.3
K	3.6	13.5–21.1
J	1.2	06.8–13.4
		02.9–06.7
		00.9–02.8
		00.2–00.8
		00.0–00.1
75th Percentile = Q 50th Percentile = O 25th Percentile = M		

Biological Sciences		
Scaled Score	Percent Achieving Score	Percentile Rank Range
15	0.1	99.9–99.9
14	1.2	98.7–99.8
13	2.5	96.2–98.6
12	5.1	91.1–96.1
11	7.2	83.9–91.0
10	12.1	71.8–83.8
9	12.9	58.9–71.1
8	16.5	42.4–58.5
7	16.7	25.7–42.3
6	13.0	12.7–25.6
5	7.9	04.8–12.6
4	3.3	01.5–04.7
3	1.3	00.2–01.4
2	0.1	00.1–00.1
1	0.0	00.0–00.0
Scaled Score Mean = 8.2 Standard Deviation = 2.39		

WHAT THE MCAT REALLY TESTS

It's important to grasp not only the nuts and bolts of the MCAT, so you'll know *what* to do on Test Day, but also the underlying principles of the test so you'll know *why* you're doing what you're doing on Test Day. We'll cover the straightforward MCAT facts later. Now it's time to examine the heart and soul of the MCAT, to see what it's really about.

THE MYTH

Most people preparing for the MCAT fall prey to the myth that the MCAT is a straightforward science test. They think something like this:

"It covers the four years of science I had to take in school: biology, chemistry, physics, and organic chemistry. It even has equations. OK, so it has Verbal Reasoning and Writing, but those sections are just to see if we're literate, right? The important stuff is the science. After all, we're going to be doctors."

Well, here's the little secret no one seems to want you to know: The MCAT is not just a science test; it's also a thinking test. This means that the test is designed to let you demonstrate your thought process, not only your thought content.

The implications are vast. Once you shift your test-taking paradigm to match the MCAT modus operandi, you'll find a new level of confidence and control over the test. You'll begin to work with the nature of the MCAT rather than against it. You'll be more efficient and insightful as you prepare for the test, and you'll be more relaxed on Test Day. In fact, you'll be able to see the MCAT for what it is rather than for what it's dressed up to be. We want your Test Day to feel like a visit with a familiar friend instead of an awkward blind date.

THE ZEN OF MCAT

Medical schools do not need to rely on the MCAT to see what you already know. Admission committees can measure your subject-area proficiency using your undergraduate coursework and grades. Schools are most interested in the potential of your mind.

In recent years, many medical schools have shifted pedagogic focus away from an information-heavy curriculum to a concept-based curriculum. There is currently more emphasis placed on problem solving, holistic thinking, and cross-disciplinary study. Be careful not to dismiss this important point, figuring you'll wait to worry about academic trends until you're actually in medical school. This trend affects you right now, because it's reflected in the MCAT. Every good tool matches its task. In this case the tool is the test, used to measure you and other candidates, and the task is to quantify how likely it is that you'll succeed in medical school.

Your intellectual potential—how skillfully you annex new territory into your mental boundaries, how quickly you build "thought highways" between ideas, how confidently and creatively you solve problems—is far more important to admission committees than your ability to recite Young's modulus for every material known to man. The schools assume they can expand your knowledge base. They choose applicants carefully because expansive knowledge is not enough to succeed in medical school or in the profession. There's something more. It's this "something more" that the MCAT is trying to measure.

Every section on the MCAT tests essentially the same higher-order thinking skills: analytical reasoning, abstract thinking, and problem solving.

Most test takers get trapped into thinking they are being tested strictly about biology, chemistry, and so on. Thus, they approach each section with a new outlook on what's expected. This constant mental gear-shifting can be exhausting, not to mention counterproductive. Instead of perceiving the test as parsed into radically different sections, you need to maintain your focus on the underlying nature of the test: It's designed to test your thinking skills, not your information-recall skills. Each test section thus presents a variation on the same theme.

WHAT ABOUT THE SCIENCE?

With this perspective, you may be left asking these questions: "What about the science? What about the content? Don't I need to know the basics?" The answer is a resounding "Yes!" You must be fluent in the different languages of the test. You cannot do well on the MCAT if you don't know the basics of physics, general chemistry, biology, and organic chemistry. We recommend that you take one year each of biology, general chemistry, organic chemistry, and physics before taking the MCAT, and that you review the content in this book thoroughly. Knowing these basics is just the beginning of doing well on the MCAT. That's a shock to most test takers. They presume that once they recall or relearn their undergraduate science, they are ready to do battle against the MCAT. Wrong! They merely have directions to the battlefield. They lack what they need to beat the test: a copy of the test maker's battle plan!

You won't be drilled on facts and formulas on the MCAT. You'll need to demonstrate ability to reason based on ideas and concepts. The science questions are painted with a broad brush, testing your general understanding.

TAKE CONTROL: THE MCAT MINDSET

In addition to being a thinking test, as we've stressed, the MCAT is a standardized test. As such, it has its own consistent patterns and idiosyncrasies that can actually work in your favor. This is the key to why test preparation works. You have the opportunity to familiarize yourself with those consistent peculiarities, to adopt the proper test-taking mindset.

The following are some overriding principles of the MCAT mindset that will be covered in depth in the chapters to come:

- Read actively and critically.
- Translate prose into your own words.

TEST TIP

Don't think of the sections of the MCAT as unrelated timed pieces. Each is a variation on the same theme, because the underlying purpose of each section and of the test as a whole is to evaluate your thinking skills. Memorizing formulas won't boost your score. Understanding fundamental scientific principles will.

TEST TIP

Those perfectionist tendencies that make you a good student and a good medical-school candidate may work against you in MCAT Land. If you get stuck on a question or passage, move on. Perfectionism is for medical school—not the MCAT. You don't need to understand every word of a passage before you go on to the questions—what's tripping you up may not even be relevant to what you'll be asked.

- Save the toughest questions for last.

- Know the test and its components inside and out.

- Do MCAT-style problems in each topic area after you've reviewed it.

- Allow your confidence to build on itself.

- Take full-length practice tests a week or two before the test to break down the mystique of the real experience.

- Learn from your mistakes—get the most out of your practice tests.

- Look at the MCAT as a challenge, the first step in your medical career, rather than as an arbitrary obstacle.

That's what the MCAT mindset boils down to: Taking control. Being proactive. Being on top of the testing experience so that you can get as many points as you can as quickly and as easily as possible. Keep this in mind as you read and work through the material in this book and, of course, as you face the challenge on Test Day.

Now that you have a better idea of what the MCAT is all about, let's take a tour of the individual test sections. Although the underlying skills being tested are similar, each MCAT section requires that you call into play a different domain of knowledge. So, though we encourage you to think of the MCAT as a holistic and unified test, we also recognize that the test is segmented by discipline and that there are characteristics unique to each section. In the overviews, we'll review sample questions and answers and discuss section-specific strategies. For each of the sections—Verbal Reasoning, Physical/Biological Sciences, and the Writing Sample—we'll present you with the following:

- **The Big Picture**
  You'll get a clear view of the section and familiarize yourself with what it's really evaluating.

- **A Closer Look**
  You'll explore the types of questions that will appear and master the strategies you'll need to deal with them successfully.

- **Highlights**
  The key approaches to each section are outlined, for reinforcement and quick review.

TEST EXPERTISE

The first year of medical school is a frenzied experience for most students. In order to meet the requirements of a rigorous work schedule, students either learn to prioritize and budget their time or else fall hopelessly behind. It's no surprise, then, that the MCAT, the test specifically designed to predict success in the first year of medical school, is a high-speed, time-intensive test. It demands excellent time-management skills as well as that sine qua non of the successful physician—grace under pressure.

It's one thing to answer a Verbal Reasoning question correctly; it's quite another to answer several correctly in a limited time frame. The same goes for Physical and Biological Sciences—it's a whole new ballgame once you move from doing an individual passage at your leisure to handling a full section under actual timed conditions. You also need to budget your time for the Writing Sample, but this section isn't as time sensitive. When it comes to the multiple-choice sections, time pressure is a factor that affects virtually every test taker.

So when you're comfortable with the content of the test, your next challenge will be to take it to the next level—test expertise—which will enable you to manage the all-important time element of the test.

THE FIVE BASIC PRINCIPLES OF TEST EXPERTISE

On some tests, if a question seems particularly difficult you'll spend significantly more time on it, as you'll probably be given more points for correctly answering a hard question. Not so on the MCAT. Remember, every MCAT question, no matter how hard, is worth a single point. There's no partial credit or "A" for effort, and because there are so many questions to do in so little time, you'd be a fool to spend 10 minutes getting a point for a hard question and then not have time to get a couple of quick points from three easy questions later in the section.

Given this combination—limited time, all questions equal in weight—you've got to develop a way of handling the test sections to make sure you get as many points as you can as quickly and easily as you can. Here are the principles that will help you do that:

> **TEST TIP**
>
> For complete MCAT success, you've got to get as many correct answers as possible in the time you're allotted. Knowing the strategies is not enough. You have to perfect your time-management skills so that you get a chance to use those strategies on as many questions as possible.

> **TEST TIP**
>
> In order to meet the stringent time requirements of the MCAT, you have to cultivate the following elements of test expertise:
>
> - Feel free to skip questions.
> - Learn to recognize and seek out questions you can do.
> - Use a process of answer elimination.
> - Remain calm.
> - Keep track of time.

1. FEEL FREE TO SKIP AROUND

One of the most valuable strategies to help you finish the sections in time is to learn to recognize and deal first with the questions that are easier and more familiar to you. That means you must temporarily skip those that promise to be difficult and time-consuming, if you feel comfortable doing so. You can always come back to these at the end, and if you run out of time, you're much better off not getting to questions you may have had difficulty with, rather than not getting to potentially feasible material. Of course, because there's no guessing penalty, always put an answer to every question on the test, whether you get to it or not. (It's not practical to skip passages, so do those in order.)

This strategy is difficult for most test takers; we're conditioned to do things in order, but give it a try when you practice. Remember, if you do the test in the exact order given, you're letting the test makers control you. You control how you take this test. On the other hand, if skipping around goes against your moral fiber and makes you a nervous wreck— don't do it. Just be mindful of the clock, and don't get bogged down with the tough questions.

2. LEARN TO RECOGNIZE AND SEEK OUT QUESTIONS YOU CAN DO

Another thing to remember about managing the test sections is that MCAT questions and passages, unlike items on the SAT and other standardized tests, are not presented in order of difficulty. There's no rule that says you have to work through the sections in any particular order; in fact, the test makers scatter the easy and difficult questions throughout the section, in effect rewarding those who actually get to the end. Don't lose sight of what you're being tested for along with your reading and thinking skills: efficiency and cleverness.

Don't waste time on questions you can't do. We know that skipping a possibly tough question is easier said than done; we all have the natural instinct to plow through test sections in their given order, but it just doesn't pay off on the MCAT. The computer won't be impressed if you get the toughest question right. If you dig in your heels on a tough question, refusing to move on until you've cracked it, well, you're letting your ego get in the way of your test score. A test section (not to mention life itself) is too short to waste on lost causes.

> **TEST TIP**
>
> Every question is worth exactly one point, but questions vary dramatically in difficulty level. Given a shortage of time, work on easy questions and then move on to the hard ones.

TEST TIP

Don't let your ego sabotage your score. It isn't easy for some of us to give up on a tough, time-consuming question, but sometimes it's better to say "uncle." Remember, there's no point of honor at stake here, but there are MCAT points at stake.

3. USE A PROCESS OF ANSWER ELIMINATION

Using a process of elimination is another way to answer questions both quickly and effectively. There are two ways to get all the answers right on the MCAT. You either know all the right answers, or you know all the wrong answers. Because there are three times as many wrong answers, you should be able to eliminate some if not all of them. By doing so you either get to the correct response or increase your chances of guessing the correct response. You start out with a 25 percent chance of picking the right answer, and with each eliminated answer your odds go up. Eliminate one, and you'll have a 33⅓ percent chance of picking the right one, eliminate two, and you'll have a 50 percent chance, and, of course, eliminate three, and you'll have a 100 percent chance. Increase your efficiency by actually crossing out the wrong choices on the screen using the strikethrough feature. Remember to look for wrong-answer traps when you're eliminating. Some answers are designed to seduce you by distorting the correct answer.

4. REMAIN CALM

It's imperative that you remain calm and composed while working through a section. You can't allow yourself to become so rattled by one hard reading passage that it throws off your performance on the rest of the section. Expect to find at least one killer passage in every section, but remember, you won't be the only one to have trouble with it. The test is curved to take the tough material into account. Having trouble with a difficult question isn't going to ruin your score—but getting upset about it and letting it throw you off track will. When you understand that part of the test maker's goal is to reward those who keep their composure, you'll recognize the importance of not panicking when you run into challenging material.

5. KEEP TRACK OF TIME

Of course, the last thing you want to happen is to have time called on a particular section before you've gotten to half the questions. Therefore, it's essential that you pace yourself, keeping in mind the general guidelines for how long to spend on any individual question or passage. Have a sense of how long you have to do each question, so you know when you're exceeding the limit and should start to move faster.

So, when working on a section, always remember to keep track of time. Don't spend a wildly disproportionate amount of time on any one question or group of questions. Also, give yourself 30 seconds or so at the end of each section to fill in answers for any questions you haven't gotten to.

SECTION-SPECIFIC PACING

Let's now look at the section-specific timing requirements and some tips for meeting them. Keep in mind that the times per question or passage are only averages; there are bound to be some that take less time and some that take more. Try to stay balanced. Remember, too, that every question is of equal worth, so don't get hung up on any one. Think about it: If a question is so hard that it takes you a long time to answer it, chances are you may get it wrong anyway. In that case, you'd have nothing to show for your extra time but a lower score.

VERBAL REASONING

Allow yourself approximately eight to ten minutes per passage and respective questions. It may sound like a lot of time, but it goes quickly. Keep in mind that some passages are longer than others. On average, give yourself about three or four minutes to read and then four to six minutes for the questions.

PHYSICAL AND BIOLOGICAL SCIENCES

Averaging over each section, you'll have about one minute and 20 seconds per question. Some questions, of course, will take more time, some less. A science passage plus accompanying questions should take about eight to nine minutes, depending on how many questions there are. Stand-alone questions can take anywhere from a few seconds to a minute or more. Again, the rule is to do your best work first. Also, don't feel that you have to understand everything in a passage before you go on to the questions. You may not need that deep an understanding to answer questions, because a lot of information may be extraneous. You should overcome your perfectionism and use your time wisely.

WRITING SAMPLE

You have exactly 30 minutes for each essay. As mentioned in discussion of the seven-step approach to this section, you should allow approximately five minutes to prewrite the essay, 23 minutes to write the essay, and two minutes to proofread. It's important that you budget your time, so you don't get cut off.

COMPUTER-BASED TESTING STRATEGIES

ARRIVE AT THE TESTING CENTER EARLY

Get to the testing center early to jump-start your brain. However, if they allow you to begin your test early, decline.

TEST TIP

For Verbal Reasoning, here are some of the important time techniques to remember:

- Spend eight to ten minutes per passage
- Allow about three to four minutes to read and four to six minutes for the questions

TEST TIP

Some suggestions for maximizing your time on the science sections:

- Spend about eight to nine minutes per passage
- Maximize points by doing the questions you can do first
- Don't waste valuable time trying to understand extraneous material

USE THE MOUSE TO YOUR ADVANTAGE

If you are right-handed, practice using the mouse with your left hand for Test Day. This way, you'll increase speed by keeping the pencil in your right hand to write on your scratch paper. If you are left-handed, use your right hand for the mouse.

KNOW THE TUTORIAL BEFORE TEST DAY

You will save time on Test Day by knowing exactly how the test will work. Click through any tutorial pages and save time.

PRACTICE WITH SCRATCH PAPER

Going forward, always practice using scratch paper when solving questions because this is how you will do it on Test Day. Never write directly on a written test.

GET NEW SCRATCH PAPER

Between sections, get a new piece of scratch paper even if you only used part of the old one. This will maximize the available space for each section and minimize the likelihood of you running out of paper to write on.

REMEMBER YOU CAN ALWAYS GO BACK

Just because you finish a passage or move on, remember you can come back to questions about which you are uncertain. You have the "marking" option to your advantage. However, as a general rule minimize the amount of questions you mark or skip.

MARK INCOMPLETE WORK

If you need to go back to a question, clearly mark the work you've done on the scratch paper with the question number. This way, you will be able to find your work easily when you come back to tackle the question.

LOOK AWAY AT TIMES

Taking the test on computer leads to faster eye-muscle fatigue. Use the Kaplan strategy of looking at a distant object at regular intervals. This will keep you fresher at the end of the test.

PRACTICE ON THE COMPUTER

This is the most critical aspect of adapting to computer-based testing. Like anything else, in order to perform well on computer-based tests you must practice. Spend time reading passages and answering questions on the computer. You often will have to scroll when reading passages.

Part I
Subject Review

CHAPTER 1

ATOMIC STRUCTURE

Chemistry is the study of the nature and behavior of matter. The **atom** is the basic building block of matter, representing the smallest unit of a chemical element. An atom in turn is composed of subatomic particles called **protons, neutrons,** and **electrons.** The protons and neutrons in an atom form the **nucleus,** the core of the atom. The electrons exist outside the nucleus in characteristic regions of space called **orbitals.** All atoms of an **element** show similar chemical properties and cannot be further broken down by chemical means.

TEACHER TIP

The building blocks of the atom are also the building blocks of knowledge for the General Chemistry on the MCAT. Understand these interactions well.

SUBATOMIC PARTICLES

A. PROTONS

Protons carry a single positive charge and have a mass of approximately one **atomic mass unit** or amu. The **atomic number** (Z) of an element equals the number of protons found in an atom of that element. All atoms of a given element have the same atomic number.

B. NEUTRONS

Neutrons carry no charge and have a mass only slightly larger than that of protons. Different **isotopes** of one element have different numbers of neutrons but the same number of protons. The **mass number** of an atom is equal to the total number of protons and neutrons. The convention $_Z^A X$ is used to show both the atomic number and mass number of an X atom, where Z is the atomic number and A is the mass number.

C. ELECTRONS

Electrons carry a charge equal in magnitude but opposite in sign to that of protons. An electron has a very small mass, approximately 1/1,837th the mass of a proton or neutron, which is negligible for most purposes. The electrons farthest from the nucleus are known as **valence electrons.** The farther the valence electrons are from the nucleus, the weaker the attractive force of the positively charged nucleus and the more likely the valence electrons are to be influenced by other atoms. Generally, the valence electrons and their activity determine the reactivity of an atom. In a neutral atom, the number of electrons is equal to the number of protons. A positive or negative charge on an atom is due to a loss or gain of electrons; the result is called an **ion.**

Some basic features of the three subatomic particles are shown in the table below.

Table 1.1

Subatomic Particle	Symbol	Relative Mass	Charge	Location
Proton	$_1^1H$	1	+1	Nucleus
Neutron	$_0^1n$	1	0	Nucleus
Electron	e	0	–1	Electron Orbitals

Example: Determine the number of protons, neutrons, and electrons in a nickel-58 atom and in a nickel-60 2+ cation.

Solution: ^{58}Ni has an atomic number of 28 and a mass number of 58. Therefore, ^{58}Ni will have 28 protons, 28 electrons, and 58 – 28, or 30, neutrons.

In the $^{60}Ni^{2+}$ species, the number of protons is the same as in the neutral ^{58}Ni atom. However, $^{60}Ni^{2+}$ has a positive charge because it has lost two electrons and thus, Ni^{2+} will have 26 electrons. Also the mass number is 2 units higher than for the ^{58}Ni atom, and this difference in mass must be due to 2 extra neutrons, thus it has a total of 32 neutrons.

ATOMIC WEIGHTS AND ISOTOPES

A. ATOMIC WEIGHTS

The atomic mass of an atom is the relative mass of that atom compared with the mass of a carbon-12 atom, which is used as a standard with an assigned mass of 12.000. Atomic masses are expressed in terms of atomic mass units (amu), with one amu defined as exactly one-twelfth the mass of the carbon-12 atom, approximately 1.66×10^{-24} grams (g). A more common convention used to define the mass of an atom is **atomic weight.** The atomic weight is the weight in grams of one mole (mol) of a given element and is expressed in terms of g/mol. A mole is a unit used to count particles and is represented by **Avogadro's number,** 6.022×10^{23} particles. For example, the atomic weight of carbon is 12.0 g/mol, which means that 6.022×10^{23} carbon atoms weigh 12.0 g (see chapter 4, Compounds and Stoichiometry).

B. ISOTOPES

For a given element, multiple species of atoms with the same number of protons (same atomic number) but different numbers of neutrons (different mass numbers) exist; these are called **isotopes** of the element. Isotopes are referred to either by the convention described above or, more commonly, by the name of the element followed by the mass number. For example, carbon-12 ($^{12}_{6}C$) is a carbon atom with 6 protons and 6 neutrons, while carbon-14 ($^{14}_{6}C$) is a carbon atom with 6 protons and 8 neutrons. Because isotopes have the same number of protons and electrons, they generally exhibit the same chemical properties.

In nature, almost all elements exist as a collection of two or more isotopes, and these isotopes are usually present in the same proportions in any sample of a naturally occurring element. The presence of these isotopes accounts for the fact that the accepted atomic weight for most elements is not a whole number. The masses listed in the periodic table are weighted averages that account for the relative abundance of various isotopes.

Example: Element Q consists of three different isotopes, A, B, and C. Isotope A has an atomic mass of 40.00 amu and accounts for 60.00 percent of naturally occurring Q. The atomic mass of isotope B is 44.00 amu and accounts for 25.00 percent of Q. Finally, isotope C has an atomic mass of 41.00 amu and a natural abundance of 15.00 percent. What is the atomic weight of element Q?

Solution: 0.60(40 amu) + 0.25(44 amu) + 0.15(41 amu) = 24.00 amu + 11.00 amu + 6.15 amu = 41.15 amu

The atomic weight of element Q is 41.15 g/mol.

BOHR'S MODEL OF THE HYDROGEN ATOM

In 1911, Ernest Rutherford provided experimental evidence that an atom has a dense, positively charged nucleus that accounts for only a small portion of the volume of the atom. In 1900, Max Planck developed the first quantum theory, proposing that energy emitted as electromagnetic radiation from matter comes in discrete bundles called quanta. The energy value of a quantum is given by the equation E = hf where h is a proportionality constant known as Planck's constant, equal to 6.626×10^{-34} J•s, and f (sometimes designated v) is the frequency of the radiation.

A. THE BOHR MODEL

In 1913, Niels Bohr used the work of Rutherford and Planck to develop his model of the electronic structure of the hydrogen atom. Starting from Rutherford's findings, Bohr assumed that the hydrogen atom consisted of a central proton around which an electron travelled in a circular orbit, and that the centripetal force acting on the electron as it revolved around the nucleus was the electrical force between the positively charged proton and the negatively charged electron.

Bohr's model used the quantum theory of Planck in conjunction with concepts from classical physics. In classical mechanics, an object, such as an electron, revolving in a circle may assume an infinite number of values for its radius and velocity. Therefore, the angular momentum (L = mvr) and kinetic energy (KE = $mv^2/2$) can take on any value. However, by incorporating Planck's quantum theory into his model, Bohr placed conditions on the value of the angular momentum. Like Planck's energy, the angular momentum of an electron is quantized according to the following equation:

$$\text{angular momentum} = n\text{h}/2\pi$$

where h is Planck's constant and n is a quantum number that can be any positive integer. As h, 2, and π are constants, the angular momentum changes only in discrete amounts with respect to the quantum number, n. Bohr then equated the allowed values of the angular momentum to the energy of the electron. He obtained the following equation:

$$\text{E} = -\text{R}_\text{H}/n^2$$

where R_H is an experimentally determined constant (known as the Rydberg constant) equal to 2.18×10^{-18} J/electron. Therefore, like angular momentum, the energy of the electron changes in discrete amounts with respect to the quantum number.

A value of zero energy was assigned to the state in which the proton and electron were separated completely, meaning that there was no attractive force between them. Therefore, the electron in any of its quantized states in the atom would have a negative energy as a result of the attractive

TEACHER TIP

When you see a formula in your review or on Test Day, focus on ratios and relationships rather than the equation as a whole. This simplifies your "calculations" to a conceptual understanding and oftentimes still gets you the right answer.

TEACHER TIP

At first glance it may not be clear that the energy (E) is directly proportional to the principle quantum number (n). Take note of the negative charge, which causes the values to approach zero from a greater negative value as n increases (thereby increasing the energy). On Test Day, be sure to consider where the variable appears in the fraction and negative signs when determining proportionality.

forces between the electron and proton. This explains the negative sign in the previous equation for energy.

B. APPLICATIONS OF THE BOHR MODEL

In his model of the structure of hydrogen, Bohr postulated that an electron can exist only in certain fixed energy states. In terms of quantum theory, the energy of an electron is **quantized.** Using this model, certain generalizations concerning the characteristics of electrons can be made. The energy of the electron is related to its orbital radius: the smaller the radius, the lower the energy state of the electron. The smallest orbit (radius) an electron can have corresponds to $n = 1$, which is the ground state of the hydrogen electron. At the **ground state** level, the electron is in its lowest energy state. The Bohr model is also used to explain the atomic emission spectrum and atomic absorption spectrum of hydrogen, and is helpful in interpretation of the spectra of other atoms.

1. Atomic Emission Spectra

At room temperature, the majority of atoms in a sample are in the ground state. However, electrons can be excited to higher energy levels, by heat or other energy, to yield the excited state of the atom. Because the lifetime of the excited state is brief, the electrons will return rapidly to the ground state, emitting energy in the form of photons. The electromagnetic energy of these photons may be determined using the following equation:

$$E = hc/\lambda$$

where h is Planck's constant, c is the velocity of light (3×10^8 m/s), and λ is the wavelength of the radiation.

The different electrons in an atom will be excited to different energy levels. When these electrons return to their ground states, each will emit a photon with a wavelength characteristic of the specific transition it undergoes. The quantized energies of light emitted under these conditions do not produce a continuous spectrum (as expected from classical physics). Rather, the spectrum is composed of light at specific frequencies and is thus known as a line spectrum, where each line on the emission spectrum corresponds to a specific electronic transition. Because each element can have its electrons excited to different distinct energy levels, each one possesses a unique **atomic emission spectrum,** which can be used as a fingerprint for the element. One particular application of atomic emissions spectroscopy is in the analysis of stars; while a physical sample cannot be taken, the light

MCAT SYNOPSIS

Note that all systems tend toward minimal energy, thus atoms of any element will generally exist in the ground state unless subjected to extremely high temperatures or irradiation.

BRIDGE

E = hf for photons in physics. This also holds true here since we know that C = fλ. This is based on the formula V = fλ for photons.

MCAT FAVORITE

Emissions from electrons in molecules or atoms dropping from an excited state to a ground state give rise to fluorescence. We see the color of the light being emitted.

from a star can be resolved into its component wavelengths, which are then matched to the known line spectra of the elements.

The Bohr model of the hydrogen atom explained the atomic emission spectrum of hydrogen, which is the simplest emission spectrum among all the elements. The group of hydrogen emission lines corresponding to transitions from upper levels $n > 2$ to $n = 2$ is known as the **Balmer series** (4 wavelengths in the visible region), while the group corresponding to transitions between upper levels $n > 1$ to $n = 1$ is known as the **Lyman series** (higher energy transitions, occur in the UV region).

When the energy of each frequency of light observed in the emission spectrum of hydrogen was calculated according to Planck's quantum theory, the values obtained closely matched those expected from energy level transitions in the Bohr model. That is, the energy associated with a change in the quantum number from an initial value n_i to a final value n_f is equal to the energy of Planck's emitted photon. Thus:

$$E = hc/\lambda = -R_H[1/(n_i)^2 - 1/(n_f)^2]$$

and the energy of the emitted photon corresponds to the precise difference in energy between the higher-energy initial state and the lower-energy final state.

2. Atomic Absorption Spectra

When an electron is excited to a higher energy level, it must absorb energy. The energy absorbed as an electron jumps from an orbital of low energy to one of higher energy is characteristic of that transition. This means that the excitation of electrons in a particular element results in energy absorptions at specific wavelengths. Thus, in addition to an emission spectrum, every element possesses a characteristic **absorption spectrum.** Not surprisingly, the wavelengths of absorption correspond directly to the wavelengths of emission since the energy difference between levels remains unchanged. Absorption spectra can thus be used in the identification of elements present in a gas phase sample.

QUANTUM MECHANICAL MODEL OF ATOMS

While the concepts put forth by Bohr offered a reasonable explanation for the structure of the hydrogen atom and ions containing only one electron (such as He^{1+} and Li^{2+}), they did not explain the structures of atoms containing more than one electron. This is because Bohr's model does not take into consideration the repulsion between multiple electrons surrounding one nucleus. Modern quantum mechanics has led to a more

MCAT FAVORITE

Absorption is the basis for the color of compounds. We see the color of the light that is NOT absorbed by the compound.

MCAT SYNOPSIS

Note that the magnitude of ΔE is the same for absorption or emission between any two energy levels. The sign of ΔE indicates whether the energy goes in or out, and therefore, whether the electron is going to an excited state (absorption) or to the ground state (emission), respectively.

rigorous and generalized study of the electronic structure of atoms. The most important difference between the Bohr model and modern quantum mechanical models is that Bohr's assumption that electrons follow a circular orbit at a fixed distance from the nucleus is no longer considered valid. Rather, electrons are described as being in a state of rapid motion within regions of space around the nucleus, called **orbitals.** An orbital is a representation of the probability of finding an electron within a given region. In the current quantum mechanical description of electrons, pinpointing the exact location of an electron at any given point in time is impossible. This idea is best described by the **Heisenberg uncertainty principle,** which states that it is impossible to determine, with perfect accuracy, the momentum and the position of an electron simultaneously. This means that if the momentum of the electron is being measured accurately, its position will change, and vice versa.

A. QUANTUM NUMBERS

Modern atomic theory states that any electron in an atom can be completely described by four **quantum numbers:** n, ℓ, m_ℓ, and m_s. Further, according to the **Pauli exclusion principle,** no two electrons in a given atom can possess the same set of four quantum numbers. The position and energy of an electron described by its quantum numbers is known as its **energy state.** The value of n limits the values of ℓ, which in turn limits the values of m_ℓ. The values of the quantum numbers qualitatively give information about the orbitals: n about the size, ℓ about the shape, and m_ℓ about the orientation of the orbital. All four quantum numbers are discussed below.

1. Principal Quantum Number

The first quantum number is commonly known as the **principal quantum number** and is denoted by the letter n. This is the quantum number used in Bohr's model that can theoretically take on any positive integer value. The larger the integer value of n, the higher the energy level and radius of the electron's orbit. The maximum number of electrons in energy level n (electron shell n) is $2n^2$. The difference in energy between adjacent shells decreases as the distance from the nucleus increases, since it is related to the expression $1/n_2^2 - 1/n_1^2$. For example, the energy difference between the third and fourth shells, $n = 3$ to $n = 4$, is less than that between the second and third shells, $n = 2$ to $n = 3$.

2. Azimuthal Quantum Number

The second quantum number is called the **azimuthal (angular momentum) quantum number** and is designated by the letter ℓ.

TEACHER TIP

A larger integer value of the principal quantum number indicates a larger radius and higher energy. This is similar to gravitational potential energy, where the higher the object is above the earth, the higher its potential energy.

MCAT SYNOPSIS

For any principal quantum number n, there will be n possible values for ℓ.

The second quantum number refers to the **subshells** or **sublevels** that occur within each principal energy level. For any given n, the value of ℓ can be any integer in the range of 0 to $n - 1$. The four subshells corresponding to $\ell = 0, 1, 2,$ and 3 are known as the s, p, d, and f subshells, respectively. The maximum number of electrons that can exist within a subshell is given by the equation $4\ell + 2$. The greater the value of ℓ, the greater the energy of the subshell. However, the energies of subshells from different principal energy levels may overlap. For example, the 4s subshell will have a lower energy than the 3d subshell because its average distance from the nucleus is smaller (see Figure 1.1).

3. Magnetic Quantum Number

The third quantum number is the **magnetic quantum number** and is designated m_ℓ. An orbital is a specific region within a subshell that may contain no more than two electrons. The magnetic quantum number specifies the particular orbital within a subshell where an electron is highly likely to be found at a given point in time. The possible values of m_ℓ are all integers from ℓ to $-\ell$, including 0. Therefore, the s subshell, where there is one possible value of m_ℓ (0), will contain 1 orbital; likewise, the p subshell will contain 3 orbitals, the d subshell will contain 5 orbitals, and the f subshell will contain 7 orbitals. The shape and energy of each orbital are dependent upon the subshell in which the orbital is found. For example, a p subshell has three possible m_ℓ values (–1, 0, +1). The three dumbbell-shaped orbitals are oriented in space around the nucleus along the x, y, and z axes and are often referred to as p_x, p_y, and p_z.

4. Spin Quantum Number

The fourth quantum number is also called the **spin quantum number** and is denoted by ms. The spin of a particle is its intrinsic angular momentum and is a characteristic of a particle, like its charge. In classical mechanics an object spinning about its axis has an angular momentum; however, this does not apply to the electron. Classical analogies often are inapplicable in the quantum world. In any case, the two spin orientations are designated $+\frac{1}{2}$ and $-\frac{1}{2}$. Whenever two electrons are in the same orbital, they must have opposite spins. Electrons in different orbitals with the same ms values are said to have **parallel** spins.

The quantum numbers for the orbitals in the second principal energy level, with their maximum number of electrons noted in parentheses, are shown in Table 1.2. Electrons with opposite spins in the same orbital are often referred to as paired.

MCAT SYNOPSIS

For any value of ℓ there will be $2\ell + 1$ possible values for m_ℓ. For any n, this produces n^2 possible values of m_ℓ, i.e., n^2 orbitals (see table below).

MCAT SYNOPSIS

For any value of n there will be a maximum of $2n^2$ electrons, i.e., two per orbital.

Table 1.2

n		2(8)		
ℓ	0(2)		1(6)	
M_ℓ	0(2)	+1(2)	0(2)	–1(2)
M_s	$+\frac{1}{2}, -\frac{1}{2}$	$+\frac{1}{2}, -\frac{1}{2}$	$+\frac{1}{2}, -\frac{1}{2}$	$+\frac{1}{2}, -\frac{1}{2}$

B. ELECTRON CONFIGURATION AND ORBITAL FILLING

For a given atom or ion, the pattern by which subshells are filled and the number of electrons within each principal level and subshell are designated by an **electron configuration.** In electron configuration notation, the first number denotes the principal energy level, the letter designates the subshell, and the superscript gives the number of electrons in that subshell. For example, $2p^4$ indicates that there are four electrons in the second (p) subshell of the second principal energy level.

When writing the electron configuration of an atom, it is necessary to remember the order in which subshells are filled. Subshells are filled from lowest to highest energy, and each subshell will fill completely before electrons begin to enter the next one. The $(n + \ell)$ rule is used to rank subshells by increasing energy. This rule states that the lower the values of the first and second quantum numbers, the lower the energy of the subshell. If two subshells possess the same $(n + \ell)$ value, the subshell with the lower n value has a lower energy and will fill first. The order in which the subshells fill is shown in the following chart.

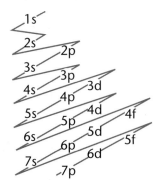

Figure 1.1

Example: Which will fill first, the 3d subshell or the 4s subshell?

Solution: For 3d, $n = 3$ and $\ell = 2$, so $(n + \ell) = 5$. For 4s, $n = 4$ and
$\ell = 0$, so $(n + \ell) = 4$. Therefore, the 4s subshell has lower

energy and will fill first. This can also be determined from the chart by examination.

To determine which subshells are filled, you must know the number of electrons in the atom. In the case of uncharged atoms, the number of electrons equals the atomic number. If the atom is charged, the number of electrons is equal to the atomic number plus the extra electrons if the atom is negative, or the atomic number minus the electrons if the atom is positive.

In subshells that contain more than one orbital, such as the 2p subshell with its 3 orbitals, the orbitals will fill according to **Hund's rule.** Hund's rule states that within a given subshell, orbitals are filled such that there are a maximum number of half-filled orbitals with parallel spins. Electrons "prefer" empty orbitals to half-filled ones because a pairing energy must be overcome for two electrons carrying repulsive negative charges to exist in the same orbital.

Example: What are the written electron configurations for nitrogen (N) and iron (Fe) according to Hund's rule?

Solution: Nitrogen has an atomic number of 7, thus its electron configuration is $1s^2\ 2s^2\ 2p^3$. According to Hund's rule, the two s-orbitals will fill completely, while the three p-orbitals will each contain one electron, all with parallel spins.

$$\underset{1s^2}{\uparrow\downarrow} \quad \underset{2s^2}{\uparrow\downarrow} \quad \underset{2p^3}{\uparrow\ \uparrow\ \uparrow}$$

Iron has an atomic number of 26, and its 4s subshell fills before the 3d. Using Hund's rule, the electron configuraton will be:

$$\underset{1s^2}{\uparrow\downarrow} \quad \underset{2s^2}{\uparrow\downarrow} \quad \underset{2p^6}{\uparrow\downarrow\ \uparrow\downarrow\ \uparrow\downarrow} \quad \underset{3s^2}{\uparrow\downarrow} \quad \underset{3p^6}{\uparrow\downarrow\ \uparrow\downarrow\ \uparrow\downarrow} \quad \underset{3d^6}{\uparrow\downarrow\ \uparrow\ \uparrow\ \uparrow\ \uparrow} \quad \underset{4s^2}{\uparrow\downarrow}$$

Iron's electron configuration is written as $1s^2\ 2s^2\ 2p^6\ 3s^2\ 3p^6\ 3d^6\ 4s^2$. Subshells may be listed either in the order in which they fill (e.g., 4s before 3d) or with subshells of the same principal quantum number grouped together, as shown here. Both methods are correct.

The presence of paired or unpaired electrons affects the chemical and magnetic properties of an atom or molecule. If the material has unpaired electrons, a magnetic field will align the spins of these electrons and weakly attract the atom. These materials are said to be **paramagnetic.** Materials that have no unpaired electrons and are slightly repelled by a magnetic field are said to be **diamagnetic.**

TEACHER TIP

Paramagnetic means that a magnetic field will cause *parallel* spins in unpaired electrons, and will therefore cause an attraction.

C. VALENCE ELECTRONS

The valence electrons of an atom are those electrons that are in its outer energy shell *or* that are available for bonding. For elements in Groups IA and IIA, only the outermost s electrons are valence electrons. For elements in Groups IIIA through VIIIA, the outermost s and p electrons in the highest energy shell are valence electrons. For transition elements, the valence electrons are those in the outermost s subshell and in the d subshell of the next-to-outermost energy shell. For the inner transition elements, the valence electrons are those in the *s* subshell of the outermost energy shell, the d subshell of the next-to-outermost energy shell, and the f subshell of the energy shell two levels below the outermost shell.

TEACHER TIP

The valence electron configuration of an atom helps us understand its properties, and can be ascertained from the Periodic Table (the only "cheat sheet" you will have on Test Day).

IIIA–VIIA elements beyond Period II might, under some circumstances, accept electrons into their empty d subshell, which gives them more than 8 valence electrons (see Exceptions to the Octet Rule in chapter 3).

Example: Which are the valence electrons of elemental iron, elemental selenium, and the sulfur atom in a sulfate ion?

Solution: Iron has 8 valence electrons: 2 in its 4s subshell and 6 in its 3d subshell.

Selenium has 6 valence electrons: 2 in its 4s subshell and 4 in its 4p subshell. Selenium's 3d electrons are not part of its valence shell.

Sulfur in a sulfate ion has 12 valence electrons: its original 6 plus 6 more from the oxygens to which it is bonded. Sulfur's 3s and 3p subshells can contain only 8 of these 12 electrons; the other 4 electrons have entered the sulfur atom's 3d subshell, which in elemental sulfur is empty (see Figure 3.1).

PRACTICE QUESTIONS

1. The image below illustrates the charged surface of an unknown substance at a certain point in time. Each arrow represents an individual dipole moment, reflecting the overall orientation of electron charge density at that point on the surface. The individual dipole moments in each parallelogram all have the same magnitude and direction.

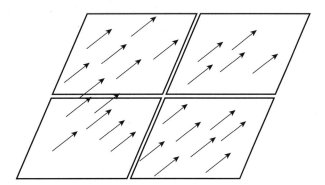

Which of the following terms best describes the magnetic properties of this substance?

A. Ferromagnetic

B. Paramagnetic

C. Diamagnetic

D. There is not enough information to determine the magnetic properties of the material.

2. Which of the following is the correct electron configuration for Zn^{2+}?

A. $1s^2 2s^2 2p^6 3s^2 3p^6 4s^0 3d^{10}$

B. $1s^2 2s^2 2p^6 3s^2 3p^6 4s^2 3d^8$

C. $1s^2 2s^2 2p^6 3s^2 3p^6 4s^2 3d^{10}$

D. $1s^2 2s^2 2p^6 3s^2 3p^6 4s^0 3d^8$

3. Which of the following quantum number sets describes a possible element?

A. $n = 2$; $l = 2$; $m_l = 1$; $m_s = +\frac{1}{2}$

B. $n = 2$; $l = 1$; $m_l = -1$; $m_s = +\frac{1}{2}$

C. $n = 2$; $l = 0$; $m_l = -1$; $m_s = -\frac{1}{2}$

D. $n = 2$; $l = 0$; $m_l = 1$; $m_s = -\frac{1}{2}$

4. What is the maximum number of electrons allowed in a single atomic energy level in terms of the principal quantum number n?

A. $2n$

B. $2n + 2$

C. $2n^2$

D. $2n^2 + 2$

5. Which of the following equations describes the maximum number of electrons that can fill a subshell?

A. $2l + 2$

B. $4l + 2$

C. $2l^2$

D. $2l^2 + 2$

6. Which of the following substances is most likely to be diamagnetic?

A. Hydrogen

B. Iron

C. Cobalt

D. Sulfur

7. An electron returns from an excited state to its ground state, emitting a photon at $\lambda = 500$ nm. If this process were repeated such that a mole of these photons were emitted, what would be the magnitude of the energy change?

A. 3.98×10^{-19} J
B. 3.98×10^{-21} J
C. 2.39×10^{5} J
D. 2.39×10^{3} J

8. Suppose an electron falls from $n = 4$ to its ground state, $n = 1$. Which of the following effects is most likely?

A. A photon is absorbed.
B. A photon is emitted.
C. The electron gains velocity.
D. The electron loses velocity.

9. Which of the following compounds is NOT a possible isotope of carbon?

A. ^{6}C
B. ^{12}C
C. ^{13}C
D. ^{14}C

10. According to the Heisenberg uncertainty principle, which of the following properties of a particle can an observer measure simultaneously?

　I. Position
　II. Momentum
　III. Velocity

A. I and II
B. I and III
C. II and III
D. I, II, and III

11. Orbitals like the one pictured below are characteristic of which of the following shells?

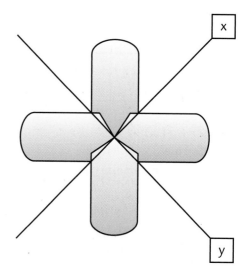

A. s
B. p
C. d
D. f

12. Which of the following electronic transitions would result in the greatest gain in energy for a single hydrogen electron, assuming that its ground state is $n = 1$?

A. An electron moves from $n = 6$ to $n = 2$.
B. An electron moves from $n = 2$ to $n = 6$.
C. An electron moves from $n = 3$ to $n = 4$.
D. An electron moves from $n = 4$ to $n = 3$.

13. Suppose a chemical species fills its orbitals as shown below. Which of the following laws of atomic physics could this compound be said to obey?

 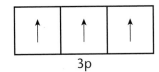

3s   3p

A. Hund's rule
B. Heisenberg uncertainty principle
C. Bohr model
D. Pauli exclusion principle

14. Which of the following correctly places the theories of atomic structure in proper chronological order, from the oldest theory to the most recent?

I. Bohr model
II. Rutherford model
III. Thomson model

A. I, II, III
B. I, III, II
C. III, II, I
D. II, III, I

15. How many total electrons are in a ^{133}Cs cation?

A. 54
B. 55
C. 78
D. 133

16. The atomic mass of hydrogen is 1.008 amu. What is the percent composition of hydrogen by isotope, assuming that hydrogen's only isotopes are ^{1}H and ^{2}D?

A. 92% H, 8% D
B. 99.2% H, 0.8% D
C. 99.92% H, 0.08% D
D. 99.992% H, 0.008% D

17. Consider the following two sets of quantum numbers, which describe two different electrons in the same atom. Which of the following best describes these two electrons?

n	l	m_l	m_s
1	1	1	+½
2	1	-1	+½

A. Parallel
B. Opposite
C. Antiparallel
D. Paired

18. The electron configuration $1s^2 2s^2 2p^6 3s^2 3p^6 4s^1 3d^5$ can describe several different transition metals. Which of the following species is represented by this configuration?

A. Cr
B. Mn$^+$
C. Fe^{2+}
D. Co^{3+}

19. Which of the following statements is NOT true of an electron's ground state?

A. The electron is at its lowest possible energy level.

B. The electron is in a quantized energy level.

C. The electron is traveling along its smallest possible orbital radius.

D. The electron is static.

20. Which of the following experimental conditions would NOT excite an electron out of the ground state?

A. Radiation
B. High temperature
C. High pressure
D. None of the above

Periodic Table of the Elements

Group**

Period

	1 IA 1A	2 IIA 2A											13 IIIA 3A	14 IVA 4A	15 VA 5A	16 VIA 6A	17 VIIA 7A	18 vIIIA 8A
1	1 H 1.008																	2 He 4.003
2	3 Li 6.941	4 Be 9.012											5 B 10.81	6 C 12.01	7 N 14.01	8 O 16.00	9 F 19.00	10 Ne 20.18
3	11 Na 22.99	12 Mg 24.31	3 IIIB 3B	4 IVB 4B	5 VB 5B	6 VIB 6B	7 VIIB 7B	8 ------- VIII ----- -- ------- 8 -------	9	10	11 IB 1B	12 IIB 2B	13 Al 26.98	14 Si 28.09	15 P 30.97	16 S 32.07	17 Cl 35.45	18 Ar 39.95
4	19 K 39.10	20 Ca 40.08	21 Sc 44.96	22 Ti 47.88	23 V 50.94	24 Cr 52.00	25 Mn 54.94	26 Fe 55.85	27 Co 58.47	28 Ni 58.69	29 Cu 63.55	30 Zn 65.39	31 Ga 69.72	32 Ge 72.59	33 As 74.92	34 Se 78.96	35 Br 79.90	36 Kr 83.80
5	37 Rb 85.47	38 Sr 87.62	39 Y 88.91	40 Zr 91.22	41 Nb 92.91	42 Mo 95.94	43 Tc (98)	44 Ru 101.1	45 Rh 102.9	46 Pd 106.4	47 Ag 107.9	48 Cd 112.4	49 In 114.8	50 Sn 118.7	51 Sb 121.8	52 Te 127.6	53 I 126.9	54 Xe 131.3
6	55 Cs 132.9	56 Ba 137.3	57 La* 138.9	72 Hf 178.5	73 Ta 180.9	74 W 183.9	75 Re 186.2	76 Os 190.2	77 Ir 190.2	78 Pt 195.1	79 Au 197.0	80 Hg 200.5	81 Tl 204.4	82 Pb 207.2	83 Bi 209.0	84 Po (210)	85 At (210)	86 Rn (222)
7	87 Fr (223)	88 Ra (226)	89 Ac~ (227)	104 Rf (257)	105 Db (260)	106 Sg (263)	107 Bh (262)	108 Hs (265)	109 Mt (266)	110 --- ()	111 --- ()	112 --- ()		114 --- ()		116 --- ()		118 --- ()

Lanthanide Series*	58 Ce 140.1	59 Pr 140.9	60 Nd 144.2	61 Pm (147)	62 Sm 150.4	63 Eu 152.0	64 Gd 157.3	65 Tb 158.9	66 Dy 162.5	67 Ho 164.9	68 Er 167.3	69 Tm 168.9	70 Yb 173.0	71 Lu 175.0
Actinide Series~	90 Th 232.0	91 Pa (231)	92 U (238)	93 Np (237)	94 Pu (242)	95 Am (243)	96 Cm (247)	97 Bk (247)	98 Cf (249)	99 Es (254)	100 Fm (253)	101 Md (256)	102 No (254)	103 Lr (257)

CHAPTER 2

THE PERIODIC TABLE

In 1869, the Russian chemist Dmitri Mendeleev published the first version of his periodic table, in which he showed that ordering the elements according to atomic weight produced a pattern in which similar properties periodically recurred. This table was later revised, using the work of the physicist Henry Moseley, to organize the elements on the basis of increasing atomic number. Using this revised table, the properties of certain elements that had not yet been discovered were predicted: A number of these predictions were later borne out by experimentation. The substance of this work is summarized in the **periodic law,** which states that the chemical properties of the elements are dependent, in a systematic way, upon their atomic numbers.

In the periodic table used today, the elements are arranged in **periods** (rows) and **groups** (columns). There are seven periods, representing the principal quantum numbers $n = 1$ to $n = 7$, and each period is filled sequentially. Groups represent elements that have the same electronic configuration in their **valence,** or outermost shell, and share similar chemical properties. The electrons in the outermost shell are called **valence electrons.** They are involved in chemical bonding and determine the chemical reactivity and properties of the element. The Roman numeral above each group represents the number of valence electrons. There are two sets of groups, designated A and B. The A elements are the **representative elements,** which have either s- or p-sublevels as their outermost orbitals. The B elements are the **nonrepresentative elements,** including the **transition elements,** which have partly filled d sublevels, and the **lanthanide** and **actinide series,** which have partly filled f-sublevels. The electron configuration for the valence electrons is given by the Roman numeral and letter designations. For example, an element in Group VA will have a valence electron configuration of s^2p^3 ($2 + 3 = 5$ valence electrons).

PERIODIC PROPERTIES OF THE ELEMENTS

The properties of the elements exhibit certain trends, which can be explained in terms of the position of the element in the periodic table, or

> **MCAT FAVORITE**
> Don't memorize the periodic table because you have access to it on Test Day. Do know about its configuration and trends.

in terms of the electron configuration of the element. All elements seek to gain or lose valence electrons so as to achieve the stable octet formation possessed by the **inert** or **noble gases** of Group VIII. Two other important trends exist within the periodic table. First, as one goes from left to right across a period, electrons are added one at a time; the electrons of the outermost shell experience an increasing amount of nuclear attraction, becoming closer and more tightly bound to the nucleus. Second, as one goes down a given column, the outermost electrons become less tightly bound to the nucleus. This is because the number of filled principal energy levels (which shield the outermost electrons from attraction by the nucleus) increases downward within each group. These trends help explain elemental properties such as atomic radius, ionization potential, electron affinity, and electronegativity.

A. ATOMIC RADII

The **atomic radius** of an element is equal to one-half the distance between the centers of two atoms of that element that are just touching each other. In general, the atomic radius decreases across a period from left to right and increases down a given group; The atoms with the largest atomic radii will be located at the bottom of groups, and in Group I.

As one moves from left to right across a period, electrons are added one at a time to the outer energy shell. Electrons within a shell cannot shield one another from the attractive pull of protons. Therefore, because the number of protons is also increasing, producing a greater positive charge attracting the valence electrons, the effective nuclear charge increases steadily across a period. This causes the atomic radius to decrease.

As one moves down a group of the periodic table, the number of electrons and filled electron shells will increase, but the number of valence electrons will remain the same. Thus, the outermost electrons in a given group will feel the same amount of effective nuclear charge, but electrons will be found farther from the nucleus as the number of filled energy shells increases. Thus, the atomic radii will increase.

B. IONIZATION ENERGY

The **ionization energy** (IE), or **ionization potential,** is the energy required to completely remove an electron from a gaseous atom or ion. Removing an electron from an atom always requires an input of energy (is endothermic; see chapter 6, Thermodynamics). The closer and more tightly bound an electron is to the nucleus, the more difficult it will be to remove, and the higher the ionization energy will be. The **first ionization energy** is the energy required to remove one valence electron from the parent atom, the **second ionization energy** is the energy needed to remove a second valence electron from the univalent ion to form the divalent ion, and so on. Successive ionization energies grow increasingly large; i.e., the second ionization energy is always greater than the first ionization energy. For example:

$$Mg(g) \longrightarrow Mg^+(g) + e^- \text{ First Ionization Energy} + 7.646 \text{ eV}$$

$$Mg^+(g) \longrightarrow Mg^{2+}(g) + e^- \text{ Second Ionization Energy} + 15.035 \text{ eV}$$

Ionization energy increases from left to right across a period as the atomic radius decreases. Moving down a group, the ionization energy decreases as the atomic radius increases. Group I elements have low ionization energies because the loss of an electron results in the formation of a stable octet.

C. ELECTRON AFFINITY

Electron affinity is the energy change that occurs when an electron is added to a gaseous atom, and it represents the ease with which the atom can accept an electron. The stronger the attractive pull of the nucleus for electrons (**effective nuclear charge, or Z_{eff}),** the greater the electron affinity will be. In discussing electron affinities, two sign conventions are used. The more common one states that a positive electron affinity value represents energy release when an electron is added to an atom; the other states that a negative electron affinity represents a release of energy. In this discussion, the first convention will be used.

Generalizations can be made about the electron affinities of particular groups in the periodic table. For example, the Group IIA elements, or **alkaline earths,** have low electron affinity values. These elements are relatively stable because their s subshell is filled. Group VIIA elements, or **halogens,** have high electron affinities because the addition of an electron to the atom results in a completely filled shell, which represents a stable electron configuration. Achieving the stable octet involves a release of energy, and the strong attraction of the nucleus for the electron leads to a high energy change. The Group VIII elements, or **noble gases,** have electron affinities on the order of zero, because they already possess a stable octet and cannot readily accept an electron. Elements of other groups generally have low values of electron affinity.

> **MCAT STRATEGY**
>
> To recall the various trends, remember this: Cesium (Cs) is the largest, most metallic, and least electronegative of all naturally occurring elements. It also has the smallest ionization energy and the least exothermic electron affinity.

> **MCAT STRATEGY**
>
> In contrast to cesium, fluorine (F) is the smallest, most electronegative element. It also has the largest ionization energy and most exothermic electron affinity.

D. ELECTRONEGATIVITY

Electronegativity is a measure of the attraction an atom has for electrons in a chemical bond. The greater the electronegativity of an atom, the greater its attraction for bonding electrons. Electronegativity values are not determined directly. The most common electronegativity scale is the Pauling electronegativity scale, with values ranging from 0.7 for the most electropositive elements, like cesium, to 4 for the most electronegative element fluorine. Electronegativities are related to ionization energies: Elements with low ionization energies will have low electronegativities because their nuclei do not attract electrons strongly, while elements with high ionization energies will have high electronegativities because of the strong pull their nuclei have on electrons. Therefore, electronegativity increases from left to right across periods. In any group, the electronegativity decreases as the atomic number increases, as a result of the increased distance between the valence electrons and the nucleus, i.e., greater atomic radius.

TYPES OF ELEMENTS

The elements of the periodic table may be classified into three categories: **metals,** located on the left side and in the middle of the periodic table; **nonmetals,** located on the right side of the table; and **metalloids (semimetals),** found along a diagonal line between the other two.

A. METALS

Metals are shiny solids (except for mercury) at room temperature, and generally have high melting points and densities. Metals have the characteristic ability to be deformed without breaking. The ability of a metal to be hammered into shapes is called **malleability** and the ability to be drawn into wires is called **ductility.** Many of the characteristic properties of metals, such as large atomic radius, low ionization energy, and low electronegativity, are due to the fact that the few electrons in the valence shell of a metal atom can easily be removed. Because the valence electrons can move freely, metals are good conductors of heat and electricity. Group IA and IIA represent the most reactive metals and will be discussed. The transition elements, also discussed later, are metals that have partially filled d orbitals.

B. NONMETALS

Nonmetals are generally brittle in the solid state and show little or no metallic luster. They have high ionization energies and electronegativities, and are usually poor conductors of heat and electricity. Most nonmetals share the ability to gain electrons easily, but otherwise they display a wide range of chemical behaviors and reactivities. The nonmetals are located on the upper-right side of the periodic table; they are separated from the metals by a line cutting diagonally through the region of the periodic table containing elements with partially filled p orbitals.

C. METALLOIDS

The metalloids or semimetals are found along the line between the metals and nonmetals in the periodic table, and their properties vary considerably. Their densities, boiling points, and melting points fluctuate widely. The electronegativities and ionization energies of metalloids lie between those of metals and nonmetals; therefore, these elements possess characteristics of both those classes. For example, silicon has a metallic luster, yet it is brittle and is not an efficient conductor. The reactivity of metalloids is dependent upon the element with which they are reacting. For example, boron (B) behaves as a nonmetal when reacting with sodium (Na) and as a metal when reacting with fluorine (F). The elements classified as metalloids are boron, silicon, germanium, arsenic, antimony, and tellurium.

MCAT SYNOPSIS

Metalloids are intermediate in properties between metals and nonmetals. Such properties include electrical conductivity, thus semimetals tend to make good semiconductors.

THE CHEMISTRY OF GROUPS

A. ALKALI METALS

The **alkali metals** are the elements of Group IA. They possess most of the physical properties common to metals, yet their densities are lower than those of other metals. The alkali metals have only one loosely bound electron in their outermost shell, giving them the largest atomic radii of all the elements in their respective periods. Their metallic properties and high reactivity are determined by the fact that they have low ionization energies; thus they easily lose their valence electron to form univalent cations. Alkali metals have low electronegativities and react very readily with nonmetals, especially halogens.

TEACHER TIP

These two groups of compounds are both metallic in nature because they both lose electrons easily from the s-orbital of their valence shell.

B. ALKALINE EARTHS

The **alkaline earths** are the elements of Group IIA, which also possess many characteristically metallic properties. Like the alkali metals, these properties are dependent upon the ease with which they lose electrons. The alkaline earths have two electrons in their outer shell and thus have smaller atomic radii than the alkali metals. However, the two valence electrons are not held very tightly by the nucleus, so they can be removed to form divalent cations. Alkaline earths have low electronegativities and low electron affinities.

C. HALOGENS

The **halogens,** Group VIIA, are highly reactive nonmetals with seven valence electrons (one short of the favored octet configuration). Halogens are highly variable in their physical properties. For instance, the halogens range from gaseous (F_2 and Cl_2) to liquid (Br_2) to solid (I_2) at room temperature. Their chemical properties are more uniform: The electronegativities of halogens are very high, and they are particularly reactive towards alkali metals and alkaline earths, which "want" to donate electrons to the halogens to form stable ionic crystals. Fluorine (F) has the highest electronegativity of all the elements.

D. NOBLE GASES

The **noble gases,** also called the **inert gases,** are found in Group VIII (also called Group 0). They are fairly nonreactive because they have a complete valence shell, which is an energetically favored arrangement. This gives them little or no tendency to gain or lose electrons, high ionization energies, and no real electronegativities. They possess low boiling points and are all gases at room temperature.

E. TRANSITION ELEMENTS

TEACHER TIP

Transition metals are seen in biological systems and are therefore seen on the MCAT. You don't need to memorize them but understand how the transition metals ionize and act.

The **transition elements,** Groups IB to VIIIB, are all considered metals; hence, they are also called the **transition metals.** These elements are very hard and have high melting points and boiling points. As one moves across a period, the five d-orbitals become progressively more filled. The d-electrons are held only loosely by the nucleus and are relatively mobile, contributing to the malleability and high electrical conductivity of these elements. Chemically, transition elements have low ionization energies and may exist in a variety of positively charged forms or **oxidation states.** This is because transition elements are capable of losing various numbers of electrons from the s- and d-orbitals of their valence shell. Theoretically, the transition metals in Group VIIIB could have eight different oxidation states, from +1 to +8; however, they typically do not exhibit so many. For instance, copper (Cu), in group IB, can exist in either the +1 or the +2 oxidation state, and manganese (Mn), in Group VIIB, occurs in the +2, +3, +4, +6, or +7 state. Because of this ability to attain positive oxidation states, transition metals form many different ionic and partially ionic compounds. The dissolved ions can form **complex ions** either with molecules of water (**hydration complexes**) or with nonmetals, forming highly colored solutions and compounds (e.g., $CuSO_4.5H_2O$), and this complexation may enhance the relatively low solubility of certain compounds (e.g., AgCl is insoluble in water, but quite soluble in aqueous ammonia due to the formation of the complex ion $[Ag(NH_3)_2]^+$). The formation of complexes causes the d-orbitals to be split into two energy sublevels. This enables many of the complexes to absorb certain frequencies of light—those containing the precise amount of energy required to raise electrons from the lower to the higher d-sublevel. The frequencies not absorbed—known as the subtraction frequencies— give the complexes their characteristic colors.

PRACTICE QUESTIONS

1. Lithium and sodium have similar chemical properties, such as the ability to form ionic bonds with chloride. Which of the following best explains this similarity?

   A. Both lithium and sodium ions are positively charged.
   B. Lithium and sodium are in the same group within the periodic table.
   C. Lithium and sodium are in the same period of the periodic table.
   D. Both lithium and sodium have low atomic weights.

2. Carbon and silicon, elements used as the basis of biologic life and synthetic computing, respectively, are often considered elements with similar chemical properties. Which of the following is true about the differences between the two elements?

   A. Carbon has a smaller atomic radius than silicon.
   B. Silicon has a smaller atomic radius than carbon.
   C. Carbon has fewer valence electrons than silicon.
   D. Silicon has fewer valence electrons than carbon.

3. One important property of any element is its atomic radius, because this can affect its chemical properties. Which of the following determines the length of an element's radius?

   I. The number of valence electrons
   II. The number of electron shells
   III. The number of neutrons in the nucleus
   A. I only
   B. III only
   C. I and II only
   D. I, II, and III

4. Ionization energy contributes to an atom's chemical reactivity. Which of the following would be an accurate ordering of ionization energies, from lowest ionization energy to highest?

   A. Be, first ionization energy → Be, second ionization energy → Li, first ionization energy
   B. Be, second ionization energy → Be, first ionization energy → Li, first ionization energy
   C. Li, first ionization energy → Be, first ionization energy → Be, second ionization energy
   D. Li, first ionization energy → Be, second ionization energy → Be, first ionization energy

5. Selenium is often an active component of scalp treatments for scalp dermatitis. What type of element is selenium?

   A. Metal
   B. Metalloid
   C. Halogen
   D. Nonmetal

6. The properties of atoms can be predicted, to some extent, by their location within the periodic table. Which of the following properties increases in the direction of the arrows shown below?

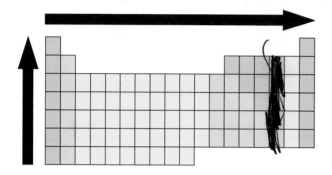

   I. Electronegativity
  II. Atomic radius
 III. First ionization energy

A. I only
B. II only
C. I and III
D. I, II, and III

7. Metals are often used for making wires that conduct electricity. Which of the following properties of many metals is most important to making them good conductors?

A. Metals are malleable.
B. Metals have high electronegativity.
C. Metals have valence electrons that can move freely.
D. Metals have high melting points.

8. In the periodic table below, which of the following is an important property of the set of elements shaded?

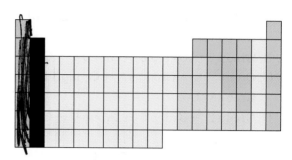

A. These elements are the best electrical conductors in the periodic table.
B. These elements form divalent cations.
C. The second ionization energy for these elements is lower than the first ionization energy.
D. The atomic radii of these elements decrease as one moves down the column.

9. Despite the fact that silicon and aluminum are adjacent in the periodic table, they react differently with 6M HCl, as demonstrated by the following reactions:[1] What best explains the difference in reactivity of silicon and aluminum?

$$Si + HCl \longrightarrow No\ Reaction$$

$$6Al + 6HCl \longrightarrow 3H_2 + 2AlCl_3$$

A. Silicon and aluminum are in different periods.
B. Silicon and aluminum are in different groups.
C. Silicon is a metalloid while aluminum is a metal.
D. Both silicon and aluminum are metalloids.

---

[1]www.chemicool.com/elements/aluminum.html;
www.chemicool.com/elements/silicon.html

10. Which of the following is the correct order of groups in terms of increasing electronegativity?

A. Group VIIA → Group VIA → Group VA → Group IIA

B. Group 7 → Group 6 → Group 5 → Group 2

C. Group IIA → Group VA → Group VIA → Group VIIA

D. Group 2 → Group 5 → Group 6 → Group 7

11. When dissolved in water, what ion is most likely to form a complex ion with H_2O?

A. Na^+

B. Fe^{2+}

C. Cl^-

D. S^{2-}

12. How many valence electrons are present in elements in the third period?

A. 2

B. 3

C. The number decreases as the atomic number increases.

D. The number increases as the atomic number increases.

13. Which of the following elements has the highest electronegativity?

A. Mg

B. Cl

C. Li

D. I

14. Of the four atoms depicted below, which has the highest electron affinity?

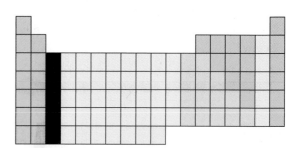

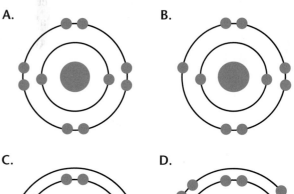

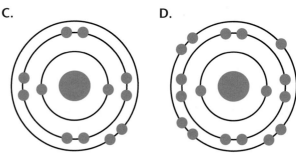

15. An atom with a large atomic radius

A. is likely to be on the right side of the periodic table.

B. is likely to have a high second ionization energy.

C. is likely to have low electronegativity.

D. is likely to form ionic bonds.

16. Which of the following atoms/ions has the largest effective nuclear charge?

A. Cl

B. Cl^-

C. K

D. K^+

17. Why do halogens often form ionic bonds with alkaline earth metals?

   A. The alkaline earth metals have much higher electron affinity than the halogens.
   B. By sharing electrons equally, the alkaline earth metals and halogens both form full octets.
   C. Within the same row, the halogens have smaller atomic radii than the alkaline earth metals.
   D. The halogens have much higher electron affinity than the alkaline earth metals.

18. What is the outermost orbital of elements in the third period?

   A. s-orbital
   B. p-orbital
   C. d-orbital
   D. f-orbital

19. A student undertakes the following experiment. In beaker A, the student places 500 mL of water and 0.500 g of AgBr. In beaker B, the student places 500 mL of ammonia and 0.500 g of AgBr. She notices that nearly none of the AgBr dissolves in beaker A, while it begins dissolving nearly immediately in beaker B. What best explains this phenomenon?

   A. Formation of a hydration complex between silver and water
   B. Ionic bonding between silver and ammonia
   C. Hydrogen bonding of bromide with water
   D. Formation of a complex between silver and ammonia

CHAPTER 3

BONDING AND CHEMICAL INTERACTIONS

The atoms of many elements can combine to form **molecules.** The atoms in most molecules are held together by strong attractive forces called **chemical bonds.** These bonds are formed via the interaction of the valence electrons of the combining atoms. The chemical and physical properties of the resulting molecules are often very different from their constituent elements. In addition to the very strong forces within a molecule, there are weaker intermolecular forces between molecules. These **intermolecular forces,** although weaker than the intramolecular chemical bonds, are of considerable importance in understanding the physical properties of many substances.

TEACHER TIP

Electronegativity (which we learned about in the last chapter) is a property that addresses how an individual atom acts within a bond and will help us understand the quality of the molecules formed from atoms with different electronegativities.

BONDING

Many molecules contain atoms bonded according to the **octet rule,** which states that an atom tends to bond with other atoms until it has eight electrons in its outermost shell, thereby forming a stable electron configuration similar to that of the Group VIII (noble gas) elements. **Exceptions** to this rule are as follows: **hydrogen,** which can have only two valence electrons (the configuration of He); **lithium** and **beryllium,** which bond to attain two and four valence electrons, respectively; **boron,** which bonds to attain six; and elements beyond the second row, such as phosphorus and sulfur, which can expand their octets to include more than eight electrons by incorporating d orbitals.

TEACHER TIP

Think of the octet rule as someone who wants to be a physician. An atom strives to be noble by gaining eight valence electrons the way a pre-med strives to be noble by graduating medical school!

When classifying chemical bonds, it is helpful to introduce two distinct types: **ionic bonds** and **covalent bonds.** In ionic bonding, an electron(s) from an atom with a smaller ionization energy is transferred to an atom with a greater electron affinity. This results in a positive and negative ion. These resulting ions are held together by electrostatic forces. In covalent bonding, an electron pair is shared between two atoms. In many cases, the bond is partially covalent and partially ionic; we call such bonds polar covalent bonds.

IONIC BONDS

When two atoms with large differences in electronegativity react, there is a complete transfer of electrons from the less electronegative atom to the more electronegative atom. The atom that loses electrons becomes a positively charged ion, or **cation,** and the atom that gains electrons becomes a negatively charged ion, or **anion.** For this transfer to occur, the difference in electronegativity must be greater than 1.7. In general, the elements of Groups I and II (low electronegativities) bond ionically to elements of Group VII (high electronegativities). Hence, ionic bonds occur between metals and nonmetals. Elements of Groups I and II give up their electrons to achieve a noble gas configuration, while Group VII elements gain an electron to achieve the noble gas configuration. For example, $Na + Cl \longrightarrow Na^+ Cl^-$ (sodium chloride). The electrostatic force of attraction between the charged ions is called an **ionic** or **electrovalent bond.**

Ionic compounds have characteristic physical properties. They have high melting and boiling points due to the strong electrostatic forces between the ions. They can conduct electricity in the liquid and aqueous states, though not in the solid state. Ionic solids form crystal lattices consisting of infinite arrays of positive and negative ions in which the attractive forces between ions of opposite charge are maximized, while the repulsive forces between ions of like charge are minimized.

COVALENT BONDS

When two or more atoms with similar electronegativities interact, the energy required to form ions is greater than the energy that would be released upon the formation of an ionic bond (i.e., the process is not energetically favorable). However, because a complete transfer of electrons cannot occur, such atoms achieve a noble gas electron configuration by **sharing** electrons in a covalent bond. The binding force between the two atoms results from the attraction that each electron of the shared pair has for the two positive nuclei.

Covalent compounds contain discrete molecular units with weak intermolecular forces. Consequently, they are low-melting solids, and do not conduct electricity in the liquid or aqueous states.

A. PROPERTIES OF COVALENT BONDS

Atoms can share more than one pair of electrons. Two atoms sharing one, two, or three electron pairs are said to be joined by a **single, double,** or **triple covalent bond,** respectively. The number of shared electron pairs between two atoms is called the **bond order;** hence a single bond has a bond order of one, a double bond has a bond order of two, and a triple bond has a bond order of three.

A covalent bond can be characterized by two features: **bond length** and **bond energy.**

1. Bond Length

Bond length is the average distance between the two nuclei of the atoms involved in the bond. As the number of shared electron pairs increases, the two atoms are pulled closer together, leading to a decrease in bond length. Thus, for a given pair of atoms, a triple bond is shorter than a double bond, which is shorter than a single bond.

2. Bond Energy

Bond energy is the energy required to separate two bonded atoms. For a given pair of atoms, the strength of a bond (and therefore the bond energy) increases as the number of shared electron pairs increases. (Bond energy is further discussed in chapter 6, Thermodynamics.)

B. COVALENT BOND NOTATION

The shared valence electrons of a covalent bond are called the **bonding electrons.** The valence electrons not involved in the covalent bond are called **nonbonding electrons.** The unshared electron pairs can also be called **lone electron pairs.** A convenient notation, called a **Lewis structure,** is used to represent the bonding and nonbonding electrons in a molecule, facilitating chemical "bookkeeping." The number of valence electrons attributed to a particular atom in the Lewis structure of a molecule is not necessarily the same as the number would be in the isolated atom, and the difference accounts for what is referred to as the **formal charge** of that atom. Often, more than one Lewis structure can be drawn for a molecule; this phenomenon is called **resonance.** Lewis structures, formal charge, and resonance are discussed in detail next.

1. Lewis Structures

A Lewis structure, or **Lewis dot symbol,** is the chemical symbol of an element surrounded by dots, each representing one of the s and/or

---

BRIDGE

We see a great example of covalent bonds in Organic Chemistry, and we can see here the inverse proportionality between bond length and strength.

	Bond length	Bond strength
C–C	longest	weakest
C=C	medium	medium
C≡C	shortest	strongest

TEACHER TIP

When dealing with Lewis Dot structures, we only deal with the eight valence electrons (s- and p-orbitals of the outer shell) on each atom. Remember that some atoms can expand their octets by utilizing the d-orbitals in this outer shell, but this will take place only with atoms in period 3 or greater.

p-valence electrons of the atom. The Lewis symbols of the elements found in the second period of the periodic table are shown below.

Table 3.1

$\cdot$Li	Lithium	$\cdot\ddot{\text{N}}\cdot$	Nitrogen
$\cdot$Be$\cdot$	Beryllium	$\cdot\ddot{\text{O}}\colon$	Oxygen
$\cdot\overset{\cdot}{\text{B}}\cdot$	Boron	$\cdot\ddot{\underset{\cdot\cdot}{\text{F}}}\colon$	Fluorine
$\cdot\overset{\cdot}{\text{C}}\cdot$	Carbon	$\colon\ddot{\text{Ne}}\colon$	Neon

Just as a Lewis symbol is used to represent the distribution of valence electrons in an atom, it can also be used to represent the distribution of valence electrons in a molecule. For example, the Lewis symbol of an F ion is $\colon\ddot{\text{F}}\colon$; the Lewis structure of an F_2 molecule is $\colon\ddot{\text{F}}$ —— $\ddot{\text{F}}\colon$.

Certain steps must be followed in assigning a Lewis structure to a molecule. These steps are outlined below, using HCN as an example.

- Write the skeletal structure of the compound (i.e., the arrangement of atoms). In general, the least electronegative atom is the central atom. Hydrogen (always) and the halogens F, Cl, Br, and I (usually) occupy the end position.

  In HCN, H must occupy an end position. Of the remaining two atoms, C is the least electronegative, and therefore occupies the central position. The skeletal structure is as follows:

$$\text{H} - \text{C} - \text{N}$$

- Count all the valence electrons of the atoms. The number of valence electrons of the molecule is the sum of the valence electrons of all atoms present:

  H has 1 valence electron;
  C has 4 valence electrons;
  N has 5 valence electrons; therefore,
  HCN has a total of 10 valence electrons.

- Draw single bonds between the central atom and the atoms surrounding it. Place an electron pair in each bond (bonding electron pair).

$$\text{H} \colon \text{C} \colon \text{N}$$

Each bond has two electrons, so $10 - 4 = 6$ valence electrons remain.

- Complete the octets (eight valence electrons) of all atoms bonded to the central atom, using the remaining valence electrons still to be assigned. (Recall that H is an exception to the Octet rule because it can have only two valence electrons.) In this example H already has two valence electrons in its bond with C.

$$:H : C : \ddot{N} :$$

- Place any extra electrons on the central atom. If the central atom has less than an octet, try to write double or triple bonds between the central and surrounding atoms using the nonbonding, unshared lone electron pairs.

The HCN structure above does not satisfy the Octet rule for C because C possesses only four valence electrons. Therefore, two lone electron pairs from the N atom must be moved to form two more bonds with C, creating a triple bond between C and N. Finally, bonds are drawn as lines rather than pairs of dots.

$$H - C \equiv N:$$

Now the Octet rule is satisfied for all three atoms, because C and N have eight valence electrons and H has two valence electrons.

2. Formal Charges

The number of electrons officially assigned to an atom in a Lewis structure does not always equal the number of valence electrons of the free atom. The difference between these two numbers is the **formal charge** of the atom. Formal charge can be calculated using the following formula:

$$\text{Formal charge} = V - \frac{1}{2} N_{\text{bonding}} - N_{\text{nonbonding}}$$

where V is the number of valence electrons in the free atom, N_{bonding} is the number of bonding electrons, and $N_{\text{nonbonding}}$ is the number of nonbonding electrons.

The formal charge of an ion or molecule equals the sum of the formal charges of the individual atoms comprising the ion or molecule.

Formal charge also contributes to stability. The lower the overall formal charge of the molecule, the more stable the molecule.

TEACHER TIP

Practicing with many molecules and remembering the "normal" amount of bonds on common central atoms will allow you to save time on Test Day from complicated equations like this. For example, the nitrogen atom here normally has three bonds and one lone pair. Here, it is sharing more than usual, so it will have a positive charge. If a molecule is selfish and is sharing less than usual, it will be negative (as we often see with oxygen atoms).

Example: Calculate the formal charge on the central N atom of $[NH_4]^+$.

Solution: The Lewis structure of $[NH_4]^+$ is

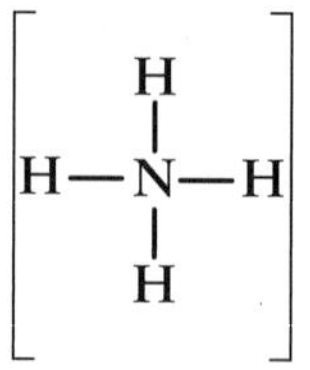

$$\left[\begin{array}{c} H \\ | \\ H-N-H \\ | \\ H \end{array} \right]$$

Nitrogen is in group VA; thus it has five valence electrons. In $[NH_4]^+$,

N has 4 bonds (i.e., eight bonding electrons and no nonbonding electrons).

So, V = 5; $N_{bonding}$ = 8; $N_{nonbonding}$ = 0

Formal charge = $5 - \dfrac{1}{2}(8) - 0 = +1$

Thus, the formal charge on the N atom in $[NH_4]^+$ is +1.

3. Resonance

For some molecules, two or more nonidentical Lewis structures can be drawn; these are called **resonance structures.** The molecule doesn't actually exist as either one of the resonance structures, but is rather a composite, or hybrid, of the two. For example, SO_2 has three resonance structures, two of which are minor: O = S – O and O – S = O. The actual molecule is a hybrid of these three structures (spectral data indicate that the two S–O bonds are identically equivalent). This phenomenon is known as resonance, and the actual structure of the molecule is called the **resonance hybrid.** Resonance structures are expressed with a double-headed arrow between them; thus,

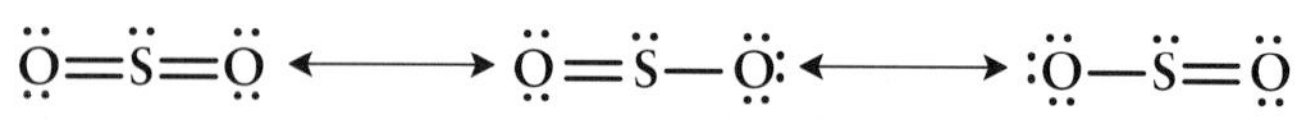

$$\ddot{O}=\ddot{S}=\ddot{O} \longleftrightarrow \ddot{O}=\ddot{S}-\ddot{O}: \longleftrightarrow :\ddot{O}-\ddot{S}=\ddot{O}$$

represents the resonance structures of SO_2.

The last two resonance structures of sulfur dioxide shown above have equivalent energy or stability. Often, nonequivalent resonance structures may be written for a molecule. In these cases, the more stable the structure, the more that structure contributes to the character of the resonance hybrid. Conversely, the less stable the resonance structure, the less that structure contributes to the resonance hybrid.

It is the structure on the left of the diagram that is the most stable. Formal charges are often useful for qualitatively assessing the stability of a particular resonance structure; the following guidelines are used:

a. A Lewis structure with small or no formal charges is preferred over a Lewis structure with large formal charges.

b. A Lewis structure in which negative formal charges are placed on more electronegative atoms is more stable than one in which the formal charges are placed on less electronegative atoms.

Example: Write the resonance structures for [NCO]⁻.

Solution: 1. C is the least electronegative of the three given atoms, N, C, and O. Therefore the C atom occupies the central position in the skeletal structure of [NCO]⁻.

$$N \ C \ O$$

2. N has 5 valence electrons;
C has 4 valence electrons;
O has 6 valence electrons;
and the species itself has one negative charge.
Total valence electrons = 5 + 4 + 6 + 1 = 16

3. Draw single bonds between the central C atom and the surrounding atoms, N and O. Place a pair of electrons in each bond.

$$N : C : O$$

4. Complete the octets of N and O with the remaining 16 − 4 = 12 electrons.

$$:\ddot{\overset{..}{N}} : C : \ddot{\overset{..}{O}} :$$

5. The C octet is incomplete. There are three ways in which double and triple bonds can be formed to complete the C octet: two lone pairs from the O atom can be used to form a triple bond between the C and O atoms;

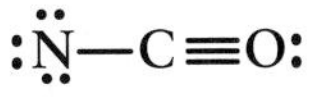

$$:\ddot{N} - C \equiv O :$$

TEACHER TIP

We spoke earlier in the book about how atoms strive for nobility. Here we can see that molecules strive to be like Switzerland. No, not cheesy—neutral! By spreading out charges amongst more than one atom, the charge gets closer to zero and therefore more stable.

or one lone electron pair can be taken from both the O and the N atoms to form two double bonds, one between N and C, and the other between O and C;

$$:\ddot{N}=C=\ddot{O}:$$

or two lone electron pairs can be taken from the N atom to form a triple bond between the C and N atoms.

$$:N\equiv C-\ddot{\underset{..}{O}}:$$

These three are all resonance structures of $[NCO]^-$.

6. Assign formal charges to each atom of each resonance structure.

   The most stable structure is:

$$:N\equiv C-\ddot{\underset{..}{O}}:$$

   because the negative formal charge is on the most electronegative atom, O.

4. Exceptions to the Octet Rule

Atoms found in or beyond the third period can have more than 8 valence electrons, because some of the valence electrons may occupy *d* orbitals. These atoms can be assigned more than four bonds in Lewis structures. When drawing the Lewis structure of the sulfate ion, giving the sulfur 12 valence electrons permits three of the five atoms to be assigned a formal charge of zero. The sulfate ion can be drawn in six resonance forms, each with the two double bonds attached to a different combination of oxygen atoms.

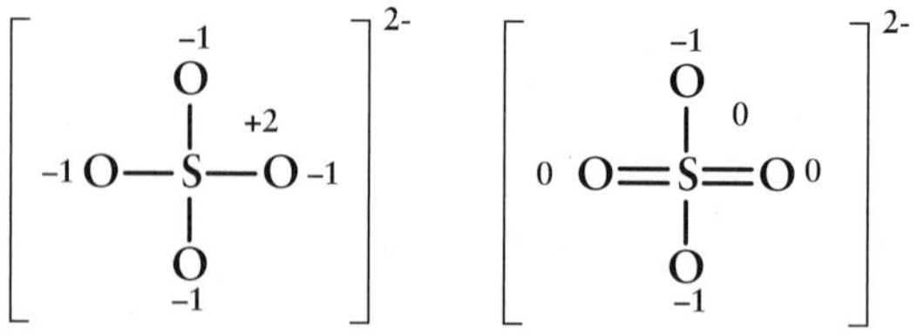

Figure 3.1

NOTE

As with all rules, the Octet "rule" has exceptions. It *always* applies to neutral atoms and anions of C, N, O, and F (which are common on the MCAT). It *often* (not always) applies to the halogens and other representative elements, but never applies to H, He, Li, Be, or neutral B and Al. Other notable exceptions are elements beyond period 3 because they have d orbitals (sulfur and phosphorous will be the most common examples seen on Test Day)

C. TYPES OF COVALENT BONDING

The nature of a covalent bond depends on the relative electronegativities of the atoms sharing the electron pairs. Covalent bonds are considered to be **polar** or **nonpolar** depending on the difference in electronegativities between the atoms.

1. Polar Covalent Bond

Polar covalent bonding occurs between atoms with small differences in electronegativity, generally in the range of 0.4 to 1.7 Pauling units. The bonding electron pair is not shared equally but pulled more toward the element with the higher electronegativity. As a result, the more electronegative atom acquires a partial negative charge, δ^-, and the less electronegative atom acquires a partial positive charge, δ^+, giving the molecule partially ionic character. For instance, the covalent bond in HCl is polar because the two atoms have a small difference in electronegativity (approximately 0.9). Chlorine, the more electronegative atom, attains a partial negative charge and hydrogen attains a partial positive charge. This difference in charge between the atoms is indicated by an arrow crossed (like a plus sign) at the positive end pointing to the negative end, as shown below:

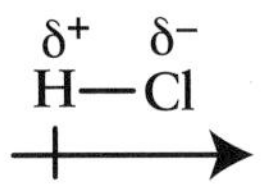

$$\overset{\delta^+ \quad \delta^-}{H-Cl}$$

Figure 3.2

TEACHER TIP

Back to that tug of war from earlier, sometimes we can see the winner before the final flag. Here, the chlorine has the flag closer to its side (therefore, a partial negative charge), but it hasn't won the match yet.

A molecule that has such a separation of positive and negative charges is called a polar molecule. The **dipole moment** itself is a vector quantity μ, defined as the product of the charge magnitude (q) and the distance between the two partial charges (r):

$$\mu = qr$$

The dipole moment is denoted by an arrow pointing from the positive to the negative charge, and is measured in Debye units (coulomb-meters).

2. Nonpolar Covalent Bond

Nonpolar covalent bonding occurs between atoms that have the same electronegativities. The bonding electron pair is shared equally, with no separation of charge across the bond. Not surprisingly, nonpolar covalent bonds occur in diatomic molecules such as H_2, Cl_2, O_2, and N_2.

3. Coordinate Covalent Bond

In a coordinate covalent bond, the shared electron pair comes from the lone pair of one of the atoms in the molecule. Once such a bond forms, it is indistinguishable from any other covalent bond. Distinguishing such a bond is useful only in keeping track of the valence electrons and formal charges. Coordinate bonds are typically found in Lewis acid-base compounds (see chapter 10, Acids and Bases). A **Lewis acid** is a compound that can accept an electron pair to form a covalent bond; a **Lewis base** is a compound that can donate an electron pair to form a covalent bond. For example, in the reaction between borontrifluoride (BF_3) and ammonia (NH_3):

$$
\begin{array}{ccc}
\underset{\displaystyle F}{\overset{\displaystyle F}{F-B}} & + & \underset{\displaystyle H}{\overset{\displaystyle H}{:N-H}} \longrightarrow \underset{\displaystyle F\ \ H}{\overset{\displaystyle F\ \ H}{F-B-N-H}}
\end{array}
$$

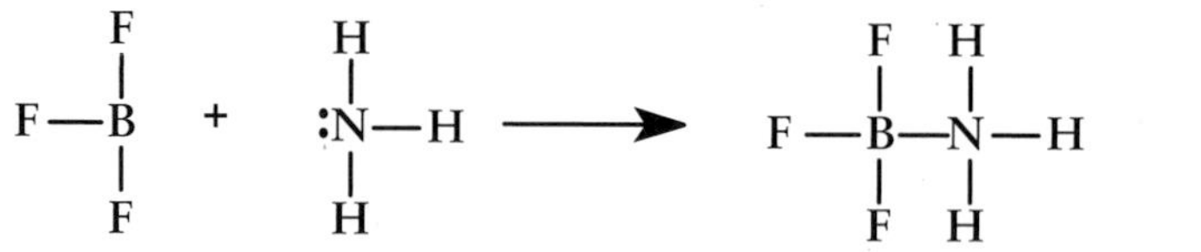

Lewis acid   Lewis base   Lewis acid–base compound

Figure 3.3

NH_3 donates a pair of electrons to form a coordinate covalent bond; thus, it acts as a Lewis base. BF_3 accepts this pair of electrons to form the coordinate covalent bond; thus, it acts as a Lewis acid.

D. GEOMETRY AND POLARITY OF COVALENT MOLECULES

1. The Valence Shell Electron-Pair Repulsion Theory

The valence shell electron-pair repulsion (VSEPR) theory uses Lewis structures to predict the molecular geometry of covalently bonded molecules. It states that the three-dimensional arrangement of atoms surrounding a central atom is determined by the repulsions between the bonding and the nonbonding electron pairs in the valence shell of the central atom. These electron pairs arrange themselves as far apart as possible, thereby minimizing repulsion.

The following steps are used to predict the geometrical structure of a molecule using the VSEPR theory.

- Draw the Lewis structure of the molecule.
- Count the total number of bonding and nonbonding electron pairs in the valence shell of the central atom.
- Arrange the electron pairs around the central atom so that they are as far apart from each other as possible. For example, the compound AX_2 has the Lewis structure, X : A : X. A has two bonding electron pairs in its valence shell. To make these electron pairs as far apart as possible, their geometric structure should be linear,

X – A – X

Valence electron arrangements are summarized in Table 3.2.

Table 3.2

Regions of Electron Density	Example	Geometric Arrangement of Electron Pairs Around the Central Atom	Shape	Angle between Electron Pairs
2	$BeCl_2$	X – A – X	linear	180°
3	BH_3	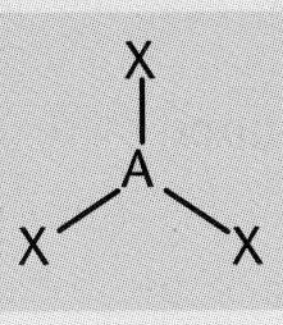	trigonal planar	120°
4	CH_4	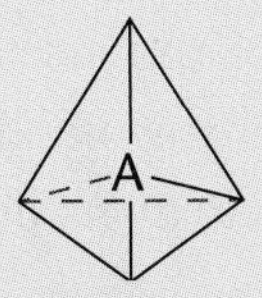	tetrahedral	109.05°
5	PCl_5	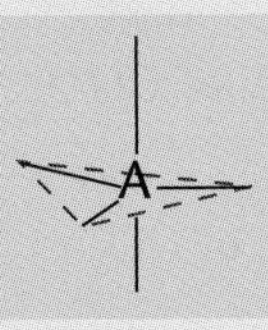	trigonal bipyramidal	90°, 120°, 180°
6	SF_6	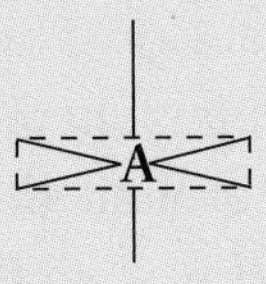	octahedral	90°, 180°

Example: Predict the geometry of NH_3.

Solution: 1. The Lewis structure of NH_3 is:

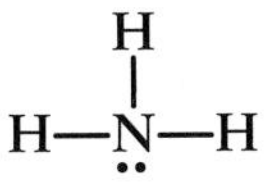

2. The central atom, N, has three bonding electron pairs and one nonbonding electron pair, for a total of four electron pairs.

3. The four electron pairs will be farthest apart when they occupy the corners of a tetrahedron. As one of the four electron pairs is a lone pair, the observed geometry is trigonal pyramidal.

TEACHER TIP

Know some of these shapes and angles on Test Day, particularly the tetrahedral shape because it is seen with carbon, nitrogen, and oxygen-common topics in both science sections of the MCAT.

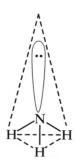

Figure 3.4

In describing the shape of a molecule, only the arrangement of atoms (not electrons) is considered. Even though the electron pairs are arranged tetrahedrally, the shape of NH_3 is pyramidal. It is not trigonal planar because the lone pair repels the three bonding electron pairs, causing them to move as far away as possible.

Example: Predict the geometry of CO_2.

Solution: The Lewis structure of CO_2 is $\ddot{O}::C::\ddot{O}$.

The double bond behaves just like a single bond for purposes of predicting molecular shape. This compound has two groups of electrons around the carbon. According to the VSEPR theory, the two sets of electrons will orient themselves 180° apart, on opposite sides of the carbon atom, minimizing electron repulsion. Therefore, the molecular structure of CO_2 is linear: $\ddot{O}=C=\ddot{O}$

2. Polarity of Molecules

A molecule with a net dipole moment is called polar, as previously mentioned, because it has positive and negative poles. The polarity of a molecule depends on the polarity of the constituent bonds and on the shape of the molecule. A molecule with nonpolar bonds is always nonpolar; a molecule with polar bonds may be polar or nonpolar depending on the orientation of the bond dipoles.

A molecule of two atoms bound by a polar bond must have a net dipole moment and therefore be polar. The two equal and opposite partial charges are localized at the ends of the molecule on the two atoms. A molecule consisting of more than two atoms bound with polar bonds may be either polar or nonpolar, because the overall dipole moment of a molecule is the vector sum of the individual bond dipole moments. If the molecule has a particular shape such that the bond dipole moments cancel each other, i.e., if the vector sum is zero, then the result is a nonpolar molecule. For instance, CCl_4 has four polar C–Cl bonds. According to the VSEPR theory, the shape of CCl_4 is tetrahedral. The four bond dipoles point to the vertices of the tetrahedron and cancel each other, resulting in a nonpolar molecule.

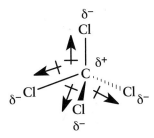

Figure 3.5. No Net Dipole Moment

However, if the orientation of the bond dipoles are such that they do not cancel out, the molecules will have a net dipole moment and therefore be polar. For instance, H_2O has two polar O–H bonds. According to the VSEPR model, its shape is angular. The two dipoles add together to give a net dipole moment to the molecule, making the H_2O molecule polar.

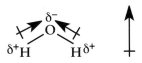

Figure 3.6. Net Dipole Moment

E. ATOMIC AND MOLECULAR ORBITALS

A description of the quantum numbers has already been given in chapter 1. The azimuthal quantum number ℓ describes the orbitals of each n shell. The shapes of these orbitals represent the probability of finding an electron at any given instant. When $\ell = 0$, the orbital is an s-orbital. s-orbitals are spherically symmetric. The 1s-orbital ($n = 1, \ell = 0$) is plotted on the following page.

FLASHBACK

Quantum numbers (chapter 1) revisited:

- For any value of n, there are n values of ℓ ($0 \rightarrow n - 1$).

- $\ell = 0 \rightarrow$ s
  $\ell = 1 \rightarrow$ p
  $\ell = 2 \rightarrow$ d

- For any value of ℓ, there are $2\ell + 1$ values of $m\ell$ (number of orbitals); values themselves will range from $-\ell$ to ℓ.

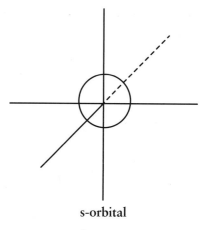

s-orbital

Figure 3.7

When $\ell = 1$, there are three possible orbitals (because the magnetic quantum number, m_ℓ may equal -1, 0, or 1). These are called p-orbitals and have a dumbbell shape. The three p-orbitals, designated p_x, p_y, and p_z, are oriented at right angles to each other; the p_x-orbital is plotted below.

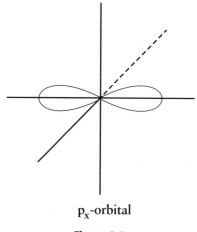

p_x-orbital

Figure 3.8

Plus and minus signs, determined from the mathematics of the wave function, are assigned to each lobe of the p-orbitals. The shapes of the five d-orbitals ($\ell = 2$, $m_\ell = -2, -1, 0, 1, 2$) and the seven f-orbitals ($\ell = 3$, $m_\ell = -3, -2, -1, 0, 1, 2, 3$) are more complex and need not be memorized.

When two atoms bond to form a molecule, the atomic orbitals interact to form a **molecular orbital** that describes the probability of finding the bonding electrons. Molecular orbitals are obtained by adding the wave functions of the atomic orbitals. Qualitatively, this is described by the **overlap** of two atomic orbitals. If the signs of the two atomic orbitals are the same, a **bonding orbital** is formed. If the signs are different, an

BRIDGE

It is the pi bonds of alkenes, alkynes, aromatic compounds, and carboxylic acid derivates that lend the functionality so important in organic chemistry.

antibonding orbital is formed. In addition, two different types of overlap are possible. When orbitals overlap head-to-head, the resulting bond is called a **sigma** (σ) bond. When the orbitals are parallel, a **pi** (π) bond is formed.

THE INTERMOLECULAR FORCES

The attractive forces that exist between molecules are collectively known as **intermolecular forces.** These include **dipole-dipole interactions, hydrogen bonding,** and **dispersion forces.** Dipole-dipole interactions and dispersion forces are often referred to as **van der Waals forces.**

1. Ion-Dipole Interactions

When dipoles are dissolved in solutions where ions are present, ions will arrange themselves with the opposite charged end of the dipole. For example, positive ions will be attracted to and bond with the negative end of the dipole and vice versa.

2. Dipole-Dipole Interactions

Polar molecules tend to orient themselves such that the positive region of one molecule is close to the negative region of another molecule. This arrangement is energetically favorable because an attractive dipole force is formed between the two molecules.

Dipole-dipole interactions are present in the solid and liquid phases but become negligible in the gas phase because the molecules are generally much farther apart. Polar species tend to have higher boiling points than nonpolar species of comparable molecular weight.

3. Hydrogen Bonding

Hydrogen bonding is a specific, unusually strong form of dipole-dipole interaction, which may be either intra- or intermolecular. When hydrogen is bound to a highly electronegative atom such as fluorine, oxygen, or nitrogen, the hydrogen atom carries little of the electron density of the covalent bond. This positively charged hydrogen atom interacts with the partial negative charge located on the electronegative atoms of nearby molecules. Substances that display hydrogen bonding tend to have unusually high boiling points compared with compounds of similar molecular formula that do not hydrogen bond. The difference derives from the energy required to break the hydrogen bonds. Hydrogen bonding is particularly important in the behavior of water, alcohols, amines, and carboxylic acids.

MCAT SYNOPSIS

These intermolecular forces are the binding forces which keep a substance together in its solid or liquid state (see chapter 8). These same forces determine whether two substances are miscible or immiscible in the solution phase (see chapter 9).

MCAT APPLICATION & REAL-WORLD CORRELATION

While van der Waals forces are the weakest of intermolecular attractions, when there are millions of these interactions like there are on the bottom of a gecko's foot due to many microfibers, there is an amazing power of adhesion that is demonstrated by the animal's ability to climb smooth vertical, even inverted, surfaces.

4. Dispersion Forces

The bonding electrons in covalent bonds may appear to be equally shared between two atoms, but at any particular point in time they will be located randomly throughout the orbital. This permits unequal sharing of electrons, causing rapid polarization and counterpolarization of the electron cloud and formation of short-lived dipoles. These dipoles interact with the electron clouds of neighboring molecules, inducing the formation of more dipoles. The attractive interactions of these short-lived dipoles are called dispersion or **London forces.**

Dispersion forces are generally weaker than other intermolecular forces. They do not extend over long distances and are therefore most important when molecules are close together. The strength of these interactions within a given substance depends directly on how easily the electrons in the molecules can move (i.e., be polarized). Large molecules in which the electrons are far from the nucleus are relatively easy to polarize and therefore possess greater dispersion forces. If it were not for dispersion forces, the noble gases would not liquefy at any temperature because no other intermolecular forces exist between the noble gas atoms. The low temperature at which the noble gases liquefy is to some extent indicative of the magnitude of dispersion forces between the atoms.

PRACTICE QUESTIONS

1. What is the character of the bond in carbon monoxide?

A. Ionic
B. Polar covalent
C. Nonpolar covalent
D. Coordinate covalent

2. Which of the following molecules has the oxygen atom with the most negative formal charge?

A. H_2O
B. CO_3^{2-}
C. O_3
D. CH_2O

3. Which of the following are the most important resonance structures for NO_2?

I.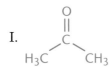

II.

III.

A. I only
B. II only
C. I and II only
D. I, II, and III

4. Order the following compounds shown from lowest to highest boiling point.

I.

II. KCl
III. Kr
IV. Isopropyl alcohol

A. I → II → IV → III
B. III → IV → I → II
C. II → IV → I → III
D. I → IV → II → III

5. What should be changed in the following ClF4- Lewis configuration?

A. The central chloride atom should have fewer electrons.
B. The central chloride should carry an additional electron pair.
C. The central chloride should carry a formal charge of –1.
D. The central chloride should have a formal charge of –2.

6. Both CO_3^{2-} and ClF_3 have three atoms bonded to a central atom. How would one best explain why CO_3 has trigonal planar geometry, while ClF_3 is trigonal bipyramidal?

A. CO_3 has multiple resonance structures, while ClF_3 does not.
B. CO_3 has a charge of –2, while ClF_3 has no charge.
C. ClF_3 has lone pairs on its central atom, while CO_3 has none.
D. CO_3 has lone pairs on its central atom, while ClF_3 has none.

7. Which of the following has the largest dipole moment?

A. HCN
B. H_2O
C. CCl_4
D. SO_2

8. Despite the fact that both C_2H_2 and NCH contain triple bonds, the lengths of these triple bonds are not equal. Which of the following best explains this finding?

A. In C_2H_2, because the triple bond is between similar atoms, it is shorter in length.

B. The two molecules have different resonance structures.

C. Carbon is more electronegative than hydrogen.

D. Nitrogen is more electronegative than carbon.

9. Which of the following best explains the phenomenon of hydrogen bonding?

A. Hydrogen has a strong affinity for holding onto valence electrons.

B. Hydrogen can only hold two valence electrons.

C. Electronegative atoms disproportionately carry shared pairs when bonded to hydrogen.

D. Hydrogen bonds have ionic character.

10. Which of the following best describes the character of the bonds in a molecule of ammonium?

A. Three polar covalent bonds

B. Four polar covalent bonds

C. Two polar covalent bonds, one coordinate covalent bond

D. Three polar covalent bonds, one coordinate covalent bond

11. Although the Octet rule dictates much of molecular structure, some atoms can exceed the Octet rule and be surrounded by more than eight electrons. Some atoms can exceed the Octet rule because they

A. already have eight electrons in their outermost electron shell.

B. do so only when bonding with transition metals.

C. have f-orbitals in which extra electrons can reside.

D. have d-orbitals in which extra electrons can reside.

12. Noble gases can liquefy as a result of

A. van der Waals force.

B. ion-dipole interaction.

C. dispersion force.

D. dipole-dipole interaction.

13. What is correct electron configuration for elemental chromium?

A. [Ar] $3p^6$

B. [Ar] $3d^5\ 4s^1$

C. [Ar] $3d^6$

D. [Ar] $3d^4\ 4s^2$

14. In the structure shown below, which atoms have the most positive charge?

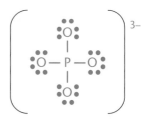

A. Phosphorous atom

B. All atoms equally

C. Four oxygens

D. Oxygen, at the peak of the trigonal pyramidal geometry

15. Which of the following is most characteristic of the bonding of $CaCl_2$?

   A. Low melting point
   B. No conduction of electricity in liquid state
   C. No conduction of electricity in aqueous state
   D. No conduction of electricity in solid state

16. The new bond formed in the reaction below is best called a(n)

   A. polar covalent bond.
   B. ionic bond.
   C. coordinate covalent bond.
   D. hydrogen bond.

17. Both BF_3 and NH_3 have three atoms bonded to the central atom. Which of the following best explains why the geometry of these two molecules is different?

   A. BF_3 has three bonded atoms and no lone pairs, which makes its geometry trigonal pyramidal.
   B. NH_3 is sp^3 hybridized, while BF_3 is sp^2 hybridized.
   C. NH_3 has one lone pair.
   D. BF_3 is nonpolar while NH_3 is polar.

18. Which of the following is a proper Lewis structure for $BeCl_2$?

19. Which of the following best describes an important property of bond energy?

   A. Bond energy increases with increasing bond length.
   B. The more shared electron pairs comprising a bond, the higher the energy of that bond.
   C. Single bonds are more difficult to break than double bonds.
   D. Bond energy and bond length are unrelated.

20. Which of the following is true about the polarity of molecules?

   A. Polarity is dependent on the vector sum of dipole moments.
   B. Polarity does not depend upon molecular geometry.
   C. If a molecule is comprised of one or more polar bonds, the molecule is polar.
   D. If a molecule is comprised of one or more nonpolar bonds, the molecule is nonpolar.

KEY CONCEPTS

Polarity

Molecular symmetry

Melting points

TAKEAWAYS

Forces that stabilize a molecule more in the solid state than in the liquid state will cause a molecule to have a higher melting point.

THINGS TO WATCH OUT FOR

Be careful not to confuse melting points with boiling points. Remember that in general, symmetry raises melting points, whereas branching lowers them.

SIMILAR QUESTIONS

1) For straight chain alkanes, which do you suppose have higher melting points: alkanes with an odd number of carbons, or those with an even number of alkanes?

2) Which molecule would you expect to melt higher, *n*–pentane or neopentane (2,2–dimethylpropane)? Why?

3) Between phenol (hydroxybenzene) and aniline (aminobenzene), which would melt higher and why?

MELTING POINTS

Arrange the following compounds in order of *increasing* melting point:

1) Separate the compounds by general polarity.
In this series, we can separate the compounds into three groups of two. The alkanes (**3** and **4**) will be the least polar, and therefore will melt the lowest; the alkenes (**1** and **5**) will be in the middle, and the aromatic compounds (**2** and **6**) will melt the highest.

---

2) Examine each grouping for trends in polarity and/or molecular symmetry.
For the lowest melting compounds, notice that cyclohexane has a higher degree of molecular symmetry than does *n*–hexane; this will cause it to melt significantly higher.

With the alkenes, the *trans* alkene has more symmetry than the *cis* alkene because the *cis* alkene has a rather large "kink" in the middle of the chain that prevents it from packing together as well in the crystal, and thus lowers its melting point.

Finally, acetanilide (**6**) is significantly more polar than aniline (**2**) because the amide carbonyl bond is highly polar, causing these molecules to stick together better and consequently raising their melting point.

Therefore, the ordering of the compounds' melting points is as follows:

3 < 4 < 5 < 1 < 2 < 6

Polarity affects melting point just as it does boiling points: more polar molecules melt higher because they tend to stick together better. Molecular symmetry also plays a more prominent role than with boiling point because another consideration is how well molecules pack or "fit together" in the crystal. The more symmetrical a molecule is, the better it packs in the crystal, just like symmetrical puzzle pieces in a jigsaw puzzle fit together better than asymmetrical pieces.

BOILING POINTS

Given the following five molecules, place them in order of increasing boiling point:

1   2   3

4   5

KEY CONCEPTS

Boiling points

Intermolecular forces

Molecular symmetry

1) Look for unusually heavy molecules.

Remember that molecular weight is one of the key determinants of boiling point. Something that is extraordinarily heavy is going to be harder to boil than something that is lighter. In this case, all the molecules are in the same general range of molecular weight, so this factor won't help us place the molecules in order.

2) Look for highly polar functional groups.

Compounds **3** and **5** are going to have higher-than-usual boiling points. Between compounds **3** and **5**, compound **3** will boil higher because it has a more polar functional group, and also the alcohol is capable of hydrogen bonding. Compound **3** will have hydrogen bonds that are a stronger version of dipole–dipole interactions.

The other factor that affects boiling point is the presence of polar functional groups. These groups help *increase* boiling point because they increase the attractions of molecules for each other.

Remember: Hydrogen bonding is the strongest type of intermolecular attraction.

3) Look for the effect of dispersion forces.

Compound **4** will boil higher than **1**, **2**, and **5** because it is longer (eight carbons versus five, which increases its London Forces); therefore, there are more opportunities for it to attract other molecules of **4**.

Although **1**, **2**, and **5** all have the same surface area, the polar group on **5** gives it a higher boiling point than **1** and **2**.

TAKEAWAYS

Remember that there are only two factors that affect relative boiling points between substances: *molecular weight* and *intermolecular forces*.

THINGS TO WATCH OUT FOR

Be sure to consider the factors in the order presented here. For example, polarity is more important than size.

SIMILAR QUESTIONS

1) How could you easily alter the structure of compound 3 to lower its boiling point?
2) How could you easily alter the structure of compound 5 to raise its boiling point?

Remember: *Dispersion forces are the only kind of intermolecular attractions that cause* ***nonpolar*** *molecules to stick together.*

---

4) Look for trends in the symmetry of molecules.
In this case, pentane, **1**, will boil higher than neopentane, **2.** This is because neopentane is more symmetrical and therefore a more compact molecule; thus, it has a less effective surface area. You can determine this by imagining a "bubble" around each molecule. Neopentane could very easily fit into a spherically shaped bubble, whereas pentane would require an elongated, elliptical bubble with a greater surface area.

If neopentane has a smaller surface area, then there are less opportunities for it to engage in dispersion-type attractions with other molecules of neopentane, making it a lower boiling compound (the actual boiling points are 36.1°C for pentane and 9.4°C for neopentane).

At this point, we're really splitting hairs. Notice that compounds **1** and **2** are merely constitutional isomers of one another. If two molecules have the same weight and are relatively nonpolar, *symmetry* is the factor that decides which one will boil higher.

---

5) Put it all together. Order the compounds as specified by the question.
The ordering of the boiling points will therefore be:

2 < **1** < **5** < **4** < **3**

CHAPTER 4

COMPOUNDS AND STOICHIOMETRY

A **compound** is a pure substance that is composed of two or more elements in a fixed proportion. Compounds can be broken down chemically to produce their constituent elements or other compounds. All elements, except for some of the noble gases, can react with other elements or compounds to form new compounds. These new compounds can react further to form yet different compounds.

MOLECULES AND MOLES

A **molecule** is a combination of two or more atoms held together by covalent bonds. It is the smallest unit of a compound displaying the properties of that compound. Molecules may contain two atoms of the same element, as in N_2 and O_2, or may be comprised of two or more different atoms, as in CO_2 and $SOCl_2$. Molecules are usually discussed in terms of molecular weights and moles.

Ionic compounds do not form true molecules. In the solid state they can be considered to be a nearly infinite, three-dimensional array of the charged particles of which the compound is composed. Because no actual molecule exists, molecular weight becomes meaningless, and the term **formula weight** is used in its place.

> ## MCAT Synopsis
>
> Ionic compounds form from combinations of elements with large electronegativity differences (and far apart on the periodic table), such as sodium with chlorine. Molecular compounds form from the combination of elements of similar electronegativity (or close to each other on the periodic table), such as carbon with oxygen.

A. MOLECULAR WEIGHT

Like atoms, molecules can be characterized by their weight. The molecular weight is the sum of the atomic weights (in amu) of the atoms in the molecule. Similarly, the formula weight of an ionic compound is found by adding the atomic weights according to the empirical formula of the substance.

Example: What is the molecular weight of $SOCl_2$?

Solution: To find the molecular weight of $SOCl_2$, add together the atomic weights of each of the atoms.

$$1S = 1 \times 32 \text{ amu} \quad = 32 \text{ amu}$$
$$1O = 1 \times 16 \text{ amu} \quad = 16 \text{ amu}$$

$$2Cl = 2 \times 35.5 \text{ amu} \quad = \underline{71 \text{ amu}}$$
$$\text{molecular weight} \quad = 119 \text{ amu}$$

B. MOLE

A mole is defined as the amount of a substance that contains the same number of particles that are found in a 12.000 g sample of carbon-12. This quantity, **Avogadro's number,** is equal to 6.022×10^{23}. One mole of a compound has a mass in grams equal to the molecular weight of that compound in amu, and contains 6.022×10^{23} molecules of the compound. For example, 62 g of H_2CO_3 represents 1 mole of carbonic acid and contains 6.022×10^{23} H_2CO_3 molecules. The mass of 1 mole of a compound is called its **molar weight** or **molar mass,** and is usually expressed as g/mol. Therefore, the molar mass of H_2CO_3 is 62 g/mol.

The following formula is used to determine the number of moles that are present:

$$\text{mol} = \frac{\text{weight of sample (g)}}{\text{molar weight (g/mol)}}$$

Example: How many moles are in 9.52 g of $MgCl_2$?

Solution: First, find the molar mass of $MgCl_2$.

1(24.31 g/mol) + 2(35.45 g/mol) = 95.21 g/mol
Now, solve for the number of moles.

$$\frac{9.52}{95.21 \text{ g/mol}} = 0.10 \text{ mol of } Mg\,Cl_2$$

C. EQUIVALENT WEIGHT

For some substances, it is useful to define a measure of reactive capacity. This expresses the fact that some molecules are more potent than others in performing certain reactions. An example of this is the ability of different acids to donate protons (H^+ ions) in solution (see chapter 10, Acids and Bases). For instance, one mole of HCl can donate one mol of hydrogen ions, while one mol of H_2SO_4 can donate two moles of hydrogen ions. This difference is expressed using the term **equivalent:** one mole of HCl contains one equivalent of hydrogen ions while one mol of H_2SO_4 contains two equivalents of hydrogen ions. To determine the number of equivalents a compound contains, a new measure of weight called **gram-equivalent weight (GEW)** was developed.

$$\text{equivalents} = \frac{\text{weight of compound}}{\text{gram equivalent weight}}$$

and

$$\text{gram equivalent weight} = \frac{\text{molar mass}}{n}$$

where n is usually either the number of hydrogens used per molecule of acid in a reaction, or the number of hydroxyl groups used per molecule of base in a reaction. This value is strictly dependent on reaction conditions. By using equivalents, it is possible to say that one equivalent of acid will neutralize one equivalent of base, a statement which may not necessarily be true when dealing with moles.

REPRESENTATION OF COMPOUNDS

A. LAW OF CONSTANT COMPOSITION

The **law of constant composition** states that any sample of a given compound will contain the same elements in the identical mass ratio. For instance, every sample of H_2O will contain two atoms of hydrogen for every atom of oxygen, or, in other words, one gram of hydrogen for every eight grams of oxygen.

B. EMPIRICAL AND MOLECULAR FORMULAS

There are two ways to express a formula for a compound. The **empirical formula** gives the simplest whole number ratio of the elements in the compound. The **molecular formula** gives the exact number of atoms of each element in the compound and is usually a multiple of the empirical formula. For example, the empirical formula for benzene is CH, while the molecular formula is C_6H_6. For some compounds, the empirical and molecular formulas are the same, as in the case of H_2O. An ionic compound, such as NaCl or $CaCO_3$, will have only an empirical formula.

C. PERCENT COMPOSITION

The percent composition by mass of an element is the weight percent of the element in a specific compound. To determine the percent composition of an element X in a compound, the following formula is used:

$$\% \text{ composition} = \frac{\text{mass of } \times \text{ in formula}}{\text{Formula weight of compound}} \times 100\%$$

The percent composition of an element may be determined using either the empirical or molecular formula. If the percent compositions are known, the empirical formula can be derived. It is possible to determine the molecular formula if both the percent compositions and molecular weight of the compound are known.

Example: What is the percent composition of chromium in $K_2Cr_2O_7$?

Solution: The formula weight of $K_2Cr_2O_7$ is:

2(39 g/mol) + 2(52 g/mol) + 7(16 g/mol) = 294 g/mol

$$\text{Percent composition of Cr} = \frac{2(52 \text{ g/mol})}{294 \text{ g/mol}} = 100$$

$$= 0.354 \times 100$$

$$= 35.4 \text{ percent}$$

Example: What are the empirical and molecular formulas of a compound that contains 40.9 percent carbon, 4.58 percent hydrogen, 54.52 percent oxygen, and has a molecular weight of 264 g/mol?

Method One: First, determine the number of moles of each element in the compound by assuming a 100-gram sample; this converts the percentage of each element present directly into grams of that element. Then convert grams to moles:

$$\# \text{mol of } C = \frac{40.9 \text{ g}}{12 \text{ g/mol}} = 3.41 \text{ mol}$$

$$\# \text{mol of } H = \frac{4.58 \text{ g}}{1 \text{ g/mol}} = 4.58 \text{ mol}$$

$$\# \text{mol of } O = \frac{54.52 \text{ g}}{16 \text{ g/mol}} = 3.41 \text{ mol}$$

Next, find the simplest whole number ratio of the elements by dividing the number of moles by the smallest number obtained in the previous step.

$$C: \frac{3.41}{3.41} = 1.00 \qquad H: \frac{4.58}{3.41} = 1.33 \qquad O: \frac{3.41}{3.41} = 1.00$$

Finally, the empirical formula is obtained by converting the numbers obtained into whole numbers (multiplying them by an integer value).

$$C_1H_{1.33}O_1 \times 3 = C_3H_4O_3$$

$C_3H_4O_3$ is the empirical formula. To determine the molecular formula, divide the molecular weight by the weight represented by the empirical formula. The resultant value is the number of empirical formula units in the molecular formula.

The empirical formula weight of $C_3H_4O_3$ is:

$3(12 \text{ g/mol}) + 4(1 \text{ g/mol}) + 3(16 \text{ g/mol}) = 88 \text{ g/mol}$

$$\frac{264 \text{ g/mol}}{88 \text{ g/mol}} = 3$$

$C_3H_4O_3 \times 3 = C_9H_{12}O_9$ is the molecular formula.

Method Two: When the molecular weight is given, it is generally easier to find the molecular formula first. This is accomplished by multiplying the molecular weight by the given percentages to find the grams of each element present in one mole of compound, then dividing by the respective atomic weights to find the mole ratio of the elements:

$$\# \text{ mol of C} = \frac{(0.409)(264) \text{ g}}{12 \text{ g/mol}} = 9 \text{ mol}$$

$$\# \text{ mol of H} = \frac{(0.458)(264) \text{ g}}{1 \text{ g/mol}} = 12 \text{ mol}$$

$$\# \text{ mol of O} = \frac{(0.5452)(264) \text{ g}}{16 \text{ g/mol}} = 9 \text{ mol}$$

Thus the molecular formula, $C_9H_{12}O_9$, is the direct result.

The empirical formula can now be found by reducing the subscript ratio to the simplest integral values.

MCAT SYNOPSIS

The molecular formula is either the same as the empirical formula or a multiple of it. To calculate the molecular formula, you need to know the mole ratio (this will give you the empirical formula) and the molecular weight (molecular wt. ÷ empirical formula wt. will give you the multiplier for the empirical formula → molecular formula conversion).

TYPES OF CHEMICAL REACTIONS

There are many ways in which elements and compounds can react to form other species; memorizing every reaction would be impossible, as well as unnecessary. However, nearly every inorganic reaction can be classified into at least one of four general categories.

MCAT SYNOPSIS

Combination reactions generally have more reactants than products.

A + B → C

A. COMBINATION REACTIONS

Combination reactions are reactions in which two or more **reactants** form one **product.** The formation of sulfur dioxide by burning sulfur in air is an example of a combination reaction.

$$S(s) + O_2(g) \rightarrow SO_2(g)$$

MCAT SYNOPSIS

Decomposition reactions generally have more product than reactants.
C → A + B

B. DECOMPOSITION REACTIONS

A **decomposition reaction** is defined as one in which a compound breaks down into two or more substances, usually as a result of heating or electrolysis. An example of a decomposition reaction is the breakdown of mercury (II) oxide (the sign Δ represents the addition of heat).

$$2HgO(s) \xrightarrow{\Delta} 2Hg(l) + O_2(g)$$

C. SINGLE DISPLACEMENT REACTIONS

MCAT SYNOPSIS

Single displacement reactions are also known as redox reactions.

Single displacement reactions occur when an atom (or ion) of one compound is replaced by an atom of another element. For example, zinc metal will displace copper ions in a copper sulfate solution to form zinc sulfate.

$$Zn(s) + CuSO_4(aq) \rightarrow Cu(s) + ZnSO_4(aq)$$

Single displacement reactions are often further classified as **redox** reactions. (These will be discussed in more detail in chapter 11, Redox Reactions and Electrochemistry.)

D. DOUBLE DISPLACEMENT REACTIONS

In double displacement reactions, also called **metathesis reactions,** elements from two different compounds displace each other to form two new compounds. This type of reaction occurs when one of the products is removed from the solution as a precipitate or gas, or when two of the original species combine to form a weak electrolyte that remains undissociated in solution. For example, when solutions of calcium chloride and silver nitrate are combined, insoluble silver chloride forms in a solution of calcium nitrate.

$$CaCl_2(aq) + 2\,AgNO_3(aq) \rightarrow Ca(NO_3)_2(aq) + 2\,AgCl(s)$$

NET IONIC EQUATIONS

Because reactions such as displacements often involve ions in solution, they can be written in ionic form. In the example where zinc is reacted with copper sulfate, the **ionic equation** would be:

$$Zn(s) + Cu^{2+}(aq) + SO_4^{2-}(aq) \rightarrow Cu(s) + Zn^{2+}(aq) + SO_4^{2-}(aq)$$

When displacement reactions occur, there are usually **spectator ions** that do not take part in the overall reaction but simply remain in solution throughout. The spectator ion in the equation above is sulfate, which does not undergo any transformation during the reaction. A **net ionic reaction** can be written showing only the species that actually participate in the reaction:

$$Zn(s) + Cu^{2+}(aq) \rightarrow Cu(s) + Zn^{2+}(aq)$$

Net ionic equations are important for demonstrating the actual reaction that occurs during a displacement reaction.

NEUTRALIZATION REACTIONS

Neutralization reactions are a specific type of double displacement that occur when an acid reacts with a base to produce a solution of a salt and water. For example, hydrochloric acid and sodium hydroxide will react to form sodium chloride and water.

$$HCl(aq) + NaOH(aq) \rightarrow NaCl(aq) + H_2O(\ell)$$

(This type of reaction will be discussed further in chapter 10, Acids and Bases.)

MCAT SYNOPSIS

Acids and bases (which we'll study later in Chapter 10) combine in neutralization reactions to produce salt and water.

BALANCING EQUATIONS

A. BALANCING EQUATIONS

Chemical equations express how much and which type of reactant must be used to obtain a given quantity of product. From the law of conservation of mass, the mass of the reactants in a reaction must be equal to the mass of the products. More specifically, chemical equations must be balanced so that there are the same number of atoms of each element in the products as there are in the reactants. **Stoichiometric coefficients** are used to indicate the number of moles of a given species involved in the reaction. For example, the reaction for the formation of water is:

$$2 H_2(g) + O_2(g) \rightarrow 2 H_2O(g)$$

The coefficients indicate that two moles of H_2 gas must be reacted with one mole of O_2 gas to produce two moles of water. In general, stoichiometric coefficients are given as whole numbers.

MCAT FAVORITE

You will rarely need to balance an equation on the MCAT. However, you need to recognize reactions that are or are not balanced.
Look at the:

1) charge of each side; and

2) number of atoms of each element.

MCAT SYNOPSIS

When balancing equations, focus on the least represented elements first, and work your way to the most represented element of the reaction (usually oxygen or hydrogen).

Example: Balance the following reaction.

$$C_4H_{10}(\ell) + O_2(g) \rightarrow CO_2(g) + H_2O(\ell)$$

Solution: First, balance the carbons in reactants and products.

$$C_4H_{10} + O_2 \rightarrow 4 CO_2 + H_2O$$

Second, balance the hydrogens in reactant and products.

$$C_4H_{10} + O_2 \rightarrow 4 CO_2 + 5 H_2O$$

Third, balance the oxygens in the reactants and products.

$$2\,C_4H_{10} + 13\,O_2 \rightarrow 8\,CO_2 + 10\,H_2O$$

Finally, check that all of the elements, and the total charges, are balanced correctly. If there is a difference in total charge between the reactants and products, then the charge will also have to be balanced. (Instructions for balancing charge are found in chapter 11.)

B. APPLICATIONS OF STOICHIOMETRY

Once an equation has been balanced, the ratio of moles of reactant to moles of product is known, and that information can be used to solve many types of stoichiometry problems. It is important to use proper units when solving such problems. If and when you are faced with doing the calculations, the units should cancel out, so that the units obtained in the answer represent those asked for in the problem.

Example: How many grams of calcium chloride are needed to prepare 72 g of silver chloride according to the following equation?

$$CaCl_2(aq) + 2AgNO_3(aq) \rightarrow Ca(NO_3)_2(aq) + 2AgCl(s)$$

Solution: Noting first that the equation is balanced, 1 mole of $CaCl_2$ yields 2 moles of AgCl when it is reacted with 2 moles of $AgNO_3$. The molar mass of $CaCl_2$ is 110 g, and the molar mass of AgCl is 144 g.

$$72\text{ g AgCl} \times \frac{1\text{ mol AgCl}}{144\text{ g AgCl}} \times \frac{1\text{ mol } CaCl_2}{2\text{ mol AgCl}} \times \frac{110\text{ g } CaCl_2}{1\text{ mol } CaCl_2}$$

Thus, 27.5 g of $CaCl_2$ are needed to produce 72 g of AgCl.

1. Limiting Reactants

When reactants are mixed, they are seldom added in the exact stoichiometric proportions as shown in the balanced equation. Therefore, in most reactions, one reactant will be consumed first. This reactant is known as the **limiting reactant** because it limits the amount of product that can be formed in the reaction. The reactant that remains after all of the limiting reagent is used is called the **excess reactant.**

Example: If 28 g of Fe react with 24 g of S to produce FeS, what would be the limiting reagent? How many grams of excess reagent would be present in the vessel at the end of the reaction?

The balanced equation is: $Fe + s \xrightarrow{\Delta} FeS$.

Solution: First, determine the number of moles for each reactant.

$$28 \text{ g Fe} \times \frac{1 \text{ mol Fe}}{56 \text{ g}} = 0.5 \text{ mol Fe}$$

$$24 \text{ g S} \times \frac{1 \text{ mol S}}{32 \text{ g}} = 0.75 \text{ mol S}$$

Because 1 mole of Fe is needed to react with 1 mole of S, and there are 0.5 moles Fe for every 0.75 moles S, the limiting reagent is Fe. Thus, 0.5 moles of Fe will react with 0.5 moles of S, leaving an excess of 0.25 moles of S in the vessel. The mass of the excess reagent will be:

$$\text{mass of S} = 0.25 \text{ mol S} \times \frac{32 \text{ g}}{1 \text{ mol S}}$$
$$= 8 \text{ g of S}$$

2. Yields

The **yield** of a reaction, which is the amount of product predicted or obtained when the reaction is carried out, can be determined or predicted from the balanced equation. There are three distinct ways of reporting yields. The **theoretical yield** is the amount of product that can be predicted from a balanced equation, assuming that all of the limiting reagent has been used, that no competing side reactions have occurred, and that all of the product has been collected. The theoretical yield is seldom obtained; therefore, chemists speak of the **actual yield,** which is the amount of product that is isolated from the reaction experimentally.

The term **percent yield** is used to express the relationship between the actual yield and the theoretical yield and is given by the following equation:

$$\text{percent yield} = \frac{\text{actual yield}}{\text{theoretical yield}} \times 100\%$$

Example: What is the percent yield for a reaction in which 27 g of Cu is produced by reacting 32.5 g of Zn in excess $CuSO_4$ solution?

Solution: The balanced equation is as follows:

$$Zn(s) + CuSO_4(aq) \rightarrow Cu(s) + ZnSO_4(aq)$$

Calculate the theoretical yield for Cu.

$$32.5 \text{ g Zn} \times \frac{1 \text{ mol Zn}}{65 \text{ g}} = 0.5 \text{ mol Zn}$$

$$0.5 \text{ mol Zn} \times \frac{1 \text{ mol Cu}}{1 \text{ mol Zn}} = 0.5 \text{ mol Cu}$$

$$0.5 \text{ mol Cu} \times \frac{64 \text{ g}}{1 \text{ mol Cu}} = 32 \text{ g Cu} = \text{theoretical yield}$$

Finally, determine the percent yield.

$$\frac{27 \text{ g}}{32 \text{ g}} \times 100\% = 84\%$$

MCAT Synopsis

When we are given excess of one reagent on the MCAT, we know that the other reactant is the limiting reagent.

PRACTICE QUESTIONS

1. Ionic compounds are

   A. formed from molecules containing two or more atoms.
   B. formed from charged particles and are measured by molecular weight.
   C. formed from charged particles, which share electrons equally.
   D. three-dimensional arrays of charged particles.

2. Which of the following has a formula weight between 74 and 75 grams per mole?

   A. KCl
   B. $C_4H_{10}O$
   C. $[LiCl]_2$
   D. BF_3

3. Which of the following is the gram equivalent weight of H_2SO_4?

   A. 98.08 g/mol
   B. 49.04 g/mol
   C. 196.2 g/mol
   D. 147.1 g/mol

4. Which of the following molecules CANNOT be expressed by the empirical formula CH?

   A. Benzene
   B. Ethyne
   C. 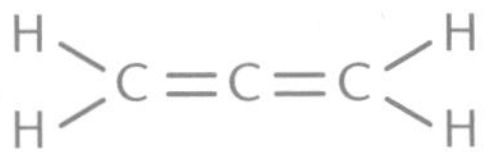
   D.

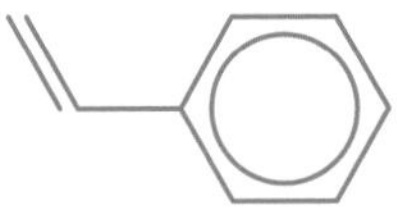

5. In which of the following compounds is the percent composition of carbon closest to 63?

   A. Acetone
   B. Ethanol
   C. C_3H_8
   D. Methanol

6. Calcium carbonate and aluminum nitrate react in solution, as demonstrated by the following reactants shown below. Which of the following answer choices best completes the equation?

   $$CaCO_3(s) + Al(NO_3)_3(aq) \longrightarrow \underline{\hspace{3cm}}$$

   A. $3CaCO_3 + Al(NO_3)_3 \longrightarrow 3CaNO_3 + Al(CO_3)_3$
   B. $CaCO_3 + 2Al(NO_3)_3 \longrightarrow Ca(NO_3)_6 + Al_2CO_3$
   C. $2CaCO_3 + Al(NO_3)_3 \longrightarrow 2CaNO_3 + Al_2(CO_3)_3$
   D. $3CaCO_3 + 2Al(NO_3)_3 \longrightarrow 3Ca(NO_3)_2 + Al_2(CO_3)_3$

7. Single displacements are chemical reactions which

   A. typically have more reactants than products.
   B. typically have more products than reactants.
   C. are often redox reactions.
   D. typically have aqueous reactants and solid products.

8. What is the most accurate characterization of the following reaction shown below?

$$Ca(OH)_2(aq) + H_2SO_4(aq) \longrightarrow CaSO_4(aq) + H_2O(l)$$

   A. Single displacement
   B. Neutralization
   C. Double displacement
   D. Redox

9. In the following reaction, if 39.03 g of Na_2S is reacted with 113.3 g of $AgNO_3$, how much, if any, of either reagent will be left over once the reaction has gone to completion?

$$Na_2S + 2\,AgNO_3 \longrightarrow Ag_2S + 2\,NaNO_3$$

   A. 41.37 g $AgNO_3$
   B. 13.00 g Na_2S
   C. 14.16 g Na_2S
   D. 74.27 g $AgNO_3$

10. How would one calculate the mass of oxygen produced in the following reaction shown below, assuming it goes to completion?

$$2\,KClO_3 \longrightarrow 2\,KCl + 3\,O_2$$

   A. $\dfrac{(\text{grams } KClO_3 \text{ consumed})(3 \text{ moles } O_2)(\text{molar mass } O_2)}{(\text{molar mass } KClO_3)(2 \text{ moles } KClO_3)}$

   B. $\dfrac{(\text{grams } KClO_3 \text{ consumed})(\text{molar mass } O_2)}{(\text{molar mass } KClO_3)(2 \text{ moles } KClO_3)}$

   C. $\dfrac{(\text{molar mass } KClO_3)(2 \text{ moles } KClO_3)}{(\text{grams } KClO_3 \text{ consumed})(\text{molar mass } O_2)}$

   D. $\dfrac{(\text{grams } KClO_3 \text{ consumed})(3 \text{ moles } O_2)}{(\text{molar mass } KClO_3)(2 \text{ moles } KClO_3)(\text{molar mass } O_2)}$

11. Aluminum metal can be used to remove tarnish from silver when the two solid metals are placed in water, according to the following reaction. Which of the following describe this reaction?

$$3\bigg/\; AgO + 2\,Al \longrightarrow 3\,Ag + Al_2O_3$$

   I. Double displacement reaction
   II. Single displacement reaction
   III. Redox reaction
   IV. Combination reaction

   A. II only
   B. IV only
   C. II and III
   D. I, II, and III

12. The following reaction is an example of the combustion of glucose to yield carbon dioxide, water, and heat. If 10 grams of glucose is reacted with excess oxygen, what is the approximate volume of liquid water that will be produced? Assume the density of water is similar to the density of water at room temperature.

$$C_6H_{12}O_6 + 6\,O_2 \longrightarrow 6\,CO_2 + 6\,H_2O + heat$$

   A. 0.6 milliliters
   B. 0.1 milliliters
   C. 1 milliliter
   D. 6 milliliters

13. Several samples of water are taken: one from the product of a combustion reaction, one from solid ice, and a final sample in the liquid phase. Which of the following would best explain why all three samples have the molecular formula H_2O?

A. Constant composition
B. Empirical formula
C. Percent composition
D. Steady-state

14. Which of the following reaction types generally have the same number of reactants and products?

I. Single displacement reaction
II. Double displacement reaction
III. Combination reaction

A. I only
B. II only
C. I and II
D. I, II, and III

15. Which of the following is the correct net ionic reaction for the reaction of copper with silver nitrate?

A. $Cu + AgNO_3 \longrightarrow Cu(NO_3)_2 + Ag$

B. $Cu + 2\,Ag^+ + NO_3^- \longrightarrow Cu^{2+} + 2\,NO_3^- + 2\,Ag^+$

C. $2\,Ag^+ + 2\,NO_3^- \longrightarrow 2\,NO_3^- + 2\,Ag$

D. $Cu + 2\,Ag^+ \longrightarrow Cu^{2+} + 2\,Ag$

16. In the process of photosynthesis, carbon dioxide and water are combined with energy to form glucose and oxygen, according to the equation shown below. What is the theoretical yield, in grams, of glucose if 30 grams of water is reacted with excess carbon dioxide and energy, in the balanced equation?

$$CO_2 + H_2O + Energy \longrightarrow C_6H_{12}O_6 + O_2$$

A. 50.02 grams glucose
B. 300.1 grams glucose
C. 30.03 grams glucose
D. 1801 grams glucose

17. One way to test for the presence of iron in solution is to add potassium thiocyanate to the solution. The resulting product is $FeSCN^{2+}$, which creates a dark red color in solution via the following net ionic equation shown below. How many grams of iron sulfate would be needed to produce 2 moles of $FeSCN^{2+}$?

$$Fe^{3+}(aq) + SCN^- \longrightarrow FeSCN^{2+}$$

A. 400 grams
B. 800 grams
C. 200 grams
D. 500 grams

CHAPTER 5

CHEMICAL KINETICS AND EQUILIBRIUM

When studying a chemical reaction, it is important to consider not only the chemical properties of the reactants, but also the **conditions** under which the reaction occurs, the **mechanism** by which it takes place, the rate at which it occurs, and the **equilibrium** (or steady state) toward which it proceeds.

CHEMICAL KINETICS

Chemical kinetics is the study of the rates of reactions, the effect of reaction conditions on these rates, and the mechanisms implied by such observations.

REACTION MECHANISMS

The **mechanism** of a reaction is the actual series of steps through which a chemical reaction occurs. Knowing the accepted mechanism of a reaction often helps to explain the reaction's rate, position of equilibrium, and thermodynamic characteristics (see chapter 6). Consider the reaction below:

> Overall reaction: $A_2 + 2B \rightarrow 2AB$

This equation seems to imply a mechanism in which two molecules of B collide with one molecule of A_2 to form two molecules of AB. But suppose instead that the reaction actually takes place in two steps.

Step 1:	$A_2 + B \rightarrow A_2B$	(Slow)
Step 2:	$A_2B + B \rightarrow 2AB$	(Fast)

Note that these two steps add up to the overall (net) reaction. A_2B, which does not appear in the overall reaction because it is neither a reactant nor a product, is called an **intermediate.** Reaction intermediates are often difficult to detect, but a proposed mechanism can be supported through kinetic experiments.

> **TEACHER TIP**
>
> Mechanisms are proposed pathways for a reaction that must coincide with rate data information from experimental observation. This is also addressed in Organic Chemistry.

The slowest step in a proposed mechanism is called the **rate-determining step,** because the overall reaction cannot proceed faster than that step.

REACTION RATES

A. DEFINITION OF RATE

Consider a reaction $2A + B \rightarrow C$, in which one mole of C is produced from every two moles of A and one mole of B. The rate of this reaction may be described in terms of either the disappearance of reactants over time, or the appearance of products over time.

$$\text{rate} = \frac{\text{decrease in concentration of reactions}}{\text{time}} = \frac{\text{increase in concentration of products}}{\text{time}}$$

Because the concentration of a reactant decreases during the reaction, a minus sign is placed before a rate that is expressed in terms of reactants. For the reaction above, the rate of reaction with respect to A is $-\Delta[A]/\Delta t$, with respect to B is $-\Delta[B]/\Delta t$, and with respect to C is $\Delta[C]/\Delta t$. In this particular reaction, the three rates are not equal. According to the stoichiometry of the reaction, A is used up twice as fast as B ($-\frac{1}{2}\Delta[A]/\Delta t = -\Delta[B]/\Delta t$), and A is consumed twice as fast as C is produced ($-\frac{1}{2}\Delta[A]/\Delta t = \Delta[C]/\Delta t$). To show a standard rate of reaction in which the rates with respect to all substances are equal, the rate for each substance should be divided by its stoichiometric coefficient.

$$\text{rate} = -\frac{1}{2}\frac{\Delta[A]}{\Delta t} = -\frac{\Delta[B]}{\Delta t} = \frac{\Delta[C]}{\Delta t}$$

In general, for the reaction

$$a A + b B \rightarrow c C + d D,$$

$$\text{rate} = -\frac{1}{a}\frac{\Delta[A]}{\Delta t} = -\frac{1}{b}\frac{\Delta[B]}{\Delta t} = \frac{1}{c}\frac{\Delta[C]}{\Delta t} = \frac{1}{d}\frac{\Delta[D]}{\Delta t}$$

Rate is expressed in the units of moles per liter per second (mol/L × sec) or molarity per second (molarity/sec).

B. RATE LAW

For nearly all forward, irreversible reactions, the rate is proportional to the product of the concentrations of the reactants, each raised to some power. For the general reaction

$$a A + b B \rightarrow c C + d D$$

the rate is proportional to $[A]^x [B]^y$, that is:

$$\text{rate} = k\,[A]^x\,[B]^y$$

This expression is the **rate law** for the general reaction above, where k is the **rate constant.** Multiplying the units of k by the concentration factors raised to the appropriate powers gives the rate in units of concentration/time. The exponents x and y are called the **orders of reaction;** x is the order with respect to A and y is the order with respect to B. These exponents may be integers, fractions, or zero, and must be determined experimentally.

MCAT SYNOPSIS

The exponents in the rate law are not equal to the stoichiometric coefficients unless the reaction actually occurs via a single step mechanism. Also note that product concentrations never appear in a rate law. Many students confuse the rate law with the equilibrium expression.

It is important to note that the exponents of the rate law are *not* necessarily equal to the stoichiometric coefficients in the overall reaction equation. (The exponents *are* equal to the stoichiometric coefficients of the rate-determining step. If one of the reactants or products in this step is an intermediate not included in the overall reaction, then calculating the rate law in terms of the original reactants is more complex.)

MCAT FAVORITE

The stoichiometric coefficients for the overall reaction will most likely be different from those for the rate-determining step, and will therefore not be the same as the order of the reaction

The **overall order of a reaction** (or the **reaction order**) is defined as the sum of the exponents, here equal to x + y.

1. Experimental Determination of Rate Law

The values of k, x, and y in the rate law equation (rate = $k\,[A]^x\,[B]^y$) must be determined experimentally for a given reaction at a given temperature. The rate is usually measured as a function of the **initial concentrations** of the reactants, A and B.

Example: Given the data below, find the rate law for the following reaction at 300 K.

$$A + B \rightarrow C + D$$

Trial	$[A]_{initial}$(M)	$[B]_{initial}$(M)	$r_{initial}$(M/sec)
1	1.00	1.00	2.0
2	1.00	2.00	8.1
3	2.00	2.00	15.9

Solution: First, look for two trials in which the concentrations of all but one of the substances are held constant.

a) In trials 1 and 2, the concentration of A is kept constant while the concentration of B is doubled. The rate increases by a factor of 8.1/2.0, approximately 4. Write down the rate expression of the two trials.

Trial 1: $r_1 = k[A]^x [B]^y = k(1.00)^x (1.00)^y$

Trial 2: $r_2 = k[A]^x [B]^y = k(1.00)^x (2.00)^y$

Divide the second equation by the first.

$$\frac{r_2}{r_1} = \frac{8.1}{2.0} = \frac{k (1.00)^x (2.00)^y}{k (1.00)^x (1.00)^y} = (2.00)^y$$

$$4 = (2.00)^y$$

$$y = 2$$

b) In trials 2 and 3, the concentration of B is kept constant while the concentration of A is doubled; the rate is increased by a factor of 15.9/8.1, approximately 2. The rate expressions of the two trials are:

Trial 2: $r_2 = k(1.00)^x (2.00)^y$

Trial 3: $r_3 = k(2.00)^x (2.00)^y$

Divide the second equation by the first.

$$\frac{r_3}{r_2} = \frac{15.9}{8.1} = \frac{k (2.00)^x (2.00)^y}{k (1.00)^x (2.00)^y} = (2.00)^y$$

$$2 = (2.00)^y$$

$$x = 1$$

So $r = k[A] [B]^2$

The order of the reaction with respect to A is 1 and with respect to B is 2; the overall reaction order is $1 + 2 = 3$.

To calculate k, substitute the values from any one of the above trials into the rate law, e.g.:

$$2.0 \text{ M/sec} = k \times 1.00 \text{ M} \times (1.00 \text{ M})^2$$
$$k = 2.0 \text{ M}^{-2} \text{ sec}^{-1}$$

Therefore, the rate law is $r = 2.0 \text{ M}^{-2} \text{ sec}^{-1} [A][B]^2$.

C. REACTION ORDERS

Chemical reactions are often classified on the basis of kinetics as zero-order, first-order, second-order, mixed-order, or higher-order reactions. The general reaction $a A + b B \rightarrow c C + d D$ will be used in the discussion next.

1. Zero-Order Reactions

A zero-order reaction has a constant rate, which is independent of the reactants' concentrations. Thus the rate law is: rate = k, where k has units of $Msec^{-1}$. An increase in temperature or a decrease in temperature is the only factor that can change the rate of a zero-order reaction.

2. First-Order Reactions

A first-order reaction (order = 1) has a rate proportional to the concentration of one reactant.

$$rate = k[A] \text{ or } rate = k[B]$$

First-order rate constants have units of sec^{-1}.

The classic example of a first-order reaction is the process of radioactive decay. The concentration of radioactive substance A at any time t can be expressed mathematically as

$$[A_t] = [A_o] e^{-kt}$$

where $[A_o]$ = initial concentration of A

$[A_t]$ = concentration of A at time t

k = rate constant

t = elapsed time

The half-life ($t_{1/2}$) of a reaction is the time needed for the concentration of the radioactive substance to decrease to one-half of its original value. Half-lives can be calculated from the rate law as follows:

$$t_{1/2} = \ln 2/k = 0.693/k$$

where k is the first order rate constant.

3. Second-Order Reactions

A second-order reaction (order = 2) has a rate proportional to the product of the concentration of two reactants, or to the square of the concentration of a single reactant; for example, $rate = k[A]^2$, $rate = k[B]^2$, or $rate = k[A][B]$. The units of second-order rate constants are $M^{-1} sec^{-1}$.

4. Higher-Order Reactions

A higher-order reaction has an order greater than 2.

5. Mixed-Order Reactions

A mixed-order reaction has a fractional order; e.g., $rate = k[A]^{1/3}$.

D. EFFICIENCY OF REACTIONS

1. Collision Theory of Chemical Kinetics

In order for a reaction to occur, molecules must collide with each other. The **collision theory of chemical kinetics** states that the rate of a reaction is proportional to the number of collisions per second between the reacting molecules.

Not all collisions, however, result in a chemical reaction. An **effective collision** (one that leads to the formation of products) occurs only if the molecules collide with correct orientation and sufficient force to break the existing bonds and form new ones. The minimum energy of collision necessary for a reaction to take place is called the **activation energy, E_a,** or the **energy barrier.** Only a fraction of colliding particles have enough kinetic energy to exceed the activation energy. This means that only a fraction of all collisions are effective. The rate of a reaction can therefore be expressed as:

$$\text{rate} = fZ$$

where Z is the total number of collisions occurring per second and f is the fraction of collisions that are effective.

TEACHER TIP

Because the transition state structure is at the highest energy state, it is only a theoretical structure and cannot be isolated. We can still use the proposed structures, however, to better understand the reactions in which they are involved.

2. Transition State Theory

When molecules collide with sufficient energy, they form a **transition state,** in which the old bonds are weakened and the new bonds are beginning to form. The transition state then dissociates into products, and the new bonds are fully formed. For a reaction $A_2 + B_2 \rightarrow 2\,AB$, the change along the reaction coordinate (a measure of the extent to which the reaction has progressed from reactants to products; see Figures 5.1 and 5.2) can be represented as follows:

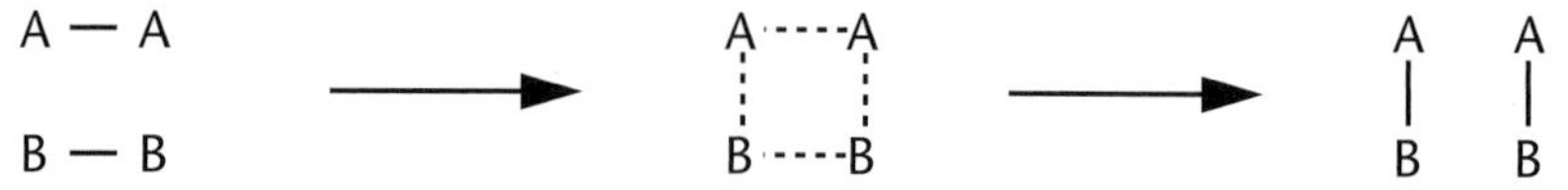

Figure 5.1

The **transition state,** also called the **activated complex,** has greater energy than either the reactants or the products and is denoted by the symbol ‡. The activation energy is required to bring the reactants to this energy level. Once an activated complex is formed, it can either dissociate into the products or revert to reactants without any additional energy input. Transition states are distinguished from intermediates in that, existing as they do at energy maxima, transition states do not have a finite lifetime.

A **potential energy diagram** illustrates the relations among the activation energy, the heats of reaction, and the potential energy of the system. The most important factors in such diagrams are the *relative* energies of the products and reactants. The **enthalpy change** of the reaction (**ΔH**) is the difference between the potential energy of the products and the potential energy of the reactants (see chapter 6). A negative enthalpy change indicates an exothermic reaction (where heat is given off) and a positive enthalpy change indicates an endothermic reaction (where heat is absorbed). The activated complex exists at the top of the energy barrier. The difference in potential energies between the activated complex and the reactants is the activation energy of the forward reaction; the difference in potential energies between the activated complex and the products is the activation energy of the reverse reaction.

For example, consider the formation of HCl from H_2 and Cl_2. The following figure, which gives the energy profile of the reaction

$$H_2 + Cl_2 \rightleftarrows 2\ HCl$$

shows that the reaction is exothermic. The potential energy of the products is less than the potential energy of the reactants; heat is evolved, and the heat of reaction is negative.

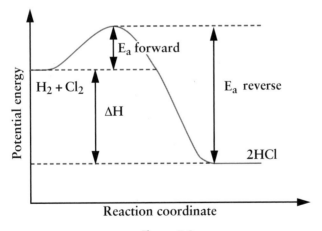

Figure 5.2

The thermodynamic properties of reactions are discussed further in chapter 6.

E. FACTORS AFFECTING REACTION RATE

The rate of a chemical reaction depends upon the individual species undergoing reaction, and upon the reaction environment. The rate of reaction will increase if either of the following occurs: an increase in the number of effective collisions, or a stabilization of the activated complex compared with the reactants.

1. Reactant Concentrations

The greater the concentrations of the reactants (the more particles per unit volume), the greater will be the number of effective collisions per unit time, and therefore the reaction rate will increase for all but zero-order reactions. For reactions occurring in the gaseous state, the partial pressures of the reactants can serve as a measure of concentration (see chapter 7).

2. Temperature

For nearly all reactions, the reaction rate will increase as the temperature of the system increases. Because the temperature of a substance is a measure of the particles' average kinetic energy, increasing the temperature increases the average kinetic energy of the molecules. Consequently, the proportion of molecules having energies greater than E_a (thus capable of undergoing reaction) increases with higher temperature.

3. Medium

The rate of a reaction may also be affected by the medium in which it takes place. Certain reactions proceed more rapidly in aqueous solution, whereas other reactions may proceed more rapidly in benzene. The state of the medium (liquid, solid, or gas) can also have a significant effect.

4. Catalysts

Catalysts are substances that increase reaction rate without themselves being consumed; they do this by lowering the activation energy. Catalysts are important in biological systems and in industrial chemistry; enzymes are biological catalysts. Catalysts may increase the frequency of collision between the reactants, change the relative orientation of the reactants making a higher percentage of collisions effective, donate electron density to the reactants, or reduce intramolecular bonding within reactant molecules. Figure 5.3 compares the energy profiles of catalyzed and uncatalyzed reactions.

The energy barrier for the catalyzed reaction is much lower than the energy barrier for the uncatalyzed reaction. Note that the rates of both the forward and the reverse reactions are increased by catalysis, because E_a of the forward and reverse reactions are lowered by the same amount. Therefore, the presence of a catalyst causes the reaction to proceed more quickly toward equilibrium.

TEACHER TIP

We know that, in many reactions, when we change the concentrations of reaction, the rate will generally increase. But be aware of the order of the reaction in each of the reactants before making this leap.

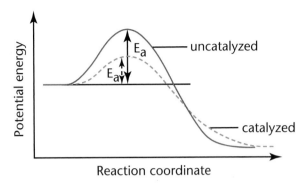

Figure 5.3

EQUILIBRIUM

THE DYNAMIC CONCEPT OF EQUILIBRIUM

So far, reaction rates have been discussed under the assumption that the reactions were **irreversible** (i.e., only proceeded in one direction), and that the reactions proceeded to completion. However, a **reversible** reaction often does not proceed to completion, because (by definition) the products can react to reform the reactants. This is particularly true of reactions occurring in closed systems, where products are not allowed to escape. When there is no **net** change in the concentrations of the products and reactants during a reversible chemical reaction, equilibrium exists. This is not to say that a reaction in equilibrium is static; change continues to occur in both the forward and reverse directions. Equilibrium can be thought of as a balance between the two reaction directions.

Consider the following reaction:

$$A \rightleftharpoons B$$

At equilibrium, the concentrations of A and B are constant, yet the reactions $A \rightarrow B$ and $B \rightarrow A$ continue to occur at equal rates.

LAW OF MASS ACTION

Consider the following *one-step* reaction:

$$2A \rightleftharpoons B + C$$

Because the reaction occurs in one step, the rates of the forward and reverse reaction are given by:

$$rate_f = k_f[A]^2 \text{ and } rate_r = k_r[B][C]$$

When $rate_f = rate_r$, equilibrium is achieved. Because the rates are equal, it can be stated that

$$k_f[A]^2 = k_r[B][C] \text{ or } \frac{k_f}{k_r} = \frac{[B][C]}{[A]^2}$$

Because k_f and k_r are both constants, this equation may be rewritten:

$$K_c = \frac{[B][C]}{[A]^2} \text{ (see below for general equation)}$$

where K_c is called the **equilibrium constant,** and the subscript c indicates that it is in terms of concentration (when dealing with gases, the equilibrium constant is referred to as K_p, and the subscript p indicates that it is in terms of pressure). For dilute solutions, K_c and K_{eq} are used interchangeably; the symbol K is also often used, although it is not completely correct to do so.

When the forward and reverse reaction rates are equal at equilibrium, the molar concentrations of the reactants and products usually are not equal. This means that the forward and reverse rate constants, k_f and k_r, are also usually unequal. For the *one-step* reaction described above:

$$k_f[A]^2 = k_r[B][C]$$

$$k_f = k_r \frac{[B][C]}{[A]^2}$$

In a reaction of more than one step, the equilibrium constant for the overall reaction is found by multiplying the equilibrium constants for each step of the reaction. When this is done, the equilibrium constant for the overall reaction is equal to the concentrations of products divided by reactants in the overall reaction, each raised to its stoichiometric coefficient.

The forward and reverse rate constants for any step n are designated k_n and k_{-n} respectively. For example, if the reaction

$$a\,A + b\,B \rightleftarrows c\,C + d\,D$$

occurs in three steps, then

$$K_c = \frac{k_1 k_2 k_3}{k_{-1} k_{-2} k_{-3}} \text{ will equal } \frac{[C]^c[D]^d}{[A]^a[B]^b}$$

This expression is known as the **Law of Mass Action.**

MCAT SYNOPSIS

For most purposes you will not need to distinguish between different K values. For dilute solutions, $K_{eq} \approx K_c$ and is calculated in terms of concentration.

Example: What is the expression for the equilibrium constant for the following reaction?

$$3\,H_2\,(g) + N_2\,(g) \rightleftarrows 2\,NH_3\,(g)$$

Solution: $K_c = \dfrac{[NH_3]^2}{[H_2]^3[N_2]}$

The **reaction quotient, Q**, is a measure of the degree to which a reaction has gone to completion. Q_c is equal to

$$\frac{[C]^c[D]^d}{[A]^a[B]^b}$$

Q_c is a constant only at equilibrium, when it is equal to K_c:

PROPERTIES OF THE EQUILIBRIUM CONSTANT

The equilibrium constant, K_{eq}, has the following characteristics:

- Pure solids and liquids do not appear in the equilibrium constant expression.

- K_{eq} is characteristic of a given system at a given temperature.

- If the value of K_{eq} is very large compared to 1, an equilibrium mixture of reactants and products will contain very little of the reactants compared to the products.

- If the value of K_{eq} is very small compared to 1 (i.e., less than 0.1), an equilibrium mixture of reactants and products will contain very little of the products compared to the reactants.

- If the value of K_{eq} is close to 1, an equilibrium mixture of products and reactants will contain approximately equal amounts of reactants and products.

MCAT SYNOPSIS

Remember our earlier warning about an oft-confused issue dealing with reaction coefficients and rate laws? Well, here the coefficients *ARE* equal to the exponents in the equilibrium expression. On Test Day, if the reaction is balanced, then the equilibrium expression should just about write itself on your scratch paper.

LE CHÂTELIER'S PRINCIPLE

The French chemist Henry Louis Le Châtelier stated that a system to which a stress is applied tends to change so as to relieve the applied stress. This rule, known as **Le Châtelier's principle**, is used to determine the direction in which a reaction at equilibrium will proceed when subjected to a stress, such as a change in concentration, pressure, temperature, or volume.

A. CHANGES IN CONCENTRATION

Increasing the concentration of a species will tend to shift the equilibrium away from the species that is added to reestablish its equilibrium concentration, and vice versa. For example, in the reaction:

$$A + B \rightleftarrows C + D$$

if the concentration of A and/or B is increased, the equilibrium will shift toward (or favor production of) C and D. Conversely, if the concentration of C and/or D is increased, the equilibrium will shift away from the production of C and D, favoring production of A and B. Similarly, decreasing the concentration of a species will tend to shift the equilibrium toward the production of that species. For example, if A and/or B is removed from the above reaction, the equilibrium will shift so as to favor increasing concentration of A and B.

This effect is often used in industry to increase the yield of a useful product or drive a reaction to completion. If D were constantly removed from the above reaction, the net reaction would produce more D and concurrently more C. Likewise, using an excess of the least expensive reactant would help to drive the reaction forward.

B. CHANGE IN PRESSURE OR VOLUME

In a system at constant temperature, a change in pressure causes a change in volume, and vice versa. Because liquids and solids are practically incompressible, a change in the pressure or volume of systems involving only these phases has little or no effect on their equilibrium. Reactions involving gases, however, may be greatly affected by changes in pressure or volume, Because gases are highly compressible.

Pressure and volume are inversely related. An increase in the pressure of a system will shift the equilibrium so as to decrease the number of moles of gas present. This reduces the volume of the system and relieves the stress of the increased pressure. Consider the following reaction:

$$N_2(g) + 3\,H_2(g) \rightleftarrows 2\,NH_3(g)$$

The left side of the reaction has four moles of gaseous molecules, whereas the right side has only two moles. When the pressure of this system is increased, the equilibrium will shift so that the side of the reaction producing fewer moles is favored. Because there are fewer moles on the right, the equilibrium will shift toward the right. Conversely, if the volume of

---

MCAT FAVORITE

LeChâtelier's principle applies to a wide variety of systems and as such, appears in many disguises in both MCAT science sections.

BRIDGE

Remember the equation:

$$CO_2 + H_2O \rightarrow HCO_3^- + H^+$$

In the tissues, there is a lot of CO_2 and the reaction shifts to the right. In the lungs, CO_2 is lost and the reaction shifts to the left. Note that blowing off CO_2 (hyperventilation) is used as a mechanism of dealing with acidosis (excess H^+).

the same system is increased, its pressure immediately decreases, which, according to Le Châtelier's principle, leads to a shift in the equilibrium to the left.

C. CHANGE IN TEMPERATURE

Changes in temperature also affect equilibrium. To predict this effect, heat may be considered as a product in an exothermic reaction and as a reactant in an endothermic reaction. Consider the following exothermic reaction:

$$A \rightleftharpoons B + heat$$

If this system were placed in an ice bath, its temperature would decrease, driving the reaction to the right to replace the heat lost. Conversely, if the system were placed in a boiling-water bath, the reaction equilibrium would shift to the left because of the increased "concentration" of heat.

Not only does a temperature change alter the position of the equilibrium, it also alters the numerical value of the equilibrium constant. In contrast, changes in the concentration of a species in the reaction, in the pressure, or in the volume, will alter the position of the equilibrium without changing the numerical value of the equilibrium constant.

MCAT SYNOPSIS

$$A + B \rightleftharpoons C + heat$$

will shift to Ⓡ	will shift to Ⓛ
• If more A or B is added	• If more C is added
• If C is taken away	• If A or B is taken away
• If pressure is applied or volume reduced (assuming A, B, and C gases)	• If pressure is reduced or volume increased (assuming A, B, and C gases)
• If temperature is reduced	• If temperature is increased

PRACTICE QUESTIONS

1. In a third-order reaction involving two reactants and two products, doubling the concentration of the first reactant causes the rate to increase by a factor of 2. If the concentration of the second reactant is cut in half, the rate of this reaction will

   A. increase by a factor of 2.
   B. increase by a factor of 4.
   C. decrease by a factor of 2.
   D. decrease by a factor of 4.

2. In a certain equilibrium process, the activation energy of the forward reaction is greater than the activation energy of the reverse reaction. What type of reaction is this?

   A. Endothermic
   B. Exothermic
   C. Spontaneous
   D. Nonspontaneous

3. The volume of a gas is increased without changing the overall number of molecules present in the system. For this system, which of the following statements is always true?

   A. Pressure decreases and temperature increases.
   B. Pressure decreases or temperature increases.
   C. If temperature decreases, then pressure decreases.
   D. If pressure decreases, then temperature decreases.

4. Carbonated beverages are produced by dissolving carbon dioxide in water to produce carbonic acid:

$$CO_2(g) + H_2O(l) \rightleftharpoons H_2CO_3(aq)$$

   When a bottle containing carbonated water is opened, the taste of the beverage gradually changes until all of the carbonation is lost. Which of the following statements best explains this phenomenon?

   A. The change in pressure and volume causes the reaction to shift to the left, thereby decreasing the amount of aqueous carbonic acid.
   B. The change in pressure and volume causes the reaction to shift to the right, thereby decreasing the amount of gaseous carbon dioxide.
   C. Carbonic acid reacts with environmental oxygen and nitrogen.
   D. Carbon dioxide reacts with environmental oxygen and nitrogen.

5. A certain chemical reaction is endothermic. It occurs spontaneously. Which of the following must be true for this reaction?

   I. $\Delta H > 0$
   II. $\Delta G < 0$
   III. $\Delta S > 0$

   A. I only
   B. I and II only
   C. II and III only
   D. I, II, and III

6. A certain ionic salt, A_3B, has a molar solubility of 10 M at a certain temperature. What is the K_{sp} of this salt at the same temperature?

A. 10^4
B. 3×10^4
C. 2.7×10^5
D. 8.1×105

7. Acetic acid dissociates in solution according to the equation, $CH_3COOH \Leftrightarrow CH_3COO^- + H^+$. If sodium acetate is added to a solution of acetic acid in excess water, what effect would be observed?

A. Decreased Ph
B. Increased Ph
C. Decreased pK_a
D. Increased pK_a

8. A certain chemical reaction follows the rate law, rate = k $[NO_2]$ $[Br_2]$. Which of the following statements describe the kinetics of this reaction?

 I. The reaction is second-order.
 II. The amount of NO_2 consumed is equal to the amount of Br_2 consumed.
 III. The rate will not be affected by the addition of a compound other than NO_2 and Br_2.

A. I only
B. III only
C. I and II only
D. I, III, and III

9. The data in the following table is collected for the combustion of the theoretical compound XH_4: $XH_4 + 2O_2 \rightarrow XO_2 + 2H_2O$. What is the rate law for the reaction described?

Trial	$[XH_4]_{initial}$ (M)	$[O_2]_{initial}$ (M)	Rate (M/min)
1	0.6	0.6	12.4
2	0.6	2.4	49.9
3	1.2	2.4	198.3

A. Rate = k $[XH_4]$ $[O_2]$
B. Rate = k $[XH_4]$ $[O_2]^2$
C. Rate = k $[XH_4]^2$ $[O_2]$
D. Rate = k $[XH_4]^2$ $[O_2]^2$

10. A solution is prepared with an unknown concentration of a theoretical compound whose K_a is exactly 1. What is the pH of this solution?

A. Higher than 7
B. Exactly 7
C. Lower than 7
D. Impossible to determine

11. Which of the following actions does NOT affect the rate of a reaction?

A. Adding/subtracting heat
B. Increasing/decreasing activation energy
C. Increasing/decreasing concentration of reactants
D. Increasing/decreasing volume of reactants

12. In a sealed 1 L container, 1 mol of nitrogen gas reacts with 3 mol of hydrogen gas to form 0.05 mol of NH_3. Which of the following is closest to the K_{eq} of the reaction?

A. 0.0001
B. 0.001
C. 0.01
D. 0.1

FOR QUESTIONS 13–15, CONSIDER THE ENERGY DIAGRAM SHOWN BELOW.

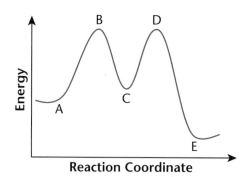

13. The overall reaction depicted by this energy diagram is

A. endothermic, because point B is higher than point A.
B. endothermic, because point C is higher than point A.
C. exothermic, because point D is higher than point E.
D. exothermic, because point A is higher than point E.

14. What process has the highest activation energy?

A. The first step of the forward reaction
B. The first step of the reverse reaction
C. The second step of the forward reaction
D. The second step of the reverse reaction

15. Which of the following components of the reaction mechanism will never be present in the reaction vessel when the reaction coordinate is at point B?

A. Reactants
B. Products
C. Intermediates
D. Catalysts

16. Consider the following two reactions. If K_{eq} for reaction 1 is equal to 0.1, what is K_{eq} for reaction 2?

$$3A + 2B \rightleftharpoons 3C + 4D \qquad \text{(Reaction 1)}$$
$$4D + 3C \rightleftharpoons 3A + 2B \qquad \text{(Reaction 2)}$$

A. 0.1
B. 1
C. 10
D. 100

17. Which of the following statements would best describe the experimental result if the temperature of the following theoretical reaction were decreased?

$$A + B \rightleftharpoons C + D \qquad \Delta H = -1.12 \text{ kJ/mol}$$

A. [C] + [D] would increase.
B. [A] + [B] would increase.
C. ΔH would increase.
D. ΔH would decrease.

18. Compound A has a K_a of approximately 10^{-4}. Which of the following compounds is most likely to react with a solution of compound A?

A. HNO_2
B. NO_2
C. NH_3
D. N_2O_5

19. The following system obeys second-order kinetics:

$2NO_2 \rightarrow NO_3 + NO$ (slow)
$NO_3 + CO \rightarrow NO_2 + CO2$ (fast)

What is the rate law for this reaction?

A. Rate = k $[NO_2]$ $[CO]$
B. Rate = k $[NO_2]^2$ $[CO]$
C. Rate = k $[NO_2]$ $[NO_3]$
D. Rate = k $[NO_2]^2$

20. The potential energy diagram below represents four different reactions. Assuming identical conditions, which of the reactions displayed proceeds the fastest?

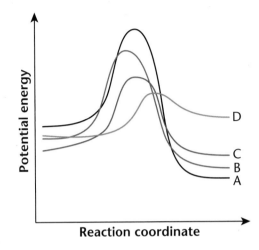

A. A
B. B
C. C
D. D

KEY CONCEPTS

Kinetics

Reaction mechanisms

Rate law

RATE LAW FROM EXPERIMENTAL RESULTS

Consider the nitration reaction of benzene, an example of electrophilic aromatic substitution:

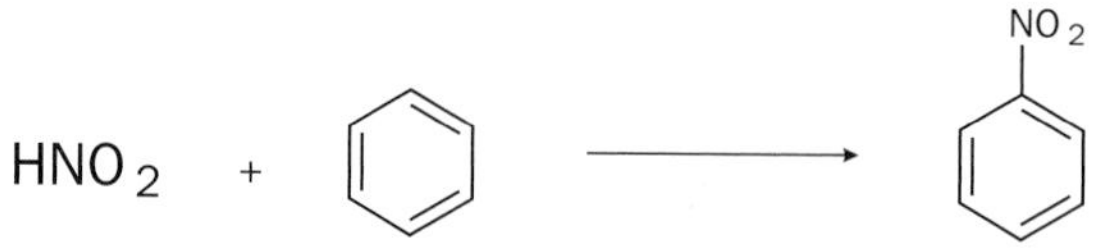

The rate data below were collected with the nitration of benzene carried out at 298 K. From this information, determine the rate law for this reaction.

Trial	$[C_6H_6]$ (M)	$[HNO_2]$ (M)	Initial Rate (M · s^{-1})
1	1.01×10^{-3}	2×10^{-2}	5.96×10^{-6}
2	4.05×10^{-3}	2×10^{-2}	5.96×10^{-6}
3	3.02×10^{-3}	6.01×10^{-2}	5.4×10^{-5}

TAKEAWAYS

Remember that the rate constant k depends only on temperature.

A shortcut to determine order is to use the following relation when you find two trials where one reagent's concentration changes, but all other concentrations are constant:

Change in rate = (Proportional change in concentration)^x, where $x =$ the order with respect to that reagent.

1) Write down the general form of the rate law.

Rate = $k[C_6H_6]^x[HNO_2]^y$

Remember: *The general form of the rate law must include a constant, k, that is multiplied by the concentrations of each of the reactants raised to a certain power.*

2) Determine the order of the reaction with respect to each reactant.

$$\frac{\text{Rate of trial 2}}{\text{Rate of trial 1}} = \frac{k[C_6H_6]_2^x[HNO_2]_2^y}{k[C_6H_6]_1^x[HNO_2]_1^y}$$

$$\frac{\text{Rate of trial 2}}{\text{Rate of trial 1}} = \left(\frac{k[C_6H_6]_2}{k[C_6H_6]_1}\right)^x \left(\frac{[HNO_2]_2}{[HNO_2]_1}\right)^y$$

$$\frac{5.96 \times 10^{-6}}{5.96 \times 10^{-6}} = \left(\frac{4.05 \times 10^{-3}}{1.01 \times 10^{-3}}\right)^x \left(\frac{2 \times 10^{-2}}{2 \times 10^{-2}}\right)^y$$

$$\frac{\text{Rate of trial 3}}{\text{Rate of trial 1}} = \left(\frac{[HNO_2]_3}{[HNO_2]_1}\right)^y$$

$$\left(\frac{5.4 \times 10^{-5}}{5.96 \times 10^{-6}}\right) = \left(\frac{6.01 \times 10^{-2}}{2.01 \times 10^{-2}}\right)^y$$

$$\left(\frac{54 \times 10^{-6}}{6 \times 10^{-6}}\right) = \left(\frac{6 \times 10^{-2}}{2 \times 10^{-2}}\right)^y$$

THINGS TO WATCH OUT FOR

Make sure that initially you select two trials where *one reagent's concentration changes*, but *all other concentrations are constant*. Otherwise, you won't come out with the correct rate law!

Choose two trials in which the concentration of one reagent is changing, but the other is not. Take the *ratio* of these two trials and set up an equation.

Cancel the rate constants because they are equal to each other. Collect terms raised to the same exponent together.

Plug and chug. Substitute numbers from the rate data table into the equation.

$1 = 4^x$

The term raised to the y power disappears because 1 raised to any power equals 1. The only way that 4^x can equal 1 is if $x = 0$.

To determine the order with respect to HNO_2, note that there are no two trials in which the concentration of benzene stays the same. However, this does not matter, because the reaction is zero order with respect to benzene.

Plug in numbers from the table as before.

Simplify the numbers to make them easy to handle. Note that 5.40×10^{-5} is the same thing as 54.0×10^{-6}.

$9 = 3^y$

The only way this equation can be true is if $y = 2$.

---

3) Write down the rate law with the correct orders.

Rate $= k[C_6H_6]^0[HNO_2]^2 = k[HNO_2]^2$

SIMILAR QUESTIONS

1) What is the value of the rate constant k for the original reaction above? What are its units?

2) Given the data below, determine the rate law for the reaction of pyridine with methyl iodide. Find the rate constant k for this reaction and its units. Use the rate law to determine what type of reaction this is.

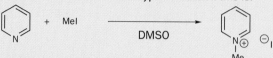

Trial	$[C_5H_5N]$ (M)	[MeI] (M)	Initial Rate (M s^{-1})
1	1×10^{-4}	1×10^{-4}	7.5×10^{-7}
2	2×10^{-4}	2×10^{-4}	3×10^{-6}
3	2×10^{-4}	4×10^{-4}	6×10^{-6}

3) Cerium(IV) is a common inorganic oxidant. Determine the rate law for the following reaction and compute the value of the rate constant k along with its units.

$$Ce^{4+} + Fe^{2+} \rightarrow Ce^{3+} + Fe^{3+}$$

Trial	$[Ce4^+]$ (M)	$[Fe^{2+}]$ (M)	Initial Rate (M s^{-1})
1	1.1×10^{-5}	1.8×10^{-5}	2×10^{-7}
2	1.1×10^{-5}	2.8×10^{-5}	3.1×10^{-7}
3	3.4×10^{-5}	2.8×10^{-5}	9.5×10^{-7}

RATE LAW FROM REACTION MECHANISMS

Often, changing the medium of a reaction can have a dramatic effect on its mechanism. In the gas phase, HCl reacts with propene according to the following reaction mechanism:

Step 1: $HCl + HCl \rightleftharpoons H_2Cl_2$ (fast, equilibrium)

Step 2: $HCl + CH_3CHCH_2 \rightleftharpoons CH_3CHClCH_3*$
(fast, equilibrium)

Step 3: $CH_3CHClCH_3* + H_2Cl_2 \rightarrow CH_3CHClCH_3$
$+ 2\,HCl$ (slow)
where CH_3CHCH_2 is propene and $CH_3CHClCH_3*$
represents an excited state of 2–chloropropane.
Based on these reaction steps, derive the rate law for this reaction.

1) Identify the slow step in the reaction and write down the rate law expression for that step.

Rate $= k_3[CH_3CHClCH_3*][H_2Cl_2]$

---

2) If intermediates exist in the rate law from step 1, use prior steps to solve for their concentration and eliminate them from the rate law.

$k_1[HCl]^2 = k_{-1}[H_2Cl_2]$

$[H_2Cl_2] = \dfrac{k_1}{k_{-1}}[HCl]^2$

$k_2[HCl][CH_3CHCH_2] = k_{-2}[CH_3CHClCH_3{}^*]$

$[CH_3CHClCH_3{}^*] = \dfrac{k_2}{k_{-2}}[HCl][CH_3CHCH_2]$

$rate = \left[k_3[\dfrac{k_2}{k_{-2}}[HCl][CH_3CHCH_2][\dfrac{k_1}{k_{-1}}HCl]^2 \right]$

Here, we are taking advantage of the fact that step 1 of the mechanism is in equilibrium; therefore, the rates of the forward and reverse reactions are equal.

Solve for the concentration of H_2Cl_2, one of the intermediates from above.

Step 2 from the mechanism is also in equilibrium, so the rates of the forward and reverse reactions are equal.

Solve for the intermediate, as above.

KEY CONCEPTS

Equilibrium

Rate laws

Reaction mechanisms

TAKEAWAYS

With reaction mechanisms, the goal is to eliminate the concentrations of intermediates because they are usually high-energy species that exist only briefly.

SIMILAR QUESTIONS

1) What are the units of the rate in the original question? Based on this, what must the units of k_{obs} be for this reaction?

2) How does this rate law differ from the one that you might expect if this reaction were to be carried out in solution, instead of in the gas phase?

3) How would the key intermediates differ between this reaction in the gas phase and in solution?

THINGS TO WATCH OUT FOR

In this case, you may assume that the stoichiometric coefficients of each reactant are equal to the order. When you are presented with rate data, you *may not* make this assumption but must use the rate data to determine order.

Plug the concentrations into the rate law for the slow step.

*Remember: Intermediates are assumed to exist for only a brief period of time because they are produced in one step and consumed in another. Therefore, their concentration cannot be measured, and so they **must** be eliminated from the rate law.*

---

3) Combine constants and simplify the rate law.

$$\text{rate} = \left[\frac{k_1 k_2 k_3}{k_{-1} k_{-2}} \right] [HCl][CH_3CHCH_2][HCl]^2$$

$$\text{rate} = k_{obs}[HCl]^3[CH_3CHCH_2],$$

$$\text{where } k_{obs} = \frac{k_1 k_2 k_3}{k_{-1} k_{-2}}$$

Combine all of the constants and concentrations.

Remember: A constant times a constant times a constant, and so on, is just another constant.

CHAPTER 6

THERMOCHEMISTRY

All chemical reactions are accompanied by energy changes. Thermal, chemical, potential, and kinetic energies are all interconvertible, as they must obey the **Law of Conservation of Energy.** Energy changes determine whether reactions can occur and how easily they will do so, thus an understanding of **thermodynamics** is essential to an understanding of chemistry. In chemistry, thermodynamics help determine whether a chemical reaction is **spontaneous,** i.e., if under a given set of conditions it can occur, by itself, without outside assistance. A spontaneous reaction may or may not proceed to completion, depending upon the rate of the reaction, which is determined by chemical kinetics (see chapter 5).

The application of thermodynamics to chemical reactions is called **thermochemistry.** Several thermodynamic definitions are very useful in thermochemistry. A **system** is the particular part of the universe being studied; everything outside the system is considered the **surroundings** or **environment.** A system may be:

- **isolated**—when it cannot exchange energy or matter with the surroundings, as with an insulated bomb reactor;
- **closed**—when it can exchange energy but not matter with the surroundings, as with a steam radiator;
- **open**—when it can exchange both matter and energy with the surroundings, as with a pot of boiling water.

A system undergoes a **process** when one or more of its properties changes. A process is associated with a change of state. An **isothermal** process occurs when the temperature of the system remains constant; an **adiabatic** process occurs when no heat exchange occurs; and an **isobaric** process occurs when the pressure of the system remains constant. Isothermal and isobaric processes are common, because it is usually easy to control temperature and pressure.

HEAT

A. DEFINITION

Heat is a form of energy that can easily transfer to or from a system, the result of a temperature difference between the system and its surroundings; this transfer will occur spontaneously from a warmer system to a cooler system. According to convention, heat absorbed by a system (from its surroundings) is considered positive, while heat lost by a system (to its surroundings) is considered negative.

Heat change is the most common energy change in chemical processes. Reactions that absorb heat energy are said to be **endothermic,** while those that release heat energy are said to be **exothermic.** Heat is commonly measured in **calories (cal),** or **joules (J),** and more commonly in kcal or kJ (1 cal = 4.184 J).

B. CALORIMETRY

Calorimetry measures heat changes. The terms **constant-volume calorimetry** and **constant-pressure calorimetry** are used to indicate the conditions under which the heat changes are measured. The heat (**q**) absorbed or released in a given process is calculated from the equation:

$$q = mc\Delta T$$

where m is the mass, c is the **specific heat.** Thermodynamics), and ΔT is the change in temperature.

Constant-Volume Calorimetry

In constant-volume calorimetry, the volume of the container holding the reacting mixture does not change during the course of the reaction. The heat of reaction is measured using a device called a bomb calorimeter. This apparatus consists of a steel bomb into which the reactants are placed. The bomb is immersed in an insulated container containing a known amount of water. The reactants are electrically ignited and heat is absorbed or evolved as the reaction proceeds. The heat of the reaction, q_{rxn}, can be determined as follows. Because no heat enters or leaves the system, the net heat change for the system is zero; therefore, the heat change for the reaction is compensated for by the heat change for the water and the bomb, which is easy to measure.

$$q_{system} = q_{rxn} + q_{water} + q_{steel} = 0$$
$$\text{Thus:} \quad q_{rxn} = -(q_{water} + q_{steel})$$
$$= -(m_{water}\, c_{water}\, \Delta T + m_{steel}\, c_{steel}\, \Delta T)$$

Note that the overall system, as defined, is adiabatic, because no net heat gain or loss occurs. However, the heat exchange between the various components makes it possible to determine the heat of reaction.

STATES AND STATE FUNCTIONS

The state of a system is described by the macroscopic properties of the system. Examples of macroscopic properties include temperature (T), pressure (P), and volume (V). When the state of a system changes, the values of the properties also change. Properties whose magnitude depends only on the initial and final states of the system, and not on the path of the change (how the change was accomplished), are known as **state functions.** Pressure, temperature, and volume are important state functions. Other examples are **enthalpy (H), entropy (S), free energy (G)** (all discussed below), and **internal energy (E** or **U).** Although independent of path, state functions are not necessarily independent of one another.

A set of **standard conditions** (25°C and 1 atm) is normally used for measuring the enthalpy, entropy, and free energy of a reaction. A substance in its most stable form under standard conditions is said to be in its **standard state.** Examples of substances in their standard states include hydrogen as $H_2(g)$, water as H_2O (ℓ), and salt as $NaCl$ (s). The changes in enthalpy, entropy, and free energy that occur when a reaction takes place under standard conditions are called the **standard enthalpy, standard entropy,** and **standard free energy** changes respectively, and are symbolized by $\Delta H°$, $\Delta S°$, and $\Delta G°$.

A. ENTHALPY

Most reactions in the lab occur under constant pressure (at 1 atm, in open containers). To express heat changes at constant pressure, chemists use the term **enthalpy (H).** The change in enthalpy (ΔH) of a process is equal to the heat absorbed or evolved by the system at constant pressure. The enthalpy of a process depends only on the enthalpies of the initial and final states, *not* on the path. Thus to find the enthalpy change of a reaction, ΔH_{rxn}, one must subtract the enthalpy of the reactants from the enthalpy of the products:

$$\Delta H_{rxn} = H_{products} - H_{reactants}$$

A positive ΔH corresponds to an endothermic process, and a negative ΔH corresponds to an exothermic process.

Unfortunately, it is not possible to measure H directly; only ΔH can be measured, and even then, only for certain fast and spontaneous processes. Thus several standard methods have been developed to calculate ΔH for any process.

1. Standard Heat of Formation

The enthalpy of formation of a compound, ΔH°_f, is the enthalpy change that would occur if one mole of a compound were formed directly from its elements in their standard states. Note that ΔH°_f of an element in its standard state is zero. The ΔH°_f of most known substances is tabulated.

2. Standard Heat of Reaction

The standard heat of a reaction, ΔH°_{rxn}, is the hypothetical enthalpy change that would occur if the reaction were carried out under standard conditions; i.e., when reactants in their standard states are converted to products in their standard states at 298K. It can be expressed as:

$$\Delta H^\circ_{rxn} = (\text{sum of } \Delta H^\circ_f \text{ of products}) - (\text{sum of } \Delta H^\circ_f \text{ of reactants})$$

TEACHER TIP

The concept of state functions and the idea of path independence is important. Applying Hess's law is a common MCAT topic.

3. Hess's Law

Hess's law states that enthalpies of reactions are additive. When thermochemical equations (chemical equations for which energy changes are known) are added to give the net equation for a reaction, the corresponding heats of reaction are also added to give the net heat of reaction. Because enthalpy is a state function, the enthalpy of a reaction does not depend on the path taken but depends only on the initial and final states. For example, consider the reaction:

$$Br_2(\ell) \rightarrow Br_2(g) \quad \Delta H = (31 \text{ kJ/mol})(1 \text{ mol}) = 31 \text{ kJ}$$

The enthalpy change of the above reaction, called the **heat of vaporization, ΔH°_{vap},** will always be 31 kJ/mol provided that the same initial and final states, $Br_2(\ell)$ and $Br_2(g)$ respectively, exist at standard conditions. $Br_2(\ell)$ could instead be decomposed to Br atoms and then recombined to form $Br_2(g)$, but because the net reaction is the same, the change in enthalpy will always be the same.

$$\begin{array}{lll} Br_2(\ell) & \rightarrow 2\,Br(g) & \Delta H_1 \\ 2\,Br(g) & \rightarrow Br_2(g) & \Delta H_2 \\ \hline \end{array}$$

$$Br_2(\ell) \rightarrow Br_2(g) \quad \Delta H = \Delta H_1 + \Delta H_2 = 31 \text{ kJ}$$

Example: Given the following thermochemical equations:

a) $C_3H_8(g) + 5\ O_2(g) \rightarrow 3\ CO_2(g) + 4\ H_2O(\ell)$ $\qquad \Delta H_a = -2220.1$ kJ

b) $C\ (graphite) + O_2(g) \rightarrow CO_2(g)$ $\qquad \Delta H_b = -393.5$ kJ

c) $H_2(g) + 1/2\ O_2(g) \rightarrow H_2O(l)$ $\qquad \Delta H_c = -285.8$ kJ

Calculate ΔH for the reaction:

d) $3\ C(graphite) + 4\ H_2(g) \rightarrow C_3H_8(g)$

Solution: Equations a, b, and c must be combined to obtain equation d. Because equation d contains only C, H_2, and C_3H_8, we must eliminate O_2, CO_2, and H_2O from the first three equations. Equation a is reversed to get C_3H_8 on the product side (this gives equation e).

Next, equation b is multiplied by 3 (this gives equation f) and c by 4 (this gives equation g). The following addition is done to obtain the required equation d: 3b + 4c + e.

e) $3\ CO_2(g) + 4\ H_2O(\ell) \rightarrow C_3H_8(g) + 5\ O_2(g)$ $\quad \Delta H_e = 2220.1$ kJ

f) $3 \times [C(graphite) + O_2(g) \rightarrow CO_2(g)]$ $\qquad \Delta H_f = 3 \times -393.5$ kJ

g) $4 \times [H_2(g) + \dfrac{1}{2}O_2(g) \rightarrow H_2O(\ell)]$ $\qquad \Delta H_g = 4 \times -285.8$ kJ

$3\ C(graphite) + 4\ H_2(g) \rightarrow C_3H_8(g)$ $\qquad \Delta H_d = -103.6$ kJ

where $\Delta H_d = \Delta H_e + \Delta H_f + \Delta H_g$.

> **TEACHER TIP**
> Make sure to switch signs when you reverse the equation and to multiply by the correct stoichiometric coefficient when doing your calculation.

It is important to note that the reverse of any reaction has an enthalpy of the same magnitude as that of the forward reaction, but its sign is opposite.

4. Bond Dissociation Energy

Heats of reaction are related to changes in energy associated with the break down and formation of chemical bonds. **Bond energy,** or **bond dissociation energy,** is an average of the energy required to break a particular type of bond in one mole of gaseous molecules. It is tabulated as the positive value of the energy absorbed as the bonds are broken. For example:

$$H_2(g) \rightarrow 2H(g) \qquad \Delta H = 436 \text{ kJ}$$

A molecule of H_2 gas is cleaved to produce two gaseous, unassociated hydrogen atoms. For each mole of H_2 gas cleaved, roughly 436 kJ of energy is absorbed by the system. The reaction is therefore endothermic.

> **MCAT SYNOPSIS**
> Because it takes energy to pull two atoms apart, bond breakage is always endothermic. Bond formation is the reverse process, and thus must always be exothermic.

For bonds found in other than diatomic molecules, many compounds have been measured and the energy requirements averaged. For example, the C–H bond dissociation energy one would find in a table (415 kJ/mol) was compiled from measurements on thousands of different organic compounds.

Bond energies can be used to estimate enthalpies of reactions. The enthalpy change of a reaction is given by:

$$\Delta H_{rxn} \quad = \quad (\Delta H \text{ of bonds broken}) - (\Delta H \text{ of bonds formed})$$
$$= \quad \text{total energy input} - \text{total energy released}$$

Example: Calculate the enthalpy change for the following reaction:

$$C(s) + 2\,H_2(g) \rightarrow CH_4(g) \qquad \Delta H = ?$$

Bond dissociation energies of H–H and C–H bonds are 436 kJ/mol and 415 kJ/mol, respectively.

$$\Delta H_f \text{ of } C(g) = 715 \text{ kJ/mol}$$

Solution: CH_4 is formed from free elements in their standard states (C in solid and H_2 in gaseous state).

Thus here, $\Delta H_{rxn} = \Delta H_f$

The reaction can be written in three steps:

a) $C(s) \rightarrow C(g)$ $\qquad\qquad\qquad \Delta H_1$
b) $2\,[H_2(g) \rightarrow 2\,H(g)]$ $\qquad\qquad 2\Delta H_2$
c) $C(g) + 4\,H(g) \rightarrow CH_4(g)$ $\qquad \Delta H_3$

and $\Delta H_f = [\Delta H_1 + 2\Delta H_2] + [\Delta H_3]$

$$\Delta H_1 \quad = \Delta H_f C(g) = 715 \text{ kJ/mol,}$$

ΔH_2 is the energy required to break the H–H bond of one mole of H_2. So:

$$\Delta H_2 \quad = \quad \text{bond energy of } H_2$$
$$= \quad 436 \text{ kJ/mol}$$

ΔH_3 is the energy released when 4 C–H bonds are formed. So:

$$\Delta H_3 \quad = \quad -(4 \times \text{bond energy of C–H})$$
$$= \quad -(4 \times 415 \text{ kJ/mol})$$
$$= \quad -1{,}660 \text{ kJ/mol}$$

(**Note:** Because energy is released when bonds are formed, ΔH_3 is negative.)

Therefore:

$$\Delta H_{rxn} = \Delta H_f = [715 + 2(436)] - (1{,}660) \text{ kJ/mol}$$
$$= -73 \text{ kJ/mol}$$

5. Heats of Combustion

One more type of standard enthalpy change which is often used is the standard heat of combustion, $\Delta H°_{comb}$. As stated earlier, a requirement for relatively easy measurement of ΔH is that the reaction be fast and spontaneous; combustion generally fits this description. The reactions used in the C_3H_8 (g) example previous were combustion reactions, and the corresponding values ΔH_a, ΔH_b, and ΔH_c were thus heats of combustion.

B. ENTROPY

Entropy (S) is a measure of the disorder, or randomness, of a system. The units of entropy are energy/temperature, commonly J/K or cal/K. The greater the order in a system, the lower the entropy; the greater the disorder or randomness, the higher the entropy. At any given temperature, a solid will have lower entropy than a gas, because individual molecules in the gaseous state are moving randomly, while individual molecules in a solid are constrained in place. Entropy is a state function, so a change in entropy depends only on the initial and final states:

$$\Delta S = S_{final} - S_{initial}$$

A change in entropy is also given by:

$$\Delta S = \frac{q_{rev}}{T}$$

where q_{rev} is the heat added to the system undergoing a reversible process (a process that proceeds with infinitesimal changes in the system's conditions) and T is the absolute temperature.

A standard entropy change for a reaction, $\Delta S°$, is calculated using the standard entropies of reactants and products:

$$\Delta S°_{rxn} = (\text{sum of } S°_{products}) - (\text{sum of } S°_{reactants})$$

The second law of thermodynamics states that all spontaneous processes proceed such that the entropy of the system plus its surroundings (i.e., the entropy of the universe) increases:

$$\Delta S_{universe} = \Delta S_{system} + \Delta S_{surroundings} > 0$$

MCAT SYNOPSIS

Combustion of large carbohydrates yields large numbers of products. The larger the reactant, the more numerous the products.

MCAT SYNOPSIS

Entropy changes accompanying phase changes (see chapter 8) can be easily estimated, at least qualitatively. For example, freezing is accompanied by a decrease in entropy as the relatively disordered liquid becomes a well-ordered solid. Meanwhile, boiling is accompanied by a large increase in entropy as the liquid becomes a much more highly disordered gas. For any substance, sublimation will be the phase transition with the greatest entropy change.

A system reaches its maximum entropy at **equilibrium,** a state in which no observable change takes place as time goes on. For a reversible process, $\Delta S_{universe}$ is zero:

$$\Delta S_{universe} = \Delta S_{system} + \Delta S_{surroundings} = 0$$

A system will spontaneously tend toward an equilibrium state if left alone.

C. GIBBS FREE ENERGY

1. Spontaneity of Reaction

The thermodynamic state function, **G** (known as the **Gibbs free energy**), combines the two factors which affect the spontaneity of a reaction—changes in enthalpy, ΔH, and changes in entropy, ΔS. The change in the free energy of a system, ΔG, represents the maximum amount of energy released by a process, occurring at constant temperature and pressure, that is available to perform useful work. ΔG is defined by the equation:

$$\Delta G = \Delta H - T\Delta S$$

where T is the absolute temperature and $T\Delta S$ represents the total amount of heat absorbed by a system when its entropy increases reversibly.

In the equilibrium state, free energy is at a minimum. A process can occur spontaneously if the Gibbs function decreases, i.e., $\Delta G < 0$.

a) If ΔG is negative, the reaction is spontaneous.
b) If ΔG is positive, the reaction is not spontaneous.
c) If ΔG is zero, the system is in a state of equilibrium;
    thus, $\Delta G = 0$ and $\Delta H = T\Delta S$.

Because the temperature is always positive, i.e., in Kelvins, the effects of the signs of ΔH and ΔS and the effect of temperature on spontaneity can be summarized as follows:

ΔH	ΔS	Outcome
–	+	Spontaneous at all temperatures
+	–	Nonspontaneous at all temperatures
+	+	Spontaneous only at high temperatures
–	–	Spontaneous only at low temperatures

It is very important to note that the **rate** of a reaction depends on the **activation energy,** not the ΔG.

> **MCAT FAVORITE**
>
> $\Delta G = \Delta H - T\Delta S$
>
> Memorize it.

> **MCAT FAVORITE**
>
> Recall that thermodynamics and kinetics are separate topic areas. When a reaction is thermodynamically spontaneous, it has no bearing on how fast it goes; it means only that it will proceed *eventually*.

> **MCAT FAVORITE**
>
> The only temperature-dependent states are when both ΔH and ΔS are either negative or positive.

2. Standard Free Energy

Standard free energy, $\Delta G°$, is defined as the ΔG of a process occurring at 25°C and 1 atm pressure, and for which the concentrations of any solutions involved are 1 M. The **standard free energy of formation** of a compound, $\Delta G°_f$, is the free-energy change that occurs when 1 mol of a compound in its standard state is formed from its elements in their standard states under standard conditions. The standard free energy of formation of any element in its most stable form (and, therefore, its standard state) is zero. The standard free energy of a reaction, $\Delta G°_{rxn}$, is the free-energy change that occurs when that reaction is carried out under standard state conditions; i.e., when the reactants in their standard states are converted to the products in their standard states, at standard conditions of T and P. For example: under standard conditions conversion of C (*diamond*) to C (*graphite*) is spontaneous. However, its rate is so slow that the rxn is never observed.

$$\Delta G°_{rxn} = \text{(sum of } \Delta G°_f \text{ of products)} - \text{(sum of } \Delta G°_f \text{ of reactants)}.$$

3. Reaction Quotient

$\Delta G°_{rxn}$ can also be derived from the equilibrium constant for the equation:

$$\Delta G° = -RT \ln K_{eq}$$

where K_{eq} is the equilibrium constant, R is the gas constant, and T is the temperature in K.

Once a reaction commences, however, the standard state conditions no longer hold. K_{eq} must be replaced by another parameter, the **reaction quotient (Q)**. For the reaction, $a\,A + b\,B \rightleftarrows c\,C + d\,D$,

$$Q = \frac{[C]^c[D]^d}{[A]^a[D]^b}$$

Likewise, ΔG must be used in place of $\Delta G°$. The relationship between the two is as follows:

$$\Delta G = \Delta G° + RT \ln Q$$

where R is the gas constant and T is the temperature in K.

4. Examples

a. Vaporization of water at one atmosphere pressure

$$H_2O(\ell) + \text{heat} \rightarrow H_2O(g)$$

MCAT SYNOPSIS

Note the similarity of this equation to Hess's law. Almost any state function could be substituted for ΔG here.

TEACHER TIP

Note that the right side of this equation is the same as that for $K_{eq,}$ and rather than representing the reaction at equilibrium it represents a snapshot of the reaction at any time.

When water boils, hydrogen bonds (H-bonds) are broken. Energy is absorbed (the reaction is endothermic), and thus ΔH is positive. Entropy increases as the closely packed molecules of the liquid become the more randomly moving molecules of a gas; thus, $T\Delta S$ is also positive. Because ΔH and $T\Delta S$ are each positive, the reaction will proceed spontaneously only if $T\Delta S > \Delta H$. This is true only at temperatures above 100°C. Below 100°C, ΔG is positive and the water remains a liquid. At 100°C, $\Delta H = T\Delta S$ and $\Delta G = 0$: an equilibrium is established between water and water vapor. The opposite is true when water vapor condenses: H-bonds are formed, and energy is released; the reaction is exothermic (ΔH is negative) and entropy decreases, as a liquid is forming from a gas ($T\Delta S$ is negative). Condensation will be spontaneous only if $\Delta H < T\Delta S$. This is the case at temperatures below 100°C; above 100°C, $T\Delta S$ is more negative than H, ΔG is positive, and condensation is not spontaneous. Again, at 100°C, an equilibrium is established.

b. The combustion of C_6H_6 (benzene)

$$2\ C_6H_6(\ell) + 15\ O_2(g) \rightarrow 12\ CO_2(g) + 6\ H_2O(g) + \text{heat}$$

In this case, heat is released (ΔH is negative) as the benzene burns and the entropy is increased ($T\Delta S$ is positive), because two gases (18 moles total) have greater entropy than a gas and a liquid (15 moles gas and 2 liquid). ΔG is negative and the reaction is spontaneous.

PRACTICE QUESTIONS

1. Consider the cooling of an ideal gas in a closed system. This process is illustrated in the pressure-volume graph shown below. This process could be called which of the following?

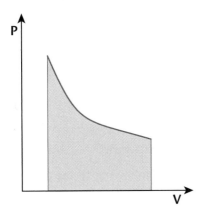

   A. Adiabatic
   B. Isobaric
   C. Isothermal
   D. None of the above

2. An ideal gas of volume 7 L undergoes an adiabatic expansion. The molar specific heat of this ideal gas at constant volume is 3 Jmol^{-1}K^{-1}. At constant pressure, its molar specific heat is 5 Jmol^{-1}K^{-1}. The structure of this ideal gas is

   A. monatomic.
   B. diatomic.
   C. triatomic.
   D. unable to be determined without more information.

3. A reaction has a positive entropy and enthalpy. What can be inferred about the progress of this reaction from this information?

   A. The reaction is spontaneous.
   B. The reaction is nonspontaneous.
   C. The reaction is at equilibrium.
   D. More information is required.

4. Pure sodium metal spontaneously combusts upon contact with room temperature water. What is true about the equilibrium constant of this combustion reaction at 25°C?

   A. $K_{eq} < 1$
   B. $K_{eq} > 1$
   C. $K_{eq} = 1$
   D. More information is required.

5. Which of the following processes has the most exothermic heat of reaction?

   A. Combustion of ethane
   B. Combustion of propane
   C. Combustion of n-butane
   D. Combustion of isobutane

6. Methanol reacts with acetic acid to form methyl acetate and water as shown below in the presence of an acid catalyst. What is the heat of formation of methyl acetate in kJ/mol?

   $$CH_3OH\ (l) + CH_3COOH\ (aq) \longrightarrow CH_3COOCH_3\ (aq) + H_2O\ (l)$$

Type of Bond	Bond Disassociation Energy (kJ/mol)
C — C	348
C — H	413
C = O	805
O — H	464
C — O	360

   A. –464 kJ/mol
   B. +464 kJ/mol
   C. –1,288 kJ/mol
   D. +1,288 kJ/mol

7. At standard temperature and pressure, a chemical process is at equilibrium. What is the free energy of reaction (ΔG) for this process?

A. $\Delta G > 0$
B. $\Delta G < 0$
C. $\Delta G = 0$
D. More information is required.

8. For a certain chemical process, $\Delta G° = -4{,}955.14$ kJ/mol. What is the equilibrium constant K_{eq} for this reaction?

A. $K_{eq} = 0.13$
B. $K_{eq} = 7.4$
C. $K_{eq} = 8.9$
D. $K_{eq} = 100$

9. Consider the chemical reaction in the vessel depicted below. The reaction is:

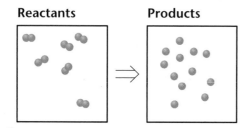

Reactants   **Products**

A. spontaneous.
B. nonspontaneous.
C. equilibrium.
D. unable to be determined without more information.

10. Suppose $\Delta G_{rxn}° = -2{,}000$ kJ/mol for a chemical reaction. At 300 K, what is the reaction quotient Q?

A. $\Delta G = -2{,}000$ kJ/mol + (300 K) (8.314 Jmol^{-1}K^{-1})ln(Q).
B. $\Delta G = -2{,}000$ kJ/mol − (300 K) (8.314 Jmol^{-1}K^{-1})ln(Q).
C. $\Delta G = -2{,}000$ kJ/mol + (300 K) (8.314 Jmol^{-1}K^{-1})log(Q).
D. $\Delta G = -2{,}000$ kJ/mol − (300 K) (8.314 Jmol^{-1}K^{-1})log(Q).

11. An ideal gas undergoes a reversible expansion at constant pressure.

Which of the following terms could describe this expansion?

I. Adiabatic
II. Isothermal
III. Isobaric

A. I only
B. I and II only
C. I and III only
D. I, II, and III

12. A chemical reaction has a negative enthalpy and negative entropy. Which of the following terms describes the energy of this reaction?

A. Exothermic
B. Endothermic
C. Endergonic
D. Exergonic

13. Consider the chemical reaction in the vessel pictured below. What can we say about the entropy of this reaction?

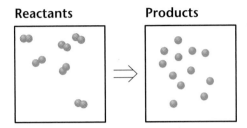

Reactants   **Products**

A. $\Delta S > 0$

B. $\Delta S < 0$

C. $\Delta S = 0$

D. More information is required to determine ΔS.

14. Which of the following statements is true of a spontaneous reaction?

A. $\Delta G > 0$ and $K_{eq} > 1$

B. $\Delta G > 0$ and $K_{eq} < 1$

C. $\Delta G < 0$ and $K_{eq} > 1$

D. $\Delta G < 0$ and $K_{eq} > 1$

15. Which of the following devices would be most appropriate to measure the heat capacity of a liquid?

A. Thermometer

B. Calorimeter

C. Barometer

D. Volumetric flask

16. Which of the following equations does not state a law of thermodynamics?

A. $\Delta E_{system} + \Delta E_{surroundings} = \Delta E_{universe}$

B. $\Delta S_{system} + \Delta S_{surroundings} = \Delta S_{universe}$

C. $\Delta H_{system} + \Delta H_{surroundings} = \Delta H_{universe}$

D. $S_{universe} = 0$ at $T = 0$ K

17. A reaction coordinate for a chemical reaction is displayed below. Which of the following terms describes the energy of this reaction?

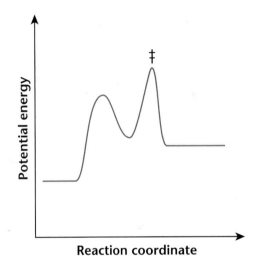

A. Endothermic

B. Exothermic

C. Endergonic

D. Exergonic

KEY CONCEPTS

Thermodynamics

Kinetics

Reaction profiles

REACTION ENERGY PROFILES

When chalcone (**A**) is subjected to reductive conditions with sodium borohydride, two products can result. The two products are the so-called "1,2–reduction" product (**B**), in which the carbonyl is reduced, and the "1,4–reduction" product (**C**), in which the conjugated alkene is reduced.

$$\left(R = 1.99\,\frac{cal}{mol\,k} \right)$$

"1,4–reduction"

C   A   B

TAKEAWAYS

The goal of a reaction profile is to give you information about energy *differences*. Make sure that you identify the important differences and their significances, as above.

The reaction profiles leading to each reduction product are both shown in the plot below.

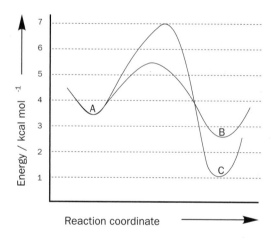

Based on the plot above, answer the following questions:

1) Which product is more thermodynamically stable? Which one forms faster?

2) Assume that **A** is in equilibrium with **C**. What will the ratio of **C** to **A** be at equilibrium?

3) How could the rate of the reaction of **A** to **C** be made closer to the rate of the reaction of **A** to **B**?

4) Which product would be favored if **A** were subjected to high temperatures for a long time? If **A** were subjected to low temperatures for only a brief period of time? Explain why for each situation.

THINGS TO WATCH OUT FOR

Be careful to take note of the units of energy on the *y*-axis if you plan on doing any computations.

1) **Look at the energy differences between the starting material and the product(s) as well as the differences between the starting material and the transition state leading to each product.**

   Notice that the energy of **C** is lower than that of **B.** Therefore, it is the more thermodynamically stable product.

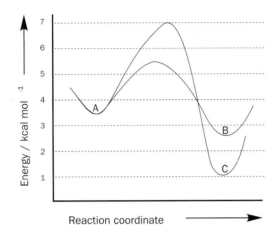

Reaction coordinate

The rate of formation of each product is determined by the difference in energy between the starting material **A** and the top of the "hump" leading to each product. Because this distance is lower for the formation of **B,** it forms faster.

2) **Note that the difference in energy between the starting material and the product(s) determines the ratio of products to reactants at equilibrium.**

$$\Delta G^\circ = -RT \ln K_{eq}$$

$$K_{eq} = e^{\frac{-\Delta G^\circ}{RT}}$$

$$K_{eq} = e^{\frac{-\Delta G^\circ}{RT}} = e^{\frac{-(-2500)}{(2)(300)}} = e^{\frac{2500}{600}}$$

$$K_{eq} = e^4 = 81 = \frac{[C]}{[A]}$$

This equation provides the relationship between K_{eq} and ΔG°. We need to rearrange it to solve for K_{eq}.

Note that $\Delta G^\circ \approx 1{,}000 - 3{,}500 = -2{,}500$ cal mol^{-1}, from the diagram, and $R = 1.99$ cal (mol K)$^{-1} \approx 2$ cal (mol K)$^{-1}$, and $T = 298 \approx 300$ K.

Let's say 2,500/600 is about equal to 4, and $e = 2.7818 \approx 3$.

Note that a negative ΔG° gives more product than reactant, as you would expect for a spontaneous reaction.

3) Consider what role(s) the addition of a catalyst might play.

Remember: *A catalyst is something that speeds up a reaction and is not consumed during a reaction. If it speeds up a reaction, it lowers the "hump" in the reaction profile. So, we could increase the rate of formation of **C** by adding a catalyst to that reaction, making the rate closer to the rate of formation of **B**.*

4) Consider the effects of temperature on the reaction(s).

At high temperatures for long times, **A** has the energy to go back and forth over and over again between **B** and **C**. Then, over time, the lowest energy product **C** would predominate, just as rolling a ball down a hill would cause it to fall to the lowest location.

Between the two products, **B** will form much faster than **C** because its energy of activation (height of the "hump") is lower. At low temperatures, the products won't have the energy to go back over the hill to get to **A,** so the faster-forming product will predominate (i.e., **B**).

SIMILAR QUESTIONS

1) What would be the ratio of **B** to **A** at equilibrium?

2) If a catalyst were added to the reaction of **A** going to **C**, as in step 3 above, would the energies of **A** and **C** be changed as a result? Why or why not?

3) There are actually intermediates involved in the reactions producing both **B** and **C**. These intermediates are shown below. Sketch how each reaction profile would look, including the involvement of these intermediates. Be sure to indicate which intermediate is relatively more stable.

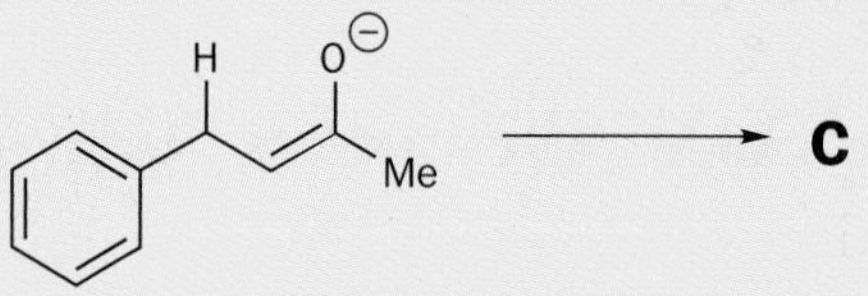

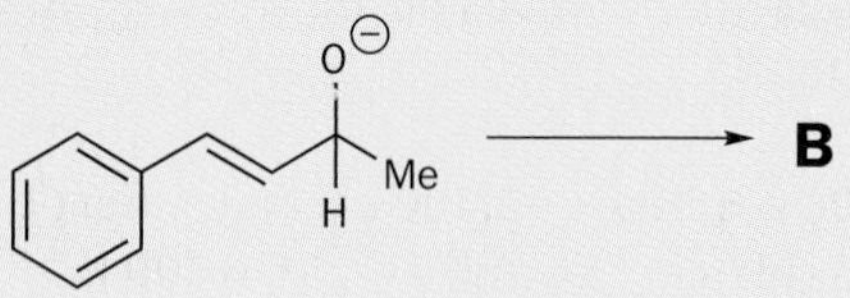

THERMODYNAMIC EQUILIBRIUM

The reaction $2NO(g) + Cl_2(g) \rightarrow 2NOCl(g)$ adheres to the following thermodynamic data:

ΔH	–77.1 kJ/mol
ΔS	–121 J/K
ΔG	–44.0 kJ/mol
K_{eq}	1.54×10^7

Suppose that, in equilibrium, NO exerts 0.6 atm of pressure and Cl_2 adds 0.3 atm, find the partial pressure of NOCl in this equilibrium. Also, find the temperature at which the thermodynamic data in the table were reported. K_{eq} is related to K_p by the following equation: $K_p = K_{eq}(RT)^{\Delta n}$ where Δn is the change in number of moles of gas evolved as the reaction moves forward. ($R = 8.314$ J/K · mol)

1) Find the temperature at which the thermodynamic data is true.
☞ $\Delta G = \Delta H - T\Delta S$
$(-44$ kJ/mol$) = (-77$ kJ/mol$) - T(-0.121$ kJ/K $\times$ mol$) \rightarrow T = 273$ K

Being able to work with the equation $\Delta G = \Delta H - T\Delta S$ is absolutely crucial for Test Day. Specifically concerning the data here, because both ΔH and ΔS are negative, the reaction will become "less spontaneous" as we increase temperature. This will help narrow down our answer choices on Test Day.

MCAT Pitfall: Notice that not all of the state functions were given in the same unit! Had you blindly put in entropy without changing its units, you would have obtained a temperature near absolute zero (0 K). At absolute zero, molecules no longer move, and it is unlikely that this reaction would have such a high equilibrium constant.

2) Find Δn.
For the equation:
$2NO(g) + Cl_2(g) \rightarrow 2NOCl(g)$
$\Delta n = 2 - (2 + 1) = -1$

3) Find K_p.
$K_p = K_{eq}(RT)^{\Delta n}$
$K_p = (1.54 \times 10^7)(18.314$ J/K·mole$)(273$ K$)^{-1}$
    $= 6785$

Use the temperature value from step 1.

KEY CONCEPTS

Thermochemistry

Gibbs free energy

Enthalpy

Entropy

Equilibrium constant, K_{eq}

Reaction quotient, Q

$\Delta G = \Delta H - T\Delta S$ (kJ/mol)

$\Delta G° = -RT \ln K_{eq}$ (kJ/mol)

$\Delta G = \Delta G° + RT \ln Q$ (kJ/mol)

TAKEAWAYS

Two equations should get you through nearly any thermochemistry question. Remember to round your numbers and to predict the ballpark for your answers wherever possible.

THINGS TO WATCH OUT FOR

Pay close attention to the units used.

You are not responsible for memorizing the equation. However, in the MCAT, you have to be able to use a brand new equation to solve for the answer.

---

4) Find the partial pressure.

$$K_p = \frac{(P^{eq}_{NOCl})^2}{(P^{eq}_{NO})^2 \left(P^{eq}_{Cl_2}\right)}$$

$$6785 = \frac{(P^{eq}_{NOCl})^2}{(0.6)^2 \cdot (0.3)}$$

$$733 = (P^{eq}_{NOCl})^2$$

$$27 \text{ atm} = P^{eq}_{NOCl}$$

Plug in the given data into the reaction quotient.

SIMILAR QUESTIONS

1) If $K_{eq} = 7.4 \times 10^{-3}$ for $CH_4(g) + 2H_2O(g) \rightarrow CO_2(g) + 4H_2(g)$, which is more plentiful, the reactants or the products?

2) If pyrophosphoric acid ($H_4P_2O_7$) and arsenous acid (H_3AsO_3) have acid dissociation constants of 3×10^{-2} and 6.6×10^{-10}, respectively, at room temperature, find the Gibbs free energy of each dissociation reaction and determine if it is spontaneous. What does this mean for the ΔH and ΔS for these reactions?

3) A chemist is given three liquid-filled flasks, each labeled with generic thermodynamic data. She is told to put one in a cold room, to put one on a Bunsen burner, and to leave one on the benchtop—whatever conditions will best facilitate the reaction. If the flasks are labeled as follows, which flask goes where?

    A $\Delta H < 0, \Delta S > 0$

    E $\Delta H < 0, \Delta S < 0$

    P $\Delta H > 0, \Delta S > 0$

BOND ENTHALPY

An unknown compound containing only carbon and hydrogen is subjected to a combustion reaction in which 2,059 kJ of heat are released. If 3 moles of CO_2 and 4 moles of steam are produced for every mole of the unknown compound reacted, find the enthalpy for a single C–H bond.

Bond	Bond Dissociation Energy (kJ/mol)
O=O	497
C=O	805
O–H	464
C–C	347

1) Write a balanced equation for the reaction.

$$C_3H_8 + 5O_2 \rightleftharpoons 3CO_2 + 4H_2O$$

The question stem tells us a few things about the reaction: it is combustion, the carbon source has the generic structure C_xH_y, and the products include 10 oxygen atoms, 3 carbon atoms, and 8 H atoms. To balance the reaction, we'd need those atoms on the left side too. Thus, we find that our unknown sample is actually propane and that we need 5 O_2 molecules.

Remember: For our purposes, it is completely acceptable to have a fractional coefficient in front of a diatomic molecule. $2C_2H_4 + (7/2)O_2 \rightarrow 3H_2O + 2CO_2$ is equivalent to $4C_2H_4 + 7CO_2 \rightarrow 6H_2O + 4CO_2$.

2) Determine which bonds are broken and which are formed.

C_3H_8: 2 C–C bonds broken, 8 C–H bonds broken
$5O_2$: 5 O=O bonds broken
$3CO_2$: 6 C=O bonds formed
$4H_2O$: 8 O–H bonds formed

Combustion of C_3H_8 will break apart the carbon backbone and the C–H bonds. The carbon is in a straight chain (as opposed to cyclic or branched), so 2 C–C bonds and 8 C–H bonds are broken. For O_2, only one O=O bond is broken. However, we have 5 moles of this reactant, and thus we have 5 O=O bonds broken. Each molecule of carbon dioxide has 2 C=O bonds, but we have 3 moles of CO_2, so we have 6 C=O bonds formed. Similarly, 8 O–H bonds are formed in the 4 moles of water produced.

KEY CONCEPTS

Hess's law:

$\Delta H_{rxn} = \Delta H_f(products) - \Delta H_f(reactants)(kJ/mol)$

Enthalpy

Bond dissociation energy

Combustion

Stoichiometry

$\Delta H_{rxn} = \Delta H_b (reactants) - \Delta H_b (products) (kJ/mol)$

ΔH_{rxn} = total energy input – total energy released (kJ/mol)

TAKEAWAYS

Consider the number of bonds before applying Hess's law. Make sure to take note of how many bonds are in a given molecule as well as how many stoichiometric equivalents of that molecule you have.

**THINGS TO
WATCH OUT FOR**

There are a number
of ways to set up the
equation for ΔH_{rxn}.
Whatever equation you
use, keep your signs
straight. Remember that
forming bonds releases
energy, whereas breaking
bonds requires energy.

3) Apply Hess's law.

☞ $\Delta H_{rxn} = \Delta H_b$ (reactants) − ΔH_b (products)

☞ ΔH_{rxn} = total energy input − total energy released

✍ −2,059 = [2(347) + 8x + 5(497)] − [6(805) + 8(464)]

−2,059 = [3,179 + 8x] − [8,542]

−2,059 + 8,542 − 3,179 = 8x

x = 413 kJ/mol

Bond dissociation energy is the energy required to break a particular type of bond in one mole of gaseous molecules. Bond energies can be used to estimate the enthalpy of reaction as given by the two equations above. When we start plugging in numbers, we are given all data except for C−H bond enthalpy. We solve for this variable (x in the above equations).

Remember: *The equation $\Delta H_{rxn} = \Delta H_b$ (reactants) − ΔH_b (products) is simply a restatement of Hess's Law. Bond enthalpy is for bond breaking and enthalpy of formation, of course, is for bond making. Changing ΔH_F to ΔH_b switches the signs and, thus, the order of the equation. Keep in mind that it can also be written as $\Delta H_{rxn} = \Delta H_b$ (bonds broken) + ΔH_b (bonds formed), but you must remember to make the bond enthalpies for the products negative because forming bonds releases energy.*

---

4) Use Avogadro's number.

✍ (413 kJ/mol) × [1 mol/(6.022 × 10²³ molecules)]

= 6.86 × 10⁻²² kJ/molecule

We see that 413 kJ are found in one mole of C−H bonds. One mole of a substance is equal to 6.022 × 10²³ molecules. Here, we simply use that conversion factor. The result tells us that 6.86 × 10⁻²² kJ are stored in each C−H bond.

SIMILAR QUESTIONS

1) Ethanol metabolism in yeast consists of the conversion of ethanol (C_2H_5OH) to acetic acid (CH_3COOH). What is the enthalpy of the reaction if 0.1 mmol of ethanol is metabolized?

2) A second metabolic process involves the net production of 2 ATP and 2 NADH from 2 ADP and 2 NAD⁺. If the conversion of these molecules is endothermic and adds 443.5 kJ to the overall enthalpy of the reaction, find the enthalpy for a "high-energy" phosphate bond.

3) Tristearin is oxidized in the body according to the following reaction: $2C_{57}H_{110}O_6 + 163O_2 \rightarrow 114CO_2 + 110H_2O$. If the standard enthalpy for this reaction is −34 MJ mol⁻¹, find the total enthalpy for the bonds in tristearin.

HEAT OF FORMATION

The heat of combustion of glucose ($C_6H_{12}O_6$) is –2,537.3 kJ/mol. If the $\Delta H°_f$ of $CO_2(g)$ is –393.5 kJ/mol, and the $\Delta H°_f$ of $H_2O(g)$ is –241.8 kJ/mol, what is the $\Delta H°_f$ of glucose?

1) Write a balanced equation for the reaction.
Unbalanced reaction: $C_6H_{12}O_6 + O_2 \rightarrow CO_2 + H_2O$
Balanced reaction: $C_6H_{12}O_6 + 6O_2 \rightarrow 6CO_2 + 6H_2O$

The unbalanced reaction to the left is typical of all hydrocarbon combustion reactions. (Unless otherwise noted, presume that combustion of carbohydrates is with oxygen gas.) Begin by balancing the carbons on the left side ($6CO_2$), then balance the hydrogens on the left side ($12H_2O$), and conclude by balancing the oxygen gas on the right side ($6O_2$).

Remember: *For our purposes, it is completely acceptable to have a fractional coefficient in front of a diatomic molecule. $2C_2H_4 + (7/2)O_2 \rightarrow 3H_2O + 2CO_2$ is equivalent to $4C_2H_4 + 7CO_2 \rightarrow 6H_2O + 4CO_2$ but the math is simpler for the former.*

2) Apply Hess's law.
☞ $\Delta H_{rxn} = \Delta H_F(\text{products}) - \Delta H_F(\text{reactants})$
$-2,537.3 = [6(-393.5) + 6(-241.8)] - [\Delta H_F(\text{glucose})]$
Rearranging to solve for $\Delta H_F(\text{glucose})$:
✍ $\Delta H_f(\text{glucose}) = 2,537.3 + [6(-393.5) + 6(-241.8)]$
$\Delta H_f(\text{glucose}) = 2,537.3 + [-2,361 + -1,450.8]$
$\Delta H_f(\text{glucose}) = 2,537.3 + [-3,811.8]$
$\Rightarrow \Delta H_f(\text{glucose}) = -1274.5$

The heat of formation is defined as the heat absorbed or released during the formation of a pure substance from the elements at a constant pressure. Therefore, by definition, diatomic gases like oxygen have a heat of formation of zero. A negative heat of formation means that heat is released to form the product, whereas a positive heat of formation means that heat is required to form the product. The overall combustion reaction of glucose releases 2,537.3 kJ/mol of heat.

KEY CONCEPTS

Hess's law:

$\Delta H_{rxn} = \Delta H_F(\text{products}) - \Delta H_F(\text{reactants})$ (kJ/mol)

Heat of formation

Combustion

TAKEAWAYS

Always identify the balanced equation for the reaction before you begin to apply Hess's law. There is a second way of thinking about Hess's law that may be applicable in some questions as well (see previous topic). The given information in the passage and/or question stem will dictate which equation to use. Finally, recall that enthalpy is a state function, and regardless of the path you take to get from the reactants to the products, the change in enthalpy will be the same.

THINGS TO WATCH OUT FOR

At least one of the wrong answer choices for thermochemistry questions will be a result from carelessness with signs. Organized scratchwork in a stepwise fashion will facilitate avoiding this problem, but perhaps more important is maintaining the ability to approximate the answer. Only experience (a.k.a. practice!) will breed such wisdom.

SIMILAR QUESTIONS

1) Given the ΔH_F of carbon dioxide and water, what other piece(s) of information must you have to calculate the ΔH_{comb} of ethane?

2) If the ΔH_F of acetylene is 226.6 kJ/mol, what is the ΔH_{comb} of acetylene?

3) If the ΔH_F of NaBr (s) is −359.9 kJ/mol, what is the sum of each ΔH_F of the following series of five reactions?

$$Na(s) \rightarrow Na(g) \rightarrow Na^+(g)$$

$$\frac{1}{2} Br_2(g) \rightarrow Br(g) \rightarrow Br^-(g)$$

$$Na^+(g) + Br^-(g) \rightarrow NaBr(s)$$

CHAPTER 7

THE GAS PHASE

Matter can exist in three different physical forms, called **phases** or **states: gas, liquid,** and **solid.** Liquids and solids will be discussed in chapter 8.

The gaseous phase, the subject of this chapter, is the simplest to understand, because all gases display similar behavior and follow similar laws regardless of their identity. The atoms or molecules in a gaseous sample move rapidly and are far apart from each other. In addition, only very weak intermolecular forces exist between gas particles; this results in certain characteristic physical properties, such as the ability to expand to fill any volume and to take on the shape of a container. Further, gases are easily, though not infinitely, compressible.

The state of a gaseous sample is generally defined by four variables: pressure (P), volume (V), temperature (T), and number of moles (n). Gas pressures are usually expressed in units of atmospheres (atm) or millimeters of mercury (mm Hg or torr), which are related as follows:

$$1 \text{ atm} = 760 \text{ mm Hg} = 760 \text{ torr}$$

Volume is generally expressed in liters (L) or milliliters (mL). The temperature of a gas is usually given in Kelvin (K, **not** °K). Gases are often discussed in terms of **standard temperature and pressure (STP),** which refers to conditions of 273.15 K (0°C) and 1 atm.

Note: It is important not to confuse **STP** with **standard conditions**— the two standards involve different temperatures and are used for different purposes. STP (0°C or 273 K) is generally used for gas law calculations; standard conditions (25°C or 298 K) is used when measuring standard enthalpy, entropy, Gibbs's free energy, and voltage.

> **MCAT FAVORITE**
> STP is different from standard state. Temperature at STP is 0°C, i.e., 273.15 K. Temperature at standard state is 25°C.

IDEAL GASES

When examining the behavior of gases under varying conditions of temperature and pressure, scientists speak of ideal gases. An ideal gas represents a hypothetical gas whose molecules have no intermolecular forces and occupy no volume. Although gases actually deviate from this idealized behavior, at relatively low pressures (atmospheric pressure) and high temperatures many gases behave in a nearly ideal fashion. Therefore, the assumptions used for ideal gases can be applied to real gases with reasonable accuracy.

A. BOYLE'S LAW

Experimental studies performed by Robert Boyle in 1660 led to the formulation of Boyle's law. His work showed that for a given gaseous sample held at constant temperature (isothermal conditions), the volume of the gas is inversely proportional to its pressure:

$$PV = k \text{ or } P_1V_1 = P_2V_2$$

where k is a proportionality constant and the subscripts 1 and 2 represent two different sets of conditions. A plot of pressure versus volume for a gas is shown in Figure 7.1.

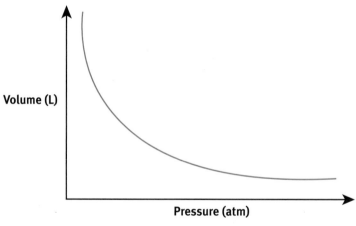

Figure 7.1

> **MCAT FAVORITE**
>
> Boyle's law, a common topic on the exam, states that pressure and volume are inversely related. When one increases, the other decreases.

> **TEACHER TIP**
>
> Remembering the shape of the graph might help you recall the relationship on Test Day. Here we can see that as pressure increases, volume decreases, and vice versa.

Example: Under isothermal conditions, what would be the volume of a 1 L sample of helium if its pressure is changed from 12 atm to 4 atm?

Solution:

$$P_1 = 12 \text{ atm} \qquad P_2 = 4 \text{ atm}$$

$$V_1 = 1 \text{ L} \qquad V_2 = X$$

$$P_1V_1 = P_2V_2$$

$$12 \text{ atm } (1 \text{ L}) = 4 \text{ atm } (X)$$

$$\frac{12}{4}L = X$$

$$X = 3 \text{ L}$$

B. LAW OF CHARLES AND GAY-LUSSAC

The law of Charles and Gay-Lussac, or simply Charles's law, was developed during the early 19th century. The law states that at constant pressure, the volume of a gas is directly proportional to its absolute temperature. The absolute temperature is the temperature expressed in Kelvin, which can be calculated from the expression $T_K = T_{°C} + 273.15$.

$$\frac{V}{T} = k \quad or \quad \frac{V_1}{T_1} = \frac{V_2}{T_2}$$

where k is a constant and the subscripts 1 and 2 represent two different sets of conditions. A plot of temperature versus volume is shown in Figure 7.2.

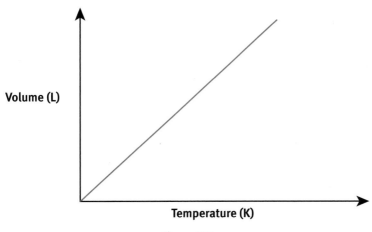

Figure 7.2

Example: If the absolute temperature of 2 L of gas at constant pressure is changed from 283.15 K to 566.30 K, what would be the final volume?

Solution:

$$T_1 = 283.15 \text{ K} \qquad V_1 = 2 \text{ L}$$

$$T_2 = 566.30 \text{ K} \qquad V_2 = X$$

$$\frac{V_1}{T_1} = \frac{V_2}{T_2}$$

$$\frac{2L}{283.15 \text{ K}} = \frac{X}{566.30 \text{ K}}$$

$$X = \frac{2L(566.30 \text{ K})}{283.15 \text{ K}}$$

$$X = 4L$$

C. AVOGADRO'S PRINCIPLE

In 1811, Amedeo Avogadro proposed that for all gases at a constant temperature and pressure, the volume of the gas will be directly proportional to the number of moles of gas present; therefore, all gases have the same number of moles in the same volume.

$$\frac{n}{V} = k \text{ or } \frac{n_1}{V_1} = \frac{n_2}{V_2}$$

The subscripts 1 and 2 once again apply to two different sets of conditions with the same temperature and pressure.

D. IDEAL GAS LAW

The ideal gas law combines the relationships outlined in Boyle's law, Charles's law, and Avogadro's principle to yield an expression which can be used to predict the behavior of a gas. The ideal gas law shows the relationship among four variables that define a sample of gas—pressure (P), volume (V), temperature (T), and number of moles (n)—and is represented by the equation

$$PV = nRT$$

The constant R is known as the **gas constant.** Under STP conditions (273.15 K and 1 atmosphere), 1 mole of gas was shown to have a volume of 22.4 L. Substituting these values into the ideal gas equation gave R = 8.21×10^{-2} L • atm/(mol • K).

The gas constant may be expressed in many other units: another common value is 8.314 J/(K • mol), which is derived when SI units of pascals (for pressure) and cubic meters (for volume) are substituted into the ideal gas law. **When carrying out calculations based on the ideal gas law, it is important to choose a value of R that matches the units of the variables.**

Example: What volume would 12 g of helium occupy at 20°C and a pressure of 380 mm Hg?

Solution: The ideal gas law can be used, but first, all of the variables must be converted to yield units that will correspond to the expression of the gas constant as 0.0821 L • atm/(mol • K).

$$P = 380 \text{ mm Hg} \times \frac{1 \text{atm}}{760 \text{ mm Hg}} = 0.5 \text{ atm}$$

$$T = 20°C + 273.15 = 293.15 \text{ K}$$

$$n = 12 \text{g He} \times \frac{1 \text{ mol He}}{4.0 \text{ g}} = 3 \text{ mol He}$$

Substituting into the ideal gas equation:

$$PV = nRT$$

$$(0.5 \text{ atm})(V) = (3 \text{ mol})(0.0821 \text{ L} \bullet \text{atm/(mol} \bullet \text{K)})(293.15 \text{ K})$$

$$V = 144.4 \text{ L}$$

In addition to standard calculations to determine the pressure, volume, or temperature of a gas, the ideal gas law may be used to determine the density and molar mass of the gas.

1. Density

Density is defined as the mass per unit volume of a substance and, for gases, is usually expressed in units of g/L. By rearrangement, the ideal gas equation can be used to calculate the density of a gas.

$$PV = nRT$$

$$\text{where} \quad n = \frac{m}{MM} \quad \frac{\text{(mass in g)}}{\text{(molar mass)}}$$

$$\text{therefore} \quad PV = \frac{m}{MM} RT$$

$$\text{and} \quad d = \frac{m}{v} = \frac{P(MM)}{RT}$$

Another way to find the density of a gas is to start with the volume of a mole of gas at STP, 22.4 L, calculate the effect of pressure and temperature on the volume, and finally calculate the density by dividing the mass by the new volume. The following equation, derived from Boyle's and Charles's laws, is used to relate changes in the temperature, volume and pressure of a gas:

$$\frac{P_1 V_1}{T_1} = \frac{P_2 V_2}{T_2}$$

where the subscripts 1 and 2 refer to the two states of the gas (at STP and under the actual conditions). To calculate a change in volume, the equation is rearranged as follows.

$$V_2 = V_1 \left(\frac{P_1}{P_2} \right) \left(\frac{T_2}{T_1} \right)$$

V_2 is then used to find the density of the gas under nonstandard conditions.

$$d = \frac{m}{V_2}$$

If you *visualize* how the changes in pressure and temperature affect the volume of the gas, you can check to be sure you have not accidentally confused the pressure or temperature value that belongs in the numerator with the one that belongs in the denominator.

Example: What is the density of HCl gas at 2 atm and 45°C?

Solution: At STP, a mole of gas occupies 22.4 liters. Because the increase in pressure to 2 atm decreases volume, 22.4 L must be multiplied by $\left(\dfrac{1\text{ atm}}{2\text{ atm}}\right)$. Because the increase in temperature increases volume, the temperature factor will be $\left(\dfrac{318\text{ K}}{273\text{ K}}\right)$.

$$V_2 = \left(\frac{22.4\text{ L}}{\text{mol}}\right)\left(\frac{1\text{ atm}}{2\text{ atm}}\right)\left(\frac{318\text{ K}}{273\text{ K}}\right) = 13.0\text{ L/mol}$$

$$d = \left(\frac{36\text{ g/mol}}{13.0\text{ L/mol}}\right) = 2.77\text{g/L}$$

2. Molar Mass

Sometimes the identity of a gas is unknown, and the molar mass (see chapter 4) must be determined in order to identify it. Using the equation for density derived from the ideal gas law, the molar mass of a gas can be determined experimentally as follows. The pressure and temperature of a gas contained in a bulb of a given volume are measured, and the weight of the bulb plus sample is found. Then, the bulb is evacuated, and the empty bulb is weighed. The weight of the bulb plus sample minus the weight of the bulb yields the weight of the sample. Finally, the density of the sample is determined by dividing the weight of the sample by the volume of the bulb. The density at STP is calculated. The molecular weight is then found by multiplying the number of grams per liter by 22.4 liters per mole.

Example: What is the molar mass of a 2 L sample of gas that weighs 8 g at a temperature of 15°C and a pressure of 1.5 atm?

$$d = \frac{8\text{ g}}{2\text{ L}} \text{ at } 15°C \text{ and } 1.5 \text{ atm}$$

$$V_{STP} = (2\text{L})\left(\frac{273\text{ K}}{288\text{ K}}\right)\left(\frac{1.5\text{ atm}}{1\text{ atm}}\right) = 2.84\text{ L}$$

$$\frac{8\text{ g}}{2.84\text{ L}} = 2.82\text{ g/L at STP}$$

$$\left(\frac{2.82\text{ g}}{\text{L}}\right)\left(\frac{22.4\text{ L}}{\text{mol}}\right) = 63.2\text{ g/mol}$$

DALTON'S LAW OF PARTIAL PRESSURES

When two or more gases are found in one vessel without chemical interaction, each gas will behave independently of the other(s). Therefore, the pressure exerted by each gas in the mixture will be equal to the pressure that gas would exert if it were the only one in the container. The pressure exerted by each individual gas is called the **partial pressure** of that gas. In 1801, John Dalton derived an expression, now known as **Dalton's Law of Partial Pressures,** which states that the total pressure of a gaseous mixture is equal to the sum of the partial pressures of the individual components. The equation is:

$$P_T = P_A + P_B + P_C + \ldots$$

The partial pressure of a gas is related to its mole fraction and can be determined using the following equations:

$$P_A = P_T X_A$$

where $\qquad X_A = \dfrac{n_A \text{ (moles of A)}}{n_T \text{ (total moles)}}$

Example: A vessel contains 0.75 mol of nitrogen, 0.20 mol of hydrogen, and 0.05 mol of fluorine at a total pressure of 2.5 atm. What is the partial pressure of each gas?

First calculate the mole fraction of each gas.

$$X_{N_2} = \frac{0.75 \text{ mol}}{1.0 \text{ mol}} = 0.75 \quad X_{H_2} = \frac{0.20 \text{ mol}}{1.0 \text{ mol}} = 0.20 \quad X_{F_2} = \frac{0.05 \text{ mol}}{1.0 \text{ mol}} = 0.05$$

Then calculate the partial pressure.

$$P_A = X_A P_T$$

$$P_{N_2} = (2.5 \text{ atm})(0.75) \qquad P_{H_2} = (2.5 \text{ atm})(0.20) \qquad P_{F_2} = (2.5 \text{ atm})(0.05)$$

$$= 1.875 \text{ atm} \qquad\qquad = 0.5 \text{ atm} \qquad\qquad = 0.125 \text{ atm}$$

REAL GASES

In general, the ideal gas law is a good approximation of the behavior of real gases, but all real gases deviate from ideal gas behavior to some extent, particularly when the gas atoms or molecules are forced into close proximity under high pressure and at low temperature, so that molecular volume and intermolecular attractions become significant.

A. DEVIATIONS DUE TO PRESSURE

As the pressure of a gas increases, the particles are pushed closer and closer together. As the condensation pressure for a given temperature is approached, intermolecular attraction forces become more and more significant until the gas condenses into the liquid state (see Gas-Liquid Equilibrium in chapter 8).

At moderately high pressure (a few hundred atmospheres) a gas's volume is less than would be predicted by the ideal gas law, due to intermolecular attraction. At extremely high pressure the size of the particles becomes relatively large compared to the distance between them, and this causes the gas to take up a larger volume than would be predicted by the ideal gas law.

B. DEVIATIONS DUE TO TEMPERATURE

As the temperature of a gas is decreased, the average velocity of the gas molecules decreases, and the attractive intermolecular forces become increasingly significant. As the condensation temperature is approached for a given pressure, intermolecular attractions eventually cause the gas to condense to a liquid state (see Gas-Liquid Equilibrium in chapter 8).

As the temperature of a gas is reduced toward its condensation point (which is the same as its boiling point), intermolecular attraction causes the gas to have a smaller volume than would be predicted by the ideal gas law. The closer the temperature of a gas is to its boiling point, the less ideal is its behavior.

C. VAN DER WAALS EQUATION OF STATE

> **MCAT SYNOPSIS**
>
> Note that if *a* and *b* are both zero, this reduces to the ideal gas law.

Several real gas equations, or gas laws, exist that attempt to correct for the deviations from ideality that occur when a gas does not closely follow the ideal gas law. The van der Waals equation is a case in point.

$$\left(P + \frac{n^2 a}{V^2}\right)(V - nb) = nRT$$

In this equation, *a* and *b* are physical constants, experimentally determined for each gas. The *a* term corrects for the attractive forces between molecules, and as such will be small in value for a gas such as helium, larger for more polarizable gases such as Xe or N_2, and larger yet for polar molecules such as HCl or NH_3. The *b* term corrects for the volume of the molecules themselves. Larger values of *b* are thus found for larger molecules. Numerical values for *a* are generally much larger than those for *b*.

Example: Find the correction in pressure necessary for the deviation from ideality for 1 mole of ammonia in a 1 liter flask at 0°C. (For NH_3, a = 4.2, b = 0.037)

Solution: According to the ideal gas law,

P = nRT/V = (1)(0.0821)(273)/(1) = 22.4 atm, while according to the van der Waals equation,

$$P = \frac{nRT}{(V-nb)} - \frac{n^2a}{V^2} = \frac{(1)(0.821)(273)}{(1-0.037)} - \frac{1^2(4.2)}{1}$$

= 23.3 – 4.2 = 19.1 atm.

The pressure is thus 3.3 atm less than would be predicted from the ideal gas law, or an error of 15 percent.

KINETIC MOLECULAR THEORY OF GASES

As indicated by the gas laws, all gases show similar physical characteristics and behavior. A theoretical model to explain the behavior of gases was developed during the second half of the 19th century. The combined efforts of Boltzmann, Maxwell, and others led to a simple explanation of gaseous molecular behavior based on the motion of individual molecules. This model is called the **Kinetic Molecular Theory of Gases.** Like the gas laws, this theory was developed in reference to ideal gases, although it can be applied with reasonable accuracy to real gases as well.

A. ASSUMPTIONS OF THE KINETIC MOLECULAR THEORY

1. Gases are made up of particles whose volumes are negligible compared to the container volume.

2. Gas atoms or molecules exhibit no intermolecular attractions or repulsions.

3. Gas particles are in continuous, random motion, undergoing collisions with other particles and the container walls.

4. Collisions between any two gas particles are elastic, meaning that there is no overall gain or loss of energy.

5. The average kinetic energy of gas particles is proportional to the absolute temperature of the gas, and is the same for all gases at a given temperature.

B. APPLICATIONS OF THE KINETIC MOLECULAR THEORY OF GASES

1. Average Molecular Speeds

According to the kinetic molecular theory of gases, the average kinetic energy of a gas particle is proportional to the absolute temperature of the gas:

$$KE = \frac{1}{2}mv^2 = \frac{3}{2}kt$$

where k is the Boltzmann constant. This equation also shows that the speed of a gas molecule is related to its absolute temperature. However, because of the large number of rapidly and randomly moving gas particles, the speed of an individual gas molecule is nearly impossible to define. Therefore, the speeds of gases are defined in terms of their average molecular speed ($\bar{c}$), which represents the mathematical average of all the speeds of the gas particles in the sample. This is given by the following equation:

$$\bar{c} = \left(\frac{3RT}{MM}\right)^{\frac{1}{2}} \quad \text{where R = gas constant}$$

$$MM = \text{molecular mass}$$

A **Maxwell-Boltzmann distribution curve** shows the distribution of speeds of gas particles at a given temperature. Figure 7.3 shows a distribution curve of molecular speeds at two temperatures, T_1 and T_2, where $T_2 > T_1$. Notice that the bell-shaped curve flattens and shifts to the right as the temperature increases, indicating that at higher temperatures more molecules are moving at high speeds.

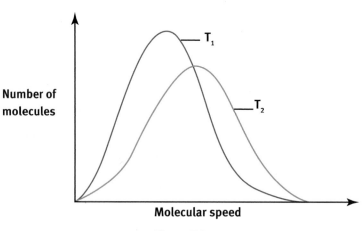

Figure 7.3

Example: What is the average speed of sulfur dioxide molecules at 37°C?

Solution: The gas constant R = 8.314 J/(K • mol) should be used and MM must be expressed in kg/mol.

$$\bar{c} = \left(\frac{3RT}{MM} \right)^{\frac{1}{2}}$$

$$\bar{c} = \left[\frac{3(8.314 \text{ J/K mol})(310.15 \text{ K})}{0.064 \text{ kg/mol}} \right]^{\frac{1}{2}}$$

$$\bar{c} = \sqrt{120871.3 \text{ J/kg}}$$

Use the conversion factor 1 J = 1 kg • m²/s²:

$$\bar{c} = \sqrt{120871.3 \text{ kg} \bullet \text{m}^2/\text{s}^2 \bullet \text{kg}}$$

$$\bar{c} = 347.7 \text{ m/s}$$

2. Graham's Law of Diffusion and Effusion

a. Diffusion

Diffusion occurs when gas molecules diffuse through a mixture. Diffusion accounts for the fact that an open bottle of perfume can quickly be smelled across a room. The kinetic molecular theory of gases predicted that heavier gas molecules diffuse more slowly than lighter ones because of their differing average speeds. In 1832, Thomas Graham showed mathematically that under isothermal and isobaric conditions, the rates at which two gases diffuse are inversely proportional to the square root of their molar masses. Thus:

$$\frac{r_1}{r_2} = \left(\frac{MM_2}{MM_1} \right)^{\frac{1}{2}} = \sqrt{\frac{MM_2}{MM_1}}$$

where r_1 and MM_1 represent the diffusion rate and molar mass of gas 1, and r_2 and MM_2 represent the diffusion rate and molar mass of gas 2.

TEACHER TIP

Diffusion is when gases mix with one another. Effusion is when a gas moves through a small hole under pressure. Both will be slower for larger molecules.

b. Effusion

Effusion is the flow of gas particles under pressure from one compartment to another through a small opening. Graham used the kinetic molecular theory of gases to show that for two gases at the same temperature, the rates of effusion are proportional to the average speeds. He then expressed the rates of effusion in terms of molar mass and found that the relationship is the same as that for diffusion:

$$\frac{r_1}{r_2} = \left(\frac{MM_2}{MM_1} \right)^{\frac{1}{2}}$$

PRACTICE QUESTIONS

1. The graph below shows a plot of PV versus P for 1 mol of ammonia gas. Experimental data was used to plot the line at pressures of 0.20 atm and above. The line was then extrapolated in order to determine the value of PV at zero pressure. Does the graph accurately describe the relationship between pressure and volume that would be seen for an ideal gas?

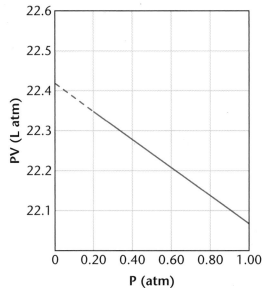

Graph of experimental results of PV versus V for 1 mol of ammonia gas. The data is extrapolated to zero pressure.

A. Yes, the graph describes an ideal gas because the value of PV at zero pressure is approximately 22.4 L.

B. Yes, the graph describes an ideal gas because the slope of the line is equal to −0.33 L.

C. No, the graph does not describe an ideal gas because as pressure increases the product of P and V deviates from 22.4 L.

D. No, the graph does not describe an ideal gas because the line is not horizontal.

2. Based on the graph in the previous question and your knowledge of gases, what conditions would be least likely to result in ideal gas behavior?

A. High pressure and low temperature
B. Low temperature and large volume
C. High pressure and large volume
D. Low pressure and high temperature

3. Calculate the density of neon gas at STP in g L^{-1}. The molar mass of neon can be approximated to 20.18 g mol^{-1}.

A. 452.3 g L^{-1}
B. 226.0 g L^{-1}
C. 1.802 g L^{-1}
D. 0.9009 g L^{-1}

4. A leak of helium gas through a small hole occurs at a rate of 3.22×10^{-5} mol s^{-1}. Will a leak of neon gas at the same temperature and pressure occur at a slower or faster rate than helium? Will a leak of oxygen gas at the same temperature and pressure occur at a slower or faster rate than helium?

A. Neon will leak faster than helium; oxygen will leak slower than helium.

B. Neon will leak faster than helium; oxygen will leak slower than helium.

C. Neon will leak slower than helium; oxygen will leak slower than helium.

D. Neon will leak slower than helium; oxygen will leak faster than helium.

5. A manometer is open to the atmosphere. The pressure of the gas in the flask can be calculated by the difference in the mercury levels in the arms of the U-shaped tube. If the atmospheric pressure is equal to 760 torr, calculate the pressure in the flask shown in below.

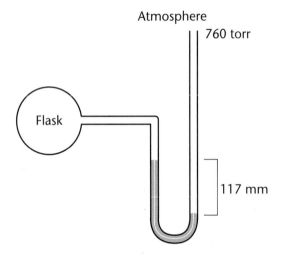

Atmosphere

760 torr

Flask

117 mm

A. 117 mm Hg
B. 877 mm Hg
C. 643 mm Hg
D. 760 mm Hg

6. A hot-air balloon rises because

A. the air molecules move faster due to the high temperature. The molecules escape through the bottom of the balloon, which forces the balloon upward.
B. the higher temperature within the balloon creates a larger volume, which decreases the density of air inside the balloon, allowing it to rise.
C. the air molecules inside the balloon circulate to increase the upward force lifting the balloon.
D. the volume inside the increasing balloon increases as a result of the increasing number of air molecules entering through the bottom of the hole.

7. A 0.04 gram piece of magnesium is placed in a beaker of hydrochloric acid. Hydrogen gas is generated according to the following equation. The gas is collected over water at 25°C, and the pressure during the experiment reads 784 mm Hg. The gas displaces a volume of 100 mL. The vapor pressure of water at 25°C is approximately 24 mm Hg. How many moles of hydrogen are produced?

$$Mg_{(s)} + 2HCl_{(aq)} \rightarrow MgCl_{2(aq)} + H_{2(g)}$$

A. 4.22×10^{-3} moles hydrogen
B. 4.08×10^{-3} moles hydrogen
C. 3.11 moles hydrogen
D. 3.2 moles hydrogen

8. Which of the following properties are true of ideal gases?

I. No volume
II. No attractive forces between them
III. No mass

A. I only
B. I and II only
C. I and III only
D. I, II, and III

9. An 8.01 g sample of $NH_4NO_{3(s)}$ is placed into an evacuated 10 L flask and heated to 227°C. After the NH_4NO_3 totally decomposes, what is the approximate pressure in the flask?

$$NH_4NO_{3(s)} \rightarrow N_2O_{(g)} + H_2O_{(g)}$$

A. 0.6 atm
B. 0.41 atm
C. 1.23 atm
D. 0.672 atm

10. In the diagram below, what is the partial pressure of each gas if all of the stopcocks are opened? Assume that the volume in the connecting tubes is negligible.

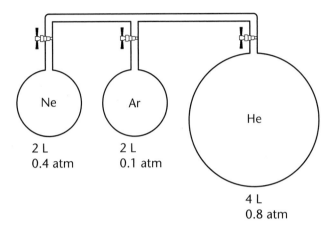

A. P_{Ne} = 0.1 atm; P_{Ar} = 0.25 atm; P_{He} = 0.25 atm
B. P_{Ne} = 0.025 atm; P_{Ar} = 0.4 atm; P_{He} = 0.1 atm
C. P_{Ne} = 0.2 atm; P_{Ar} = 0.1 atm; P_{He} = 0.4 atm
D. P_{Ne} = 0.1 atm; P_{Ar}= 0.025 atm; P_{He}= 0.4 atm

11. The kinetic molecular theory states that

A. the average kinetic energy of a molecule of gas is directly proportional to the temperature of the gas in Kelvin.
B. collisions between gas molecules are inelastic.
C. elastic collisions result in a loss of energy.
D. all gas molecules have the same kinetic energy.

12. Use the velocity distribution curves shown below to answer the question. The plots of two gases at STP are shown. One of the gases is 1 L of helium and the other is 1 L of bromine. Which plot corresponds to each gas and why?

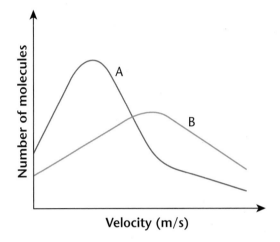

A. Curve A is helium and curve B is bromine because helium has a smaller molar mass than bromine.
B. Curve A is helium and curve B is bromine because the average kinetic energy of bromine is greater than the average kinetic energy of helium.
C. Curve A is bromine and curve B is helium because helium has a smaller molar mass than bromine.
D. Curve A is bromine and curve B is helium because the average kinetic energy of bromine is greater than the average kinetic energy of helium.

13. A balloon at standard temperature and pressure contains 0.2 moles of oxygen and 0.6 moles of nitrogen. What is the partial pressure of oxygen in the balloon?

A. 0.2 atm
B. 0.3 atm
C. 0.6 atm
D. 0.25 atm

14. The temperature at the center of the sun can be estimated based on the approximation that the gases at the center of the sun have an average molar mass equal to 2 g/mole. Approximate the temperature at the center of the sun using these additional values: the pressure equals 1.3×10^9 atm and the density at the center equals 1.2 g/cm³.

A. $2.6 \times 10^7 °C$
B. $2.6 \times 10^{10} °C$
C. $2.6 \times 10^4 °C$
D. $2.6 \times 10^6 °C$

15. Which of the following are true about the gaseous state of matter?

  I. Gases are compressible.
 II. Gases readily conduct electricity.
III. Gases assume the volume of their container.
 IV. Gas particles exist as diatomic molecules.

A. I and II only
B. I and III only
C. I, III, and IV
D. I, II, III, and IV

16. A gas at a temperature of 27°C has a volume of 60 mL. What temperature change is needed to increase this gas to a volume of 90 mL?

A. Reduce temperature by 150°C
B. Increase temperature by 150°C
C. Reduce temperature by 40.5°C
D. Increase temperature by 40.5°C

17. Gases X and Y are contained in a moveable piston system. They are beneath the pistons in an enclosed space. They react completely to form gas XY, and the reaction is not reversible. What movement will the pistons exhibit during the reaction?

A. They will move up due to an increase in the volume of gas.
B. They will move up due to the energy given off by the reaction.
C. They will not move.
D. They will move down due to a decrease in the volume of gas.

18. A gaseous mixture contains nitrogen and helium and has a total pressure of 150 torr. The nitrogen particles comprise 80 percent of the gas and the helium particles make up the other 20 percent of the gas. What is the pressure exerted by each individual gas?

A. 100 torr nitrogen, 50 torr helium
B. 120 torr nitrogen, 30 torr helium
C. 30 torr nitrogen, 150 torr helium
D. 50 torr nitrogen, 100 torr helium

19. In which of the following situations is it impossible to predict how the pressure will change for the gas sample?

A. Gas is cooled at a constant volume
B. Gas is heated at a constant volume
C. Gas is heated and the volume is simultaneously increased
D. Gas is cooled and the volume is simultaneously increased

CHAPTER 8

PHASES AND PHASE CHANGES

When the attractive forces between molecules (i.e., van der Waals forces) overcome the kinetic energy that keeps them apart, the molecules move closer together such that they can no longer move about freely, entering the **liquid** or **solid** phase. Because of their smaller volume relative to gases, liquids and solids are often referred to as the **condensed phases.**

LIQUIDS

In a liquid, atoms or molecules are held close together with little space between them. As a result, liquids have definite volumes and cannot easily be expanded or compressed. However, the molecules can still move around and are in a state of relative disorder. Consequently, the liquid can change shape to fit its container, and its molecules are able to **diffuse** and **evaporate.**

One of the most important properties of liquids is their ability to mix, both with each other and with other phases, to form **solutions** (see chapter 9). The degree to which two liquids can mix is called their **miscibility.** Oil and water are almost completely **immiscible;** that is, their molecules tend to repel each other due to their polarity difference. Oil and water normally form separate layers when mixed, with oil on top because it is less dense. Under extreme conditions, such as violent shaking, two immiscible liquids can form a fairly homogeneous mixture called an **emulsion.** Although they look like solutions, emulsions are actually mixtures of discrete particles too small to be seen distinctly.

SOLIDS

In a solid, the attractive forces between atoms, ions, or molecules are strong enough to hold them rigidly together; thus the particles' only motion is vibration about fixed positions, and the kinetic energy of solids is predominantly vibrational energy. As a result, solids have definite shapes and volumes.

TEACHER TIP

Because the molecules in liquids and solids are much closer together than those in gases, intermolecular forces are very important and there is no such thing as "ideal" behavior. However, due to these forces, the behavior is predictable in other ways than the gases.

A solid may be **crystalline** or **amorphous.** A crystalline solid, such as NaCl, possesses an ordered structure; its atoms exist in a specific three-dimensional geometric arrangement with repeating patterns of atoms, ions, or molecules. An amorphous solid, such as glass, has no ordered three-dimensional arrangement, although the molecules are also fixed in place.

Most solids are crystalline in structure. The two most common forms of crystals are **metallic** and **ionic** crystals.

Ionic solids are aggregates of positively and negatively charged ions; there are no discrete molecules. The physical properties of ionic solids include high melting points, high boiling points, and poor electrical conductivity in the solid phase. These properties are due to the compounds' strong electrostatic interactions, which also cause the ions to be relatively immobile. Ionic structures are given by empirical formulas that describe the ratio of atoms in the lowest possible whole numbers. For example, the empirical formula $BaCl_2$ gives the ratio of barium to chloride within the crystal.

Metallic solids consist of metal atoms packed together as closely as possible. Metallic solids have high melting and boiling points as a result of their strong covalent attractions. Pure metallic structures (consisting of a single element) are usually described as layers of spheres of roughly similar radii.

The repeating units of crystals (both ionic and metallic) are represented by **unit cells.** There are many types of unit cells. We will now consider only the three cubic unit cells: **simple cubic, body-centered cubic,** and **face-centered cubic.**

TEACHER TIP

The crystal structures allow for a balance of both attractive and repulsive forces to minimize energy. The ionic solids often have extremely strong attractive forces as we saw in chapter 4, thereby causing extremely high meting points.

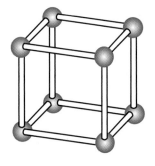

simple cubic

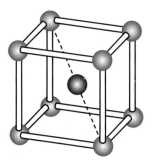

body-centered cubic

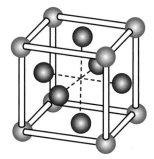

face-centered cubic

Figure 8.1

simple cubic

body-centered cubic

face-centered cubic

Figure 8.2

Atoms are represented as points, but are actually adjoining spheres. Each unit cell is surrounded by similar units. In the ionic unit cell, the spaces between points (anions) are filled with other ions (cations).

PHASE EQUILIBRIA

In an isolated system, phase changes (solid to liquid to gas) are reversible, and an equilibrium exists between phases. For example, at 1 atm and 0°C in an isolated system, an ice cube floating in water is in equilibrium. Some of the ice may absorb heat and melt, but an equal amount of water will release heat and freeze. Thus, the relative amounts of ice and water remain constant.

A. GAS-LIQUID EQUILIBRIUM

The temperature of a liquid is related to the average kinetic energy of the liquid molecules; however, the kinetic energy of the molecules will vary. A few molecules near the surface of the liquid may have enough energy to leave the liquid phase and escape into the gaseous phase. This process is known as **evaporation** (or **vaporization**). Each time the liquid loses a high-energy particle, the temperature of the remaining liquid decreases; thus, evaporation is a cooling process. Given enough kinetic energy, the liquid will completely evaporate.

If a cover is placed on a beaker of liquid, the escaping molecules are trapped above the solution. These molecules exert a countering pressure, which forces some of the gas back into the liquid phase; this process is called **condensation.** Atmospheric pressure acts on a liquid in a similar fashion as a solid lid. As evaporation and condensation proceed, an equilibrium is reached in which the rates of the two processes become equal. Once this equilibrium is reached, the pressure that the gas exerts over the liquid is called the **vapor pressure** of the liquid. Vapor pressure increases as temperature increases, because more molecules have sufficient kinetic energy to escape into the gas phase. The temperature

TEACHER TIP
As with all equilibriums, we know that the rates of the forward and reverse processes will be the same.

at which the vapor pressure of the liquid equals the external pressure is called the **boiling point.**

B. LIQUID-SOLID EQUILIBRIUM

The liquid and solid phases can also coexist in equilibrium (e.g., the ice-water mixture previously discussed). Even though the atoms or molecules of a solid are confined to definite locations, each atom or molecule can undergo motions about some equilibrium position. These motions (vibrations) increase when heat is applied. If atoms or molecules in the solid phase absorb enough energy in this fashion, the solid's three-dimensional structure breaks down and the liquid phase begins. The transition from solid to liquid is called **fusion** or **melting.** The reverse process, from liquid to solid, is called **solidification, crystallization,** or **freezing.** The temperature at which these processes occur is called the **melting point** or **freezing point,** depending on the direction of the transition. Whereas pure crystals have distinct, very sharp melting points, amorphous solids, such as glass, tend to melt over a larger range of temperatures, due to their less-ordered molecular distribution.

C. GAS-SOLID EQUILIBRIUM

A third type of phase equilibrium is that between a gas and a solid. When a solid goes directly into the gas phase, the process is called **sublimation.** Dry ice (solid CO_2) sublimes; the absence of the liquid phase makes it a convenient refrigerant. The reverse transition, from the gaseous to the solid phase, is called **deposition.**

D. THE GIBBS FUNCTION

The thermodynamic criterion for each of the above equilibria is that the change in Gibbs free energy must equal zero; $\Delta G = 0$. For an equilibrium between a gas and a solid:

$$\Delta G = G(g) - G(s),$$
$$\text{so } G(g) = G(s) \text{ at equilibrium.}$$

The same is true of the Gibbs functions for the other two equilibria.

E. HEATING CURVES

When a compound is heated, the temperature rises until the melting or boiling points are reached. Then the temperature remains constant as the compound is converted to the next phase, i.e., liquid or gas, respectively. Once the entire sample is converted, then the temperature begins to rise again (Figure 8.3).

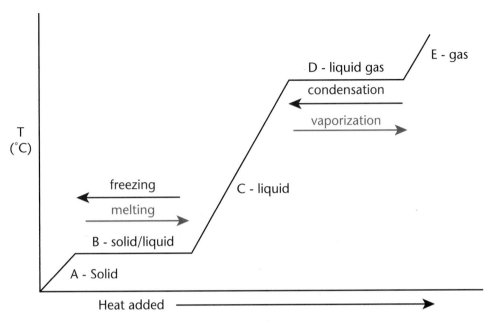

Figure 8.3: Heating Curves

PHASE DIAGRAMS

A. SINGLE COMPONENT

A standard **phase diagram** depicts the phases and phase equilibria of a substance at defined temperatures and pressures. In general, the gas phase is found at high temperature and low pressure; the solid phase at low temperature and high pressure; and the liquid phase is found at high temperature and high pressure. A typical phase diagram is shown in Figure 8.4.

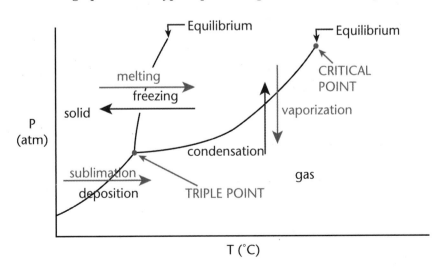

Figure 8.4: Gas-Liquid Equilibrium

MCAT SYNOPSIS

Every pure substance has a characteristic phase diagram.

MCAT FAVORITE

You should be able to identify and explain each area and every line of a phase diagram.

149

MCAT SYNOPSIS

H_2O is a unique molecule because of its different properties, ice floats and ice skates flow smoothly over ice. This all "boils" down to the slope of the solid-liquid equilibrium line in its phase diagram. Because the density of ice is less than that of liquid H_2O, an increase in pressure (at a constant temperature) will actually melt ice (the opposite of the substance seen in Figure 8.4)

The three phases are demarcated by lines indicating the temperatures and pressures at which two phases are in equilibrium. Line A represents freezing/melting, line B evaporation/condensation, and line C sublimation/deposition. The intersection of the three lines is called the **triple point.** At this temperature and pressure, unique for a given substance, all three phases are in equilibrium. The point at B is known as the **critical point,** the temperature and pressure above which no distinction between liquid and gas is possible.

B. MULTIPLE COMPONENTS

The phase diagram for a mixture of two or more components (Figure 8.5) is complicated by the requirement that the composition of the mixture, as well as the temperature and pressure, must be specified. Consider a solution of two liquids, A and B. The vapor above the solution is a mixture of the vapors of A and B. The pressures exerted by vapor A and vapor B on the solution are the vapor pressures that each exerts above its individual liquid phase. **Raoult's law** (described later in this chapter) enables one to determine the relationship between the vapor pressure of vapor A and the concentration of liquid A in the solution.

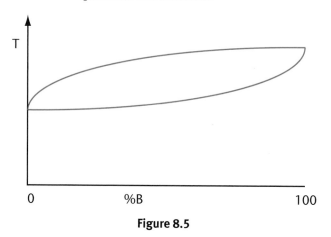

Figure 8.5

Curves such as this show the different compositions of the liquid phase and the vapor phase above a solution; the upper curve is that of the vapor while the lower curve is that of the liquid. It is this difference in composition that forms the basis of distillation, an important separation technique in organic chemistry.

COLLIGATIVE PROPERTIES

Colligative properties are physical properties derived solely from the number of particles present, not the nature of those particles. These properties are usually associated with dilute solutions (see chapter 9).

A. FREEZING-POINT DEPRESSION

Pure water (H_2O) freezes at 0°C; however, for every mole of solute particles dissolved in 1 L of water, the freezing point is lowered by 1.86°C. This is because the solute particles interfere with the process of crystal formation that occurs during freezing; the solute particles lower the temperature at which the molecules can align themselves into a crystalline structure.

The formula for calculating this **freezing-point depression** is:

$$\Delta T_f = K_f m$$

where ΔT_f is the freezing-point depression, K_f is a proportionality constant characteristic of a particular solvent, and m is the molality of the solution (mol solute/kg solvent; see chapter 9). The K_f for water—which you do not need to memorize for the MCAT—is $1.86°Cm^{-1}$. Each solvent has its own characteristic K_f.

B. BOILING-POINT ELEVATION

A liquid boils when its vapor pressure equals the atmospheric pressure. If the vapor pressure of a solution is lower than that of the pure solvent, more energy (and consequently a higher temperature) will be required before its vapor pressure equals atmospheric pressure. The extent to which the boiling point of a solution is raised relative to that of the pure solvent is given by the following formula:

$$\Delta T_b = K_b m$$

where ΔT_b is the boiling-point elevation, K_b is a proportionality constant characteristic of a particular solvent, and m is the molality of the solution. The K_b for water is $0.51°Cm^{-1}$.

REAL-WORLD ANALOGY

In cold climates, roads are often salted during snowstorms to decrease the freezing point of water, thereby lessening the formation of ice.

C. OSMOTIC PRESSURE

Consider a container separated into two compartments by a semipermeable membrane (which, by definition, selectively permits the passage of certain molecules). One compartment contains pure water, while the other contains water with dissolved solute. The membrane allows water but not solute to pass through. Because substances tend to flow, or **diffuse,** from higher to lower concentrations (which increases entropy), water will diffuse from the compartment containing pure water to the compartment containing the water-solute mixture. This net flow will cause the water level in the compartment containing the solution to rise above the level in the compartment containing pure water.

Because the solute cannot pass through the membrane, the concentrations of solute in the two compartments can never be equal. However, the pressure exerted by the water level in the solute-containing compartment will eventually oppose the influx of water; thus, the water level will rise only to the point at which it exerts a sufficient pressure to counterbalance the tendency of water to flow across the membrane. This pressure is defined as the **osmotic pressure** (Π) of the solution, and is given by the formula:

$$\Pi = \mathbf{MRT}$$

where M is the molarity of the solution (see chapter 9), R is the ideal gas constant, and T is the temperature on the Kelvin scale. This equation clearly shows that molarity and osmotic pressure are directly proportional, i.e., as the concentration of the solution increases, the osmotic pressure also increases. Thus, the osmotic pressure depends only on the amount of solute, not its identity.

D. VAPOR-PRESSURE LOWERING (RAOULT'S LAW)

When solute B is added to pure solvent A, the vapor pressure of A above the solvent decreases (see Figure 8.4). If the vapor pressure of A above pure solvent A is designated by $P°_A$ and the vapor pressure of A above the solution containing B is P_A, the vapor pressure decreases as follows:

$$\Delta P = P°_A - P_A$$

In the late 1800s, the French chemist François Marie Raoult determined that this vapor pressure decrease is also equivalent to:

$$\Delta P = X_B P°_A$$

where X_B is the mole fraction of the solute B in solvent A. Since $X_B = 1 - X_A$ and $\Delta P = P°_A - P_A$, substitution into the above equation leads to the common form of Raoult's law:

$$P_A = X_A P°_A$$

Similarly, the expression for the vapor pressure of the solute in solution (assuming it is volatile) is given by:

$$P_B = X_B P°_B$$

Raoult's law holds only when the attraction between molecules of the different components of the mixture is equal to the attraction between the molecules of any one component in its pure state. When this condition does not hold, the relationship between mole fraction and vapor pressure will deviate from Raoult's law. Solutions that obey Raoult's law are called **ideal solutions.**

PRACTICE QUESTIONS

1. The phase diagram below illustrates what substance?

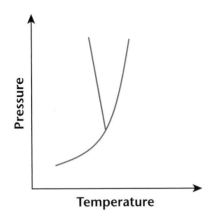

A. CO_2
B. NaCl
C. Ne
D. H_2O

2. Living cells are comprised of a significant amount of water. Which of the following best explains why frostbite—the result of freezing living tissue—is so harmful to living cells?

A. Water is very dense at 4° Celsius.
B. Water is not very dense at 4° Celsius.
C. Water is less dense at 0° Celsus than at 4° Celsius.
D. Water is more dense at 0° Celsius than at 4° Celsius.

3. What phase change occurs to the ice beneath an ice skater as pressure is applied by the skates?

A. Condensation
B. Crystallization
C. Deposition
D. Melting

4. Which of the following proportionalities best describes the relationship between intermolecular forces and heat of vaporization for a given substance?

A. Intermolecular forces are proportional to ΔH_{vap}.
B. Intermolecular forces are inversely proportional to ΔH_{vap}.
C. The relationship between intermolecular forces and ΔH_{vap} cannot be generalized.
D. There is no relationship between intermolecular forces and ΔH_{vap}.

5. What molecule below is likely to have the highest melting point?

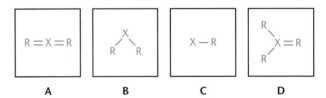

A. A
B. B
C. C
D. D

6. Which of the following physical conditions favor a gaseous state for most substances?

A. High pressure and high temperature
B. Low pressure and low temperature
C. High pressure and low temperature
D. Low pressure and high temperature

7. When ambient pressure increases, the heating/coiling curve for a substance will be shifted in which of the following directions?

A. Up
B. Down
C. Right
D. Left

8. Which of the following best explains the mechanism by which solute particles affect the melting point of ice?

A. Melting point elevates because the kinetic energy of the substance increases.
B. Melting point elevates because the kinetic energy of the substance decreases.
C. Melting point depresses because solute particles interfere with lattice formation.
D. Melting point depresses because solute particles enhance lattice formation.

9. A viscous substance is most likely to have a

A. low precipitation rate.
B. high heat of vaporization.
C. low heat of fusion.
D. high critical mass.

10. Fractional distillation of crude oil involves heating the oil at very high temperatures to the gaseous state, then allowing parts of the oil to condense at different temperatures. Which hydrocarbon component of crude oil would you predict is the last to vaporize?

A. Gasoline
B. Natural gas
C. Propane
D. Tar

11. In the figure below, what phase change is represented by the arrow?

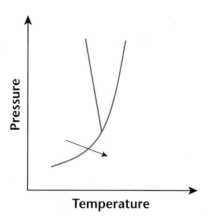

A. Condensation
B. Deposition
C. Sublimation
D. Vaporization

12. It is impossible to skate on dry ice because it has a

A. positive solid/liquid equilibrium line slope.
B. negative solid/liquid equilibrium line slope.
C. positive liquid/gas equilibrium line slope.
D. negative liquid/gas equilibrium line slope.

13. Which of the following best describes the chemical activity depicted by the region X on the heating/cooling curve for a substance shown below?

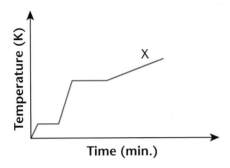

A. Average kinetic energy of the particles is changing.
B. Particles are locked in a lattice-like state.
C. Particles are in a liquid state.
D. Particle size is decreasing.

14. Which of the following statements best explains the effect of sweating on body temperature in animals?

A. Condensation of sweat leads to the gain of low-energy molecules.
B. Condensation of sweat leads to the loss of high-energy molecules.
C. Evaporation of sweat leads to the gain of low-energy molecules.
D. Evaporation of sweat leads to the loss of high-energy molecules.

15. Which of the following situations would most favor the change of water from a liquid to a solid?

  I. Decreased solute concentration of a substance
 II. Decreased temperature of a substance
III. Decreased pressure on a substance

A. I only
B. II only
C. I and II only
D. I, II, and III

16. A person feels warmer on a humid day compared with a very dry one, even though the temperature on both days is the same. On the humid day, the person is experiencing the process of

A. condensation.
B. evaporation.
C. transpiration.
D. sublimation.

17. Rain is a form of

A. condensation.
B. evaporation.
C. transpiration.
D. sublimation.

18. The heats of vaporization of four substances are given below. Which of these substances has the lowest boiling point?

Comparative Heats of Vaporization

Liquid	Heat Required (cal/g)
Chlorine	67.4
Ether	9.4
Carbon dioxide	72.2
Ammonia	295.0

A. Chlorine
B. Ether
C. Carbon dioxide
D. Ammonia

KEY CONCEPTS

Dalton's law

$P_A = X_A P_{Total}$ (atm)

Mole fraction

$$X_A = \frac{(\text{moles of } A)}{(\text{total \# of moles in container})}$$

PARTIAL PRESSURES

32 g of oxygen, 28 g of nitrogen, and 22 g of carbon dioxide are confined in a container with partial pressures of 2 atm, 2 atm and 1 atm respectively. A student added 57 g of a halogen gas to this container and observed that the total pressure increased by 3 atm. Can you identify this gas?

1) Determine the number of moles for each gas.

$MW_{oxygen} = 32$ g/mol

$MW_{nitrogen} = 28$ g/mol

$MW_{carbon\ dioxide} = 44$ g/mol

$$n = \frac{mass}{MW}$$

$n_{oxygen} = 1$ mole

$n_{nitrogen} = 1$ mole

$n_{carbon\ dioxide} = 0.5$ moles

This is a more complicated style of partial pressure question, yet the first step is still the basic one of identifying the number of moles for each gas.

TAKEAWAYS

Partial pressure questions will require manipulation of the formulas above, so the key is to always keep track of what is given to you and what the question is asking for.

2) Solve for the relevant variable.

$P_A = X_A P_{Total}$

$$X_A = \frac{P_A}{P_{Total}}$$

$$X_A = \frac{3}{8}$$

All partial pressure questions boil down to this formula. The relevant variable here is the mole fraction of the halogen gas. The partial pressure of the gas is 3 atm, and the total pressure is 8 atm.

THINGS TO WATCH OUT FOR

Dalton's law assumes that the gases do not react with each other.

3) Use the mole fraction X_A to solve for the number of moles and the MW of the halogen gas.

$$X_A = \frac{(\text{moles of } A)}{(\text{total \# of moles in container})}$$

\# moles of $A = (X_A)(\text{total \# of moles})$

$$n_A = \left(\frac{3}{8}\right)(2.5 + n_A)$$

$8n_A = 7.5 + 3n_A$

$5n_A = 7.5$

$n_A = 1.5$

$$MW = \frac{57\ g}{1.5\ mol}$$
MW of 38 g/mol

The mole fraction of a substance is the number of moles of the substance as a fraction of the total number of moles in the container:

$$X_A = \frac{(\text{moles of } A)}{(\text{total \# of moles in container})}$$

Rearranging the formula, we have # moles of $A = (X_A)(\text{total \# of moles})$. Note that the total number of moles is not known, but we can express it algebraically as $2.5 + n_A$, where n_A is defined as the number of moles of A.

This *MW* corresponds to F_2. Of course, on Test Day you will roughly round such that 60 g = 1.5 mole and look for the halogen gas using your calculated *MW* of 40 g/mol. Again, the only gas possible is F_2.

SIMILAR QUESTIONS

1) 64 g of oxygen, 14 g of nitrogen, and 66 g of carbon dioxide are confined in a container. If the total pressure is 10 atm, what is the partial pressure of each gas?

2) The partial pressure of nitrogen is 2 atm. If its mole fraction is 2/10 and the only other gas in the container is oxygen, how many moles of oxygen are in the container?

3) An unknown substance's mole fraction is 4/10. If its partial pressure is 5 atm, what is the sum pressure of all the other gases in the container?

CHAPTER 9

SOLUTIONS

Solutions are **homogeneous** (everywhere the same) mixtures of substances that combine to form a single phase, generally the liquid phase. Many important chemical reactions, both in the laboratory and in nature, take place in solution (including almost all reactions in living organisms).

NATURE OF SOLUTIONS

A solution consists of a **solute** (e.g., NaCl, NH_3, or $C_{12}H_{22}O_{11}$) dispersed (dissolved) in a **solvent** (e.g., H_2O or benzene). The solvent is the component of the solution whose phase remains the same after mixing. If the two substances are already in the same phase, the solvent is the component present in greater quantity. Solute molecules move about freely in the solvent and can interact with other molecules or ions; consequently, chemical reactions occur easily in solution.

A. SOLVATION

The interaction between solute and solvent molecules is known as **solvation** or **dissolution;** when water is the solvent, it is called **hydration** and the resulting solution is known as an **aqueous solution.** Solvation is possible when the attractive forces between solute and solvent are stronger than those between the solute particles. For example, when NaCl dissolves in water, its component ions dissociate from one another and become surrounded by water molecules. Because water is polar, ion-dipole interactions can occur between the Na^+ and Cl^- ions and the water molecules. For nonionic solutes, solvation involves van der Waals forces between the solute and solvent molecules. The general rule is that like dissolves like; ionic and polar solutes are soluble in polar solvents, and nonpolar solutes are soluble in nonpolar solvents.

B. SOLUBILITY

The **solubility** of a substance is the maximum amount of that substance that can be dissolved in a particular solvent at a particular temperature. When this maximum amount of solute has been added, the solution is

MCAT SYNOPSIS

Note that "dilute" is a relative term.

in equilibrium and is said to be **saturated;** if more solute is added, it will not dissolve. For example, at 18°C, a maximum of 83 g of glucose ($C_6H_{12}O_6$) will dissolve in 100 mL of H_2O. Thus the solubility of glucose is 83 g/100 mL. If more glucose is added, it will remain in solid form, precipitating to the bottom of the container. A solution in which the proportion of solute to solvent is small is said to be **dilute,** and one in which the proportion is large is said to be **concentrated.**

C. AQUEOUS SOLUTIONS

The most common class of solutions are the aqueous solutions, in which the solvent is water. The aqueous state is denoted by the symbol (*aq*). In discussing the chemistry of aqueous solutions, it is useful to know how soluble various salts are in water; this information is given by the solubility rules below.

1. All salts of alkali metals are water soluble.

2. All salts of the ammonium ion (NH_4^+) are water soluble.

3. All chlorides, bromides, and iodides are water soluble, with the exceptions of Ag^+, Pb^{2+}, and Hg_2^{2+}.

4. All salts of the sulfate ion (SO_4^{2-}) are water soluble, with the exceptions of Ca^{2+}, Sr^{2+}, Ba^{2+}, and Pb^{2+}.

5. All metal oxides are insoluble, with the exception of the alkali metals and CaO, SrO , and BaO, all of which hydrolyze to form solutions of the corresponding metal hydroxides.

6. All hydroxides are insoluble, with the exception of the alkali metals and Ca^{2+}, Sr^{2+}, and Ba^{2+}.

7. All carbonates (CO_3^{2-}), phosphates (PO_4^{3-}), sulfides (S^{2-}), and sulfites (SO_3^{2-}) are insoluble, with the exception of the alkali metals and ammonium.

IONS

Ionic solutions are of particular interest to chemists because certain important types of chemical interactions—acid-base reactions and oxidation-reduction reactions, for instance—take place in ionic solutions. Ions and their properties in solution will be introduced here; the chemical reactions mentioned are discussed in detail in chapter 10, Acids and Bases, and chapter 11, Redox Reactions and Electrochemistry.

A. CATIONS AND ANIONS

Ionic compounds are made up of **cations** and **anions,** where a cation is a positive ion and an anion is a negative ion. The nomenclature of ionic compounds is based on the names of the component ions.

1. For elements (usually metals) that can form more than one positive ion, the charge is indicated by a Roman numeral in parentheses following the name of the element.

    Fe^{2+} Iron (II) Cu^+ Copper (I)

    Fe^{3+} Iron (III) Cu^{2+} Copper (II)

2. An older but still commonly used method is to add the endings **-ous** or **-ic** to the root of the Latin name of the element, to represent the ions with lesser or greater charge respectively.

    Fe^{2+} Ferrous Cu^+ Cuprous

    Fe^{3+} Ferric Cu^{2+} Cupric

3. Monatomic anions are named by dropping the ending of the name of the element and adding **-ide.**

    H^- Hydride S^{2-} Sulfide

    F^- Fluoride N^{3-} Nitride

    O^{2-} Oxide P^{3-} Phosphide

4. Many polyatomic anions contain oxygen and are therefore called **oxyanions**. When an element forms two oxyanions, the name of the one with less oxygen ends in **-ite** and the one with more oxygen ends in **-ate.**

    NO_2^- Nitrite SO_3^{2-} Sulfite

    NO_3^- Nitrate SO_4^{2-} Sulfate

5. When the series of oxyanions contains four oxyanions, prefixes are also used. **Hypo-** and **per-** are used to indicate less oxygen and more oxygen, respectively.

    ClO^- Hypochlorite

    ClO_2^- Chlorite

    ClO_3^- Chlorate

    ClO_4^- Perchlorate

6. Polyatomic anions often gain one or more H^+ ions to form anions of lower charge. The resulting ions are named by adding the word **hydrogen** or **dihydrogen** to the front of the anion's name. An older method uses the prefix **bi-** to indicate the addition of a single hydrogen ion.

HCO_3^- Hydrogen carbonate or bicarbonate

HSO_4^- Hydrogen sulfate or bisulfate

$H_2PO_4^-$ Dihydrogen phosphate

B. ION CHARGES

Metals, which are found in the left part of the periodic table, generally form positive ions, whereas nonmetals, which are found in the right part of the periodic table, generally form negative ions. Note, however, the existence of anions that contain metallic elements, e.g., MnO_4^- (permanganate) and CrO_4^{2-} (chromate). All elements in a given group tend to form monatomic ions with the same charge. Thus ions of alkali metals (Group I) usually form cations with a single positive charge, the alkaline earth metals (Group II) form cations with a double positive charge, and the halides (Group VII) form anions with a single negative charge. Though other main group elements follow this trend, the intermediate electronegativity of such elements (making them less likely to form ionic compounds) and the transition from metallic to nonmetallic character complicates the picture.

C. ELECTROLYTES

The electrical conductivity of aqueous solutions is governed by the presence and concentration of ions in solution. Therefore, pure water does not conduct an electrical current well because the concentrations of hydrogen and hydroxide ions are very small. Solutes whose solutions are conductive are called **electrolytes.** A solute is considered a **strong electrolyte** if it dissociates completely into its constituent ions. Examples of strong electrolytes include ionic compounds, such as NaCl and KI, and molecular compounds with highly polar covalent bonds that dissociate into ions when dissolved, such as HCl in water. A **weak electrolyte,** on the other hand, ionizes or hydrolyzes incompletely in aqueous solution and only some of the solute is present in ionic form. Examples include acetic acid and other weak acids, ammonia and other weak bases, and $HgCl_2$. Many compounds do not ionize at all in aqueous solution, retaining their molecular structure in solution, which usually limits their solubility. These compounds are called nonelectrolytes and include many nonpolar gases and organic compounds, such as oxygen and sugar.

MCAT SYNOPSIS

Oxyanions of transition metals like the MnO^{4-} and CrO_4^{2-} ions have an inordinately high oxidation number on the metal. As such, they tend to gain electrons in order to reduce this oxidation number, and thus make good oxidizing agents. (See chapter 11.)

MCAT SYNOPSIS

Because electrolytes ionize in solution, they will produce a larger effect on colligative properties (see chapter 8) than one would expect from the given concentration.

CONCENTRATION

A. UNITS OF CONCENTRATION

Concentration denotes the amount of solute dissolved in a solvent. The concentration of a solution is most commonly expressed as **percent composition by mass, mole fraction, molarity, molality,** or **normality**.

TEACHER TIP
Know the different ways to express concentration.

1. Percent Composition by Mass

The percent composition by mass (percent) of a solution is the mass of the solute divided by the mass of the solution (solute plus solvent), multiplied by 100.

Example: What is the percent composition by mass of a salt water solution if 100 g of the solution contains 20 g of NaCl?

Solution:

$$\frac{20 \text{g NaCl}}{100 \text{ g}} \times 100 = 20\% \text{ NaCl solution}$$

2. Mole Fraction

The mole fraction ($\mathbf{X}$) of a compound is equal to the number of moles of the compound divided by the total number of moles of all species within the system. The sum of the mole fractions in a system will always equal 1.

Example: If 92 g of glycerol is mixed with 90 g of water, what will be the mole fractions of the two components? (MW of H_2O = 18; MW of $C_3H_8O_3$ = 92.)

Solution:

$$90 \text{ g water} = 90 \text{ g} \times \frac{1 \text{ mol}}{18 \text{ g}} = 5 \text{ mol}$$

$$92 \text{ g glycerol} = 92 \text{ g} \times \frac{1 \text{ mol}}{92 \text{ g}} = 1 \text{ mol}$$

$$\text{Total mol} = 5 + 1 = 6 \text{ mol}$$

$$X_{\text{water}} = \frac{5 \text{ mol}}{6 \text{ mol}} = 0.833$$

$$X_{\text{glycerol}} = \frac{1 \text{ mol}}{6 \text{ mol}} = 0.167$$

$$X_{\text{water}} + X_{\text{glycerol}} = 0.833 + 0.167 = 1$$

3. Molarity

The molarity (**M**) of a solution is the number of moles of solute per liter of **solution.** Solution concentrations are usually expressed in terms of molarity. Molarity depends on the volume of the solution, not on the volume of solvent used to prepare the solution.

Example: If enough water is added to 11 g of $CaCl_2$ to make 100 mL of solution, what is the molarity of the solution?

Solution:

$$\frac{11 \text{ g } CaCl_2}{110 \text{ g } CaCl_2/\text{mol } CaCl_2} = 0.1 \text{ mol } CaCl_2$$

$$100 \text{ mL} \times \frac{1L}{1,000 \text{ mL}} = 0.1 \text{ L}$$

$$\text{molarity} = \frac{0.1 \text{ mol}}{0.1 \text{ L}} = 1 \text{ M}$$

4. Molality

The molality (**m**) of a solution is the number of moles of solute per kilogram of **solvent**. For dilute aqueous solutions at 25°C the molality is approximately equal to the molarity, because the density of water at this temperature is 1 kilogram per liter. However, note that this is an approximation and true only for **dilute aqueous** solutions.

Example: If 10 g of NaOH are dissolved in 500 g of water, what is the molality of the solution?

Solution:

$$\frac{10 \text{ g NaOH}}{40 \text{ g NaOH/mol NaOH}} = 0.25 \text{ mol NaOH}$$

$$500 \text{ g} \times \frac{1kg}{1,000 \text{ g}} = 0.5 \text{ kg}$$

$$\text{molality} = \frac{0.25 \text{ mol}}{0.5 \text{ kg}} = 0.5 \text{ mol/kg} = 0.50 \text{ m}$$

5. Normality

The normality (**N**) of a solution is equal to the number of gram equivalent weights of solute per liter of solution. A gram equivalent weight, or equivalent, is a measure of the reactive capacity of a molecule (see chapter 4, Compounds and Stoichiometry).

To calculate the normality of a solution, we must know for what purpose the solution is being used, because it is the concentration of the reactive species with which we are concerned. Normality is unique among concentration units in that it is reaction dependent. For example, a 1 molar solution of sulfuric acid would be 2 normal for acid-base reactions (because each mole of sulfuric acid provides 2 moles of H^+ ions) but is only 1 normal for a sulfate precipitation reaction (because each mole of sulfuric acid only provides 1 mole of sulfate ions).

B. DILUTION

A solution is **diluted** when solvent is added to a solution of high concentration to produce a solution of lower concentration. The concentration of a solution after dilution can be conveniently determined using the equation below:

$$M_i V_i = M_f V_f$$

where M is molarity, V is volume, and the subscripts i and f refer to initial and final values, respectively.

> **MCAT FAVORITE**
> This equation is worthy of memorization. Note that it works for any units of concentration, not just molarity, if we replace the M with C for concentration.

Example: How many mL of a 5.5 M NaOH solution must be used to prepare 300 mL of a 1.2 M NaOH solution?

Solution:
$$5.5 \text{ M} \times V_i = 1.2 \text{ M} \times 0.3 \text{ L}$$
$$V_i = \frac{1.2 \text{ M} \times 0.3 \text{ L}}{5.5 \text{ M}}$$
$$V_i = 0.065 \text{ L} = 65 \text{ mL}$$

SOLUTION EQUILIBRIA

The process of solvation, like other reversible chemical and physical changes, tends toward an equilibrium. Immediately after solute has been introduced into a solvent, most of the change taking place is dissociation, because no dissolved solute is initially present. However, according to Le Châtelier's principle, as solute dissociates, the reverse reaction (precipitation of the solute) also begins to occur. Eventually an equilibrium is reached, with the rate of solute dissociation equal to the rate of precipitation, and the net concentration of the dissociated solute remains unchanged regardless of the amount of solute added.

An ionic solid introduced into a polar solvent dissociates into its component ions. The dissociation of such a solute in solution may be represented by

$$A_mB_n(s) \rightleftarrows mA^{n+}(aq) + nB^{m-}(aq)$$

A. THE SOLUBILITY PRODUCT CONSTANT

A slightly soluble ionic solid exists in equilibrium with its saturated solution. In the case of AgCl, for example, the solution equilibrium is as follows:

$$AgCl(s) \rightleftarrows Ag^+(aq) + Cl^-(aq)$$

The **ion product, I.P.,** of a compound in solution is defined as follows:

$$I.P. = [A^{n+}]^m[B^{m-}]^n$$

The same expression for a saturated solution at equilibrium defines the **solubility product constant, K_{sp}.**

$$K_{sp} = [A^{n+}]^m[B^{m-}]^n \text{ in a saturated solution}$$

However, I.P. is defined with respect to initial concentrations and does not necessarily represent either an equilibrium or a saturated solution, while K_{sp} does; at any point other than at equilibrium, the ion product is often referred to as Q_{sp}.

Each salt has its own distinct K_{sp} at a given temperature. If at a given temperature a salt's I.P. is equal to its K_{sp}, the solution is saturated, and the rate at which the salt dissolves equals the rate at which it precipitates out of solution. If a salt's I.P. exceeds its K_{sp}, the solution is supersaturated (holding more salt than it should be able to at a given temperature) and unstable. If the supersaturated solution is disturbed by adding more salt, other solid particles, or jarring the solution by a sudden decrease in temperature, the solid salt will precipitate until I.P. equals the K_{sp}. If I.P. is less than K_{sp}, the solution is unsaturated and no precipitate will form.

Example: The solubility of $Fe(OH)_3$ in an aqueous solution was determined to be 4.5×10^{-10} mol/L. What is the value of the K_{sp} for $Fe(OH)_3$?

Solution: The molar solubility (the solubility of the compound in mol/L) is given as 4.5×10^{-10} M. The equilibrium concentration of each ion can be determined from the molar solubility and the balanced dissociation reaction of $Fe(OH)_3$. The dissociation reaction is:

$$Fe(OH)_3(s) \rightleftarrows Fe^{3+}(aq) + 3OH^-(aq)$$

Thus, for every mol of $Fe(OH)_3$ that dissociates, one mol of Fe^{3+} and three mol of OH^- are produced. Since the solubility is 4.5×10^{-10} M, the K_{sp} can be determined as follows:

$$K_{sp} = [Fe^{3+}][OH^-]^3$$

$[OH^-] = 3[Fe^{3+}];$ $[Fe^{3+}] = 4.5 \times 10^{-10}$ M

$$K_{sp} = [Fe^{3+}](3[Fe^{3+}])^3 = 27[Fe^{3+}]^4$$

$$K_{sp} = (4.5 \times 10^{-10})[3(4.5 \times 10^{-10})]^3 = 27(4.5 \times 10^{-10})^4$$

$$K_{sp} = 1.1 \times 10^{-36}$$

MCAT SYNOPSIS

Every slightly soluble salt of general formula MX_3 will have $K_{sp} = 27x^4$, where x is the molar solubility.

Example: What are the concentrations of each of the ions in a saturated solution of $PbBr_2$, given that the K_{sp} of $PbBr_2$ is 2.1×10^{-6}? If 5 g of $PbBr_2$ are dissolved in water to make 1 L of solution at 25°C, would the solution be saturated, unsaturated, or supersaturated?

Solution: The first step is to write out the dissociation reaction:

$$PbBr_2(s) \rightleftarrows Pb^{2+}(aq) + 2Br^-(aq)$$

$$K_{sp} = [Pb^{2+}][Br^-]^2.$$

Let x equal the concentration of Pb^{2+}. Then 2x equals the concentration of Br^- in the saturated solution at equilibrium (as $[Br^-]$ is 2 times $[Pb^{2+}]$).

$$(x)(2x)^2 = 4x^3$$

$$2.1 \times 10^{-6} = 4x^3$$

Solving for x, the concentration of Pb^{2+} in a saturated solution is 8.07×10^{-3} M and the concentration of Br^- (2x) is 1.61×10^{-2} M.

Next, we convert 5 g of $PbBr_2$ into moles:

$$5 \text{ g} \times \frac{1 \text{ mol PbBr}_2}{367 \text{ g}} = 1.36 \times 10^{-2} \text{ mol}$$

MCAT SYNOPSIS

Every slightly soluble salt of general formula MX_2 will have $K_{sp} = 4x^3$, where x is the molar solubility.

1.36×10^{-2} mol of $PbBr_2$ is dissolved in 1 L of solution, so the concentration of the solution 1.36×10^{-2} M. Because this is higher than the concentration of a saturated solution, this solution would be supersaturated.

B. FACTORS AFFECTING SOLUBILITY

The solubility of a substance varies depending on the temperature of the solution, the solvent, and, in the case of a gas-phase solute, the pressure. Solubility is also affected by the addition of other substances to the solution.

The solubility of a salt is considerably reduced when it is dissolved in a solution that already contains one of its ions, rather than in a pure solvent. For example, if a salt such as CaF_2 is dissolved in a solution already containing Ca^{2+} ions, the dissociation equilibrium will shift toward the production of the solid salt. This reduction in solubility, called the **common ion effect,** is another example of Le Châtelier's principle.

Example: The K_{sp} of AgI in aqueous solution is 1×10^{-16} mol/L. If a 1×10^{-5} M solution of $AgNO_3$ is saturated with AgI, what will be the final concentration of the iodide ion?

Solution: The concentration of Ag^+ in the original $AgNO_3$ solution will be 1×10^{-5} mol/L. After AgI is added to saturation, the iodide concentration can be found by the formula:

$$1 \times 10^{-16} = [Ag^+][I^-]$$

$$= (1 \times 10^{-5})[I^-]$$

$$[I^-] = 1 \times 10^{-11} \text{ mol/L}$$

If the AgI had been dissolved in pure water, the concentration of both Ag^+ and I^- would have been 1×10^{-8} mol/L. The presence of the common ion, silver, at a concentration one thousand times higher than what it would normally be in a silver iodide solution, has reduced the iodide concentration to one thousandth of what it would have been otherwise. An additional 1×10^{-11} mol/L of silver will, of course, dissolve in solution along with the iodide ion, but this will not significantly affect the final silver concentration, which is much higher.

MCAT SYNOPSIS

Every slightly soluble salt of general formula MX will have $K_{sp} = x^2$, where x is the molar solubility.

PRACTICE QUESTIONS

1. An aqueous solution is prepared by mixing 70 grams of a solid into 100 grams of water. The solution has a boiling point of 101.11° C. What is the molar mass of the solute? (K_b = 0.512° C)

  A. 322.58 g/mol
  B. 32.26 g/mol
  C. 123.24 g/mol
  D. 233.59 g/mol

2. Which of the following phases of solvent and solute, respectively, can form a solution?

  I. Solid solvent, gaseous solute
  II. Solid solvent, solid solute
  III. Gaseous solvent, gaseous solute

  A. I and II only
  B. II and III only
  C. I and III only
  D. I, II, and III

3. Two organic liquids, below, are combined to form a solution. Based on the structures, will the solution closely obey Raoult's law?

Benzene   **Toluene**

  A. Yes, the liquids differ due to the additional methyl group on toluene and therefore will not deviate from Raoult's law.
  B. Yes, the liquids are very similar and therefore will not deviate from Raoult's law.
  C. No, the liquids differ due to the additional methyl group on toluene and therefore will deviate from Raoult's law.
  D. No, the liquids both contain benzene rings which will interact with each other and cause deviation from Raoult's law.

4. The diagram below shows two arms separated by an impermeable membrane. If the membrane were replaced with a semipermeable one which allowed water molecules to move across, the level of liquid in the two branches would

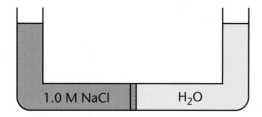

A. decrease on the right and increase on the left.

B. remain the same on both sides.

C. increase on the right and decrease on the left.

D. stay the same on the right and increase on the left.

5. The process of formation of a liquid solution can be better understood by breaking the process into three steps, below. The overall energy change to form a solution can be estimated by taking the sum of each of the three steps. Identify whether the steps are most likely to be endothermic or exothermic.

Step 1: Break up the solute into individual components.

Step 2: Make room for the solute in the solvent by overcoming intermolecular forces in the solvent.

Step 3: Allow solute-solvent interactions to occur to form the solution.

A. Endothermic, exothermic, endothermic

B. Exothermic, endothermic, endothermic

C. Exothermic, exothermic, endothermic

D. Endothermic, endothermic, exothermic

6. The entropy change when a solution forms can be expressed by the term $\Delta S°_{soln}$. When an ion dissolves and water molecules are ordered around it, the ordering would be expected to make a negative contribution to $\Delta S°_{soln}$. An ion that has more charge density will have a greater hydration effect, or ordering of water molecules. Based on this information, which of the following compounds will have the most negative $\Delta S°_{soln}$?

A. KCl

B. LiF

C. CaS

D. NaCl

7. A 0.01 M solution of a nonelectrolyte has an osmotic pressure of 15 mm Hg. What is the osmotic pressure of a 0.02 M solution of $Mg(NO_3)_2$? The temperature of both solutions is the same.

A. 15 mm Hg

B. 30 mm Hg

C. 45 mm Hg

D. 90 mm Hg

8. Vitamins A and C both have many functions in the body. They are essential for normal function, and deficiencies can lead to medical illness. While people can regularly consume large amounts of vitamin C and experience virtually no negative effects, those who consume large amounts of vitamin A can contract hypervitaminosis, an illness with various consequences. Which of the following best explains the differences between vitamins A and C?

Vitamin A   Vitamin C

A. Vitamin A is hydrophobic and will not be excreted in the urine. Therefore, ingesting large amounts will be toxic. Vitamin C is hydrophilic and will be excreted. Therefore, large amounts will exit the body and cause no damage.

B. Vitamin A is a larger molecule than vitamin C and will accumulate much more rapidly due to its large size. Consumption of large amounts of vitamin A will be toxic to the body.

C. Vitamin A contains more methyl groups that are toxic to cells when large amounts of vitamin A are consumed.

D. Vitamin A's long carbon chain causes it to interact with lipids in membrane bilayers and disrupt the transport of other molecules. Therefore, large amounts of vitamin A will impede too much transport in the body and lead to illness.

9. A 3 gram sugar cube is dissolved in a cup of hot water at 80° C. The cup of water contains 300 mL of water. What is the mass percentage of sugar in the resulting solution? (Sugar = $C_{12}H_{22}O_{11}$, density of water at 80° C = 0.975 g/ml)

A. 0.52%
B. 1.02%
C. 1.52%
D. 2.02%

10. Which of the following combinations of liquids would be expected to have a vapor pressure higher than the vapor pressure predicted by Raoult's law?

A. Ethanol and hexane
B. Acetone and water
C. Isopropanol and methanol
D. Nitric acid and water

11. The salt KCl is dissolved in a beaker of water that you are holding. You can feel the solution cool as the KCl dissolves. You can conclude which of the following?

A. $\Delta S°_{soln}$ is large enough to overcome the unfavorable $\Delta H°_{soln}$.
B. KCl is mostly insoluble in water.
C. $\Delta S°_{soln}$ must be negative when KCl dissolves.
D. Boiling point depression will occur in this solution.

12. What will give the greatest increase in the boiling point of water when it is dissolved in 1 kg H_2O?

A. 0.4 mol calcium sulfate
B. 1 mol acetic acid
C. 0.25 mol iron(III) nitrate
D. 1.1 mol sucrose

13. At sea level and 25°C, the solubility of oxygen gas in water is 1.25×10^{-3} M. In a U.S. city that lies high above sea level, the atmospheric pressure is 0.8 atm. What is the solubility of oxygen in water there?

A. 1.05×10^{-3} M
B. 1.56×10^{-3} M
C. 1×10^{-3} M
D. 1.25×10^{-3} M

14. Lead is a dangerous element that exists in the environment in large quantities due to man-made pollution. Lead poisoning has many symptoms, including mental retardation in children. If a body of water is polluted with lead ions at 30 ppb (parts per billion), what is the concentration of lead in molarity? The density of water is 1 g/mL, ppb equals grams per 10^9 grams of solution.

A. 6.2×10^{-7} M Pb^{2+}
B. 1.4×10^{-10} M Pb^{2+}
C. 1.4×10^{-7} M Pb^{2+}
D. 6.2×10^{-6} M Pb^{2+}

15. Which of the following statements are correct?

  I. NaF is an electrolyte.
  II. Glucose is a nonelectrolyte.
  III. CH_3OH is a weak electrolyte.
  IV. CH_3CH_2COOH is a weak electrolyte.

A. III only
B. I and III only
C. I, II, and IV only
D. I, II, III, and IV

16. Which of the following is not a colligative property?

A. Boiling point elevation
B. Vapor pressure of a mixture
C. Osmotic pressure
D. Entropy of dissolution

17. The following equilibrium exists when AgBr is in solution. Calculate the solubility of AgBr in g/L in a solution of 0.001 M NaBr.

$$AgBr_{(s)} \longleftrightarrow Ag^+_{(aq)} + Br^-_{(aq)}$$
$$Ksp = 7.7 \times 10^{-13}$$

A. 1.4×10^{-7} g/L
B. 7.7×10^{-10} g/L
C. 7.7×10^{-13} g/L
D. 2.8×10^{-7} g/L

18. When ammonia, NH_3, is a solvent, complex ions can form. For example, dissolving AgCl in NH_3 will result in the complex ion $Ag(NH_3)^{2+}$. What effect would you expect the formation of complex ions to have on the solubility of a compound like AgCl in NH_3?

A. The solubility of AgCl will increase because complex ion formation will cause more ions to exist in solution that interact with AgCl to cause it to dissociate.
B. The solubility of AgCl will increase because complex ion formation will consume Ag^+ molecules and cause the equilibrium to shift away from solid AgCl.
C. The solubility of AgCl will decrease because Ag^+ ions are in complexes and the Ag^+ ions that are not complexed will want to associate with Cl^- to form solid AgCl.
D. The solubility of AgCl will decrease because complex ion formation will consume Ag^+ molecules and cause the equilibrium to shift toward the solid AgCl.

19. Detergents are compounds that are dissolved in water. They are also able to dissolve hydrophobic stains such as oil and grease on clothing and other fabrics. Detergents can fulfill both hydrophilic and hydrophobic functions because they

A. contain a hydrophobic core molecule that is encased in a hydrophilic shell.
B. can ionize into two parts: one part is ionic and the other part is hydrophobic.
C. have two states: in water they are ionic, and in hydrophobic solvents they circularize to form a nonpolar ring structure.
D. have two functionally distinct parts: one side is a hydrophobic chain while the other side is a polar ionic end.

NORMALITY AND MOLARITY

What volume of a 2 M solution of lithium aluminum hydride in ether is necessary to reduce 1 mole of methyl 5-cyanopentanoate to the corresponding amino alcohol? What if a 2 N (with respect to H^-) solution were used instead?

1) Determine the number of equivalents of reagent necessary to accomplish the desired transformation.

There are two functional groups that need to be reduced in the molecule, the nitrile and the ester.

The ester will require two moles of hydride to be reduced to the alcohol.

The nitrile will also require two moles of hydride because it proceeds through an imine intermediate.

2) Compute the necessary volume of the given solution.

$$4 \text{ mol hydride} \times \left(\frac{1 \text{ mol LiAlH}_4}{4 \text{ mol hydride}} \right) = 1 \text{ mol LiAlH}_4$$

$$\frac{1 \text{ mol LiAlH}_4}{(2 \text{ mol LiAlH}_4 \text{ L}^{-1})} = 0.5 \text{ L}$$

$$\frac{1 \text{ mol LiAlH}_4}{(0.5 \text{ mol LiAlH}_4 \text{ L}^{-1})} = 2 \text{ L of 2 N solution}$$

Don't forget that one mole of lithium aluminum hydride contains four moles of hydride.

So, we'll need 500 mL of the 2 M solution.

With the 2 N solution, things get a little trickier. If the solution is 2 N with respect to H^-, that means that each liter of solution contains 2 moles of hydride, or 0.5 moles of $LiAlH_4$.

Remember: *Normality refers to equivalents per unit volume, not necessarily moles of compound per unit volume.*

SIMILAR QUESTIONS

1) Determine the volumes necessary for the same reaction as that in the initial question if 4 M and 4 N solutions of lithium aluminum hydride were used instead.

2) If the following molecule were subjected to $LiAlH_4$ reduction as well, what would the product be? How much of the 2 M solution would be necessary? The 2 N solution?

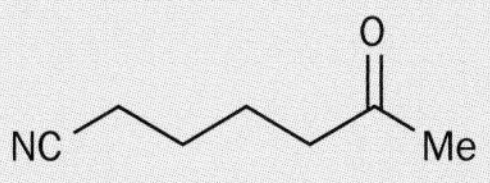

3) Diisobutylaluminum hydride (DIBAL) is a common alternate hydride reducing agent. Its structure is shown below. How much of a 2.5 M solution would be necessary to carry out the same reaction described above? A 2.5 N solution?

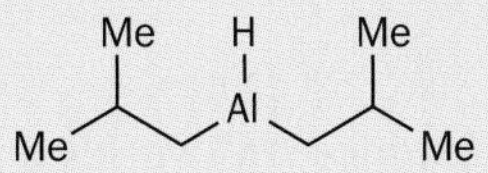

KEY CONCEPTS

pH

Molar solubility

Common Ion effect

Le Châtelier's principle

$k_{sp} = [A^+]_{sat}^x [B^-]_{sat}^y$

TAKEAWAYS

The value of K_{sp} does not change when a common ion is present; it is a constant that is dependent on temperature. The molar solubility of the salt, however, does change if a common ion is present. To find the change in molar solubility due to the common ion effect, you must find the K_{sp} of the substance first.

THINGS TO WATCH OUT FOR

Be careful when applying Le Châtelier's principle in cases of precipitation and solvation. For a solution at equilibrium (i.e., saturated), adding more solid would not shift the equilibrium to the right. More solid does not dissociate to raise the ion concentrations; the solid just piles up at the bottom.

MOLAR SOLUBILITY

The molar solubility of iron(III) hydroxide in pure water at 25°C is 9.94×10^{-10} mol/L. How would the substance's molar solubility change if placed in an aqueous solution of pH 10.0 at 25°C?

1) Identify the balanced equation for the dissociation reaction.

The generic dissociation reaction may be expressed as:

$$A_xB_y(s) \rightarrow xA^+(aq) + yB^-(aq)$$

Plugging in for iron(III) hydroxide, the reaction expression is:

$$Fe(OH)_3(s) \rightarrow Fe^{+3}(aq) + 3OH^-(aq)$$

This step allows us to see how many moles of ions are added to the solution per mole dissolved.

2) Find the K_{sp} expression for the dissociation reaction.

☞ Generic: $K_{sp} = [xA^+]_{sat}^x [yB^-]_{sat}^y$

$Fe(OH)_3$: $K_{sp} = [Fe^{+3}] [OH^-]^3$

K_{sp} is merely an equilibrium constant just like K, and it is given the special name "solubility product" because it tells us how soluble a solid is.

Recall that the concentrations are those at equilibrium, thus the solution is saturated. A saturated solution contains the maximum concentration of dissolved solute.

Remember: Like all K's, a substance's K_{sp} varies only with temperature.

3) Calculate molar solubility of each product by assuming that you're starting with x mols of reactant.

x mol $Fe(OH)_3 \rightarrow x$ mol $Fe^{+3} + 3x$ mol OH^-

Use the balanced equation from step 1 to determine the appropriate coefficients. For each mole of iron hydroxide dissolved, four ions are created: one Fe^{+3} and three OH^-.

4) Plug the molar solubility for each product into the K_{sp} equation:

$Fe(OH)_3$: $K_{sp} = [Fe^{+3}] [OH^-]^3$

$K_{sp} = [x] [3x]^3 = 27x^4$ ($x = 9.94 \times 10^{-10}$)

$K_{sp} = 27(9.94 \times 10^{-10})^4 = 2.64 \times 10^{-35}$

Simply plug in the coefficients from step 3 into the K_{sp} equation. The molar solubility, x, was given in the question stem. Thus, to calculate K_{sp}, plug in 9.94×10^{-10}. Now that we are armed with the K_{sp}, we can find the change in molar solubility due to the common ion.

---

5) If a common ion is present in a solution, it must also be accounted for in the K_{sp} equation:

$Fe(OH)_3$: $K_{sp} = [Fe^{+3}] [OH^-]^3$

$2.64 \times 10^{-35} = x(3x + 10^{-4})^3 \approx x(10^{-4})^3$

$2.64 \times 10^{-35} = x10^{-12}$

$x = 2.64 \times 10^{-23}$

A solution of pH 10.0 has an OH^- concentration of 10^{-4}. Although iron hydroxide will also contribute to the solution's total concentration of OH^-, its contribution will be negligible relative to the 10^{-4} already present in solution; thus, when plugging in for the $[OH^-]$, we can approximate that it equals 10^{-4}. For the pH 10.0 solution, the molar solubility is on the order of 10^{-23} mol/L, a steep decrease from the 10^{-9} in pure water. This is due to the common ion effect. Look at it from the perspective of Le Châtelier's principle: the addition of more OH^- will shift the reaction to the left, so that less iron hydroxide will dissociate.

SIMILAR QUESTIONS

1) Given a substance's K_{sp}, how would you solve for its molar solubility in pure water? What if a common ion were also present in solution?

2) Given a table listing substances and their solubility constants, how would you determine which substance was most soluble in pure water?

3) Given that the sulfate ion can react with acid to form hydrogen sulfate, how would the molar solubility of sulfate salts be affected by varying a solution's pH?

CHAPTER 10

ACIDS AND BASES

Many important reactions in chemical and biological systems involve two classes of compounds called **acids** and **bases.** Acids and bases cause color changes in certain compounds called **indicators,** which may be in solution or on paper. A particular common indicator is litmus paper, which turns red in acidic solution and blue in basic solution. A more extensive discussion of the chemical properties of acids and bases is outlined below.

DEFINITIONS

A. ARRHENIUS DEFINITION

The first definitions of acids and bases were formulated by Svante Arrhenius toward the end of the 19th century. Arrhenius defined an acid as a species that produces H^+ (a proton) in an aqueous solution, and a base as a species that produces OH^- (a hydroxide ion) in an aqueous solution. These definitions, though useful, fail to describe acidic and basic behavior in nonaqueous media.

> **TEACHER TIP**
> This is the most specific definition of acids and bases, and the least useful.

B. BRØNSTED-LOWRY DEFINITION

A more general definition of acids and bases was proposed independently by Johannes Brønsted and Thomas Lowry in 1923. A Brønsted-Lowry acid is a species that donates protons, while a Brønsted-Lowry base is a species that accepts protons. For example, NH_3 and Cl^- are both Brønsted-Lowry bases because they accept protons. However, they cannot be called Arrhenius bases because in aqueous solution they do not dissociate to form OH^-. The advantage of the Brønsted-Lowry concept of acids and bases is that it is not limited to aqueous solutions.

> **TEACHER TIP**
> This is the more general and most useful of the three definitions. It is all about the proton (H^+). It is seen frequently on the MCAT.

Brønsted-Lowry acids and bases always occur in pairs, called **conjugate acid-base pairs.** The two members of a conjugate pair are related by the transfer of a proton. For example, H_3O^+ is the conjugate acid of the base H_2O, and NO_2^- is the conjugate base of HNO_2.

$$H_3O^+(aq) \rightleftarrows H_2O(aq) + H^+(aq)$$
$$HNO_2(aq) \rightleftarrows NO_2^-(aq) + H^+(aq)$$

TEACHER TIP

This is the most general and inclusive definition, and is sometimes seen on the MCAT.

C. LEWIS DEFINITION

At approximately the same time as Brønsted and Lowry, Gilbert Lewis also proposed definitions of acids and bases. Lewis defined an acid as an electron-pair acceptor, and a base as an electron-pair donor. Lewis's are the most inclusive definitions. Just as every Arrhenius acid is a Brønsted-Lowry acid, every Brønsted-Lowry acid is also a Lewis acid (and likewise for bases). However, the Lewis definition encompasses some species not included within the Brønsted-Lowry definition. For example, BCl_3 and $AlCl_3$ can each accept an electron pair and are therefore Lewis acids, despite their inability to donate protons.

NOMENCLATURE OF ARRHENIUS ACIDS

The name of an acid is related to the name of the parent anion (the anion that combines with H^+ to form the acid). Acids formed from anions whose names end in **-ide** have the prefix **hydro-** and the ending **-ic.**

F^-	Fluoride	HF	Hydrofluoric acid
Br^-	Bromide	HBr	Hydrobromic acid

MCAT SYNOPSIS

Some exceptions to the rules exist. For instance, MnO_4^- is called permanganate even though there are no "manganate" or "manganite" ions.

Acids formed from oxyanions are called **oxyacids.** If the anion ends in **-ite** (less oxygen), then the acid will end with **-ous acid.** If the anion ends in **-ate** (more oxygen), then the acid will end with **-ic acid.** Prefixes in the names of the anions are retained. Some examples:

ClO^-	Hypochlorite	HClO	Hypochlorous acid
ClO_2^-	Chlorite	$HClO_2$	Chlorous acid
ClO_3^-	Chlorate	$HClO_3$	Chloric acid
ClO_4^-	Perchlorate	$HClO_4$	Perchloric acid
NO_2^-	Nitrite	HNO_2	Nitrous acid
NO_3^-	Nitrate	HNO_3	Nitric acid

PROPERTIES OF ACIDS AND BASES

A. HYDROGEN ION EQUILIBRIA (pH AND pOH)

Hydrogen ion concentration, $[H^+]$, is generally measured as **pH,** where:

$$pH = -\log[H^+] = \log(1/[H^+])$$

Likewise, hydroxide ion concentration, $[OH^-]$, is measured as **pOH** where:

$$pOH = -\log[OH^-] = \log(1/[OH^-])$$

MCAT SYNOPSIS

Recall that a fundamental property of logarithms is that the log of a product is equal to the sum of the logs, i.e., $\log(xy) = \log x + \log y$.

In any aqueous solution, the H_2O solvent dissociates slightly:

$$H_2O(\ell) \rightleftarrows H^+(aq) + OH^-(aq)$$

This dissociation is an equilibrium reaction and is therefore described by a constant, K_w, the water dissociation constant.

$$K_w = [H^+][OH^-] = 10^{-14}$$

Rewriting this equation in logarithmic form gives:

$$pH + pOH = 14$$

In pure H_2O, $[H^+]$ is equal to $[OH^-]$, because for every mole of H_2O that dissociates, one mole of H^+ and one mole of OH^- are formed. A solution with equal concentrations of H^+ and OH^- is neutral, and has a pH of 7($-\log 10^{-7}$ = 7). A pH below 7 indicates a relative excess of H^+ ions, and therefore an acidic solution; a pH above 7 indicates a relative excess of OH^- ions, and therefore a basic solution.

Math Note: Estimating p-Scale Values

A useful skill for various problems involving acids and bases, as well as their corresponding buffer solutions, is the ability to quickly convert pH, pOH, pK_a, and pK_b into nonlogarithmic form and vice versa.

When the original value is a power of 10, the operation is relatively simple; changing the sign on the exponent gives the corresponding p-scale value directly. For example:

If $[H^+] = 0.001$, or 10^{-3}, then pH = 3.

If $K_b = 1 \times 10^{-7}$, then $pK_b = 7$.

More difficulty arises (in the absence of a calculator) when the original value is not an exact power of 10; exact calculation would be excessively onerous, but a simple method of approximation exists. If the nonlogarithmic value is written in proper scientific notation, it will look like: $n \times 10^{-m}$, where n is a number between 1 and 10. The log of this product can be written as: $\log(n \times 10^{-m}) = -m + \log n$, and the negative log is thus $m - \log n$. Now, because n is a number between 1 and 10, its logarithm will be a fraction between 0 and 1, thus $m - \log n$ will be between $m - 1$ and m. Further, the larger n is, the larger the fraction log n will be, and therefore the closer to $m - 1$ our answer will be.

Example: If $Ka = 1.8 \times 10^{-5}$, then $pKa = 5 - \log 1.8$. Because 1.8 is small, its log will be small, and the answer will be closer to 5 than to 4. (The actual answer is 4.74.)

MCAT SYNOPSIS

Other important properties of logarithms include:

$\text{Log } x^n = n\text{Log } x$, and $\text{Log } 10^x = x$. From these two properties one can derive the particularly useful relationship: $-\text{Log } 10^{-x} = x$.

TEACHER TIP

Learning how to estimate is an important skill.

B. STRONG ACIDS AND BASES

Strong acids and bases are those that completely dissociate into their component ions in aqueous solution. For example, when NaOH is added to water, it dissociates completely:

$$NaOH(s) + excess\ H_2O(\ell) \rightarrow Na^+(aq) + OH^-(aq)$$

Hence, in a 1 M solution of NaOH, complete dissociation gives 1 mole of OH^- ions per liter of solution.

$$pH = 14 - (-\log[OH^-]) = 14 + \log[1] = 14$$

Virtually no undissociated NaOH remains. Note that the $[OH^-]$ contributed by the dissociation of H_2O is considered to be negligible in this case. The contribution of OH^- and H^+ ions from the dissociation of H_2O can be neglected only if the concentration of the acid or base is greater than 10^{-7} M. For example, the pH of a 1×10^{-8} M HCl solution (HCl is a strong acid) might appear to be 8, since $[-\log (1 \times 10^{-8})] = 8$. However, a pH of 8 is in the basic pH range, and an HCl solution is not basic. The discrepancy arises from the fact that at low HCl concentrations, H^+ from the dissociation of water does contribute significantly to the total $[H^+]$. The $[H^+]$ from the dissociation of water is less than 1×10^{-7} M due to the common ion effect. The total concentration of H^+ can be calculated from $K_w = (x + 1 \times 10^{-8})(x) = 1.0 \times 10^{-14}$, where $x = [H^+] = [OH^-]$ (both from the dissociation of water molecules).

Solving for x gives $x = 9.5 \times 10^{-8}$ M,
so $[H^+]_{total} = (9.5 \times 10^{-8} + 1 \times 10^{-8})$ M $= 1.05 \times 10^{-7}$ M
and pH $= -\log (1.05 \times 10^{-7}) = 6.98$, slightly less than 7, as should be expected for a very dilute, yet acidic solution.

Strong acids commonly encountered in the laboratory include $HClO_4$ (perchloric acid), HNO_3 (nitric acid), H_2SO_4 (sulfuric acid), and HCl (hydrochloric acid). Commonly encountered strong bases include NaOH (sodium hydroxide), KOH (potassium hydroxide), and other soluble hydroxides of Group IA and IIA metals. Calculation of the pH and pOH of strong acids and bases assumes complete dissociation of the acid or base in solution: $[H^+]$ = normality of strong acid and $[OH^-]$ = normality of strong base.

C. WEAK ACIDS AND BASES

Weak acids and bases are those that only partially dissociate in aqueous solution. A weak monoprotic acid, HA, in aqueous solution will achieve

TEACHER TIP

Be sure to think about the answer and whether it makes sense. As seen here, a basic pH for an acidic solution should make you think about what might be wrong with your answer.

MCAT FAVORITE

The K_w, like all equilibrium constants, will change if the temperature changes. This will change the pH scale. In other words, our pH scale of 1–14 is only valid at 25°C.

the following equilibrium after dissociation (H_3O^+ is equivalent to H^+ in aqueous solution.):

$$HA(aq) + H_2O(\ell) \rightleftarrows H_3O^+(aq) + A^-(aq)$$

The **acid dissociation constant, K_a,** is a measure of the degree to which an acid dissociates.

$$K_a = \frac{[H_3O^+][A^-]}{[HA]}$$

The weaker the acid, the smaller the K_a. Note that K_a does not contain an expression for the pure liquid, water.

A weak monovalent base, BOH, undergoes dissociation to give B^+ and OH^-. The **base dissociation constant, K_b,** is a measure of the degree to which a base dissociates. The weaker the base, the smaller its K_b. For a monovalent base, K_b is defined as follows:

$$K_b = \frac{[B^+][OH^-]}{[BOH]}$$

A **conjugate acid** is defined as the acid formed when a base gains a proton. Similarly, a **conjugate base** is formed when an acid loses a proton. For example, in the HCO_3^-/CO_3^{2-} conjugate acid/base pair, CO_3^{2-} is the conjugate base and HCO_3^- is the conjugate acid:

$$HCO_3^-(aq) \rightleftarrows H^+(aq) + CO_3^{2-}(aq)$$

To find the K_a of the conjugate acid HCO_3^-, the reaction with water must be considered.

$$HCO_3^-(aq) + H_2O(\ell) \rightleftarrows H_3O^+(aq) + CO_3^{2-}(aq)$$

Likewise, for the K_b of CO_3^{2-}:

$$CO_3^{2-}(aq) + H_2O(\ell) \rightleftarrows HCO_3^-(aq) + OH^-(aq)$$

In a conjugate acid/base pair formed from a weak acid, the conjugate base is generally stronger than the conjugate acid. Thus, for HCO_3^- and CO_3^{2-}, the reaction of CO_3^{2-} (the conjugate base) in water to produce HCO_3^- (the conjugate acid) and OH^- occurs to a great extent (i.e., is more favorable) than the reverse reaction.

The equilibrium constants for these reactions are as follows:

$$K_a = \frac{[H^+][CO_3^{2-}]}{[HCO_3^-]} \text{ and } K_b = \frac{[HCO_3^-][OH^-]}{[CO_3^{2-}]}$$

Adding the two reactions shows that the net reaction is simply the dissociation of water:

$$H_2O(\ell) \rightleftarrows H^+(aq) + OH^-(aq)$$

The equilibrium constant for this net reaction is $K_w = [H^+][OH^-]$, which is the product of K_a and K_b. Thus, if the dissociation constant either for an acid or for its conjugate base is known, then the dissociation constant for the other can be determined, using the equation:

$$K_a \times K_b = K_w = 1 \times 10^{-14}$$

Thus K_a and K_b are inversely related. In other words, if K_a is large (the acid is strong), then K_b will be small (the conjugate base will be weak), and vice versa.

D. APPLICATIONS OF K_a AND K_b

To calculate the concentration of H^+ in a 2 M aqueous solution of acetic acid, CH_3COOH ($K_a = 1.8 \times 10^{-5}$) , first write the equilibrium reaction:

$$CH_3COOH(aq) \rightleftarrows H^+(aq) + CH_3COO^-(aq)$$

Next, write the expression for the acid dissociation constant:

$$K_a = \frac{[H^+]\left[CH_3COO^-\right]}{[CH_3COOH]} = 1.8 \times 10^{-5}$$

Because acetic acid is a weak acid, the concentration of CH_3COOH at equilibrium is equal to its initial concentration, 2 M, less the amount dissociated, x. Likewise $[H^+] = [CH_3COO^-] = x$, because each molecule of CH_3COOH dissociates into one H^+ ion and one CH_3COO^- ion. Thus, the equation can be rewritten as follows:

$$K_a = \frac{[X][X]}{[2-X]} = 1.8 \times 10^{-5}$$

We can approximate that $2 - x \approx 2$ because acetic acid is a weak acid, and only slightly dissociates in water. This simplifies the calculation of x:

$$K_a = \frac{[X][X]}{[2.0]} = 1.8 \times 10^{-5}$$

$$X = 6 \times 10^{-3} M$$

The fact that [x] is so much less than the initial concentration of acetic acid (2 M) validates the approximation; otherwise, it would have been necessary to solve for x using the quadratic formula. (A rule of thumb is that the approximation is valid as long as x is less than 5 percent of the initial concentration.)

SALT FORMATION

Acids and bases may react with each other, forming a salt and (often, but not always) water, in what is termed a **neutralization reaction** (see chapter 4). For example,

$$HA + BOH \rightarrow BA + H_2O$$

The salt may precipitate out or remain ionized in solution, depending on its solubility and the amount produced. Neutralization reactions generally go to completion. The reverse reaction, in which the salt ions react with water to give back the acid or base, is known as **hydrolysis.**

Four combinations of strong and weak acids and bases are possible:

1. strong acid + strong base: e.g., $HCl + NaOH \rightarrow NaCl + H_2O$
2. strong acid + weak base: e.g., $HCl + NH_3 \rightarrow NH_4Cl$
3. weak acid + strong base: e.g., $HClO + NaOH \rightarrow NaClO + H_2O$
4. weak acid + weak base: e.g., $HClO + NH_3 \rightleftarrows NH_4ClO$

TEACHER TIP
Remember the reaction types discussed in the Compounds and Stoichiometry chapter? Well, here is our neutralization reaction.

The products of a reaction between equal concentrations of a strong acid and a strong base are a salt and water. The acid and base neutralize each other, so the resulting solution is neutral (pH = 7), and the ions formed in the reaction do not react with water. The product of a reaction between a strong acid and a weak base is also a salt but usually no water is formed because weak bases are usually not hydroxides; however, in this case, the cation of the salt will react with the water solvent, reforming the weak base. This reaction constitutes hydrolysis. For example:

$$HCl(aq) + NH_3(aq) \rightleftarrows NH_4^+(aq) + Cl^-(aq) \text{ Reaction I}$$
$$NH_4^+(aq) + H_2O(aq) \rightleftarrows NH_3(aq) + H_3O^+(aq) \text{ Reaction II}$$

NH_4^+ is the conjugate acid of a weak base (NH_3), and is therefore stronger than the conjugate base (Cl^-) of the strong acid HCl. NH_4^+ will thus react with OH^-, reducing the concentration of OH^-. There will thus be an excess of H^+, which will lower the pH of the solution.

On the other hand, when a weak acid reacts with a strong base the solution is basic, due to the hydrolysis of the salt to reform the acid, with the concurrent formation of hydroxide ion from the hydrolyzed water molecules. The pH of a solution containing a weak acid and a weak base depends on the relative strengths of the reactants. For example, the acid HClO has a $K_a = 3.2 \times 10^{-8}$, and the base NH_3 has a $K_b = 1.8 \times 10^{-5}$.

Thus an aqueous solution of HClO and NH_3 is basic because K_a for HClO is less than K_b for NH_3.

POLYVALENCE AND NORMALITY

The relative acidity or basicity of an aqueous solution is determined by the relative concentrations of **acid** and **base equivalents.** An acid equivalent is equal to one mole of H^+ (or H_3O^+) ions; a base equivalent is equal to one mole of OH^- ions. Some acids and bases are polyvalent, that is, each mole of the acid or base liberates more than one acid or base equivalent. For example, the diprotic acid H_2SO_4 undergoes the following dissociation in water:

$$H_2SO_4(aq) \rightarrow H^+(aq) + HSO_4^-(aq)$$
$$HSO_4^-(aq) \rightleftarrows H^+(aq) + SO_4^{2-}(aq)$$

One mole of H_2SO_4 can thus produce two acid equivalents (two moles of H^+). The acidity or basicity of a solution depends upon the concentration of acidic or basic equivalents that can be liberated. The quantity of acidic or basic capacity is directly indicated by the solution's normality (see chapter 9, Solutions). Because each mole of H_3PO_4 can liberate three moles (equivalents) of H^+, a 2 M H_3PO_4 solution would be 6 N (6 normal).

Another useful measurement is equivalent weight. For example, the gram molecular weight of H_2SO_4 is 98 g/mol. Because each mole liberates two acid equivalents, the gram equivalent weight of H_2SO_4 would be $\frac{98}{2}$ = 49g; that is, the dissociation of 49 g of H_2SO_4 would release one acid equivalent. Common polyvalent acids include H_2SO_4, H_3PO_4, and H_2CO_3.

AMPHOTERIC SPECIES

An **amphoteric,** or **amphiprotic,** species is one that can act either as an acid or a base, depending on its chemical environment. In the Brønsted-Lowry sense, an amphoteric species can either gain or lose a proton. Water is the most common example. When water reacts with a base, it behaves as an acid:

$$H_2O + B^- \rightleftarrows HB + OH^-$$

When water reacts with an acid, it behaves as a base:

$$HA + H_2O \rightleftarrows H_3O^+ + A^-$$

> ## FLASHBACK
>
> Recall that we spoke about gram equivalent weights in the Compounds and Stoichiometry chapter, and about normality and all units of concentration in the Solutions chapter.

The partially dissociated conjugate base of a polyprotic acid is usually amphoteric (e.g., HSO_4^- can either gain an H^+ to form H_2SO_4, or lose an H^+ to form SO_4^{2-}). The hydroxides of certain metals, e.g., Al, Zn, Pb, and Cr, are also amphoteric. Furthermore, species that can act as either oxidizing or reducing agents (see chapter 11, Redox Reactions and Electrochemistry) are considered to be amphoteric as well, because by accepting or donating electron pairs they act as Lewis acids or bases, respectively.

TITRATION AND BUFFERS

Titration is a procedure used to determine the molarity of an acid or base. This is accomplished by reacting a known volume of a solution of unknown concentration with a known volume of a solution of known concentration. When the number of acid equivalents equals the number of base equivalents added, or vice versa, the **equivalence point** is reached. It is important to emphasize that, while a strong acid/strong base titration will have an equivalence point at pH 7, the equivalence point **need not** always occur at pH 7. Also, when titrating polyprotic acids or bases, there are several equivalence points, as each different acidic or basic species is titrated separately (see Polyprotic Acids and Bases later in this chapter).

The equivalence point in a titration is estimated in two common ways: either by using a graphical method, plotting the pH of the solution as a function of added titrant by using a **pH meter** (e.g. Figure 10.1), or by watching for a color change of an added **indicator.** Indicators are weak organic acids or bases that have different colors in their undissociated and dissociated states. Indicators are used in low concentrations and therefore do not significantly alter the equivalence point. The point at which the indicator actually changes color is not the equivalence point but is called the end point. If the titration is performed well, the volume difference (and therefore the error) between the end point and the equivalence point is usually small and may be corrected for, or ignored.

FLASHBACK

Le Châtelier's principle:

$HIN \rightleftharpoons H^+ + IN^-$

(color 1) (color 2)

Adding H^+ shifts equilibrium to left. Adding OH^- removes H^+ and therefore shifts equilibrium to the right.

MCAT SYNOPSIS

An easy way to calculate the volume added to reach the endpoint is by use of the formula: $V_A N_A = V_B N_B$, where V is for volume, N is for normality (see chapter 9), A is for acid, and B is for base.

A. STRONG ACID AND STRONG BASE

Consider the titration of 10 mL of a 0.1 N solution of HCl with a 0.1 N solution of NaOH. Plotting the pH of the reaction solution versus the quantity of NaOH added gives the following curve:

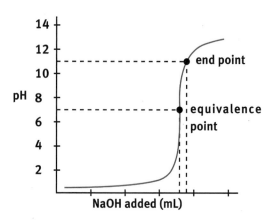

Figure 10.1. Titration of HCl with NaOH

Because HCl is a strong acid and NaOH is a strong base, the equivalence point of the titration will be at pH 7 and the solution will be neutral. Note that the endpoint shown is close to, but not exactly equal to, the equivalence point; selection of a better indicator, say one that changes colors at pH 8, would have given a better approximation.

In the early part of the curve (when little base has been added), the acidic species predominates, and so the addition of small amounts of base will not appreciably change either the [OH⁻] or the pH. Similarly, in the last part of the titration curve (when an excess of base has been added), the addition of small amounts of base will not change the [OH⁻] significantly, and the pH remains relatively constant. The addition of base most alters the concentrations of H⁺ and OH⁻ near the equivalence point, and thus the pH changes most drastically in that region.

B. WEAK ACID AND STRONG BASE

Titration of a weak acid, HA, with a strong base produces the following titration curve:

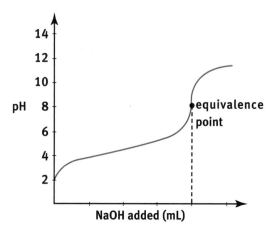

Figure 10.2. Titration of a Weak Acid, HA, with NaOH

Comparing Figure 10.2 with Figure 10.1 shows that the initial pH of the weak acid solution is greater than the initial pH of the strong acid solution. The pH changes most significantly early on in the titration, and the equivalence point is in the basic range.

C. BUFFERS

A **buffer solution** consists of a mixture of a weak acid and its salt (which consists of its conjugate base and a cation), or a mixture of a weak base and its salt (which consists of its conjugate acid and an anion). Two examples of buffers are: a solution of acetic acid (CH_3COOH) and its salt, sodium acetate ($CH_3COO^-Na^+$); and a solution of ammonia (NH_3) and its salt, ammonium chloride ($NH_4^+Cl^-$). Buffer solutions have the useful property of resisting changes in pH when small amounts of acid or base are added.

Consider a buffer solution of acetic acid and sodium acetate:

$$CH_3COOH \rightleftarrows H^+ + CH_3COO^-$$

When a small amount of NaOH is added to the buffer, the OH^- ions from the NaOH react with the H^+ ions present in the solution; subsequently, more acetic acid dissociates (equilibrium shifts to the right), restoring the $[H^+]$. Thus, an increase in $[OH^-]$ does not appreciably change pH. Likewise, when a small amount of HCl is added to the buffer, H^+ ions from the HCl react with the acetate ions to form acetic acid. Thus $[H^+]$ is kept relatively constant and the pH of the solution is relatively unchanged.

The **Henderson-Hasselbalch equation** is used to estimate the pH of a solution in the buffer region where the concentrations of the species and its conjugate are present in approximately equal concentrations. For a weak acid buffer solution:

$$pH = pK_a + \log \frac{[\text{conjugate base}]}{[\text{weak acid}]}$$

Note that when [conjugate base] = [weak acid] (in a titration, halfway to the equivalent point) the pH = pK_a because the log 1 = 0. Likewise, for a weak base buffer solution:

$$pOH = pK_b + \log \frac{[\text{conjugate acid}]}{[\text{weak base}]}$$

and pOH = pK_b when [conjugate acid] = [weak base].

> **MCAT SYNOPSIS**
>
> The Henderson-Hasselbalch equation is also useful in the creation of buffer solutions other than those formed during the course of a titration. By careful selection of the weak acid (or base) and its salt, a buffer at almost any pH can be produced.

D. POLYPROTIC ACIDS AND BASES

The titration curve for a polyprotic acid or base looks different from that for a monoprotic acid or base. Figure 10.3 shows the titration of Na_2CO_3 with HCl in which the polyprotic acid H_2CO_3 is the ultimate product.

In region I, little acid has been added and the predominant species is CO_3^{2-}. In region II, more acid has been added and the predominant species are CO_3^{2-} and HCO_3^-, in relatively equal concentrations. The flat part of the curve is the first buffer region, corresponding to the pK_a of HCO_3^- ($K_a = 5.6 \times 10^{-11}$ implies $pK_a = 10.25$).

Region III contains the equivalence point, at which all of the CO_3^{2-} is titrated to HCO_3^-. As the curve illustrates, a rapid change in pH occurs at the equivalence point; in the latter part of region III, the predominant species is HCO_3^-.

In region IV, the acid has neutralized approximately half of the HCO_3^-, and now H_2CO_3 and HCO_3^- are in roughly equal concentrations. This flat region is the second buffer region of the titration curve, corresponding to the pK_a of H_2CO_3 ($K_a = 4.3 \times 10^{-7}$ implies $pK_a - 6.37$). In region V, the equivalence point for the entire titration is reached, as all of the HCO_3^- is converted to H_2CO_3. Again, a rapid change in pH is observed near the equivalence point as acid is added.

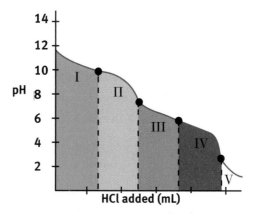

Figure 10.3. Titration of Na_2CO_3 with HCl

PRACTICE QUESTIONS

1. Which of the following is NOT a Brønsted-Lowry base?

A.

B. F⁻

C.

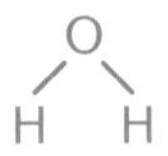

D.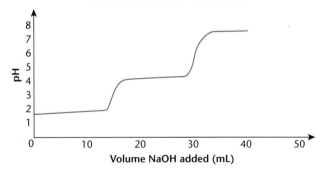

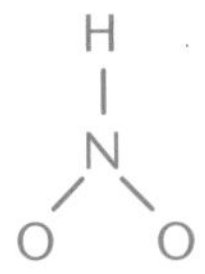

2. What is the pH of a solution containing 5 mM H_2S?

A. 1
B. 1.5
C. 2
D. 4

3. Which of the following is chloric acid?

A. $HClO_3$
B. ClO_3^-
C. $HClO_2$
D. $HClO$

4. Which of the following is the weakest base of those provided?

A. KOH
B. $Ca(OH)_2$
C. CH_3NH_2
D. NaH

5. The function of a buffer is to

A. speed up reactions between acids and bases.
B. resist changes in pH when small amounts of acid or base are added.
C. slow down reactions between acids and bases.
D. keep pH constant throughout an acid/base reaction.

6. What is the pH of the following solution shown below?

$pK_b = 3.45$	$[NH_4^+] = 70$ mM	$[NH_3] = 712$ mM

A. 4.45
B. 7.55
C. 9.55
D. 10.65

Questions 7–9 are based on the titration curve of acid X shown below:

Titration Curve of Weak Acid X

7. What is the approximate value of the first pK_a on the cuve above?

A. 1.9
B. 2.9
C. 3.8
D. 4.1

191

8. Where is the second equivalence point on the previous curve?

   A. pH = 3
   B. pH = 4.1
   C. pH = 5.9
   D. pH = 7.2

9. What is the approximate value of the second pK_a on the previous curve?

   A. 3.6
   B. 4.1
   C. 5.5
   D. 7.2

10. What is the approximate gram equivalent weight of phosphoric acid?

   A. 25 g
   B. 33 g
   C. 49 g
   D. 98 g

11. What is the $[H^+]$ of a 2M aqueous solution of a weak acid "HXO_2" with $K_a = 3.2 \times 10^{-5}$?

   A. 8×10^{-3} M
   B. 6.4×10^{-5} M
   C. 1.3×10^{-4} M
   D. 4×10^{-3} M

12. Which of the following is NOT true of an amphoteric species?

   A. It can act as a base or an acid depending on its environment.
   B. It can act as an oxidizing or reducing agent depending on its environment.
   C. It is always protic.
   D. It is always a nonpolar species.

13. What is the approximate pH of a 1.2×10^{-5} M aqueous solution of NaOH?

   A. 4.85
   B. 7.5
   C. 9.15
   D. 12.45

High-Yield Problems

ACIDS AND BASES

PH AND PK$_a$

What is the pH of the resulting solution if 4 g of sodium acetate (CH_3CO_2Na) is dissolved in 0.5 L of water? (The pK$_a$ of acetic acid, CH_3CO_2H, is 4.74.)

KEY CONCEPTS

Acids and bases

Chemical equilibrium

1) Convert masses to concentrations.

Molecular weight of sodium acetate in g mol^{-1}: $23 + 2(12) + 3(1) + 2(16) = 82$

The concentration of a solution is usually expressed in units of moles per liter.

Choose numbers that are easy to work with, i.e., 80 g mol^{-1} instead of 82 g mol^{-1}. Remember, you won't have a calculator on Test Day! Moles of sodium acetate:
$$\frac{4\,g}{80\,g\,mol^{-1}} = \frac{1}{20}\,mol = 0.05\,mol.$$

$$Concentration = \frac{0.05\,mol}{0.5\,L} = 0.1\,M$$

Remember: Moles, not grams, *are the "common currency" of chemistry problems dealing with reactions. Concentration, usually in units of moles per liter, is the essential quantity for these acid–base problems.*

TAKEAWAYS

Keep in mind that K$_b$ is nothing more than an *equilibrium constant* for the reaction of a base picking up a proton from water. So, all of the things that are true for K$_{eq}$ are true for K$_b$, especially that K$_{eq}$ only depends on temperature. At constant temperature, *it never changes* (as the name suggests), even if the concentrations of the species in solution change.

2) Choose the constant that will make most sense for the reaction in question and compute its value.

$$-\log(K_a \times K_b) = -\log(10^{-14})$$
$$-\log K_a + -\log K_b = -\log 10^{-14} = 14$$
$$pK_a + pK_b = 14$$
$$pK_b = 14 - pK_a = 9$$
$$K_b = 10^{-pK_b} = 10^{-9}$$

Now we need to decide which constant we will use, K$_a$ or K$_b$. Here's where a little common sense goes a long way. If you think about sodium acetate, you should realize that it is the conjugate base of acetic acid. Therefore, we need the value of K$_b$ for sodium acetate. Even though we are given the pK$_a$ of acetic acid, getting the K$_b$ from this information is no sweat.

In water, K$_a \times$ K$_b$ is always equal to K$_w$, or 10^{-14}. Take the negative logarithm of both sides.

Remember that $\log(a \times b) = \log a + \log b$ and that $\log 10^x = x$.

Don't forget that $-\log(\text{whatever}) = p(\text{whatever})$. We will want to find K$_b$ because sodium acetate is the conjugate base of acetic acid.

Plug in the pK$_a$ from above (to make our lives easier, let's say $4.74 \approx 5$).

193

Remember: The p-scale is a hugely important value for acid-base problems. Remember that p(something) = –log(something).

---

3) Write down the appropriate chemical reaction and set up a table.

Here we need to set up a table to reflect the data we've collected. This is the "putting it all together" step and is crucial.

Our table will be as follows:

	$H_2O\ (\ell) + CH_3CO_2^-\ (aq) \rightarrow CH_3CO_2H\ (aq) + OH^-\ (aq)$			
Initial	–	0.1	0	0
Change	–	$-x$	$+x$	$+x$
Equilibrium	–	$0.1 - x$	x	x

Initial: The idea is that we're going to take some sodium acetate, dump it into water, and see what happens. Our initial row in the table shows the concentrations that we have before any reaction takes place. That means that we'll start with the amount of sodium acetate we computed, 0.1 M. There's no acetic acid or hydroxide because no reaction has happened yet.

Change: Here's where all the action happens. As our acetate reacts with water, the concentration is going to decrease by some amount. We don't know what that will be yet, so let's just call it *x*. If the acetate concentration goes *down* by *x*, the concentrations of acetic acid and hydroxide must go *up* by the same amount, so we put *x*'s in their columns.

Equilibrium: This is the easy part. Just add up all of the columns above. Our completed table will look like the table at left.

*Remember: **Always, always, always** make sure that **any** chemical reaction you write down is **balanced**. This means to make sure that **mass** is balanced (the number of atoms on either side of the reaction) and that **charge** is balanced. Also, the concentration of pure liquids (e.g., water) and pure solids is never taken into account in equilibria.*

---

4) Plug the equilibrium concentrations from the table into the appropriate acidity or basicity expression.

$$K_b = \frac{[CH_3CO_2]_{eq}[OH^-]_{eq}}{[CH_3CO_2^-]_{eq}} = \frac{x\,x}{0.1-x} = \frac{x^2}{0.1-x} = 10^{-9}$$

We know that K_b is just the K_{eq} for the reaction in our table above. Plug in the numbers from the table.

5) Simplify the expression from step 4 and solve it.

$$\frac{x^2}{0.1} = 10^{-9}$$

$$x^2 = (0.1)(10^{-9}) = 10^{-10}$$

$$x = 10^{-5}$$

Let's make our lives easier (*and* save ourselves time on Test Day) by assuming that x is much, much smaller than 0.1, so that $0.1 - x \approx 0.1$.

Now why would we want to assume that x is very, very small? Well, remember that sodium acetate is a weak base because it has a K_b value. So, if it's a weak base, it won't react much with water, thus making x a very small number.

Remember: Don't forget to check the assumption we made to simplify our equation. Because $x = 10^{-5}$, which is indeed much less than 0.1 (by a factor of 10,000), our assumption holds.

SIMILAR QUESTIONS

1) What would be the pH if the initial concentration of sodium acetate in the opening question was halved? If it were doubled?

2) Compute the pH of the resulting solution if 0.1 mol of *pure NaOH* were added to 1 L of water. How does this pH compare to that of the solution with sodium acetate?

3) What would the pH of the solution be if just enough HCl were added to the solution in the original problem to consume all of the sodium acetate?

6) Answer the question.

$$-\log[OH^-] = -\log[10^{-5}] = 5 = pOH$$

$$pH = 14 - 5 = 9$$

This step is trickier than it sounds and is where many, many mistakes are committed. Here's where attention to detail counts. You don't want to slog through all of the work above and then mess up at the end, when 99 percent of the work is done!

Think about what you've solved for. What is x? Well, if we look at the table, we see that x is the concentration of hydroxide. So, if we take the negative log of the hydroxide ion concentration, we get the pOH.

Remember that $pH + pOH = 14$. The actual pH is 8.89. So, all of our assumptions and roundings didn't affect the answer much, but saved us a lot of time in computation!

Remember: Always ask yourself whether your final answer makes sense. The MCAT isn't a computation test, it's a test of critical thinking. Here, we have a base being dissolved in water, so at the end of the day, the pH better be above 7, which it is.

HIGH-YIELD PROBLEMS

KEY CONCEPTS

Titration

Acids and bases

Equivalence point

Half-equivalence point

pH

TAKEAWAYS

Setting up the tables as shown makes quick work of titration pH questions. Remember to make approximations and use numbers that are easy to work with in order to minimize the computation necessary to get to the answer.

TITRATION

Hydrazoic acid, HN_3, is a highly toxic compound that can cause death in minutes if inhaled in concentrated form. 100 mL of 0.2 M aqueous solution of HN_3 (pK_a = 4.72) is to be titrated with a 0.5 M solution of NaOH.

a) What is the pH of the HN_3 solution before any NaOH is added?

b) The *half-equivalence* point of a titration is where half the titrant necessary to get to the equivalence point has been added. How much of the NaOH solution will be needed to get to the half-equivalence point? What is the pH at the half-equivalence point?

c) What is the pH at the equivalence point?

1) Determine the pH before the titration.
What you need to ask yourself in each stage of this problem is which species is present, H^+ or OH^-, and where is it coming from? Before the titration begins, we have H^+ around because, as the name of the compound suggests, hydrazoic acid is *acidic*. The major source of H^+ is from the hydrazoic acid itself, so we can set up a table as follows:

	$H_2O\ (\ell) + HN_3(aq) \rightarrow H_3O^+(aq) + OH^-(aq)$			
Initial	–	0.2	0	0
Change	–	$-x$	$+x$	$+x$
Equilibrium	–	$0.2 - x$	x	x

$$K_a = \frac{[H_3O^+][N_3^-]}{[HN_3]} = \frac{X^2}{0.2-X} = \frac{X^2}{0.2} = 10^{-5}$$

$$X^2 = 2 \times 10^{-1} \times 10^{-5} = 2 \times 10^{-6}$$

$$\Rightarrow X = \sqrt{0.2 \times 10^{-6}} \approx 1.4 \times 10^{-3}$$

$$\Rightarrow [H_3O^+]_{eq} = 1.4 \times 10^{-3}$$

$$\Rightarrow pH = -\log[H_3O^+] = -\log(1.4 \times 10^{-3}) = 3 - \log(1.4)$$

$$2 < pH < 3$$

Plug in the concentrations from the table. We know the pK_a is around 5, so the K_a must be 10^{-5}. Whenever exponents or logarithms are involved, *use numbers that are easy to work with*. Make the approximation that $0.2 - x \approx 0.2$ because HN_3 is a weak acid.

If you must take a square root, try and get the power of 10 to be even to make matters simple. Remember from the table that x is the hydronium ion concentration.

Remember that $-\log[a \times 10^{-b}] = b - \log[a]$ = somewhere between $b - 1$ and b.

2) Find the equivalence point and half-equivalence point.

mol HN_3 = 0.1 L × 0.2 mol L^{-1} = 0.02 mol HN_3

$$\frac{0.02 \text{ mol NaOH}}{0.5 \text{ mol L}^{-1}} = 0.04 \text{ L NaOH solution}$$

$$K_a = \frac{[H_3O^+][N_3^-]}{[HN_3]} = [H_3O^+] = [H_3O^+]$$

Compute the number of moles of HN_3 that you start with.

Each mole of HN_3 will react with one mole of OH^-. Therefore, the equivalence point is reached when 40 mL of the NaOH solution are added and the half-equivalence point is at 40/2 = 20 mL. We could go through the whole rigamarole of setting up another table to figure out the pH at the half-equivalence point, or we could use a little common sense to avoid computation. At the half-equivalence point, half of the HN_3 has been consumed and converted to N_3^-. Therefore, the HN_3 and N_3 concentrations are equal.

Because $[HN_3] = [N_3^-]$, $K_a = [H_3O^+]$, and pH = pK_a = 4.72.

Remember: Whenever possible, avoid computation!

3) Determine the reactive species at the equivalence point to find the pH.

$$K_b = \frac{K_w}{K_a} = \frac{10^{-14}}{10^{-5}} = 10^{-9}$$

Remember that $K_a \times K_b = K_w = 10^{-14}$. Now we can set up our table:

		$H_2O\,(\ell) + N_3(aq)^- \rightarrow HN_3(aq) + OH^-(aq)$		
Initial	–	0.15	0	0
Change	–	$-x$	$+x$	$+x$
Equilibrium	–	$0.15 - x$	x	x

Remember that the volume of our solution has increased by 40 mL, so the concentration of N_3^- is $\frac{0.02 \text{ mol}}{(0.1 + 0.04) \text{ L}} \approx 0.15$ M.

$$K_b = \frac{[HN_3][OH^-]}{[N_3^-]} = \frac{x^2}{0.15 - x} = \frac{x^2}{0.15} = 10^{-9}$$

$x^2 = 0.15 \times 10^{-9} = 0.15 \times 10^{-10} \approx 1.6 \times 10^{-10} \approx 160 \times 10^{-12}$

$\Rightarrow x = \sqrt{160 \times 10^{-12}} = 4\sqrt{10} \times 10^{-6} \approx 12 \times 10^{-6} = 1.2 \times 10^{-5}$

$\Rightarrow [OH^-]_{eq} = 1.2 \times 10^{-5}$

$\Rightarrow pOH = -\log([OH^-]) = -\log(1.2 \times 10^{-5}) = 5 - \log(1.2) \approx 5$

$\Rightarrow pH = 14 - pOH = 14 - 5 = 9$

At the equivalence point, all of the HN_3 has been consumed, leaving only N_3^- behind. Because N_3^- is a Brønsted–Lowry *base*, we need to worry about OH^-, not H_3O^+.

Make the approximation that $0.15 - x \approx 0.15$.

Here, let's say that 1.6 is close to 1.5 to make the square root computation trivial.

Note that pH + pOH = 14 in water. Remember to ask yourself whether or not a result makes sense. Here, because we have a basic species (N_3^-), the pH should be above 7, which it is.

CHAPTER 11

REDOX REACTIONS AND ELECTROCHEMISTRY

Electrochemistry is the study of the relationships between chemical reactions and electrical energy. **Electrochemical reactions** include spontaneous reactions that produce electrical energy, and nonspontaneous reactions that use electrical energy to produce a chemical change. Both types of reactions always involve a transfer of electrons with conservation of charge and mass.

OXIDATION-REDUCTION REACTIONS

A. OXIDATION AND REDUCTION

The law of conservation of charge states that an electrical charge can be neither created nor destroyed. Thus, an isolated loss or gain of electrons cannot occur; **oxidation** (loss of electrons) and **reduction** (gain of electrons) must occur simultaneously, resulting in an electron transfer called a **redox reaction.** An **oxidizing agent** causes another atom in a redox reaction to undergo oxidation, and is itself reduced. A **reducing agent** causes the other atom to be reduced, and is itself oxidized.

KAPLAN EXCLUSIVE

OIL RIG stands for "Oxidation Is Loss, Reduction Is Gain," of electrons that is.

Alternatively, reduction is just what it sounds like: reduction of charge.

B. ASSIGNING OXIDATION NUMBERS

It is important, of course, to know which atom is oxidized and which is reduced. **Oxidation numbers** are assigned to atoms in order to keep track of the redistribution of electrons during a chemical reaction. From the oxidation numbers of the reactants and products, it is possible to determine how many electrons are gained or lost by each atom. The oxidation number of an atom in a compound is assigned according to the following rules:

TEACHER TIP

Don't forget that you'll have the periodic table available on Test Day. Beware of transition metals but realize we can often figure their oxidation by default.

1. **The oxidation number of free elements is zero.** For example, the atoms in N_2, P_4, S_8, and He all have oxidation numbers of zero.
2. **The oxidation number for a monatomic ion is equal to the charge of the ion.** For example, the oxidation numbers for Na^+, Cu^{2+}, Fe^{3+}, Cl^-, and N^{3-} are +1, +2, +3, –1, and –3, respectively.
3. **The oxidation number of each Group IA element in a compound is +1. The oxidation number of each Group IIA element in a compound is +2.**

4. **The oxidation number of each Group VIIA element in a compound is –1, except when combined with an element of higher electronegativity.** For example, in HCl, the oxidation number of Cl is –1; in HOCl, however, the oxidation number of Cl is +1.

5. **The oxidation number of hydrogen is –1 in compounds with less electronegative elements than hydrogen (Groups IA and IIA.)** Examples include NaH and CaH_2. The more common oxidation number of hydrogen is +1.

6. **In most compounds, the oxidation number of oxygen is –2.** This is not the case, however, in molecules such as OF_2. Here, because F is more electronegative than O, the oxidation number of oxygen is +2. Also, in peroxides such as BaO_2, the oxidation number of O is –1 instead of –2 because of the structure of the peroxide ion, $[O\text{–}O]^{2-}$. (Note that Ba, a group IIA element, can not be a +4 cation.)

7. **The sum of the oxidation numbers of all the atoms present in a neutral compound is zero. The sum of the oxidation numbers of the atoms present in a polyatomic ion is equal to the charge of the ion.** Thus, for $SO_4{}^{2-}$, the sum of the oxidation numbers must be –2.

Example: Assign oxidation numbers to the atoms in the following reaction in order to determine the oxidized and reduced species and the oxidizing and reducing agents.

$$SnCl_2 + PbCl_4 \rightarrow SnCl_4 + PbCl_2$$

Solution: All these species are neutral, so the oxidation numbers of each compound must add up to zero. In $SnCl_2$, because there are two chlorines present, and chlorine has an oxidation number of –1, Sn must have an oxidation number of +2. Similarly, the oxidation number of Sn in $SnCl_4$ is +4; the oxidation number of Pb is +4 in $PbCl_4$ and +2 in $PbCl_2$. Notice that the oxidation number of Sn goes from +2 to +4; it loses electrons and thus is oxidized, making it the reducing agent. Because the oxidation number of Pb has decreased from +4 to +2, it has gained electrons and been reduced. Pb is the oxidizing agent. The sum of the charges on both sides of the reaction is equal to zero, so charge has been conserved.

C. BALANCING REDOX REACTIONS

By assigning oxidation numbers to the reactants and products, one can determine how many moles of each species are required for conservation of

---

MCAT SYNOPSIS

The conventions of formula writing put cation first and anion second. Thus NaH implies H^- while HCl implies H^+.

charge and mass, which is necessary to balance the equation. To balance a redox reaction, both the net charge and the number of atoms must be equal on both sides of the equation. The most common method for balancing redox equations is the **half-reaction method,** also known as the **ion-electron method,** in which the equation is separated into two half-reactions—the oxidation part and the reduction part. Each half-reaction is balanced separately, and they are then added to give a balanced overall reaction. Consider a redox reaction between $KMnO_4$ and HI in an acidic solution.

$$MnO_4^- + I^- \rightarrow I_2 + Mn^{2+}$$

Step 1: Separate the two half-reactions.

$$I^- \rightarrow I_2$$
$$MnO_4^- \rightarrow Mn^{2+}$$

Step 2: Balance the atoms of each half-reaction. First, balance all atoms except H and O. Next, in an acidic solution, add H_2O to balance the O atoms and then add H^+ to balance the H atoms. (In a basic solution, use OH^- and H_2O to balance the O's and H's.)

To balance the iodine atoms, place a coefficient of 2 before the I^- ion.

$$2 I^- \rightarrow I_2$$

For the permanganate half-reaction, Mn is already balanced. Next, balance the oxygens by adding $4H_2O$ to the right side.

$$MnO_4^- \rightarrow Mn^{2+} + 4H_2O$$

Finally, add H+ to the left side to balance the 4 H_2Os. These two half-reactions are now balanced.

$$MnO_4^- + 8 H^+ \rightarrow Mn^{2+} + 4 H_2O$$

Step 3: Balance the charges of each half-reaction. The reduction half-reaction must consume the same number of electrons as are supplied by the oxidation half. For the oxidation reaction, add 2 electrons to the right side of the reaction:

$$2 I^- \rightarrow I_2 + 2e^-$$

For the reduction reaction, a charge of +2 must exist on both sides. Add 5 electrons to the left side of the reaction to accomplish this:

$$5 e^- + 8 H^+ + MnO_4^- \rightarrow Mn^{2+} + 4 H_2O$$

> **TEACHER TIP**
>
> This type of methodical, step-by-step approach is great for the MCAT. Chances are you'll come up with your answer only halfway through the process.

Next, both half-reactions must have the same number of electrons so that they will cancel. Multiply the oxidation half by 5 and the reduction half by 2.

$$5(2I^- \rightarrow I_2 + 2e^-)$$
$$2(5e^- + 8H^+ + MnO_4^- \rightarrow Mn^{2+} + 4 H_2O)$$

Step 4: Add the half-reactions:

$$10 \ I^- \rightarrow 5 \ I_2 + 10 \ e^-$$
$$16 \ H^+ + 2 \ MnO_4^- + 10 \ e^- \rightarrow 2 \ Mn^{2+} + 8 \ H_2O$$

The final equation is:

$$10 \ I^- + 10 \ e^- + 16 \ H^+ + 2 \ MnO_4^- \rightarrow 5 \ I_2 + 2 \ Mn^{2+} +$$
$$10 \ e^- + 8 \ H_2O$$

To get the overall equation, cancel out the electrons and any H_2Os, H^+s, or OH^-s that appear on both sides of the equation.

$$10 \ I^- + 16 \ H^+ + 2 \ MnO_4^- \rightarrow 5 \ I_2 + 2 \ Mn^{2+} + 8 \ H_2O$$

Step 5: Finally, confirm that mass and charge are balanced. There is a +4 net charge on each side of the reaction equation, and the atoms are stoichiometrically balanced.

ELECTROCHEMICAL CELLS

Electrochemical cells are contained systems in which a redox reaction occurs. There are two types of electrochemical cells, **galvanic cells** (also known as **voltaic cells**), and **electrolytic cells.** Spontaneous reactions occur in galvanic cells, and nonspontaneous reactions in electrolytic cells. Both types contain **electrodes** at which oxidation and reduction occur. For all electrochemical cells, the electrode at which oxidation occurs is called the **anode,** and the electrode where reduction occurs is called the **cathode.**

A. GALVANIC CELLS

A redox reaction occurring in a **galvanic cell** has a negative ΔG and is therefore a **spontaneous reaction.** Galvanic cell reactions supply energy and are used to do work. This energy can be harnessed by placing the oxidation and reduction half-reactions in separate containers called **half-cells.** The half-cells are then connected by an apparatus that allows for the flow of electrons.

A common example of a galvanic cell is the Daniell cell in Figure 11.1.

In the Daniell cell, a zinc bar is placed in an aqueous $ZnSO_4$ solution, and a copper bar is placed in an aqueous $CuSO_4$ solution. The anode of

KAPLAN EXCLUSIVE

A way to remember which electrode is which is: AN OX and a RED CAT. Another easy way to remember this is by the spelling of the words: oxidAtion and reduCtion

MCAT SYNOPSIS

Galvanic cells are commonly used as batteries; to be economically viable, batteries must be spontaneous!

this cell is the zinc bar where $Zn(s)$ is oxidized to $Zn^{2+}(aq)$. The cathode is the copper bar, and it is the site of the reduction of $Cu^{2+}(aq)$ to $Cu(s)$. The half-cell reactions are written as follows:

$$Zn(s) \rightarrow Zn^{2+}(aq) + 2e^- \rightarrow (anode)$$
$$Cu^{2+}(aq) + 2e \rightarrow Cu(s) \rightarrow (cathode)$$

If the two half-cells were not separated, the Cu^{2+} ions would react directly with the zinc bar and no useful electrical work would be obtained. To complete the circuit, the two solutions must be connected. Without connection, the electrons from the zinc oxidation half reaction would not be able to get to the copper ions, thus a wire (or other conductor) is necessary. If only a wire were provided for this electron flow, the reaction would soon cease anyway because an excess negative charge would build up in the solution surrounding the cathode and an excess positive charge would build up in the solution surrounding the anode. This charge gradient is dissipated by the presence of a **salt bridge,** which permits the exchange of cations and anions. The salt bridge contains an inert electrolyte, usually KCl or NH_4NO_3, whose ions will not react with the electrodes or with the ions in solution. At the same time the anions from the salt bridge (e.g., Cl^-) diffuse from the salt bridge of the Daniell cell into the $ZnSO_4$ solution to balance out the charge of the newly created Zn^{2+} ions, the cations of the salt bridge (e.g., K^+) flow into the $CuSO_4$ solution to balance out the charge of the SO_4^{2-} ions left in solution when the Cu^{2+} ions deposit as copper metal.

MCAT FAVORITE

The purpose of the salt bridge is to exchange anions and cations to balance, i.e., dissipate, newly generated charges.

During the course of the reaction, electrons flow from the zinc bar (anode) through the wire and the voltmeter, toward the copper bar (cathode). The anions (Cl^-) flow externally (via the salt bridge) into the $ZnSO_4$, and the cations (K^+) flow into the $CuSO_4$. This flow depletes the salt bridge and, along with the finite quantity of Cu^{2+} in the solution, accounts for the relatively short lifetime of the cell.

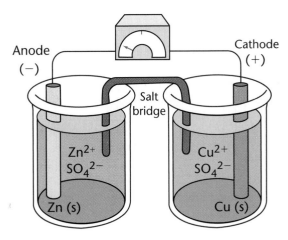

Figure 11.1: Daniell Cell

A **cell diagram** is a shorthand notation representing the reactions in an electrochemical cell. A cell diagram for the Daniell cell is as follows:

$$Zn(s) \mid Zn^{2+}(xM\ SO_4{}^{2-}) \parallel Cu^{2+}(yM\ SO_4{}^{2-}) \mid Cu(s)$$

The following rules are used in constructing a cell diagram:

1. The reactants and products are always listed from left to right in the form:

   anode | anode solution ‖ cathode solution | cathode

2. A single vertical line indicates a phase boundary.

3. A double vertical line indicates the presence of a salt bridge or some other type of barrier.

B. ELECTROLYTIC CELLS

A redox reaction occurring in an **electrolytic cell** has a positive ΔG and is therefore **nonspontaneous.** In **electrolysis,** electrical energy is required to induce reaction. The oxidation and reduction half-reactions are usually placed in one container.

An example of an electrolytic cell, in which molten NaCl is electrolyzed to form Cl_2 (g) and Na (ℓ), is shown in Figure 11.2.

In this cell, Na^+ ions migrate towards the cathode, where they are reduced to Na (ℓ). Similarly, Cl^- ions migrate towards the anode, where they are oxidized to Cl_2 (g). This cell is used in industry as the major means of sodium and chlorine production. Note that sodium is a liquid at the temperature of molten NaCl; it is also less dense than the molten salt, and thus is easily removed as it floats to the top of the reaction vessel.

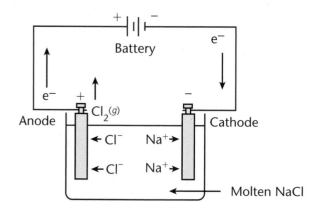

Figure 11.2: Example of an Electrolytic Cell

C. ELECTRODE CHARGE DESIGNATIONS

The anode of an **electrolytic cell** is considered **positive,** because it is attached to the positive pole of the battery and so attracts anions from the solution. The anode of a **galvanic cell,** on the other hand, is considered **negative** because the **spontaneous** oxidation reaction that takes place at the galvanic cell's anode is the original source of that cell's negative charge, i.e., is the source of electrons. In spite of this difference in designating charge, oxidation takes place at the anode in both types of cells, and electrons always flow through the wire from the anode to the cathode.

In a galvanic cell, charge is spontaneously created as electrons are released by the oxidizing species at the anode; because this is the source of electrons, the anode of a galvanic cell is considered the negative electrode.

In an electrolytic cell, electrons are forced through the cathode where they encounter the species that is to be reduced. Here it is the cathode that is providing electrons, and thus the cathode of an electrolytic cell is considered the negative electrode. Alternatively, one can think of the cathode as the electrode attached to the negative pole of the battery (or other power source) used for the electrolysis.

In either case, a simple mnemonic is that the CAThode attracts the CATions. In the Daniell cell, for example, the electrons created at the anode as the zinc oxidizes travel through the wire to the copper half cell where they attract copper (II) cations to the cathode.

One common topic in which this distinction arises is electrophoresis, a technique often used to separate amino acids based on their isoelectronic points, or pIs. The positively charged amino acids, i.e., those that are protonated at the pH of the solution, will migrate toward the cathode; negatively charged amino acids, i.e., those that are deprotonated at the solution pH, migrate instead toward the anode.

REDUCTION POTENTIALS AND THE ELECTROMOTIVE FORCE

A. REDUCTION POTENTIALS

Sometimes when electrolysis is carried out in an aqueous solution, water rather than the solute is oxidized or reduced. For example, if an aqueous solution of NaCl is electrolyzed, water may be reduced at the cathode to

> **MCAT SYNOPSIS**
>
> In an electrolytic cell, the anode is positive and the cathode is negative. In a galvanic cell, the anode is negative and the cathode is positive. However, in both types of cells, reduction occurs at the cathode and oxidation occurs at the anode.

> **TEACHER TIP**
>
> A reduction potential is exactly what it sounds like: It tells us how likely a compound is to be reduced. The higher the value, the more likely it is to be reduced.

produce $H_2(g)$ and OH^- ions, instead of Na^+ being reduced to $Na(s)$, as occurs in the absence of water. The species in a reaction that will be oxidized or reduced can be determined from the **reduction potential** of each species, defined as the tendency of a species to acquire electrons and be reduced. Each species has its own intrinsic reduction potential; the more positive the potential, the greater the specie's tendency to be reduced.

A reduction potential is measured in volts (V) and is defined relative to the **standard hydrogen electrode (SHE),** which is arbitrarily given a potential of 0 volts. **Standard reduction potential, (E°),** is measured under **standard conditions:** 25°C, a 1 M concentration for each ion participating in the reaction, a partial pressure of 1 atm for each gas that is part of the reaction, and metals in their pure state. The relative reactivities of different half-cells can be compared to predict the direction of electron flow. A higher or more positive E° means a greater tendency for reduction to occur, while a lower E° means a greater tendency for oxidation to occur.

Example: Given the following half-reactions and E° values, determine which species would be oxidized and which would be reduced.

$Ag^+ + e \rightarrow Ag\ (s)$ E° = +0.8 V

$Tl^+ + e- \rightarrow Tl\ (s)$ E° = −0.34 V

Solution: Ag+ would be reduced to Ag(s) and Tl(s) would be oxidized to Tl^+, because Ag^+ has the higher E°. Therefore, the reaction equation would be:

$Ag^+ + Tl(s) \rightarrow Tl^+ + Ag(s)$

which is the sum of the two spontaneous half-reactions.

It should be noted that reduction and oxidation are opposite processes. Therefore, in order to obtain the oxidation potential of a given half-reaction, the reduction half-reaction and the sign of the reduction potential are both reversed. For instance, from the example above, the oxidation half reaction and oxidation potential of Tl(s) are:

$Tl(s) \rightarrow Tl^+ + e^-$ E° = +0.34 V

B. THE ELECTROMOTIVE FORCE

Standard reduction potentials are also used to calculate the **standard electromotive force (EMF or E°$_{cell}$)** of a reaction, the difference in potential between two half-cells. The EMF of a reaction is determined by adding the standard reduction potential of the reduced species and the standard oxidation potential of the oxidized species. When adding standard potentials, *do not* multiply by the number of moles oxidized or reduced.

$$\text{EMF} = E°_{red} + E°_{ox} \qquad \text{(Equation 1)}$$

The standard EMF of a galvanic cell is positive, while the standard EMF of an electrolytic cell is negative.

Example: Given that the standard reduction potentials for Sm^{3+} and $[RhCl_6]^{3-}$ are –2.41 V and +0.44 V respectively, calculate the EMF of the following reaction:

$Sm^{3+} + Rh + 6\ Cl^- \rightarrow [RhCl_6]^{3-} + Sm$

Solution: First, determine the oxidation and reduction half-reactions. As written, the Rh is oxidized and the Sm^{3+} is reduced. Thus the Sm^{3+} reduction potential is used as is, while the reverse reaction for Rh, $[RhCl_6]^{3-} \rightarrow Rh + 6\ Cl^-$, applies and the oxidation potential of $[RhCl_6]^{3-}$ must be used. Then, using Equation 1, the EMF can be calculated to be (–2.41 V) + (–0.44 V) = –2.85 V. The cell is thus electrolytic as written. From this result, it is evident that the reaction would proceed spontaneously to the left, in which case the Sm would be oxidized while $[RhCl_6]^{3-}$ would be reduced.

THERMODYNAMICS OF REDOX REACTIONS

A. EMF AND GIBBS FREE ENERGY

The thermodynamic criterion for determining the spontaneity of a reaction is ΔG, Gibbs free energy, the maximum amount of useful work produced by a chemical reaction. In an electrochemical cell, the work done is dependent on the number of coulombs and the energy available. Thus, ΔG and EMF are related as follows:

$$\Delta G = -nFE_{cell} \qquad \text{(Equation 2)}$$

where n is the number of moles of electrons exchanged, F is Faraday's constant, and E_{cell} is the EMF of the cell. **Keep in mind that if Faraday's constant is expressed in coulombs (J/V), then ΔG must be expressed in J, not kJ.**

> **TEACHER TIP**
>
> In this equation we must change the sign of the second value because it is an oxidation potential, the exact opposite of a reduction potential. This equation can also be written as EMF = $E°_{cathode}$ − $E°_{anode}$ (using only reduction potential) and still get the same result.

> **FLASHBACK**
>
> Recall that if ΔG is positive, the reaction is not spontaneous; if ΔG is negative, the reaction is spontaneous.

If the reaction takes place under standard conditions (25°C, 1 atm pressure, and all solutions at 1M concentration), then the ΔG is the standard Gibbs free energy and E_{cell} is the standard cell potential. The above equation then becomes:

$$\Delta G° = -nFE°_{cell} \qquad \text{(Equation 3)}$$

B. THE EFFECT OF CONCENTRATION ON EMF

Thus far, only the calculations for the EMF of cells in unit concentrations (all the ionic species present have a molarity of 1 and all gases are at a pressure of 1 atm) have been discussed. However, concentration does have an effect on the EMF of a cell: EMF varies with the changing concentrations of the species involved. It can also be determined by the use of the **Nernst equation:**

$$E_{cell} = E°_{cell} - (RT/nF)(\ln Q)$$

Q is the reaction quotient for a given reaction. For example, in the following reaction:

$$a A + b B \rightarrow c C + d D$$

the reaction quotient would be:

$$Q = \frac{[C]^c[D]^d}{[A]^a[B]^b}$$

The EMF of a cell can be measured by a **voltmeter.** A **potentiometer** is a kind of voltmeter that draws no current, and gives a more accurate reading of the difference in potential between two electrodes.

C. EMF AND THE EQUILIBRIUM CONSTANT (K_{eq})

For reactions in solution, $\Delta G°$ can be determined in another manner, as follows:

$$\Delta G° = -RT \ln K_{eq} \qquad \text{(Equation 4)}$$

where R is the gas constant 8.314 J/(K•mol), T is the temperature in K, and K_{eq} is the equilibrium constant for the reaction.

If Equations 3 and 4 are combined, then:

$$\Delta G° = -nFE°_{cell} = -RT \ln K_{eq}$$

or simply:

$$nFE°_{cell} = RT \ln K_{eq} \qquad \text{(Equation 5)}$$

If the values for n, T, and K_{eq} are known, then the $E°_{cell}$ for the redox reaction can be readily calculated.

MCAT SYNOPSIS

If $E°_{cell}$ is positive, then ln K is positive. This means that K must be greater than one, and that the equilibrium must lie toward the right, i.e., products are favored.

PRACTICE QUESTIONS

1. An electrolytic cell is filled with water. Which of the following will move toward the cathode of such a cell?

   I. H^+ ions
   II. O^{2-} ions
   III. Electrons

   A. I only
   B. II only
   C. I and III
   D. I, II, and III

2. The anode of a certain galvanic cell is composed of copper. What metal from the data below can be used at the cathode?

Reaction	Reduction Potential
$Hg^{2+} + 2e^- \longrightarrow Hg$	+0.85 V
$Cu^+ + e^- \longrightarrow Cu$	+0.52 V
$Zn^{2+} + 2e^- \longrightarrow Zn$	−0.76 V
$Al^{3+} + 3e^- \longrightarrow Al$	−1.66 V

   A. Hg
   B. Al
   C. Zn
   D. None of the above

3. Considering the following equation, what species acts as an oxidizing agent?

   $3Na(s) + H_3N(aq) \rightarrow Na_3N(s) + H_2(g)$

   A. H^+
   B. H_2N
   C. Na
   D. Na^+

4. How many electrons are involved in the following unbalanced reaction?

   $Cr_2O_7^{2-} + H^+ + e^- \rightarrow 2Cr^{2+} + H_2O$

   A. 2
   B. 8
   C. 12
   D. 16

QUESTIONS 5 AND 6 REFER TO THE FOLLOWING HALF–REACTIONS:

$O_2 + 4H^+ + 4e^- \rightarrow 2H_2O + 1.23$ V (Reaction 1)

$PbO_2 + 4H^+ + 2e^- \rightarrow Pb^{2+} + 2H_2O + 1.46$ V (Reaction 2)

5. If the two half–reactions above combine to form a spontaneous system, what is the net balanced equation of the full reaction?

   A. $2PbO_2 + 4H^+ \rightarrow Pb^{2+} + O_2 + 2H_2O$
   B. $PbO_2 \rightarrow Pb^{2+} + O_2 + 2e^-$
   C. $Pb^{2+} + O_2 + 2H_2O \rightarrow 2PbO_2 + 4H^+$
   D. $Pb^{2+} + O_2 + 2e^- \rightarrow PbO_2$

6. Find the standard potential of the following reaction:

   $Pb^{2+} + O_2 + 2H_2O \rightarrow 2PbO_2 + 4H^+$

   A. +0.23 V
   B. −0.23 V
   C. −1.69 V
   D. +2.69 V

7. A certain electrochemical cell produces elemental sodium from a solution of sodium chloride. How many electrons must be donated by the electric current?

   A. 3
   B. 2
   C. 1
   D. 0

8. Rusting occurs due to the oxidation–reduction reaction of iron with environmental oxygen:

$$4Fe(s) + 3O_2(g) \rightarrow 2Fe_2O_3(s)$$

Some metals, such as copper, are unlikely to react with oxygen. Which of the following best explains this observation?

A. Iron has a more positive reduction potential, making it more likely to donate electrons to oxygen.

B. Iron has a more positive reduction potential, making it more likely to accept electrons from oxygen.

C. Iron has a less positive reduction potential, making it more likely to donate electrons to oxygen.

D. Iron has a less positive reduction potential, making it more likely to accept electrons from oxygen.

9. Lithium aluminum hydride ($LiAlH_4$) is often used in laboratories because of its tendency to donate a hydride ion. Which of the following properties does $LiAlH_4$ exhibit?

A. Strong reducing agent
B. Strong oxidizing agent
C. Strong acid
D. Strong base

10. If the value of $E°_{cell}$ is known, what other data are needed to calculate ΔG?

A. Equilibrium constant
B. Reaction quotient
C. Temperature of the system
D. Number of moles of reactant

11. Which of the following compounds is least likely to be found in the salt bridge of a galvanic cell?

A. NaCl
B. SO_3
C. $MgSO_3$
D. NH_4NO_3

12. What is the oxidation number of chlorine in NaClO?

A. –1
B. 0
C. +1
D. +2

13. The following cell maintains a pH of 7. What is the ratio of the volume of hydrogen produced to the volume of oxygen produced?

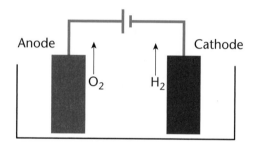

A. 2:1
B. 1:2
C. 1:1
D. 1:4

14. Which of the following is most likely to increase the rate of an electrolytic reaction?

A. Increasing the resistance in the circuit
B. Increasing the volume of electrolyte
C. Increasing the current
D. Increasing the pH

15. The following electronic configurations represent elements in their neutral form. Which element is the strongest oxidizing agent?

A. $1s^2 2s^2 p^6 3s^2 p^6 4s^2$
B. $1s^2 2s^2 p^6 3s^2 p^6 4s^2 3d^5$
C. $1s^2 2s^2 p^6 3s^2 p^6 4s^2 3d^{10} 4p^1$
D. $1s^2 2s^2 p^6 3s^2 p^6 4s^2 3d^5 4p^5$

BALANCING REDOX REACTIONS

Balance the following reaction that takes place in basic solution.

$$ZrO(OH)_2(s) + SO_3^{2-}(aq) \rightleftharpoons Zr(s) + SO_4^{2-}(aq)$$

1) Separate the overall reaction into two half-reactions.

$$ZrO(OH)_2 \rightleftharpoons Zr$$
$$SO_3^{2-} \rightleftharpoons SO_4^{2-}$$

Break the reactions up by looking at atoms other than hydrogen and oxygen.

2) Balance the oxygens in each reaction by adding the necessary number of moles of water to the appropriate side.

$$ZrO(OH)_2 \rightleftharpoons Zr(s) + 3\,H_2O$$
$$H_2O + SO_3^{2-} \rightleftharpoons SO_4^{2-}$$

3) Balance hydrogen by adding the necessary number of H⁺ ions to the appropriate side of each reaction.

$$4\,H^+ + ZrO(OH)_2 \rightleftharpoons Zr + 3\,H_2O$$
$$H_2O + SO_3^{2-} \rightleftharpoons SO_4^{2-} + 2\,H^+$$

4) If the reaction is carried out in basic solution, "neutralize" each equivalent of H⁺ with one equivalent of OH⁻.

$$4\,OH^- + 4\,H^+ + ZrO(OH)_2 \rightleftharpoons Zr + 3\,H_2O + 4\,OH^-$$
$$2\,OH^- + H_2O + SO_3^{2-} \rightleftharpoons SO_4^{2-} + 2\,H^+ + 2\,OH^-$$
$$4\,H_2O + ZrO(OH)_2 \rightleftharpoons Zr + 3\,H_2O + 4\,OH^-$$
$$2\,OH^- + H_2O + SO_3^{2-} \rightleftharpoons SO_4^{2-} + 2\,H_2O$$

Combine each mole of H⁺ and OH⁻ into one mole of water and simplify each reaction.

Remember: *Don't forget to add OH⁻ to each side of both reactions!*

5) Balance the overall charge in each reaction using electrons.

$$4\,e^- + 4\,H_2O + ZrO(OH)_2 \rightleftharpoons Zr + 3\,H_2O + 4\,OH^-$$
$$2\,OH^- + H_2O + SO_3^{2-} \rightleftharpoons SO_4^{2-} + 2\,H_2O + 2\,e^-$$

The top equation has a total charge of 4⁻ on the right from the 4 moles of hydroxide, so 4 electrons need to be added to the left side of the equation. In the bottom equation, there is a total charge of 4⁻ on the left, 2⁻ from the 2 moles of hydroxide, and 2⁻ from the 2 moles of sulfite anion (SO_3^{2-}).

KEY CONCEPTS

Oxidation

Reduction

Balancing electrochemical half-reactions

TAKEAWAYS

Don't fall into the trap of simply balancing mass in these reactions. If oxidation and reduction are occurring, you must go through this procedure to balance the reaction.

THINGS TO WATCH OUT FOR

These kinds of problems can be extremely tedious. You must take extra care to avoid careless addition and subtraction errors!

SIMILAR QUESTIONS

1) Which atom is being oxidized in the original equation? Which is being reduced? Identify the oxidizing and reducing agents.

2) A *disproportionation* is a redox reaction in which the same species is both *oxidized* and *reduced* during the course of the reaction. One such reaction is shown below. Balance the reaction, assuming that it takes place in acidic solution:

$PbSO_4(s) \rightarrow Pb(s) + PbO_2(s) + SO_4^{2-}(aq)$

3) Dentists often use zinc amalgams to make temporary crowns for their patients. It is absolutely vital that they keep the zinc amalgam dry. Any exposure to water would cause pain to the patient and might even crack a tooth. The reaction of zinc metal with water is shown below:

$Zn(s) + H_2O(\ell) \rightarrow Zn^{2+}(aq) + H_2(g)$

Balance this reaction, assuming that it takes place in basic solution. Why would exposure to water cause the crown, and perhaps the tooth, to crack?

Remember: Don't forget to account for all charges in this step, including the charge contributed by molecules other than H^+ and OH^-.

---

6) Multiply each reaction by the necessary integer to ensure that equal numbers of electrons are present in each reaction.

$$4\,e^- + 4\,H_2O + ZrO(OH)_2 \rightleftharpoons Zr + 3\,H_2O + 4\,OH^-$$
$$4\,OH^- + 2\,H_2O + 2\,SO_3^{2-} \rightleftharpoons 2\,SO_4^{2-} + 4\,H_2O + 4\,e^-$$

Here, the lowest common multiple among the four electrons in the top reaction and the two in the bottom is four electrons, so we must multiply everything in the bottom reaction by 2.

---

7) Combine both reactions and simplify by eliminating redundant molecules on each side of the reaction.

$$4\,e^- + 4\,H_2O(\ell) + ZrO(OH)_2(s) + 4\,OH^-(aq) + 2\,H_2O(\ell) + 2\,SO_3^{2-}(aq)$$
$$\rightleftharpoons Zr(s) + 3\,H_2O(\ell) + 4\,OH^-(aq) + 2\,SO_4^{2-}(aq) + 4\,H_2O(\ell) + 4\,e^-$$

$$4\,e^- + 6\,H_2O(\ell) + ZrO(OH)_2(s) + 4\,OH^-(aq) + 2\,SO_3^{2-}(aq)$$
$$\rightleftharpoons Zr(s) + 7\,H_2O(\ell) + 4\,OH^-(aq) + 2\,SO_4^{2-}(aq) + 4\,e^-$$

$$ZrO(OH)_2(s) + 2\,SO_3^{2-}(aq) \rightleftharpoons Zr(s) + 2\,SO_4^{2-}(aq) + H_2O(\ell)$$

Combine common terms on each side of the net reaction.

Eliminate the redundant water molecules, as well as the electrons and excess hydroxide equivalents.

Check to make sure that the reaction is balanced, in terms of both *mass* (number of atoms on each side) and *overall charge*.

*Remember: This last step is **extremely important**. If mass and charge aren't balanced, then you made an error in one of the previous steps.*

ELECTROCHEMICAL CELLS

A galvanic cell is to be constructed using the MnO_4^- | Mn^{2+} ($E°_{red}$ = 1.49 V) and Zn^{2+} | Zn ($E°_{red}$ = –0.76 V) couples placed in an acidic solution. Assume that all potentials given are measured against the standard hydrogen electrode at 298 K and that all reagents are present in 1 M concentration (their standard states). What is the maximum possible work output of this cell per mole of reactant if it is used to run an electric motor for one hour at room temperature (298 K)? During this amount of time, how much Zn metal would be necessary to run the cell, given a current of 5 A?

1) Determine which half-reaction is occurring at the anode and which is occurring at the cathode of the cell.

$MnO_4^-(aq) + 5\ e^- \rightarrow Mn^{2+}(aq)$ $E°_{red}$ = 1.49 V

$Zn^{2+}(aq) + 2\ e^- \rightarrow Zn(s)$ $E°_{red}$ = – 0.76 V

Compare the standard reduction potentials for both reactions. The permanganate reduction potential is greater than the zinc potential, so it would prefer to be reduced and zinc-oxidized. Therefore, the zinc is being oxidized at the anode and the manganese is being reduced at the cathode.

Remember: **O**xidation occurs at the **a**node. *(Hint: they both start with a vowel.)*

2) Write a balanced reaction for the cell.

$MnO_4^- \rightarrow Mn^{2+}$

$8\ H^+ + MnO_4^- \rightarrow Mn^{2+} + 4\ H_2O$

$8\ H^+ + MnO_4^- + 5\ e^- \rightarrow Mn^{2+} + 4\ H_2O$

$Zn \rightarrow Zn^{2+} + 2\ e^-$

$16\ H^+ + 2\ MnO_4^- + 10\ e^- \rightarrow 2\ Mn^{2+} + 8\ H_2O$
$5\ Zn \rightarrow 5\ Zn^{2+} + 10\ e^-$

$16\ H^+(aq) + 2\ MnO_4^-(aq) + 5\ Zn(s) \rightarrow 2\ Mn^{2+}(aq)$
$+ 5\ Zn^{2+}(aq) + 8\ H_2O(\ell)$

Balance the reactions one at a time.

Balance oxygen with water, and then hydrogen with acid (H^+).

Balance overall charge with electrons.

This one is easy; all you have to do is balance electrons.

SIMILAR QUESTIONS

1) How could you alter the cell setup to reverse the direction of current flow?

2) What would the cell potential be if Mn^{2+} and Zn^{2+} were at 2 M concentration and the MnO_4^- concentration remained at 1 M? Would changing the amount of zinc metal present in the cell change this potential? Why or why not?

3) Compute the minimum mass of potassium permanganate ($KMnO_4$) necessary to run the cell for the same amount of time as specified above.

To combine both equations, we need to multiply each by the appropriate integer to get to the lowest common multiple of 2 and 5, which is 10.

Now add the equations up to get the balanced cell equation, and you're golden.

---

3) Calculate the standard potential for the cell as a whole.

$$E^\circ_{cell} = 1.49 \text{ V} - (-0.76 \text{ V}) = 2.25 \text{ V}$$

Use the equation $E^\circ_{cell} = E^\circ_{cathode} - E^\circ_{anode}$. Because the standard potential for the cell is positive, this confirms that this is a galvanic (or voltaic) cell—once you hook up the electrodes and immerse them in the designated solutions, current will start to flow on its own.

---

4) Compute ΔG° for the cell.

$$\Delta G^\circ = -(10 \text{ mol e}^-)(10^5 \text{ C mol}^{-1})(2.25 \text{ V}) = -2.25 \times 10^6 \text{ J mol}^{-1}$$
$$\Rightarrow \text{maximum work output per mole of reactant} = 2.25 \times 10^3 \text{ KJ mol}^{-1}$$

Use the equation $\Delta G^\circ = -nFE^\circ_{cell}$. The upper limit on the amount of work a reaction can perform is the same thing as ΔG°.

· **Remember:** *Power is work over time, and 1 h = 3,600 s ≈ 4 × 10³ s.*

---

5) Use Faraday's constant to determine the number of moles of electrons transferred and to do any stoichiometric calculations.

$$4 \times 10^3 \text{ s} (5 \text{ C s}^{-1})(10^{-5} \text{ mol e}^- \text{ C}^{-1}) = 0.2 \text{ mol e}^-$$
$$0.2 \text{ mol e}^- \left(\frac{1 \text{ mol Zn}}{2 \text{ mol e}^-} \right) = 0.1 \text{ mol Zn} \times (70 \text{ g mol}^{-1}) = 7 \text{ g Zn}$$

Remember that current is charge passing though a point per unit of time, and Faraday's constant tells us how many coulombs of charge make up one mole of electrons.

The balanced half-reaction is used to determine the necessary mole ratio.

THE NERNST EQUATION

A galvanic cell is created at 298 K using the following net reaction:

$$2 H^+(aq) + Ca(s) \rightarrow Ca^{2+}(aq) + H_2(g)$$

Fluoride anions are added to the anode section of the cell only until precipitation is observed. Right at this point, the concentration of fluoride is 1.4×10^{-2} M, the pH is measured to be 0, the pressure of hydrogen gas is 1 atm, and the measured cell voltage is 2.96 V. Given this information, compute the K_{sp} of CaF_2 at 298 K.

Additional information:

$$R = 8.314 \text{ J (mol K)}^{-1}$$
$$Ca^{2+}(aq) + 2 e^- \rightarrow Ca(s) \quad E^\circ_{red} = -2.76 \text{ V}$$
$$2 H^+(aq) + 2 e^- \rightarrow H_2(g) \quad E^\circ_{red} = 0.00 \text{ V}$$
$$F = 96\,485 \text{ C mol}^{-1}$$

1) Write down the expression for the K_{sp}.

$$CaF_2(s) \rightarrow Ca^{2+}(aq) + 2 F^-(aq)$$
$$K_{eq} = [Ca^{2+}][F^-]^2 = K_{sp}$$

The first part of this problem begins as with any other solubility problem: we need to right down the expression for the K_{sp}.

We're given the concentration of fluoride right when precipitation begins, so we can plug that right into the K_{sp} expression above. All we need is the concentration of Ca^{2+} ions, and we're golden.

---

2) Separate the net cell reaction into half reactions, and find E°_{cell}.

$$Ca(s) \rightarrow Ca^{2+}(aq) + 2 e^- \qquad E^\circ = 2.76 \text{ V}$$
$$2 H^+(aq) + 2 e^- \rightarrow H_{2\,(g)} \qquad E^\circ = 0 \text{ V}$$
NET: $2 H^+(aq) + Ca(s) \rightarrow Ca^{2+}(aq) + H_2(g)$
$$E^\circ_{cell} = 0.00 \text{ V} - (-2.76 \text{ V}) = 2.76 \text{ V}$$

Now we know what the standard potential for the cell is. Our only problem is that, in the situation given in the problem, we are in *nonstandard conditions*, because the concentration of fluoride is not 1 M.

Remember: *Remember that $E^\circ_{cell} = E^\circ_{cathode} - E^\circ_{anode}$.*

KEY CONCEPTS

Oxidation and reduction

Electrochemistry

Equilibrium

Solubility equilibria

Nernst equation

$E^\circ_{cell} = E^\circ_{cathode} - E^\circ_{anode}$ (V)

TAKEAWAYS

Remember what the superscript "°" means: that a reaction is at standard conditions. This means that reagents are at 1 M or 1 atm, depending on their phase. If you are working with an electrochemical cell where the concentrations are nonstandard, you must apply the Nernst equation to determine what the effect on the cell voltage will be.

THINGS TO WATCH OUT FOR

Don't forget to check signs during problems that require computation. When logarithms and exponents are involved, one small sign error can have a massive impact on the answer!

SIMILAR QUESTIONS

1) If the K_{sp} of copper(I) bromide is 4.2×10^{-8}, compute the concentration of bromide necessary to cause precipitation in an electrochemical cell with the Cu|Cu$^+$ and H$^+$|H$_2$ couples. Assume the conditions are as follows: $E°_{red}$ of Cu$^+$ = 0.521 V; pH = 0; $P_{H2 (g)}$ = 1 atm; T = 298 K; E_{cell} when precipitation begins = 0.82 V.

2) Compute the equilibrium constant at 298 K for the cell comprised of the Zn^{2+} | Zn ($E_{red}°$ = −0.76 V) and MnO$_4^-$ | Mn^{2+} ($E_{red}°$ = 1.49 V) couples. Given this number, comment on the oxidizing ability of the permanganate anion.

3) A buffer solution is prepared that is 0.15 M in acetic acid and 0.05 M in sodium acetate. If oxidation is occuring at a platinum wire with 1 atm of H$_2$ bubbling over it that is submerged in the buffer solution, and the wire is connected to a standard Cu^{2+} | Cu half cell ($E_{red}°$ = 0.34 V), the measured cell voltage is 0.592 V. Based on this information, compute the pK_a of acetic acid.

3) Apply the Nernst equation.

$$E = E° - \frac{RT}{nF} \ln Q$$

$$Q = \frac{[Ca^{2+}]Ph_{2 (g)}}{[H^+]^2} = [Ca^{2+}]$$

$$E = E° - \frac{RT}{nF} \ln [Ca^{2+}]$$

$$E - E° = -\frac{RT}{nF} \ln [Ca^{2+}]$$

$$-\left(\frac{nF}{RT}\right)(E - E°) = \ln [Ca^{2+}]$$

$$-\left(\frac{2 \times 10^5}{8 \times 300}\right)(2.96 - 2.76) = \ln [Ca^{2+}]$$

$$-\left(\frac{2 \times 10^5}{8 \times 300}\right)2 \times 10^{-1} = \ln [Ca^{2+}]$$

$$-20 = \ln [Ca^{2+}]$$

$$-20 = 2.3 \log[Ca^{2+}]$$

$$-8 = \log[Ca^{2+}]$$

$$[Ca^{2+}] = 10^{-8}$$

The reaction quotient (Q) in this case is of the cell reaction. Recall that the pressure of hydrogen gas is 1 atmosphere. As the pH = 0, [H$^+$] = 10^{-0} = 1.0 M.

Rearrange the Nernst equation to solve for ln[Ca^{2+}].

Start plugging in numbers. Here, n = 2 mol e$^-$, from the cell equation; F = 96,485 ≈ 100,000 C mol^{-1}; T = 298 ≈ 300 K; R ≈ 8 J (mol K)$^{-1}$; and 2.96 − 2.76 = 0.2 = 2×10^{-1} V.

Here, assume −16.7 ≈ −20.

Recall that ln x = 2.3 log x. Assume that 2.3 ≈ 2.5 so that $-\frac{20}{2.5} \approx -8$.

Remember: *When you absolutely must do computation, choose numbers that are easy to work with.*

4) Plug the concentrations into the K_{sp} expression and solve.

$$K_{sp} = [Ca^{2+}][F^-]^2$$
$$K_{sp} = (10^{-8})(10^{-2})^2 = 10^{-12}$$

The "actual" value for the K_{sp} is 3.9×10^{-11}, so we are quite close.

PART II
PRACTICE SECTIONS

INSTRUCTIONS FOR TAKING THE PRACTICE SECTIONS

Before taking each Practice Section, find a quiet place where you can work uninterrupted. Take a maximum of 70 minutes per section (52 questions) to get accustomed to the length and scope.

Keep in mind that the actual MCAT will not feature a section made up of General Chemistry questions alone, but rather a Physical Sciences section made up of both General Chemistry and Physics questions. Use the following three sections to hone your General Chemistry skills.

Good luck!

PRACTICE SECTION 1

Time—70 minutes

QUESTIONS 1–52

Directions: Most of the questions in the following General Chemistry Practice Section are organized into groups, with a descriptive passage preceding each group of questions. Study the passage, then select the single-best answer to the question in each group. Some of the questions are not based on a descriptive passage; you must also select the best answer to these questions. If you are unsure of the best answer, eliminate the choices that you know are incorrect, then select an answer from the choices that remain.

Period	1 IA 1A	2 IIA 2A											13 IIIA 3A	14 IVA 4A	15 VA 5A	16 VIA 6A	17 VIIA 7A	18 vIIIA 8A
1	1 H 1.008																	2 He 4.003
2	3 Li 6.941	4 Be 9.012											5 B 10.81	6 C 12.01	7 N 14.01	8 O 16.00	9 F 19.00	10 Ne 20.18
3	11 Na 22.99	12 Mg 24.31	3 IIIB 3B	4 IVB 4B	5 VB 5B	6 VIB 6B	7 VIIB 7B	8 ------- VIII ----- --	9	10 8 -------	11 IB 1B	12 IIB 2B	13 Al 26.98	14 Si 28.09	15 P 30.97	16 S 32.07	17 Cl 35.45	18 Ar 39.95
4	19 K 39.10	20 Ca 40.08	21 Sc 44.96	22 Ti 47.88	23 V 50.94	24 Cr 52.00	25 Mn 54.94	26 Fe 55.85	27 Co 58.47	28 Ni 58.69	29 Cu 63.55	30 Zn 65.39	31 Ga 69.72	32 Ge 72.59	33 As 74.92	34 Se 78.96	35 Br 79.90	36 Kr 83.80
5	37 Rb 85.47	38 Sr 87.62	39 Y 88.91	40 Zr 91.22	41 Nb 92.91	42 Mo 95.94	43 Tc (98)	44 Ru 101.1	45 Rh 102.9	46 Pd 106.4	47 Ag 107.9	48 Cd 112.4	49 In 114.8	50 Sn 118.7	51 Sb 121.8	52 Te 127.6	53 I 126.9	54 Xe 131.3
6	55 Cs 132.9	56 Ba 137.3	57 La* 138.9	72 Hf 178.5	73 Ta 180.9	74 W 183.9	75 Re 186.2	76 Os 190.2	77 Ir 190.2	78 Pt 195.1	79 Au 197.0	80 Hg 200.5	81 Tl 204.4	82 Pb 207.2	83 Bi 209.0	84 Po (210)	85 At (210)	86 Rn (222)
7	87 Fr (223)	88 Ra (226)	89 Ac~ (227)	104 Rf (257)	105 Db (260)	106 Sg (263)	107 Bh (262)	108 Hs (265)	109 Mt (266)	110 --- ()	111 --- ()	112 --- ()		114 ()		116 ()		118 ()

	58 Ce 140.1	59 Pr 140.9	60 Nd 144.2	61 Pm (147)	62 Sm 150.4	63 Eu 152.0	64 Gd 157.3	65 Tb 158.9	66 Dy 162.5	67 Ho 164.9	68 Er 167.3	69 Tm 168.9	70 Yb 173.0	71 Lu 175.0
Lanthanide Series*														

	90 Th 232.0	91 Pa (231)	92 U (238)	93 Np (237)	94 Pu (242)	95 Am (243)	96 Cm (247)	97 Bk (247)	98 Cf (249)	99 Es (254)	100 Fm (253)	101 Md (256)	102 No (254)	103 Lr (257)
Actinide Series~														

PASSAGE I (QUESTIONS 1–9)

Acid rain is a meteorological phenomenon that is defined as any type of precipitation that is unusually acidic. Rain is naturally slightly acidic (pH = 5.2) due to the reaction of water with environmental CO_2 gas to produce carbonic acid. Experts agree that it is mainly a result of pollution, particularly sulfur and nitrogen compounds that react in the atmosphere to produce acids. These reactions are shown below:

$$SO_2 + OH\cdot \rightarrow HOSO_2\cdot$$
$$HOSO_2\cdot + O_2 \rightarrow HO_2\cdot + SO_3$$
$$SO_3 + H_2O \rightarrow H_2SO_4$$
$$NO_2 + OH\cdot \rightarrow HNO_3$$

A college chemistry student was studying outside one day, sipping on a glass of purified water with a pH of 7, when a sudden rainstorm occurred. Wanting to protect his books, he ran inside with them, leaving the glass out on the ledge of his deck. While studying inside, he reviewed the section on acids and bases and decided to run some tests on the glass of water outside, which had collected approximately 100 mL of rainwater mixed with 300 mL of purified water.

1. The acidity of rain is based on the acidity of the contaminating pollutants. Would H_2SO_4 or HNO_3 produce a more acidic rain?

   A. H_2SO_4, because it has a lower pK_a.
   B. HNO_3, because it has a lower pK_a.
   C. H_2SO_4, because it has a greater pK_a.
   D. HNO_3, because it has a greater pK_a.

2. What is the approximate concentration of H^+ in normal rain due to the reaction between $CO_{2(g)}$ and $H_2O_{(l)}$?

   A. 8×10^{-3} M
   B. 6×10^{-5} M
   C. 7×10^{-6} M
   D. 2×10^{-7} M

3. Under which of the following classifications of "acid" does H_2SO_4 fall?

   I. Arrhenius
   II. Brønsted-Lowry
   III. Lewis

   A. I only
   B. II only
   C. II and III only
   D. I, II, and III

4. Suppose a few drops of acid rain fell on an open cut in the student's hand. Would the bicarbonate (HCO_3^-) that exists in blood have any effect?

   A. Yes, bicarbonate will buffer by accepting a H^+ ion.
   B. Yes, bicarbonate will buffer by donating a H^+ ion.
   C. No, bicarbonate does not act as a buffer.
   D. There is not enough information in the passage to determine the correct answer.

5. If the rainwater that mixed with the pure water had original concentrations of $[H_2SO_4]$ = 2×10^{-3} M, $[HNO_3]$ = 3.2×10^{-3} M, what is the approximate final pH of the glass of water?

   A. 1.2
   B. 2.8
   C. 3.4
   D. 4.6

6. Which of the following is an incorrect pair of an acid and its conjugate base?

   A. $H_2SO_4 : HSO_4^-$
   B. $CH_3COOH : CH_3COO^-$
   C. $H_3O^+ : H_2O$
   D. $H_2CO_3 : CO_2$

7. With which of the following statements would the student most likely NOT agree?

A. Acid rain has increased in frequency and intensity over the past 150 years.

B. Radicals play an integral role in the development of acid rain.

C. Acid rain lessens the conductive capabilities of water.

D. Acid rain is dangerous to the environment even though rain is naturally acidic.

QUESTIONS 8–9 ARE BASED ON THE FOLLOWING TITRATION CURVE SHOWN BELOW:

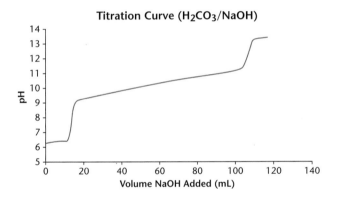

8. What is the approximate ratio of $pK_{a1} : pK_{a2}$ for H_2CO_3?

A. 9.0 : 13.0

B. 7.8 : 12.0

C. 6.3 : 10.3

D. 6.0 : 11.1

9. What is the approximate ratio of equivalence points for H_2CO_3?

A. 9.0 : 13.0

B. 7.8 : 12.0

C. 6.3 : 10.3

D. 6.0 : 11.1

PASSAGE II (QUESTIONS 10–17)

The specific heat of a substance, c, measures the amount of heat required to raise the temperature of the mass of substance by a specific number of degrees. In certain cases, the chemical literature reports specific heat in terms of moles. Specific heat differs from heat capacity, a measurement of the amount of heat required to change the temperature of an object by a specific number of degrees.

In SI units, specific heat indicates the number of joules of heat needed to raise the temperature of 1 gram of the substance by 1 degree Kelvin. The specific heat of water reported in the chemical literature is 4.184 $Jg^{-1}K^{-1}$. Specific heat can be measured by a calorimeter, a device that insulates a sample from atmospheric conditions in order to measure the change in the sample material's temperature over a set interval.

A student used a coffee cup calorimeter to compare the specific heat of water to the specific heat of a commercial fruit punch. The punch is made from a mixture of sugar water and powder flavoring. The student's coffee cup calorimeter used a stack of two foam coffee cups and a thermometer, which the student stuck through a hole in a plastic lid covering the top cup in the stack. Such calorimeters are inexpensive and accurate experimental substitutes for industrial bomb calorimeters, which hold samples at constant volume to measure water temperature changes under high-pressure conditions.

To calibrate the calorimeter, the student combined known quantities of hot and cold water in the coffee cup until the thermometer read a steady temperature, as described in Table 1.

	Hot Water	Cold Water
Volume	100 mL	100 mL
Start Temp	90°C	20°C
End Temp	54°C	54°C

Table 2 summarizes the specific heat data the student collected for the water and the fruit punch using the calibrated coffee cup setup.

Trial	1	2	3
Water (mL)	200 mL	200 mL	200 mL
Punch (g)	0 g	0 g	4 g
Sugar (g)	0 g	16 g	16 g
Start Temp	20.5°C	20.5°C	21°C
End Temp	89°C	91.5°C	91°C

10. Which of the following values reports the molar specific heat of water from the chemical literature?

A. 4.184 $Jmol^{-1}K^{-1}$
B. 75.31 $Jmol^{-1}K^{-1}$
C. 4184 $Jmol^{-1}K^{-1}$
D. 75310 $Jmol^{-1}K^{-1}$

11. What measurement is also an intrinsic property of fruit punch?

A. Mass
B. Heat
C. Enthalpy
D. Viscosity

12. What is the heat capacity of the student's coffee cup calorimeter?

A. 4.184 J/°C
B. 24.6 J/°C
C. 861 J/°C
D. 0.0246 J/°C

13. Suppose the student breaks his glass alcohol thermometer in the lab. The lab instructor's only available replacement is a mercury thermometer. How would this change to the experimental set-up affect the student's measurements?

A. The calorimeter would measure a higher specific heat.
B. The calorimeter would measure a lower specific heat.
C. The thermometer would give a less-precise specific heat measurement.
D. There would be no change to the specific heat measurement.

14. Which of the following rationales best explains why the student calibrated the coffee cup calorimeter before the experiment?

A. The coffee cup calorimeter can absorb heat.
B. The coffee cup calorimeter does not dry between uses.
C. The coffee cup calorimeter's thermometer does not produce precise values.
D. The coffee cup calorimeter contents do not always reach equilibrium.

15. Suppose the student decided to compare his sugar water measurements to those from a salt water sample, in which 16 g NaCl replace the 16 g table sugar in Trial 2. How would the specific heat of this salt water differ from that of sugar water?

   A. The calorimeter would measure a lower specific heat.
   B. The calorimeter would measure a higher specific heat.
   C. The calorimeter would measure the same specific heat.
   D. The calorimeter would decompose.

16. Which of the following experimental quantities must remain constant in Trial 1 in order for the student to obtain a specific heat for water close to the literature value?

   I. Pressure
   II. Mass
   III. Heat

   A. I only
   B. I and III only
   C. II and III only
   D. I, II, and III

17. For which of the following laboratory measurements would a bomb calorimeter be more useful than a coffee cup calorimeter?

   A. To measure the specific heat of salt water
   B. To measure the specific heat of ethanol
   C. To measure the specific heat of water vapor
   D. To measure the specific heat of copper

QUESTIONS 18–21 ARE NOT BASED ON A DESCRIPTIVE PASSAGE.

18. Given the balanced equation, $Mg(s) + 2HCl(aq) \rightarrow MgCl_2(aq) + H_2(g)$, how many liters of hydrogen gas is produced at STP if 3 moles HCl are reacted with excess magnesium?

   A. 1.2 L
   B. 33.6 L
   C. 2.4 L
   D. 44.8 L

19. Increasing the temperature of a system at equilibrium favors the

   A. exothermic reaction, decreasing its rate.
   B. exothermic reaction, increasing its rate.
   C. endothermic reaction, increasing its rate.
   D. endothermic reaction, decreasing its rate.

20. Which type of radiation has neither mass nor charge?

   A. Alpha
   B. Beta
   C. Gamma
   D. Delta

21. Iron rusts more easily than aluminum or zinc because the latter two

   A. form self-protective oxides.
   B. form extremely reactive oxides.
   C. are better reducing agents.
   D. are good oxidizing agents.

PASSAGE III (QUESTIONS 22–29)

Product BD can be prepared by the following reaction mechanism, which is known to exhibit first-order kinetics with respect to each of the reactants:

1. $AB(g) + C(g) \rightleftharpoons A(g) + BC(aq)$(fast)
2. $BC(aq) + D(aq) + heat \rightleftharpoons BCD(aq)$ (slow)
3. $BCD(aq) + heat \rightleftharpoons C(aq) + BD(aq) +$ heat(fast)

To determine the effect of heat on the overall reaction, a scientist mixed one equivalent each of compounds AB, C, and D with excess water in identical reaction flasks at five different temperatures. The scientist then recorded the rate of formation of the product at each temperature, as well as the final concentration of that product when the reaction reached equilibrium, shown in Table 1:

Temperature	Rate of Formation of BD	[BD] at Equilibrium
40°C	6.5 mmol/hr	37 mM
80°C	18.1 mmol/hr	965 mM
100°C	24.9 mmol/hr	1.16 M
120°C	31.2 mmol/hr	1.19 M
150°C	37.5 mmol/hr	1.21 M

The scientist ran a second experiment in which she omitted the equivalent of Compound C from the reaction mixture. The results of this second experiment are shown in Table 2:

Temperature	Rate of Formation of BD	[BD] at Equilibrium
40°C	0.02 mmol/hr	37 mM
80°C	0.13 mmol/hr	965 mM
100°C	0.47 mmol/hr	1.16 M
120°C	1.23 mmol/hr	1.19 M
150°C	29.3 mmol/hr	1.21 M

22. Compound C's most likely role in this reaction is to

A. donate an electron to Compound B.
B. accept an electron from Compound B.
C. decrease the amount of energy required for Compound D to bind with Compound B.
D. decrease the amount of energy required for Compound A to dissociate from Compound B.

23. Which of the following compounds could the scientist add to the initial reaction mixture to increase the yield of product BD?

A. Compound A
B. Compound B
C. Compound C
D. Compound D

24. Which of the following graphs best demonstrates the effect of temperature on the equilibrium constant of the reaction in the passage?

A.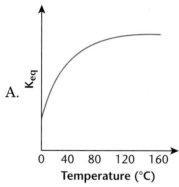

B.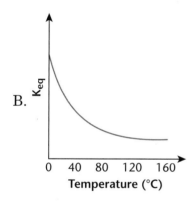

C.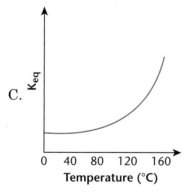

D.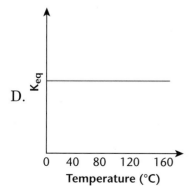

25. The scientist runs a third experiment in which she adds two equivalents of aqueous compound A to one equivalent each of compound BC and compound D at 80°C. What is the expected rate of formation of product BD under these conditions?

A. 9.1 mmol/hr
B. 18.1 mmol/hr
C. 36.2 mmol/hr
D. 54.3 mmol/hr

26. If no catalyst is present, what is the approximate minimum temperature range in which the reaction in the passage would immediately reach its activation energy?

A. 40–80°C
B. 80–100°C
C. 100–120°C
D. 120–150°C

27. What reaction type best describes step 1 of the reaction mechanism in the passage?

A. Double replacement
B. Single replacement
C. Combination
D. Decomposition

28. What step of the reaction mechanism from the passage would be affected most by a change in pressure?

A. Step 1
B. Step 2
C. Step 3
D. All steps to a roughly equal extent

29. Which of the following statements must be true for the overall reaction in the passage?

   I. $\Delta H > 0$
  II. $\Delta G > 0$
 III. $\Delta S < 0$

A. I only
B. III only
C. I and II only
D. I, II, and III

PASSAGE IV (QUESTIONS 30–36)

A few years before Dmitri Mendeleev published the first rendition of the modern periodic table, the English chemist John Newlands suggested the concept of periodicity when he arranged all of the then-known elements by increasing atomic weights and found that every eighth element exhibited similar properties. He dubbed his principle the "Law of Octaves" and created a chart in which the elements would be organized into groups of seven. In this chart (below), the eighth element would appear immediately to the right of the previous element that shares its properties:

H	F	Cl	Co/Ni	Br	Pd	I	Pt/Ir
Li	Na	K	Cu	Rb	Ag	Cs	Tl
G	Mg	Ca	Zn	Sr	Cd	Ba/V	Pb
B	Al	Cr	Y	Ce/Le	U	Ta	Th
C	Si	Ti	In	Zn	Sn	W	Hg
N	P	Mn	As	Di/Mo	Sb	Nb	Bi
O	S	Fe	Se	Ro/Ru	Te	Au	Os

Newlands's discovery was initially dismissed as a coincidence. Soon afterward, Mendeleev created a more elaborate table that was eventually refined into the version that is common today. This table also arranged the elements by molecular weight, but refuted the idea of octaves. It was capable of accommodating the s-block (groups 1A and 2A), the p-block (groups 3A to 8A), the d-block (transition metals), and the f-block (lanthanoids and actinoids). In anticipation of the discovery of more elements, Mendeleev left several empty spaces in the table; for instance, he predicted the discovery of two elements with mass between 65 and 75 amu and a third element with mass between 40 and 50 amu.

30. Several of the atomic mass calculations were inaccurate during the time that periodicity was first discovered. Which of the following pairs of elements were arranged incorrectly by mass on Newlands's table?

A. Gold and platinum
B. Manganese and iron
C. Yttrium and indium
D. Tantalum and tungsten

31. Which of the following most strongly discredits the accuracy of the law of octaves?

A. The discovery of all of the naturally occurring elements in the s-block and the p-block.
B. The discovery of most of the naturally occurring elements in the d-block and the f-block.
C. J. J. Thomson's discovery of the electron.
D. Ernest Rutherford's discovery of the nucleus.

32. Mendeleev's table was modified several times after its initial publication. Which of the following findings did NOT require modification of the existing entries in the table?

   I. A unique element is characterized by a specific number of protons.
  II. Electrons are arranged in orbitals and energy levels.
 III. The atomic mass of Gallium is approximately 70 amu.

A. II only
B. III only
C. II and III only
D. I, II, and III

33. Assuming that all known elements at the time were accounted for in Newland's table of elements, which of the following had not been discovered when Newlands published his table?

A. f-block elements
B. Halogens
C. Metalloids
D. Noble gases

34. Mendeleev predicted the existence of an element with atomic mass of 44. If his prediction were correct, which of the following properties would it exhibit?

A. Its atomic radius would be larger than calcium's atomic radius.
B. Its ionic radius would be larger than calcium's atomic radius.
C. It would lose an electron less readily than calcium would.
D. It would accept an electron less readily than calcium would.

35. What element on Newlands's table had the largest atomic radius?

A. Uranium
B. Cesium
C. Bismuth
D. Osmium

36. Which of the following, if true, would most strengthen the claim that Newlands should be credited as the inventor of the modern periodic table?

A. Although most scientists dismissed Newlands's theory, it was widely accepted within his home country of England.
B. Mendeleev approved of Newlands's work upon reading about it a few years after he formulated his own periodic table.
C. Mendeleev created his version of the periodic table in an attempt to refute Newlands's theory.
D. Newlands created a refined version of his system that was similar to Mendeleev's table, but failed to publish it before Mendeleev.

PASSAGE V (QUESTIONS 37–44)

A student inserts a sliding divider into a simple cylinder to perform a series of three experiments with an unknown gas. The gas exhibits ideal behavior. Before each experiment, the divider is reset so that $V_1 = V_2$ and the contents are at STP. The total volume of the cylinder is 2 L. The student's cylinder apparatus is illustrated below:

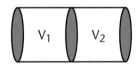

Experiment 1
The student increases the temperature of the gas in V_1 to 45°C while keeping the temperature of V_2 constant.

Experiment 2
The student uses mechanical force to move the central divider in the cylinder such that $3V_1 = V_2$. The temperature of the gas and the cylinder remains constant throughout this experiment.

Experiment 3

The student releases half of the molar contents of V_2, and does not change the molar contents of V_1.

While these experiments are being performed in near-ideal conditions (can be assumed to be ideal), an equation was derived in 1873 by Johannes van der Waals to account for the nonideal behavior of gases:

$$\left(p + \frac{a}{V^2}\right)(V - b) = kT$$

37. In Experiment 1, what is the final volume of 1 mol of gas in V_1?

   A. 164R L
   B. 318R L
   C. 358R L
   D. 403R L

38. Which of the following graphs most accurately illustrates the relationship between volume (V) and temperature (T) in experiment 1, assuming isobaric conditions?

A.
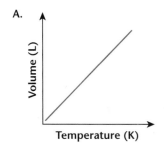

B.
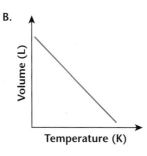

C.
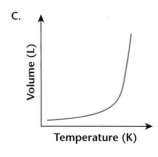

D.
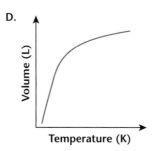

39. In experiment 2, what is the final pressure of the gas with volume V_1?

   A. 0.5 atm
   B. 1.5 atm
   C. 2 atm
   D. 3 atm

40. In the van der Waals equation for nonideal gas behavior, "a" corrects for

   A. intermolecular repulsive forces.
   B. the volume of the molecules themselves.
   C. minute changes in atmospheric pressures.
   D. intermolecular attractive forces.

41. What is the temperature of 64 g of pure O_2 gas in a 3 atm, 2L environment?

   A. 1.5/R K
   B. 2/R K
   C. 3/R K
   D. 6/R K

42. The student removes the partition, creating a cylinder with V = 2L. If there are 0.5 mol CO_2(g), 1.5 mol NO(g), and 1 mol Cl_2(g), in the cylinder, what is the partial pressure of the NO(g) at 300 K?

   A. 115R atm
   B. 225R atm
   C. 375R atm
   D. 450R atm

43. Under which of the following conditions do the contents of V_1 behave most like an ideal gas?

   A. High temperature, low pressure
   B. Low volume, high pressure
   C. Low temperature, high volume
   D. Low temperature, high pressure

44. Which of the following is the most likely result of experiment 3 after re-equilibration with the new molar concentrations?

A. V_1 will expand and V_2 will shrink.
B. P_2 will be greater than P_1.
C. Neither V nor P will change because they are unrelated to molar concentration.
D. P_1 will be greater than P_2.

PASSAGE VI (QUESTIONS 45–52)

Patients often use antacids to counteract potential adverse effects caused by an excess of stomach acid. Most antacids are weak bases whose primary function is to neutralize the hydrochloric acid in the stomach. Because of their simplicity, a wide variety of such drugs is available on the market; however, some are more effective than others. The drug typically reacts with the antacid to produce a conjugate acid and a conjugate base, as in the following examples:

Reaction 1

$Mg(OH)_2(s) + HCl(aq) \rightarrow MgCl_2(aq) + H_2O(l)$

Reaction 2

$Al_2(CO_3)_3(s) + 6HCl(aq) \rightarrow 2AlCl_3(aq) + 3H_2CO_3(aq)$

A student attempted to test the efficacy of various antacids by adding 1 gram of each drug to a beaker containing 100 mL of 0.1 M HCl. He noticed that stronger antacids tend to leave larger precipitates, so he determined that the strength of an antacid could be estimated by measuring the mass of the precipitate after complete neutralization and comparing it with the molecular weight of the reactant. His results were fairly accurate for magnesium salts, aluminum salts, and calcium salts (Group A); however, they disagreed with published results for sodium salts and potassium salts (Group B).

After inspecting the student's experimental setup, the professor pointed out a flaw in the student's reasoning. The student then decided to redesign his experiment; in the second setup, he chemically combined various quantities of antacid along with a standard amount of HCl and measured the pH of the resulting solutions. This time, he determined that an HCl sample was completely neutralized when its pH was equal to 7. The "overall efficacy" of each antacid was quantified as the number of moles of HCl that can be neutralized by one gram of antacid.

45. Which of the following does NOT describe reaction 1?

A. Double-displacement reaction
B. Neutralization reaction
C. Oxidation-reduction reaction
D. Acid-base reaction

46. What is the approximate percent composition of the cation in the conjugate base of the acid from reaction 1?

A. 10%
B. 25%
C. 75%
D. 90%

47. If the student tested each of the following antacids, which would yield the greatest overall efficacy?

A. $Al_2(CO_3)_3$
B. $Al(OH)_3$
C. $Al(HCO_3)_3$
D. $AlPO_4$

48. Which of the following is true about $NaHCO_3$ in the following reaction?

$$NaHCO_3(s) + HCl(aq) \rightarrow NaCl(aq) + H_2CO_3(aq)$$

A. Because one of the products of the reaction is an acid, $NaHCO_3$ does not function as an antacid.

B. Because one of the products of the reaction is a weaker acid than HCl, $NaHCO_3$ is capable of raising the pH of the stomach but cannot neutralize the acid completely.

C. Because H_2CO_3 decomposes into $H_2O(l)$ and $CO_2(g)$, $NaHCO_3$ is an effective antacid.

D. Because H_2CO_3 decomposes into $H_2O(l)$ and $CO_2(g)$, $NaHCO_3$ is capable of raising the pH of the stomach but cannot neutralize the acid completely.

49. Antacid AX reacts with HCl to yield a mixture with a pH of 5.4 according to the equation below. What is the limiting reagent?

$$AX(s) + HCl(aq) \rightarrow ACl(aq) + HX(aq)$$

A. HCl
B. Antacid
C. Conjugate base of HCl
D. Conjugate acid of antacid

50. When the student tested magnesium hydroxide with his first experimental setup, approximately how much antacid remained at the end of the reaction?

A. 750 mg
B. 500 mg
C. 200 mg
D. 300 mg

51. The student noticed that stronger antacids often leave larger precipitates when they are present as an excess reagent because a stronger antacid

A. neutralizes more acid, which subsequently produces a larger precipitate.

B. produces more product, which subsequently appears in the precipitate.

C. requires more of the reactant, higher quantities of unreacted material are usually present in the precipitate.

D. requires less of the reactant, so higher quantities of unreacted material are usually present in the precipitate.

52. Which of the following best explains why the student's initial results were correct for group A but incorrect for group B?

A. Group A contains very strong bases, while group B contains slightly weaker bases.

B. Group A contains compounds that dissociate into multiple ions, while group B contains compounds that dissociate into only two ions.

C. Group A contains compounds with insignificant solubility, while group B contains compounds with considerable solubility.

D. Group A contains cations with a +1 oxidation state, while group B contains cations with a +2 or +3 oxidation state.

PRACTICE SECTION 2

Time—70 minutes

QUESTIONS 1–52

Directions: Most of the questions in the following General Chemistry Practice Section are organized into groups, with a descriptive passage preceding each group of questions. Study the passage, then select the single-best answer to the question in each group. Some of the questions are not based on a descriptive passage; you must also select the best answer to these questions. In you are unsure of the best answer, eliminate the choices that you know are incorrect, then select an answer from the choices that remain.

PASSAGE I (QUESTIONS 1–9)

Swimming pools are filled with water containing a number of dissolved ions for the purpose of purification and maintenance of pH. One chemical that is added to pools, chlorine, is used to kill bacteria and harmful contaminants and can be added to pools in a number of ways. Calcium hypochlorite, $Ca(OCl)_2$, is an inorganic chlorinating agent that contributes chlorine and calcium ions to the water.

Other chemicals and materials in swimming pools can also contribute calcium ions to the water. The concentration of calcium and other ions must be closely monitored so that the water does not become saturated with a particular compound. The solubility product constant, termed K_{sp}, describes the amount of salt in moles that can be dissolved in one liter of solution to reach saturation. No more salt can dissolve after reaching the point of saturation.

Plaster that lines swimming pools is a form of hydrated calcium sulfate, $CaSO_4$. The calcium from chlorinating agents along with the calcium from plaster that lines swimming pools makes it necessary to monitor the concentrations of Ca^{2+} and SO_4^{2-} to make sure that saturation is not reached. The following equation describes the dissociation of calcium sulfate in water:

$$CaSO_4 \longleftrightarrow Ca^{2+} + SO_4^{2-}$$

The K_{sp} value for the discussed dissociation reaction can be calculated by determining the values of $[Ca^{2+}]$ and $[SO_4^{2-}]$ in a saturated solution. If the K_{sp} value is known, the ion concentrations in swimming pools can be used with the K_{sp} value to predict whether or not the levels are at or near saturation.

1. If the K_{sp} of $CaSO_4$ is calculated to be 4.93×10^{-5} at 25°C, what is the minimum amount of $CaSO_4$ that can be added to 3.75×10^5 L of water to create a saturated solution?

   A. 2.63×10^3 grams
   B. 3.58×10^5 grams
   C. 7.16×10^5 grams
   D. 2.52×10^3 grams

2. Which of the following compounds, when dissolved in water, has the highest concentration of calcium for one mole of the compound?

   A. $CaCO_3$ ($K_{sp} = 4.8 \times 10^{-9}$)
   B. CaF_2 ($K_{sp} = 3.9 \times 10^{-11}$)
   C. $Ca_3(PO_4)_2$ ($K_{sp} = 1 \times 10^{-25}$)
   D. $Ca(IO_3)_2$ ($K_{sp} = 6.47 \times 10^{-6}$)

3. The K_{sp} of $CaSO_4$ can be calculated by determining the concentration of a saturated solution of $CaSO_4$. The following graph shows the relationship between concentration and conductivity for $CaSO_4$, which was determined by finding the conductance for four $CaSO_4$ solutions of known concentration. Using the graph, estimate the concentration of a saturated solution that has a conductivity of 2.5×10^3 µS/cm and then calculate the experimental K_{sp} for a saturated solution of $CaSO_4$:

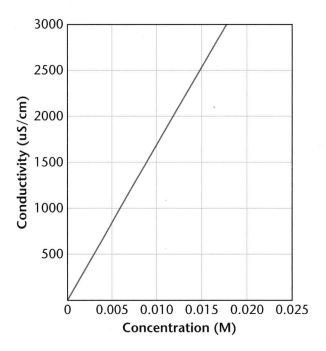

A. 2.25×10^{-4} M²
B. 1.5×10^{-2} M²
C. 3×10^{-2} M²
D. 1.22×10^{-1} M²

4. In the experiment, a probe was used to measure the conductivities in each solution. The probe generates a potential difference between two electrodes and reads the current that is produced as a voltage. The computer then outputs the conductivity. If several different solutions were all heated from room temperature to 75° Celsius, how would the conductivity of the solutions change and would the K_{sp} be affected?

A. The conductivity would increase and the K_{sp} would increase.
B. The conductivity would decrease and the change in K_{sp} cannot be determined.
C. The conductivity would increase and the change in K_{sp} cannot be determined.
D. The conductivity would decrease and the change in K_{sp} cannot be determined.

5. Instead of using calcium hypochlorite to introduce chlorine into the water, the owner of a water park, Jim, decides to bubble Cl_2 gas into the pool. Will Jim's decision affect the solubility of the plaster that is lining the pools at his water park?

A. Yes, the chlorine gas will increase the solubility of $CaSO_4$ in the plaster as compared with $Ca(OCl)_2$ because it will react with molecules of SO_4^{2-} and shift the equilibrium to the right.
B. Yes, the chlorine gas will increase the solubility of $CaSO_4$ in the plaster as compared with $Ca(OCl)_2$ because Cl_2 will not cause the same common ion effect that occurred with $Ca(OCl)_2$.
C. Yes, the chlorine gas will decrease the solubility of $CaSO_4$ in the plaster as compared with $Ca(OCl)_2$ because the absence of Ca^{2+} from the $Ca(OCl)_2$ will eliminate the common ion effect.
D. No, the chlorine gas will not change the solubility of $CaSO_4$ in the plaster as compared with $Ca(OCl)_2$.

6. $Ca(OCl)_2$ contributes OCl⁻ to the water, which acts to kill bacteria by destroying enzymes and contents of the cells through oxidation. In its ionic form, OCl⁻ exists in the following equilibrium:

$$HOCl \rightleftharpoons H^+ + OCl^-$$

In order for cleaning to occur properly, the pH must be at the right level to allow enough of the oxidizing agent, HOCl, to be present. If the pH is raised by the addition of sodium carbonate to the water, what will happen to the oxidizing power of the HOCl?

A. The higher pH will break the HOCl compound into single atoms and will eliminate its oxidizing power.

B. The pH cannot be raised due to the buffering system in the pool, and thus the oxidizing power of the chlorine will remain the same.

C. Fewer H⁺ ions will be present and the reaction will shift right. This will decrease the number of HOCl molecules and thus decrease the oxidizing power of chlorine.

D. A high pH will lower the concentration of H⁺ by associating H⁺ with OCl⁻. This will increase the number of HOCl molecules and increase the oxidizing power of chlorine.

7. Due to changes in climate and poor management of ion content in the water, the swimming pool has now become supersaturated with calcium sulfate. What combination of events could have caused this to occur?

A. Cooling of the pool followed by addition of calcium sulfate

B. Warming of the pool followed by addition of calcium sulfate

C. Addition of calcium sulfate followed by cooling of the pool and then subsequent warming of the pool

D. Warming of the pool followed by addition of calcium sulfate and then cooling of the pool

8. Water "hardness" refers to the content of calcium and magnesium in water. When referring to swimming pools, water hardness mainly refers to calcium. One way to measure the balance of ions is to use the Langelier saturation index. The Langelier saturation index is derived from a combination of the following two equilibrium equations. Which of the following accurately expresses the combination of the two equilibrium equations in terms of [H⁺]?

$$HCO_3^- \rightleftharpoons H^+ + CO_3^{2-}$$
$$pK_{a2} = 10.33$$

$$CaCO_3 \rightleftharpoons Ca^{2+} + CO_3^{2-}$$
$$pK_{sp} = 8.35$$

A. $[H^+] = \left(\dfrac{K_{sp}}{K_{a2}}\right) \times [Ca^{2+}][HCO_3^-]$

B. $[H^+] = \left(\dfrac{K_{a2}}{K_{sp}}\right) \times [Ca^{2+}][HCO_3^-]$

C. $[H^+] = \left(\dfrac{K_{sp}}{K_{a2}}\right) \times \left(\dfrac{[Ca^{2+}]}{[HCO_3^-]}\right)$

D. $[H^+] = \left(\dfrac{K_{sp}}{K_{a2}}\right) \times \left(\dfrac{[HCO_3^-]}{[Ca^{2+}]}\right)$

9. Phenol red is the most widely used indicator to determine the pH of water in swimming pools. The pKa_2 of phenol red is equal to 7.96. The acidic form of phenol red appears yellow and the basic form of phenol red appears red. In addition, the absorptivity (how strongly a species absorbs light) of the basic form is around three times greater than the acidic form. The color-changing region is indicated by an orange color. Due to the difference in absorptivity between different forms of phenol red, at what pH would the color change (to orange) be most likely to occur?

A. pH of 4
B. pH of 7.5
C. pH of 8.5
D. pH of 11

PASSAGE II (QUESTIONS 10–17)

Hydrogen is the first element of the periodic table. It contains one proton and one electron. According to one early model of the hydrogen atom developed in the early 20th century by Niels Bohr, that electron is found in any one of an infinite number of energy levels. These energy levels are sometimes called quanta, in that they can be described by a principal quantum number, n, that always has an integer value. As the electron moves from one energy level to another (n = 1 to n → 8, or vice versa) it absorbs or emits some discrete quantity of energy accordingly. This quantity is directly proportional to the frequency of the light radiation that results from the energy change.

It took some time for atomic physicists to arrive at Bohr's conclusions. They struggled to reconcile empirical data about light radiation from hydrogen atoms with their understanding that light photons moved and behaved as particles according to Newtonian mechanics. One discovery that led to Bohr's

quantum mechanics was a new quantitative interpretation of light emissions from hydrogen atoms. Hydrogen atoms emit light in characteristic patterns known as line spectra. These patterns are noncontinuous but predictable. In the early 1880s, Theodore Balmer derived a mathematical relationship between the energy emissions of a hydrogen atom and the wavelengths of light they radiated during transitions:

$$\lambda = B[m^2/(m^2 - 2^2)] = B[m^2/(m^2 - n^2)], \text{ where } B = 364.56 \text{ nm}, m > 2, \lambda \text{ is the wavelength, } n \text{ is equal to 2.}$$

The spectrum he used, which is now known as the Balmer series, is illustrated below:

The Rydberg equation is a more general version of this equation that applies to all possible energy level transitions in a hydrogen atom. Physicists used the Rydberg equation to detect other series of energy transitions in other regions of the light spectrum. One such series is the Lyman series, which accounts for transitions from excited states to n = 1, the ground state.

10. What is the proper electron configuration of hydrogen in its elemental state?

A. $1s^0$
B. $1s^1$
C. $1s^2$
D. None of the above

11. If an electron is promoted from n = 2 to n = 5, as Balmer observed, which of the following possibilities best describes the source of the line spectra observed?

    A. A photon is absorbed.
    B. A photon is emitted.
    C. An electron is absorbed.
    D. An electron is emitted.

12. What region of the light spectrum corresponds to the characteristic emissions in the Balmer series?

    A. UV
    B. Visible
    C. Infrared
    D. X-ray

13. One Balmer spectral line, the n = 3 to n = 2 transition, is a common reference point in astronomy for hydrogen gas emissions. The characteristic wavelength of this emission in the scientific literature is 656.3 nm. What color is this light emission?

    A. Red
    B. Blue-green
    C. Violet
    D. The emission is not in the visible spectrum.

14. What name best describes the absorption line spectrum pictured below?

    A. Lyman series
    B. Balmer series
    C. Bohr series
    D. None of the above

15. Suppose a scientist tried to obtain a Balmer series with a sample of deuterium. How would this sample change the appearance of the emissions in the line spectrum?

    A. Fewer emission lines
    B. More emission lines
    C. Same number of emission lines with split peaks
    D. Same number of emission lines without split peaks (that is, no change in appearance)

16. At high resolution, some of the emissions in the Balmer series appear as doublets. Which of the following best explains this result, which was not predicted by any of the models in the passage?

    A. The models in the passage do not account for relativistic effects.
    B. The models in the passage do not account for high wavelengths.
    C. The models in the passage do not account for the atomic number.
    D. The models in the passage do not account for other particles in the atom.

17. When n > 6, the Balmer series features violet light emissions at wavelengths outside the range of the visible spectrum. Which of the following best accounts for this finding?

    A. Energy levels are narrower as n → 1 and wider as n → 8.
    B. Energy levels are wider as n → 1 and narrower as n → 8.
    C. Energy differences between levels are larger as n → 1 and smaller as n → 8.
    D. Energy differences between levels are smaller as n → 1 and larger as n → 8.

QUESTIONS 18–22 ARE NOT BASED ON A DESCRIPTIVE PASSAGE.

18. Which of the following pairs of particles would be accelerated in a particle accelerator?

   A. Gamma ray and neutron

   B. Gamma ray and beta particle

   C. Beta particle and neutron

   D. Alpha and beta particles

19. What volume of 0.5 M KOH would be necessary to neutralize 15 mL of 1 M nitrous acid?

   A. 15 mL

   B. 30 mL

   C. 45 mL

   D. 60 mL

20. Why does high, but not low, pressure cause a deviation from the ideal gas law?

   A. Higher pressure decreases the interatomic distance to the point where intermolecular forces reduce the volume below that predicted by the ideal gas equation.

   B. Low pressure increases the atomic radius of a gas making it more stable whereas high pressure compresses the gas particles decreasing their stability.

   C. Low pressure does cause a significant deviation from the ideal gas law because the increased interatomic distance means that no particles ever collide.

   D. Low pressure does cause a significant deviation because a low pressure implies a reduction in temperature via Charles's law, which increases the power of intermolecular forces.

21. What type of molecular geometry is NOT able to result in a nonpolar structure?

   A. Bent

   B. Diatomic covalent

   C. Trigonal planar

   D. Square planar

22. A parent and daughter nucleus are isotypes of the same element. Therefore, the ratio of alpha to beta decays that produced the daughter nucleus must be which of the following?

   A. 2:3

   B. 2:1

   C. 1:2

   D. 1:1

PASSAGE III (QUESTIONS 23–30)

Many new consumer electronics and electric cars utilize a type of rechargeable battery that extracts its power from the movement of a lithium ion (Li^+) between the cathode and the anode of a galvanic cell. In most cases, the anode is composed of graphite, the cathode is composed of a CoO_2^- complex, and the electrolyte contains a lithium salt in an organic solvent. Following are the half-reactions, where $Li_{1-x}CoO_2$ is the simplest form of the chemical formula $Li(CoO_2)_{1/(1-x)}$ (which represents a complex of one lithium ion with several metal oxide molecules):

$$LiCoO_2 \leftrightharpoons Li_{1-x}CoO_2 + xLi^+ + xe^- \quad \text{(cathode)}$$
$$xLi^+ + xe^- + 6C \leftrightharpoons Li_xC_6 \quad\quad\quad\quad \text{(anode)}$$

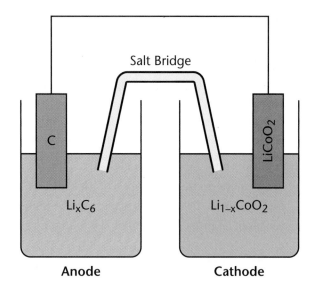

Salt Bridge

C

LiCoO₂

Li_xC_6

$Li_{1-x}CoO_2$

Anode   Cathode

The value of x is equal to the following ratio:

$$\frac{\text{(Present potential energy of the battery)}}{\text{(Original potential energy of the battery)}}$$

When the battery is fully charged, x equals 1. When the battery is fully discharged, x equals 0.

To study the change in a battery's performance over time, a scientist repeatedly charged and discharged cell 1 while leaving cell 2 intact. After several cycles of charging and discharging, the energy-storage capacity of cell 1 deteriorated significantly faster than the capacity of cell 2. Upon further testing, cell 1 was found to contain approximately equal concentrations of lithium oxide and cobalt(II) oxide. The constituents of cell 2 were not analyzed. The scientist hypothesized that the deterioration of cell 1 was caused primarily by the conversion of integral cell components into lithium oxide and cobalt(II) oxide.

23. What is the net overall equation for the cell?

A. $LiCoO_2 + 6C \rightleftharpoons Li_xC_6 + Li_{1-x}CoO_2$
B. $LiCoO_2 + xLi^+ + 6C \rightleftharpoons Li_xC_6 + Li_{1-x}CoO_2$
C. $Li^+ + 6C \rightleftharpoons Li_xC_6$
D. $LiCoO_2 + xLi^+ \rightleftharpoons Li_{1-x}CoO_2$

24. Which of the following is true about the overall potential of the cell when the battery is in use after a complete charge?

A. $E°_{cathode} + E°_{anode} < 0$
B. $E°_{cathode} + E°_{anode} > 0$
C. $E°_{cathode} + E°_{anode} < 1$
D. $E°_{cathode} + E°_{anode} > 1$

25. Which of the following identifies the oxidized and then the reduced species in the forward reaction.

A. Oxidized: Li^+/Reduced: Co^{4+}
B. Oxidized: C/Reduced: Li
C. Oxidized: $C^{x/6}$/Reduced: Co^{4+}
D. Oxidized: Co^{3+}/Reduced: C

26. Which of the following is true about the equilibrium constant of the reaction?

A. The forward reaction exhibits a positive $E°_{cell}$, which suggests a spontaneous process. Because discharging is spontaneous and charging is not, K_{eq} is high during discharging.
B. An increasing value of x will push the cathode reaction to the left and the anode reaction to the right; therefore, charging and discharging will have no net effect on K_{eq}.
C. Discharging is a spontaneous reaction, which requires reduction to occur at the cathode and oxidation to occur at the anode. Because this is only true for the reverse reaction, K_{eq} is low during discharging.
D. Based on the information in the passage, is impossible to predict the effects of charging and discharging on K_{eq}.

27. A certain battery is equipped with a mechanism that calculates its remaining energy by approximating the concentration of various lithium-cobalt-oxygen complexes. The analysis finds that the predominant species in the battery are $LiCoO_2$ and $Li(CoO_2)_2$. If the battery originally stored 100 J of potential energy, how much does it currently store?

A. 100 J
B. 50 J
C. 33 J
D. 0 J

28. Which of the following lithium species carry an oxidation number of +1?

   I. Li from $LiCoO_2$
   II. Li from $Li_{1-x}CoO_2$
   III. Li from Li_xC_6

A. I only
B. II only
C. I and III only
D. I, II, and III

29. Which of the following best explains the appearance of lithium oxide and cobalt(II) oxide in cell 1?

A. A small number of lithium ions occasionally combined with $LiCoO_2$ to produce lithium oxide and cobalt(II) oxide.
B. Because of the energy released by the system, a few $LiCoO_2$ molecules decomposed into lithium oxide and cobalt(II) oxide every time the battery was used.
C. Various constituents of the cell combined with environmental oxygen to produce lithium oxide and cobalt(II) oxide.
D. Various constituents of the cell combined with water to produce lithium oxide and cobalt(II) oxide.

30. If the scientist's hypothesis is correct, which of the following methods would be most likely to effectively measure the deterioration in the energy-storage capacity of a cell (like the one in cell 1)?

A. Determining the value of x for a fully charged battery
B. Determining the value of x for a fully discharged battery
C. Measuring the concentration of cobalt(II) oxide in a fully discharged battery
D. Measuring the concentration of Li_xC_6 in a fully charged battery

PASSAGE IV (QUESTIONS 31–37)

Water is the most abundant liquid on Earth, covering over three-fourths of its surface. Compared with other liquids, it is quite extraordinary. Its chemical structure and resulting phase change properties made the chances for the evolution of life on earth a possibility. Due to their polarity, water molecules have the ability to form hydrogen bonds with one another and with other polar substances. As a result of these forces, water forms a crystalline lattice in its solid state, as depicted by the illustration below. The larger circles represent oxygen and the smaller circles represent hydrogen in the lattice.

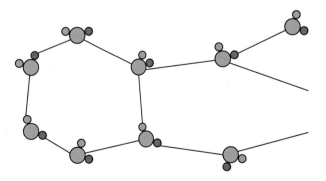

Ammonia is very similar in structure to water. Because of this similarity, many biologists have wondered whether ammonia would be a suitable substitute for water in living systems. The ammonia molecule is composed of hydrogen atoms covalently bonded to nitrogen. As the oxygen in the water molecule has a slightly negative charge, so does the nitrogen atom in ammonia. Some scientists have argued that ammonia-based life could evolve on other planets in a similar manner as life developed on Earth. Others argue that ammonia's heat of vaporization, 295 cal/g, is low compared with water, making it an unlikely candidate for the evolution of life. Modern science agrees that ammonia-based life on other planets will probably not be found to have evolved, if it exists, in the same manner as life on Earth.

31. One could infer from the passage that no form of life based on ammonia has yet been found because its

A. evaporation rate would be too high.

B. condensation rate would be too high.

C. rate of deposition would be too high.

D. rate of sublimation would be too low.

32. Had water not formed a crystalline lattice upon freezing and instead followed the common phase change pathways of most other compounds, one could logically infer that

A. life could not have evolved in a liquid environment.

B. life would have evolved in a gaseous environment.

C. soils would hold greater amounts of liquid water.

D. soils would hold greater amounts of gaseous water.

1. When the water molecules shown in the previous illustration undergo sublimation, what best explains this phenomenon?

A. The attractive forces between the water molecules overcome the kinetic energy that keeps them apart.

B. The kinetic energy of the water molecules overcomes the attractive forces that keep them together.

C. The hydrogen bonds between the water molecules form at a more rapid rate in the solid phase.

D. The hydrogen bonds between the water molecules form at a more rapid rate in the liquid phase.

34. A change in which intrinsic property of water would most affect its polarity?

A. Atomic electronegativity

B. Chirality

C. Intermolecular forces

D. Solubility

35. How would one explain the negative slope of the water-solid equilibrium line in the phase diagram for water, shown below?

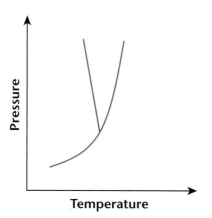

Temperature

A. Water is more dense at 4° Celsius than at 0.
B. Water's solid lattice collapses under pressure.
C. The triple point determines the slope of the phase-change line.
D. Liquid water is less dense than ice.

36. According to the passage, which of the following is true about a molecule of water undergoing evaporation?

A. The water molecule has more energy than an ammonia molecule.
B. Water evaporation is faster than an ammonia evaporation.
C. The water molecule has less energy than an ammonia molecule.
D. Both A and B

37. What would the addition of an ionic compound do to the lattice structure shown in the illustration above?

A. Collapse the structure
B. Enhance cohesive forces in the structure
C. Enhance crystallization
D. Both B or C

PASSAGE V (QUESTIONS 38–45)

There are many elements in the periodic table that play an integral role in the everyday functions of the human body. While the most obvious of these are carbon, hydrogen, nitrogen, and oxygen, we also have various essential uses for phosphorus. Its physical and chemical properties have made it the perfect candidate to play a role in the molecule that acts as the body's primary location for short-term storage of energy, adenosine-5′-triphosphate (ATP).

Some metabolic syndromes can cause a phosphate ion to be drawn from the blood into the bones and teeth, where the majority of phosphorus exists. The ensuing deficiency of phosphate in the blood can lead to dysfunction of the brain and muscle tissue, which can cause death in severe cases. Scientists are attempting to cure this disease by designing a biologic molecule whose properties and actions are similar to those of phosphate. One way to do this is to find an element that has similar physical and chemical properties to phosphorus.

38. Which of the following is most likely to act as a stronger reducing agent than phosphorus?

A. Na
B. Cs
C. O
D. Bi

39. Which of the following, on average, have more space between two nuclei placed side-by-side than phosphorus?

  I. K
 II. Pb
III. F

A. I only
B. I and II
C. II and III
D. I, II, and III

40. Which of the following is NOT a property of phosphorus, according to the classifications of types of elements?

A. Brittle in the solid state
B. Poor electrical conductivity
C. Does not show much luster
D. Is generally malleable

41. Which of the following is the correct electron orbital configuration of phosphorus?

A. $1s^2 2s^2 3s^2 2p^6 3p^3$
B. $1s^2 2s^2 2p^6 3s^2 3p^3$
C. $1s^2 2s^2 2p^6 3p^5$
D. $1s^2 2s^2 2p^6 3s^2 3d^{10} 3p^6$

42. Which of the following statements is true about the density of alkali metals and alkaline earth metals?

A. Alkaline earth metals are less dense because they contain unfilled subshells.
B. Alkaline earth metals are less dense because their nuclei contain fewer neutrons.
C. Alkali metals are less dense because they contain fewer orbitals.
D. Alkali metals are less dense because they have a loosely bound electron in their outer shell.

43. Which of the following is NOT a correct characterization of the properties of halogens?

A. At room temperature, halogens naturally exist only in the gaseous and liquid states.
B. Halogens are highly likely to react with alkali metals.
C. Halogens can form stable ionic crystals with alkaline earth metals.
D. In their neutral form, halogens always have an outer shell of p^5.

44. Which of the following contributes most to the malleability shown by transition elements?

A. Natural softness as compared to other metals
B. High electrical conductivity
C. Loosely held d-electrons
D. High melting points

45. Which of the following best explains why scientists closely examine metalloids when trying to find a biologic to replace phosphorus?

A. Phosphorus is a metalloid.
B. Metalloids often behave as semiconductors.
C. Some metalloids exhibit similar bonding capabilities to phosphorus.
D. Metalloids exhibit flexibility in their properties so they can be manipulated easily.

PASSAGE VI (QUESTIONS 46–52)

Aerobic and anaerobic bacteria undergo different types of metabolism, and the properties of their metabolisms are unique. Some anaerobic bacteria are methane-producing bacteria. These bacteria have been studied to determine the relevance of their potential use in generating biological energy or "biogas."

These methane-producing bacteria typically feed off of animal manure or other natural waste. In the process of utilizing animal waste, manure is collected from different types of animals including swine and cows. The manure is separated by phase and contains proteins, carbohydrates, and fats; bacteria then break down components into fatty acids.[1]

"Methanogens" are the particular type of anaerobic bacteria that undertake the final steps of breaking down the fatty acids into simple products: methane and carbon dioxide. A common reactant is acetic acid, which breaks down according to the following reaction shown below:

$$CH_3COOH \longrightarrow CH_4 + CO_2$$

Other fatty acids can be used as substrates for these methane-generating reactions, including propionate and butyrate. Methanogenic bacteria can also convert carbon dioxide and hydrogen gas to form methane and water. At the end of this process, which typically takes place at 95° Celsius, methane can be used to generate energy as an alternative to fossil fuels.

46. What type of reaction is presented in the passage?

A. Combination reaction
B. Single-displacement reaction
C. Decomposition reaction
D. Combustion reaction

47. If the reaction begins with 120 grams of acetic acid, what is the theoretical yield, in grams, of methane?

A. 32.05 grams
B. 64.1 grams
C. 40.92 grams
D. 29.12 grams

48. What piece of evidence would support the passage's argument that the decomposition of fatty acids can create energy serving as an alternative to fossil fuel?

A. Anaerobic bacteria can break down fatty acids efficiently at room temperature.
B. Methane gas can be compressed and transported.
C. The reaction generates gaseous products.
D. The reaction is exothermic.

49. What formula best demonstrates how to calculate the number of grams of acetic acid necessary to produce 88.02 grams of carbon dioxide?

A. $\dfrac{(88.02 \text{ grams})(\text{molecular weight } CH_3COOH)}{(\text{molecular weight } CO_2)}$

B. $\dfrac{(88.02 \text{ grams})(2 \text{ moles } CH_3COOH)(\text{molecular weight } CH_3COOH)}{(\text{molecular weight } CO_2)(1 \text{ mole } CO_2)}$

C. $\dfrac{(\text{molecular weight } CH_3COOH)}{(88.02 \text{ grams})(\text{molecular weight } CO_2)}$

D. $\dfrac{(2 \text{ moles } CH_3COOH)(\text{molecular weight of } CO_2)(\text{molecular weight } CH_3COOH)}{(88.02 \text{ grams})(1 \text{ mole } CO_2)}$

---

[1] Information for this entire passage taken primarily from:
www.thepigsite.com/articles/4/waste-and-odor/914/manure-to-energy-the-utah-project ($C_6H_{13}O_5 + xH_2O \rightarrow COOH–(CH_2)_n–CH_3 \rightarrow 4CH_4 + 2CO_2$)
With contributions from:
extension.missouri.edu/xplor/agguides/agengin/g01881.htm ($H_2 + CO_2 \rightarrow H_2O + CH_4$)
books.google.com/books?id=ndPuyf4BsXYC&pg=PA26&lpg=PA26&dq=methane+and+bacteria+equation&source=web&ots=sbBVmswS MF&sig=6pQeW_uEd6WiSvcgPuHf_YdYQ4M&hl=en&sa=X&oi=book_result&resnum=5&ct=result
$CH_3COOH \rightarrow CH_4 + CO_2$ $CO_2 + 4H_2 \rightarrow CH_4 + 2H_2O$

50. One form of acetic acid, which is typically used as a salt, is called acetate. Sodium acetate can react with other chemical compounds in solution, an example of which is demonstrated below. What is the correct net ionic equation for this reaction?

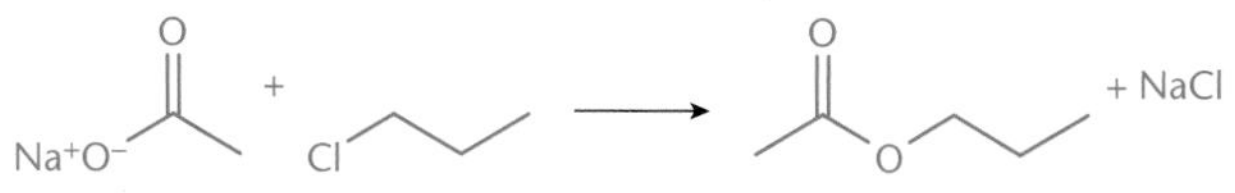

A. $Na^+ + CH_3COO^- + Cl^- + CH_3CH_2CH_2^+ \longrightarrow$
   $CH_3COOCH_2CH_2CH_3 + Na^+ + Cl^-$

B. $CH_3COO^- + Cl^- + CH_3CH_2CH_2^+ \longrightarrow$
   $CH_3COOCH_2CH_2CH_3 + Cl^-$

C. $CH_3COO^- + CH_3CH_2CH_2^+ \longrightarrow$
   $CH_3COOCH_2CH_2CH_3$

D. $CH_3COO^- + CH_3CH_2CH_2Cl \longrightarrow$
   $CH_3COOCH_2CH_2CH_3 + Cl^-$

51. As described in the passage, methanogenic bacteria can utilize hydrogen gas to produce methane. At standard temperature and pressure, if there are 3 liters of hydrogen gas and 2 liters of carbon dioxide available to the bacteria, what would be the theoretical yield, in moles, of methane?

A. 0.134 moles
B. 0.0893 moles
C. 0.067 moles
D. 0.268 moles

52. What is the percent yield if 8.02 g of methane is formed from the reaction of 50 liters of hydrogen gas, with excess carbon dioxide at standard temperature and pressure?

A. 86.2%
B. 14.4%
C. 43.1%
D. 64.7%

PRACTICE SECTION 3

Time—70 minutes

QUESTIONS 1–52

Directions: Most of the questions in the following General Chemistry Practice Section are organized into groups, with a descriptive passage preceding each group of questions. Study the passage, then select the single-best answer to the question in each group. Some of the questions are not based on a descriptive passage; you must also select the best answer to these questions. In you are unsure of the best answer, eliminate the choices that you know are incorrect, then select an answer from the choices that remain.

Period	1 IA 1A	2 IIA 2A											13 IIIA 3A	14 IVA 4A	15 VA 5A	16 VIA 6A	17 VIIA 7A	18 vIIIA 8A
1	1 H 1.008																	2 He 4.003
2	3 Li 6.941	4 Be 9.012											5 B 10.81	6 C 12.01	7 N 14.01	8 O 16.00	9 F 19.00	10 Ne 20.18
3	11 Na 22.99	12 Mg 24.31	3 IIIB 3B	4 IVB 4B	5 VB 5B	6 VIB 6B	7 VIIB 7B	8	9 ------ VIII -----	10	11 IB 1B	12 IIB 2B	13 Al 26.98	14 Si 28.09	15 P 30.97	16 S 32.07	17 Cl 35.45	18 Ar 39.95
4	19 K 39.10	20 Ca 40.08	21 Sc 44.96	22 Ti 47.88	23 V 50.94	24 Cr 52.00	25 Mn 54.94	26 Fe 55.85	27 Co 58.47	28 Ni 58.69	29 Cu 63.55	30 Zn 65.39	31 Ga 69.72	32 Ge 72.59	33 As 74.92	34 Se 78.96	35 Br 79.90	36 Kr 83.80
5	37 Rb 85.47	38 Sr 87.62	39 Y 88.91	40 Zr 91.22	41 Nb 92.91	42 Mo 95.94	43 Tc (98)	44 Ru 101.1	45 Rh 102.9	46 Pd 106.4	47 Ag 107.9	48 Cd 112.4	49 In 114.8	50 Sn 118.7	51 Sb 121.8	52 Te 127.6	53 I 126.9	54 Xe 131.3
6	55 Cs 132.9	56 Ba 137.3	57 La* 138.9	72 Hf 178.5	73 Ta 180.9	74 W 183.9	75 Re 186.2	76 Os 190.2	77 Ir 190.2	78 Pt 195.1	79 Au 197.0	80 Hg 200.5	81 Tl 204.4	82 Pb 207.2	83 Bi 209.0	84 Po (210)	85 At (210)	86 Rn (222)
7	87 Fr (223)	88 Ra (226)	89 Ac~ (227)	104 Rf (257)	105 Db (260)	106 Sg (263)	107 Bh (262)	108 Hs (265)	109 Mt (266)	110 --- ()	111 --- ()	112 --- ()		114 --- ()		116 --- ()		118 --- ()

Lanthanide Series*	58 Ce 140.1	59 Pr 140.9	60 Nd 144.2	61 Pm (147)	62 Sm 150.4	63 Eu 152.0	64 Gd 157.3	65 Tb 158.9	66 Dy 162.5	67 Ho 164.9	68 Er 167.3	69 Tm 168.9	70 Yb 173.0	71 Lu 175.0
Actinide Series~	90 Th 232.0	91 Pa (231)	92 U (238)	93 Np (237)	94 Pu (242)	95 Am (243)	96 Cm (247)	97 Bk (247)	98 Cf (249)	99 Es (254)	100 Fm (253)	101 Md (256)	102 No (254)	103 Lr (257)

PASSAGE I (QUESTIONS 1–8)

The blood-brain barrier is a unique part of the human nervous system. Endothelial cells lining blood vessels in the central nervous system are more tightly attached to one another than in other parts of the human body. As a result, there is limited permeability of both small and large molecules from the circulation into the cerebrospinal fluid (CSF).

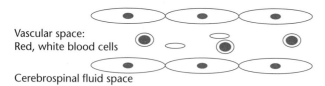

Vascular space:
Red, white blood cells

Cerebrospinal fluid space

These tightly sealed endothelial cells have both advantages and disadvantages in the human system. The central nervous system is a fragile, essential part of the human body, and the endothelial cells serve as a barrier. Multiple characteristics of any given molecule affect its permeability: its polarity, size, weight, charge, and degree of protein binding in the blood. Nonpolar molecules pass more effectively from the bloodstream into the CSF. Smaller particles, such as water, and small, charged particles will also move with varying ease across this barrier. Water moves freely, but charged ions can take hours to equilibrate between the systemic circulation and the cerebrospinal fluid.

When disease afflicts the central nervous system it is necessary to deliver drugs to the cerebrospinal fluid for delivery into the tissues of the brain and spinal cord. On the other hand, some extremely effective chemotherapeutic agents, such as cisplatin, are beneficial when they do not cross the blood-brain barrier because they are neurotoxic when they penetrate the central nervous system. Alternatively, when beginning general anesthesia for a surgical procedure it is essential that anesthetic agents penetrate from the systemic circulation into the cerebrospinal fluid to alter consciousness and systemic muscle tone during the procedure.

1. Based on the passage, which of the following characteristics would be essential for any pharmaceutical intended for use as a general anesthetic?

   A. The molecule should be nonpolar.
   B. The molecule should be directly delivered to the CNS without going through the systemic circulation first.
   C. The molecule should be polar.
   D. The molecule should be slow-acting.

2. What can be logically inferred from the passage about charge and its effect on a molecule's permeability of the blood-brain barrier?

   A. Charged molecules are more likely to associate with one another tightly in the blood stream, inhibiting diffusion into the cerebrospinal fluid.
   B. Uncharged molecules are more likely to be able to diffuse between endothelial cells.
   C. Uncharged molecules are less likely to be transported through endothelial cells.
   D. Charged molecules are more soluble in the bloodstream than in the cerebrospinal fluid.

3. What can be logically inferred from the passage about the role of the blood-brain barrier in supporting human life?

   A. A permeable central nervous system is essential in allowing diffusion of nutrients from the peripheral circulation into the CNS.
   B. The micro-environment of the CNS is similar to that of the systemic circulation.
   C. The blood-brain barrier limits the flow of damaged or infected cells from the cerebrospinal fluid into the systemic circulation.
   D. The blood-brain barrier adaptively protects the CNS from toxins or other possible insults originating in the systemic circulation.

4. Based on the information in the passage, what type of intermolecular force has the most influence on molecules that pass easily through the blood-brain barrier?

A. Ion-dipole interactions
B. Dipole-dipole interactions
C. Hydrogen bonding
D. Dispersion forces

5. Which of the following statements are NOT true when relating formal charge with permeation across the blood-brain barrier?

  I. A formal charge of zero guarantees permeability through the blood-brain barrier.
  II. A negative formal change on one or more atoms in a molecule will improve its permeability of the blood-brain barrier.
  III. Two molecules, both with formal charges of zero, will be equally permeable through the blood-brain barrier.

A. I only
B. III only
C. II and III only
D. I, II, and III

6. Cisplatin, a commonly used chemotherapeutic agent, is $PtCl_2(NH_3)_2$. What type of bond forms between each of the NH_3 groups and the central platinum?

A. Coordinate covalent bond
B. Polar covalent bond
C. Nonpolar covalent bond
D. Ionic bond

7. Phenytoin, shown below, is an anti-seizure medicine. It is one of many drugs that is actively transported *out* of the central nervous system by cellular transporters. What would be the best estimate of the geometry around the central carbon to which the arrow points?

A. Square planar
B. Tetrahedral
C. Trigonal pyramidal
D. Octahedral

8. Which of the following best describes the relationship between resonance structures and molecular polarity?

A. The most stable resonance structures maximize polarity.
B. If a molecule has more than one important resonance structure, it is more likely to be a polar molecule than another molecule without such resonance structures.
C. The most important resonance structures spread out and minimize formal charge.
D. Resonance structures will counterbalance the natural polarity of a bond.

PASSAGE II (QUESTIONS 9–16)

The human body is a dynamic system that has to deal with significant environmental threats on a daily basis. One type of threat is from the effects of reactive oxygen species (ROS). ROS are ions or small molecules containing oxygen that have unpaired valence shell electrons. The superoxide anion, O_2^-, is a toxic threat, becoming lethal at intracellular levels of just 1 nM. It spontaneously forms O_2 and H_2O_2, but is also able to react with NO to form peroxynitrite. Peroxynitrite can cause extreme cellular damage. The enzyme NADPH oxidase produces the superoxide anion in the body to combat invading microorganisms. Because of the threat that it poses in such small quantities, the body has developed ways to dispose of this chemical.

The superoxide anion puts the concept of compartmentalization is on display. It would be a waste of energy to both produce and destroy superoxide in the same cell, so it is only produced in phagocytes (immune cells that ingest infectious agents), and is broken down in any other cell of the body. In two steps, the enzyme superoxide dismutase (SOD) uses iron or other metals to create oxygen and hydrogen peroxide from superoxide and hydrogen ions:

Step 1: $Fe^{3+} - SOD + O_2^- \rightarrow Fe^{2+} - SOD + O_2$
Step 2: $Fe^{2+} - SOD + O_2^- + 2H^+ \rightarrow Fe^{3+} - SOD + H_2O_2$

A graduate student at a local university was given the task of determining the kinetics of this reaction. Her results are shown in table 1 below:

Trial	$[H^+]_{initial}$ (M)	$[O_2^-]_{initial}$ (M)	$r_{initial}$ (M/sec)
1	1	1	2.04
2	1	2	7.98
3	4	1	8.09

The potential energy diagram for the reaction is shown in figure 1 below:

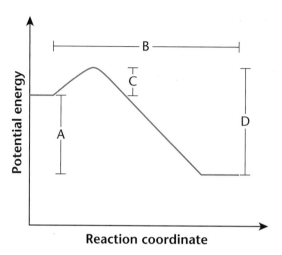

Reaction coordinate

FOR QUESTIONS 9–14, ASSUME BOTH STEPS OF THE REACTION ARE IRREVERSIBLE.

9. What is the order of H^+ in Step 2 of the above reaction?

   A. 0
   B. 1
   C. 2
   D. 3

10. What is the rate of step 2 of the reaction if the following concentrations of reactants exist? Assume the rate constant, k = 0.50.

   $$[H^+] = 2 \text{ M}, [O_2^-] = 2 \text{ M}$$

   A. 2.5 M/sec
   B. 4 M/sec
   C. 8 M/sec
   D. 10 M/sec

11. What function might Fe^{2+}–SOD play in the overall reaction?

    A. A substance used to create a product in the reaction

    B. A substance that is created in the reaction

    C. A substance that increases the rate of the reaction

    D. A short-lived, unstable molecule in the reaction

12. Which of the following is NOT true when describing the kinetics of the previous overall reaction?

    A. The rate of the reaction is proportional to the number of collisions between reacting molecules.

    B. In some effective collisions, all of the colliding particles do not have enough kinetic energy to exceed activation energy.

    C. A transition state is formed when old bonds are breaking and new bonds are forming.

    D. The activated complex has greater energy than either products or reactants.

13. What section of the diagram in figure 1 represents the forward activation energy?

    A. A
    B. B
    C. C
    D. D

14. What section of the diagram in figure 1 represents the enthalpy change during the reaction?

    A. A
    B. B
    C. C
    D. D

FOR QUESTIONS 15–16, ASSUME BOTH STEPS OF THE REACTION ARE REVERSIBLE.

15. What is the equilibrium constant for the overall reaction in the passage? Will an increase in pressure raise or lower the equilibrium constant? Assume $[O_2^-] = 3$ M, $[H^+] = 1$ M, $[H_2O_2] = 1$ M, $[O_2] = 2$ M.

    A. 0.22; raise
    B. 0.27; lower
    C. 2.2; raise
    D. 2.7; lower

16. What would best explain the equilibrium shift to the right in reaction 2?

    A. Increase in volume
    B. Addition of product
    C. Increase in pressure
    D. Decrease in temperature

QUESTIONS 17–21 ARE NOT BASED ON A DESCRIPTIVE PASSAGE.

17. Latent heat flux is the loss of heat by the surface of a body of water caused by evaporation. To determine the latent heat flux over the Atlantic Ocean, one would need to know

    A. ΔH_{fusion} of water.
    B. $\Delta H_{vaporization}$ of water.
    C. $\Delta H_{sublimation}$ of water.
    D. $\Delta H_{ionization}$ of water.

18. A particle is constrained to move in a circle with a 10-meter radius. At one instant, the particle's speed is 10 meters per second and is increased at a rate of 10 meters per second squared. What is the angle between the particle's velocity and acceleration vectors?

    A. 0°
    B. 30°
    C. 45°
    D. 60°

19. What compound would not be considered an electrolyte?

A. AgCl

B. CaO

C. LiI

D. HBr

20. Aluminum has a lower electronegativity than iron, but reacts extremely slowly with oxygen in moist air because of a hard, protective aluminum oxide coat that protects all exposed surfaces. Under which of the following conditions would aluminum be more readily eroded?

A. Immersed in a solution of HCl

B. Immersed in a bath of hot sodium metal

C. Immersed in a solution of NH_3

D. Immersed in a solution of NaOH

21. Two gases, X and Y, are combined in a closed container. At STP, the average velocity of a gas A molecule is twice that of a gas B molecule. Gases A and B are most likely which of the following?

A. He and Ar

B. He and Kr

C. Ne and Ar

D. Ne and Kr

PASSAGE III (QUESTIONS 22–29)

Dry ice forms when carbon dioxide gas is cooled to −78° C at atmospheric pressure. After becoming solid, it reforms gas when heat is added as shown in the reversible reaction below:

CO_2 (solid, −78°C) + heat (120kJ/mol) ↔ CO_2 (gas, 25°C)

An experiment was done to test the change, over three days, in a block of dry ice placed in a rigid container at room temperature at 1 atmosphere of pressure. The container was closed to the outside environment for the duration of the experiment. The only components in the container were the dry ice and air (g). No liquid in the container was detected over the three-day period. The apparatus and results of the experiment are shown in Figure 1 below.

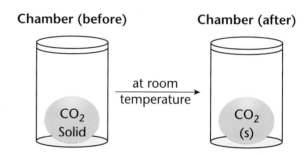

As a solid carbon dioxide has many uses, not the least of which is cooling its surroundings. This transfer of energy is a main method by which coolants operate in many mechanical devices. The phase diagram for carbon dioxide is a major reason for its unique behaviors. The phase diagram for carbon dioxide is shown in Figure 2 below.

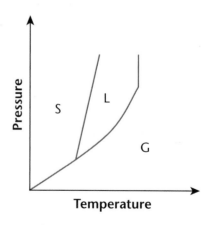

22. Which of the following best describes the equation in the passage?

   A. Evaporation
   B. Condensation
   C. Deposition
   D. Sublimation

23. Referring to Figure 2, if liquid carbon dioxide were subject to increasing pressure at a constant temperature, it would

   A. become solid.
   B. become gaseous.
   C. gain kinetic energy.
   D. lose kinetic energy.

24. It can be inferred from the results of the experiment that the air in the container

   A. lost kinetic energy.
   B. gained kinetic energy.
   C. gained volume.
   D. lost volume.

25. When the dry ice molecules shown undergo phase changes, which of the following is a likely cause?

   A. The attractive forces between the carbon dioxide molecules overcome the kinetic energy that keeps them apart.
   B. The kinetic energy of the carbon dioxide molecules overcomes the attractive forces that keep them together.
   C. The hydrogen bonds between the carbon dioxide molecules form at a more rapid rate in the solid phase.
   D. The hydrogen bonds between the carbon dioxide molecules form at a more rapid rate in the liquid phase.

26. The process shown in the experiment from the passage was

   A. endothermic, and the dry ice gained potential energy.
   B. endothermic, and the dry ice lost potential energy.
   C. exothermic, and the dry ice gained potential energy.
   D. exothermic, and the dry ice lost potential energy.

27. If the experiment from the passage were allowed to continue until all the carbon dioxide changed phase, one could logically predict that the air in the container would have

   A. increased in pressure.
   B. decreased in volume.
   C. become a solid.
   D. increased in temperature.

28. In the heating/cooling curve for carbon dioxide shown below, what represents the location of the phase change described in the passage?

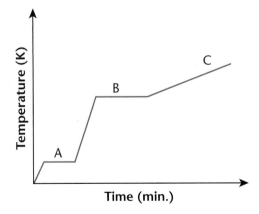

   A. A
   B. B
   C. C
   D. None of the above

29. In the phase diagram for carbon dioxide shown below, what represents the phase change shown in the experiment in the passage?

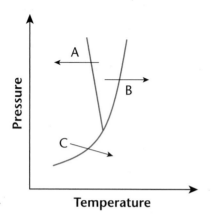

A. A
B. B
C. C
D. None of the above

QUESTIONS 30–36 ARE NOT BASED ON A DESCRIPTIVE PASSAGE.

30. Which of the following will result in a negative free energy change for a reaction?

A. The enthalpy change is negative.
B. The entropy change is positive.
C. The enthalpy change is negative and the entropy change is negative.
D. The enthalpy change is negative and the entropy change is positive.

31. Compared to the atomic radius of calcium, the atomic radius of gallium is

A. larger, because increased electron charge requires that the same force be distributed over a greater number of electrons.
B. smaller, because gallium gives up more electrons, decreasing its size.
C. smaller, because increased nuclear charge causes the electrons to be held more tightly.
D. larger, because its additional electrons increases the volume of the atom.

32. Under which conditions would water vapor demonstrate behavior closest to an ideal gas?

A. High pressure, low temperature
B. Low pressure, low temperature
C. High pressure, high temperature
D. Low pressure, high temperature

33. If the pressure of an ideal gas in a closed container is halved while the volume is held constant, the temperature of the gas

A. decreases by a factor of 2.
B. decreases by a factor of 4.
C. remains the same.
D. increases by a factor of 4.

34. "Greenhouse gases" are gases that will absorb IR radiation and trap energy between the Earth and the atmosphere. CO_2 and H_2O both strongly absorb radiation and are thus considered greenhouse gases, while N_2 and O_2 do not. One quality of greenhouse gases is that

A. they are composed of polar molecules.
B. they have a permanent dipole moment.
C. they experience hydrogen bonding.
D. they have polar covalent bonds.

35. What element contains unpaired electrons in its most common ionized state?

A. Fluorine
B. Aluminum
C. Zinc
D. Iron

36. Which of the following is the correct electron configuration for chromium in the ground state?

A. $[Ar]3d^45s^2$
B. $[Kr]4d^55s^1$
C. $[Ar]4s^14p^5$
D. $[Ar]3d^54s^1$

PASSAGE IV (QUESTIONS 37–45)

Decompression sickness involves symptoms that arise from exposure to a rapid decrease in ambient pressure. Decompression sickness can occur in multiple scenarios of decreased pressure and is most prevalent when divers return to the surface of water after a deep dive. If a diver ascends quickly and does not carry out decompression stops, gas bubbles can form in the body and create a multitude of adverse symptoms.

A diver experiences an increase in pressure when submerged many feet under water. Inert gases in the high-pressure environment dissolve into body tissues and liquids. When a diver comes back to the water's surface and the pressure decreases, the excess gas dissolved in the body comes out of solution. Gas bubbles form if inert gas comes out of the body too quickly. These bubbles are unable to leave through the lungs and subsequently cause symptoms such as itching skin, rashes, joint pain, paralysis, and even death.

At sea level the pressure exerted on one square inch is equal to 14.7 pounds, or 1 atm. In water,

an additional 1 atm of pressure is exerted for every 33 feet (about 10 m) below sea level. In addition to the decompression sickness, there are other conditions of which divers must be aware that arise from specific gases as a result of the high-pressure environment. For example, increased concentrations of nitrogen in the body lead to nitrogen narcosis. A diver with nitrogen narcosis feels intoxicated and experiences loss of decision-making skills due to nitrogen's anesthetic quality. The table below provides a list of gases and their corresponding solubility constants in water at 298 K.

Gas	k (M torr^{-1})
CO_2	4.48×10^{-5}
O_2	1.66×10^{-6}
He	5.1×10^{-7}
H_2	1.04×10^{-6}
N_2	8.42×10^{-7}

37. What theory could be used to determine the amount of oxygen that is dissolved in water at sea level?

A. Henry's law
B. Boyle's law
C. Raoult's law
D. Le Châtelier's principle

38. What is the solubility (g/L) of N_2 in water (25° C) when the N_2 partial pressure is 0.634 atm?

A. 3.19×10^{-1} g/L
B. 1.5×10^{-2} g/L
C. 1.14×10^{-2} g/L
D. 1.5×10^{-5} g/L

39. Helium is mixed with oxygen in the scuba tanks of divers in order to dilute the oxygen. Why is helium chosen over other gases for this purpose?

A. It is not a diatomic gas.

B. It is less soluble in aqueous solutions and so does not dissolve in body tissues and fluids.

C. It can react with other gases that may dissolve in the body to reverse gas bubble formation.

D. It is present only in trace amounts in water.

40. A scuba tank is filled with 0.32 kg O_2 that is compressed to a volume of 2.8 L. If the temperature of the tank equilibrates with the water at 13° Celsius, what is the pressure inside the tank?

A. 111 atm

B. 83.9 atm

C. 54.6 atm

D. 290 atm

41. Which of the following would you recommend for a diver suffering from decompression sickness?

A. Administration of helium gas

B. Administration of a gas and air mixture, which contains 50 percent nitrous oxide

C. Confinement in a hypobaric chamber

D. Confinement in a hyperbaric chamber

42. The underwater environment in the world's oceans is rapidly changing. Recent years have seen drastic shifts in the ecosystem due to human activity and its impact on the environment. Many populations of fish that rely heavily upon oxygen are declining at extraordinary rates, whereas other ocean species that can survive in oceanic regions of oxygen-depletion are on the rise. What is the most likely explanation, based on scientific theory, for the decline in dissolved oxygen in the world's oceans?

A. Carbon dioxide pollution has increased ocean acidity.

B. A new species of predator shark preys on fish in oxygen-rich regions.

C. The average temperature of the oceans is rapidly increasing.

D. Increased rainfall has added water to oceans without adding more oxygen.

43. A scuba tank contains 0.38 kg of oxygen gas under high pressure. What volume would the oxygen occupy at STP?

A. 0.27 L

B. 35 L

C. 266 L

D. 11 L

44. At 1 atm, the solubility of pure nitrogen in the blood at normal body temperature (37 °C) is 6.2×10^{-4} M. If a diver is at a depth where the pressure is equal to 3 atm and breathes air (78% N_2), calculate the concentration of nitrogen in the diver's blood.

A. 1.3×10^{-3} M

B. 1.4×10^{-3} M

C. 1.5×10^{-5} M

D. 1.9×10^{-3} M

45. Consider two scuba tanks at sea level and 25 °C. Tank 1 is filled with oxygen, and tank 2 is filled with a mixture of oxygen and helium. Will there be a difference in the root-mean-square velocities between these two tanks?

A. Yes, tank 2 has a higher root-mean-square velocity.

B. Yes, tank 1 has a higher root-mean-square velocity.

C. No, they will have the same root-mean-square velocity.

D. The root-mean-square velocity cannot be calculated for the tanks.

PASSAGE V (QUESTIONS 46–52)

Sodium fluoride is used in toothpastes to reduce the virulence of bacteria that cause *dental caries*, also known as cavities. Most U.S. residents are exposed to sodium fluoride, and its use has been correlated with a decline in the incidence of dental caries in most of the population. Although there is debate over the mechanism by which sodium fluoride acts to reduce dental caries, it has been established that the fluoride ion is the main contributor to its efficacy.

Fluoride is the ionic form of the element fluorine. The fluoride ion has a high degree of electronegativity and so holds a negative charge in solution. It thus forms relatively stable bonds with positive ions such as H^+ and Na^+. Fluoride inhibits carinogenic bacteria from metabolizing carbohydrates and thus prevents subsequent production of acid in the oral cavity. The decrease of acidity reduces erosion of tooth enamel, which would otherwise lead to fissures and irregular surface changes in the tooth.

In a variety of laboratory studies, certain types of *Streptococci* bacteria, a main culprit in the formation of caries, are adversely affected when exposed to fluoride ion concentrations of varying levels. In particular, it was found that *Streptococcus sobrinus*, the more virulent species of the *Streptococci*, produces less acid when exposed to fluoride than *Streptococcus sobrinus*, the less virulent form. The reasons for the link of reduced acid production to fluoride levels are still unclear.

46. Based on the passage, which of the following can be definitively stated about the action of fluoride ions on oral health?

A. F- prevents bacteria from forming dental caries.

B. F- kills populations of bacteria that cause dental caries.

C. F- is related to killing populations of bacteria that form dental caries.

D. F- is related to less acid production and reduces the risk of dental caries.

47. Based on the passage, what is a possible mechanism by which fluoride could act upon *Streptococci* bacteria to reduce their production of acid?

A. Fluoride adds enamel to the developing tooth structure.

B. Fluoride fills and closes fissures within the enamel topography.

C. Fluoride adds electrons to bacterial respiration reactions.

D. Fluoride pulls electrons from bacterial respiration reactions.

48. What property contributes to the high electronegativity found in the fluorine atom?

A. Small atomic radius

B. Small number of protons in the nucleus

C. Large number of electrons in the orbit

D. Large number of electron shells in the orbit

49. Which of the following is the correct electronic structure notation for fluoride?

    A. $1s^2 2s^2 2p^5$
    B. $1s^2 2s^2 2p^4$
    C. $[He]2s^2 2p^6$
    D. $[Ne]2p^6$

50. According to Heisenberg, what can be accurately, quantitatively determined in a neutral atom when the location of the electron is found?

    A. Electron momentum
    B. Velocity of electron
    C. Mass of electron
    D. None of the above

51. What is the effective nuclear charge on the outermost electron in fluoride?

    A. 0
    B. –1
    C. +1
    D. +1/2

52. What electrons are most available for bonding in the fluoride ion?

    A. 3s
    B. 2p
    C. 1s
    D. 2s

ANSWERS AND EXPLANATIONS

CHAPTER 1: ATOMIC STRUCTURE

1. A

The material is ferromagnetic (A). Ferromagnetism refers, loosely, to the ability of a surface to attract an external magnetic field. It is characteristic of iron (Fe), from which it derives its name. More specifically, paramagnetism describes the tendency of electrons to align with the same spin in the presence of a strong magnetic field. Strongly paramagnetic materials, including transition metals, are usually called ferromagnetic. Transition metals like iron are characterized by a "sea" of electrons moving freely about the surface, which makes it easier for all these electrons to align in one direction. (This electron "sea" is an imprecise model, but good enough for the MCAT.) It is harder for more stable elements (e.g., oxygen, halogens, noble gases) to align their electrons in one orientation because their orbitals are nearly filled; these substances are known as diamagnetic. This particular problem requires a qualitative assessment of this unknown substance's magnetic properties. The electrons in the figure are aligned in a very regular arrangement, so the surface is either paramagnetic or ferromagnetic. While ferromagnetic substances are also paramagnetic (B), large networks of aligned electrons are characteristic of ferromagnetic compounds only. The individual dipole moments of a diamagnetic substance (C) do not align in any organized pattern.

2. A

The 3d subshell is more stable when full, so it will fill with 10 electrons before any fill the 4s subshell. The 4s subshell then fills later, as it indicates an energy level further from the nucleus. (D) accounts for fewer electrons than those actually present in Zn^{2+}.

3. B

Quantum number ℓ, for angular momentum, cannot be higher than n – 1, ruling out (A). The m_i number, which describes the chemical's magnetic properties, can only be an integer value between $-\ell$ and ℓ, and cannot be equal to 1 if $\ell = 0$, ruling out (C) and (D).

4. C

If you did not know this formula by heart, you can calculate it using your knowledge of the four quantum numbers. For the s shell, the principal quantum number is n = 0; n = 1 for the p shell; and n = 2 for the d shell. (Larger values of n suggest higher energy levels further from the nucleus of the atom, as we know energy is quantized—that is, it differs by discrete amounts—between shells.)

5. B

4l + 2 describes the number of electrons in terms of the azimuthal quantum number l, which ranges from 0 to n – 1, where n is the principal quantum number. (C) resembles the equation which describes the maximum number of electrons in an energy level, which is equal to $2n^2$. Note that this equation is in terms of the principal quantum number n rather than the azimuthal quantum number l.

6. D

Sulfur is diamagnetic, as opposed to ferromagnetic (iron, cobalt) or paramagnetic (hydrogen). Ferromagnetism refers, loosely, to the ability of a surface to attract an external magnetic field. It is characteristic of iron (Fe), from which it derives its name. More specifically, paramagnetism describes the tendency of valence electrons to align with the same spin in the presence of a strong magnetic field. Strongly paramagnetic materials, including transition metals, are usually called ferromagnetic. Transition metals like iron are characterized by a "sea" of electrons moving freely about the surface, which makes it easier for all these electrons to align in one direction. (This electron "sea" is an imprecise model, but good enough for the MCAT.) It is harder for more stable elements (e.g., oxygen, halogens, noble gases) to align their electrons in one orientation because their orbitals are nearly filled; these substances are known as diamagnetic. Sulfur has a similar atomic structure to oxygen, so it is also diamagnetic.

7. D

The problem requires the MCAT favorite equation $E = hf$, where $h = 6.626 \times 10^{-34}$ (Planck's constant) and f is the frequency of the photon. (Memorize Planck's constant!) One can calculate the frequency of the photon using the provided wavelength, 500 nm, with the equation $f = c/\lambda$, where $c = 3 \times 10^8$ m/s, the speed of light. Here, $f = (3 \times 10^8$ m/s$)/500 \times 10^{-9}$ m, or 6×10^{14} s^{-1} (1 Hz = 1 s^{-1}). That leads to $E = hf$, or $E = (6.626 \times 10^{-34}) \times (6 \times 10^{14}$ Hz$) = 3.98 \times 10^{-19}$ J. (Don't worry about memorizing the units

of Planck's constant—energy is always in joules). But the problem includes an additional trick, in that the answer must account for a mole of photons. The $E = hf$ equation works for a single photon only. Thus the answer must account for this using Avogadro's number, i.e., 6.022×10^{23} photons. Multiply 3.98×10^{-19} J/photon × 6.022×10^{23} photons = 2.39×10^3 J total.

8. B

(C) and (D) are out of scope. There is not enough information to determine how the velocity of the electron will change. There will be some energy change, however, as the electron must lose energy to return to the minimum energy ground state. That will require emitting radiation in the form of a photon (B). Absorbing a photon (A) is opposite.

9. A

Recall that the superscript (i.e., the A in ^AC) refers to the mass number of an electron, which is equal to the number of protons plus the number of neutrons present in an element. (Sometimes a text will list the atomic number, Z, or total number of protons, under the mass number A.) According to the periodic table, carbon contains 6 protons, i.e., its atomic number Z = 6. An isotope contains the same number of protons and a different number of neutrons as the element. Carbon is most likely to have an atomic number of 12, for 6 protons and 6 neutrons. It cannot have 6 protons and 0 neutrons, or it would likely collapse under the stress of the positive charge. That means (A) is an impossible isotope. (B), (C), and (D) are all possible isotopes, as reflected by the atomic number A of carbon, which is usually reported as just under 13 amu. Carbon-12 and carbon-14 (as in 6 protons, 8 neutrons, the isotope used in carbon-14 radioactive dating) are carbon's most common isotopes.

10. C

Make sure to read the question carefully: (A) and (D) (opposite) violate the Heisenberg uncertainty principle, which states that you cannot know the position and momentum of a particle simultaneously. The Heisenberg uncertainty principle refers explicitly to particle position and momentum, but momentum depends on velocity (recall from Newtonian mechanics that p = mv), so you can calculate its momentum and its velocity at the same time. (B), which pairs position and velocity, is a distortion, as a known velocity implies a known momentum.

11. C

Orbital shapes such as that in the figure are derived from a wave function, which estimates the probability that an electron will be found within the illustrated space at a given moment in time. The electron is more likely to be found in its more dense regions of space. Here, it is best to rely on qualitative experience with orbital pictures, though quantum numbers also suggest orbital shape. The s-orbital is spherical, and p-orbitals are like s-orbitals split by a central plane in one dimension (x, y, or z) where no electron will be found. This plane creates an overall lobed or "bowling pin" shape, and is known as a nodal plane (for the node of the wave function, or for "no electron," for MCAT purposes). Two nodal planes in two different directions split the d-orbital, and three nodal planes in three directions split the f-orbital. This image suggests two splits, for four total lobes, indicating a d-orbital.

12. B

If an electron falls from a higher energy level to a lower energy level, it emits a photon of a specific wavelength. That is, the transition emits light energy. That rules out (A) and (D), which are opposite. As an electron moves from n = 1 to outer energy levels, there is less difference in the energy levels. In other words, there is a larger energy difference between n = 2 and n = 3 than there is between n = 3 and n = 4. Though the transition in (C) would absorb energy, the transition in (B) would require absorbing more energy because it must compensate for a larger energy difference.

13. A

The MCAT covers qualitative topics from the Atomic Structure unit more often than its quantitative topics. It is critical to be able to distinguish the fundamental principles that determine electron organization, which are usually known by the name of the scientist who discovered them. The Heisenberg uncertainty principle (B) refers to the momentum and position of a single electron, and the Bohr model (C) was an early attempt to describe the behavior of the single electron in a hydrogen atom. (D) is a tempting distortion, but (A) is more complete. Nitrogen, the smallest element with half-filled p subshell, is often used as an example of Hund's rule in general chemistry textbooks. Hund's rule is really a corollary of the Pauli exclusion principle, in that the Pauli exclusion principle suggests that each orbital contains two electrons of opposite spin. Additional electrons must fill new orbitals so the compound remains stable in its ground state.

14. C

The Thomson model (1904) was the early "plum pudding" idea of the atom. The Rutherford model (1911) is most like the stick and ball drawings familiar from nuclear physics (or biohazard symbols). The Bohr model of the hydrogen atom came later in the early 20th century and accounted for quantized energy levels. A basic understanding of the chronology of atomic theory will increase your understanding of the underlying physical principles that the MCAT will likely test.

15. A

This problem requires distinguishing the atomic number from the mass number. Here, the mass number is equal to the number of protons plus the number of neutrons. Usually the number of neutrons is calculated by subtracting the atomic number, or the number of protons listed on the periodic table, from the mass number. If the atom is uncharged, the number of protons is the same as the number of electrons. A Cs^+ cation has one fewer electron than the uncharged species. Here it is simplest to use the atomic number from the periodic table, 55, and subtract one, for a total of 54 electrons. (A) is the uncharged species, (C) is the number of neutrons, and (D) is the mass number.

16. B

Set up a system of two algebraic equations, where x and y are the percentages of H (mass = 1 amu) and D (mass = 2 amu) respectively. Your setup should look like the following:

x + y = 1 (proportion H(x) + proportion D(y) in whole, i.e., x% + y% = 100%)

1x + 2y = 1.008 (the total atomic mass).

Substitute one variable for the other so the atomic mass is in terms of one variable (e.g., 1 – y = x), then solve for the other percentage ([1 – y] + 2y = 1.008; simplifies to 0.008 = y, or 0.8% D). That, plus 99.2% H makes 100%. These isotope calculations are straightforward if you have memorized the method, so they are an MCAT favorite. Remember to convert from proportions to percentages.

17. A

The answer choices refer to the magnetic spin of the two electrons. The quantum number m_s repre-sents this property, as a measure of the electrons' relative intrinsic angular momentum. These electrons' spins are parallel, in that their spins are aligned in the same direction (i.e., $m_s = +\frac{1}{2}$ for both species. This implies that (B) and (C) are opposite. They would suppose that $m_s = +\frac{1}{2}$ for one electron and $-\frac{1}{2}$ for the other. Paired (D) refers to electrons of opposite spin in the same orbital.

18. B

Cr, Fe^{2+}, and Co^{3+} all have 24 total electrons. They are isoelectronic, in that they have the same number of total electrons. Under standard electron configuration rules, this total might suggest an overall configuration $1s^22s^22p^63s^23p^64s^23d^4$. In fact, the 3d subshell fills first, as it is lower in energy than the 4s subshell, so the configuration is actually more like $[Ar]4s^03d^6$. In fact, this arrangement is not precise in the case of Cr. (Keep in mind that electron configuration is an imprecise atomic model.) If the subshells are "filling up," the 3d shell attains maximum stability if it is half-filled with 5 unpaired d electrons of parallel spin (Hund's rule). In rare cases, one and only one electron is "promoted" to achieve maximum stability in the orbitals, i.e., $[Ar]4s^13d^5$. For the isoelectronic cations, electrons are actually removed from previously filled larger neutral atomic species. Neutral Fe has 26 electrons, or $[Ar]4s^03d^8$, and Co has 27, or $[Ar]4s^03d^9$. You cannot promote one electron in either of these atomic arrangements and benefit from Hund's rule in the 3d subshell. Thus, its valence electrons "stay put," so to speak, where they already are. For Fe^{2+} and Co^{3+}, this means that the configuration is actually $[Ar]4s^03d^6$, While Mn^+ is isoelectronic to the other answer choices, it is actually extremely unlikely in nature; Mn^{2+} and Mn^{4+} are far more common. Neutral Mn is $[Ar]4s^03d^7$, which makes Mn^{2+}, or $[Ar]4s^03d^5$, unusually stable, and Mn^+, or $[Ar]4s^03d^6$ unstable. (You cannot promote if you are removing electrons to form cations, only if you are "filling up.") Electron configuration in the transition metals can be confusing, but is essential practice for Test Day.

19. D

Electrons are assumed to be in motion in any energy level, even in the ground state. The electron's principal quantum number, or energy level, is n = 1. It must be an integer value in both the ground and excited states. This number gives a relative indication of the electron's distance from the nucleus, so it must have the smallest radius of all the energy levels. The further the electron moves from the nucleus, the greater energy it needs to overcome its attractive forces.

20. C

High pressure is unlikely to excite an electron out of the ground state unless it causes an extreme change in temperature, which would add enough energy to the system to promote the electron.

CHAPTER 2: THE PERIODIC TABLE

1. B

First recall that the periodic table is organized with periods (rows) and groups (columns). This method of organization allows elements to be organized such that some chemical properties can be predicted based on an element's position in the table. Groups (columns) are particularly significant because they represent sets of elements with the same outer electron configuration. In other words, all elements within the same group will have the same configuration of *valence electrons*, which in turn will dictate many of the chemical properties of those similar elements. Although (A) is true, it does not explain the similarity in chemical properties as effectively as (B); most other metals—similar to lithium and sodium or not—produce positively-charged ions. (C) is not true, because periods are rows and lithium and sodium are in the same column. Finally, although lithium and sodium have relatively low atomic weights (D), their chemical properties are better explained by their valence electron configurations.

2. A

This question assesses understanding of a key periodic trend: atomic radii. As one moves from left to right across a period (row), atomic radii decrease. This occurs because, as more protons are added to the nucleus and more electrons are added within the same shell, there is no increased shielding between the protons and electrons (though there is increased attractive electrostatic force). This effect decreases the atomic radius. In contrast, as one moves from top to bottom down a group (column), extra electron shells have accumulated, despite the fact that the valence configurations remain identical. These extra electron shells provide shielding between the positive nucleus and the outermost electrons, decreasing the electrostatic forces and increasing the atomic radius. Because carbon and silicon are in the same group, and silicon is further down the period table, it will have a larger atomic radius because of its extra electron shell. (C) and (D) are incorrect because all elements in the same group have the same number of valence electrons.

3. C

The number of valence electrons (item I) does have an impact on the atomic radius. As one moves across a period (row) and valence electrons are added, along with protons in the atom's nucleus, the electrons are more strongly attracted to the central protons. This attraction tightens the atom, shrinking the atomic radius. The number of electron shells is also significant, as demonstrated by the trend when moving down a group (column). As more electron shells (item II) are added which separate the positively charged nucleus from the outermost electrons, the electrostatic forces are weakened and the atomic radius increases. The number of neutrons (item III) is irrelevant.

4. C

Ionization energy is related to the same set of forces that explain atomic radius, as well as the rules governing maintenance of a full valence shell octet. The first set of rules dictates that the stronger the attractive forces between the outer electron (the electron to be ionized) and the positively charged nucleus, the more energy will be required to ionize. As a result, strong attractive forces, which make the atomic radius smaller toward the right of a period or the top of a group, will also increase the first ionization energy. With this information alone, one could guess that the ionization energy for beryllium (Be) should be higher than that for Li (lithium), eliminating (C) and (D). Secondly, the first ionization energy is always lower than the second ionization energy. This property holds true for the same reasons previously discussed. For example, once removing one electron from beryllium, the ion is Be^{+1}, which has one more proton in its nucleus than it has electrons surrounding it. Thus, there is a heightened electrostatic force between the positive nucleus and the now less-negative electron cloud, meaning that all remaining electrons will be held more tightly than that first electron. Removing a second electron will be more difficult than the initial electron removal, making the second ionization energy higher than the first. To quantify these differences, the first ionization energy for Li is 520.2 kJ/mol, the first ionization energy for Be is 899.5 kJ/mol, and the second ionization energy for Be is 1757.1 kJ/mol.

5. D

Selenium is to the right of the diagonal line that separates metals and nonmetals, but it is not adjacent to this line and thus is not a metalloid. In its period, Ge is the rightmost metal, while As is a metalloid. Se is the only nonmetal in the fourth period, and to its right is the halogen, Br. Alkali metals are in the first column, Group IA, of which Se is not a member.

6. C

The trend in the periodic table demonstrated by the figure is correct for increasing electronegativity and first ionization energy. Electronegativity describes how strong of an attraction an element will have for electrons in a bond. A nucleus with a stronger electrostatic pull due to its positive charge will have a higher electronegativity; this is represented with an arrow pointing right because nuclear charge increases toward the right side of a period. This mirrors the trend for ionization energies, since a stronger nuclear pull will also lead to an increased first ionization energy (the forces make it more difficult to remove an electron). The vertical arrow can be explained by the size of the atoms. As size decreases, the proximity of the outermost electrons to the positive inner nucleus increases, making the positive charge more effective at attracting new electrons in a chemical bond; this leads to higher electronegativity. Similarly, the more effective the positive nuclear charge, the higher the first ionization energy. Thus, items I and III follow the trends. Atomic radius (item II) follows the opposite trend.

7. C

Although metals have high melting points (D), the most significant property contributing to their ability to conduct electricity is the fact that they have valence electrons that can move freely (C). Metals have large atomic radii and low ionization energies, as well as low electronegativity, all of which contribute to the ability of their outermost electrons to be easily removed. Because electricity is carried by currents of electrons, this free movement of outer electrons is the most important characteristic in making them good conductors. Although it is important that metals are malleable (A) and maybe even more important that they have ductility (they can be easily made into wires), (C) is still the best answer explaining their ability to conduct electricity effectively.

8. B

This group of elements—the alkaline earth metals—is chemically important because its constituents form divalent cations, or ions with a +2 charge. All of the elements in Group IIA have two electrons in their outermost s orbital, making their outermost shell have much less than a complete octet. Because loss of these two electrons would then leave a full octet as the outermost shell, becoming a divalent cation is a stable configuration for all of the alkaline earth metals. Although some of these elements might have metallic properties, including conduction, the best conductors in the periodic table are the metals, not Group IIA, so (A) is incorrect. (C) is incorrect because, although forming a divalent cation is a stable configuration for the alkaline earths, the second ionization energy is still always higher than the first due to the increased positive nuclear charge when compared with the outer negative charge from the electrons. (D) is incorrect because atomic radii increase when moving down a group of elements since the number of electron shells increases.

9. C

A few of the solutions are simple to eliminate. Both aluminum and silicon are in the third period, so (A) is incorrect. Silicon is a metalloid while aluminum is a metal (D); in the periodic table, they're on opposite sides of the diagonal line that separates these two groups of elements. Both (B) and (C) are true; however, (C) better describes the difference in reactivity. Metalloids are an unusual set of elements within the periodic table with widely varying physical and chemical properties, which make them definitively different from the elements to their left (the metals) and those to the right (the nonmetals). The metalloids can have widely different densities, boiling points, melting points, appearance, and conductivities. Additionally, many of the metalloids will react differently with different elements and have chemical properties quite different from elements nearby in the periodic table.

10. C

First eliminate (B) and (D) because they represent the notation for periods, not groups. All groups are named with Roman numerals and then use the letters A or B to indicate whether they are representative elements (s or p as outermost orbitals) or nonrepresentative elements (d- or f- orbitals outermost). Next, the correct trend for increasing electronegativity moves from left to right across the periodic table, making (C) correct. This trend occurs because, when moving to the right across the periodic table, electrons are added to the same outermost valence shell, and protons are added to the nucleus. Because there are no new electron shells between the nucleus and the outer electrons, there is no increase in shielding when moving across the periodic table. This means that there is now a stronger electrostatic force between the positive nucleus and the negative outermost electrons, which decreases the atomic radius and increases the attractive forces for new electrons.

11. B

Iron, Fe^{2+}, is a transition metal. Transition metals can often form more than one ion—iron, for example, can be Fe^{2+} or Fe^{3+}. The transition metals, in these multiple different states, can often form hydration complexes, or complexes with water. Part of the significance of these complexes is that when a transition metal can form a complex, its solubility within this complexed solvent will increase.

Although other ions, such as (A) or (C), can dissolve readily in water, they do not typically form complexes with water. S^{2-} (D) is not a transition metal, so it is unlikely to form a complex with water.

12. D

This question is simple if you recall that periods are the horizontal rows of the periodic table, while columns are the vertical groupings. Within one period, an additional valence electron is added with each step toward the right side of the table (D).

13. B

This question requires knowledge of the trends of electronegativity within the periodic table. Electronegativity increases as one moves from left to right across periods, i.e., when protons are added to the nucleus and additional electrons are added to the same valence shell. Electronegativity *decreases* as one moves down the periodic table, because there are more electron shells separating the nucleus from the outermost electrons. The noble gases, however, also have extremely low electronegative since they already have full valence shells and do not have an affinity for holding on to additional electrons. The most electronegative atom in the periodic table is fluoride. Remembering this fact will guide you to recall the electronegativity trend, and might help you quickly identify the answer choice closest in proximity to fluoride. (B) chlorine is the most electronegative here. Though I (D) will be fairly electronegative, its higher atomic radius and position further down on the periodic table makes it less electronegative than Cl. Mg and Li (A) and (C) are elements with very low electronegativity; because they have only two and one valence electrons, respectively, they are more likely to lose these electrons in a bond than to gain electrons, since the loss of electrons would leave them with a full octet. This propensity to lose/not hold tightly electrons in a bond defines low electronegativity.

14. B

Electron affinity is related to several factors, including atomic size (radius) and filling of the valence shell. As atomic radius increases, the distance between the inner protons in the nucleus and the outermost electrons increases, thereby decreasing the attractive forces between protons and electrons. Additionally, as more electron shells are added from period to period, these shells shield the outermost electrons increasingly from inner protons. As a result, increased atomic radius will lead to lower electron affinity. Since atoms are in a low-energy state when their outermost valence electron shell is filled, atoms needing only 1–2 electrons to complete this shell will have high electron affinities. In contrast, atoms with already full valence shells—with a full octet of eight electrons—will have very low electron affinity since adding an extra electron would require a new shell. It is clear that (C) and (D) will likely have lower electron affinities than (A) and (B) because there is an extra electron shell "shielding" the nucleus from the outer electrons. (A)'s valence electron shell is already full with a complete octet, granting it extremely low electron affinity. (B) has one electron missing from its outermost shell, as does (D). This valence electron configuration is conducive to wanting to accept electrons readily or to having a high electron affinity. (B) is the configuration of chlorine, while (D) is bromine. (B) is a better answer than (D), however, because the additional shell of electrons shielding the nucleus in (D) will decrease its electron affinity when compared with (B).

15. C

Electronegativity is a property that describes an atom's attraction for bonding electrons. Highly electronegative atoms pull bonding electrons closely; atoms with low electronegativity, meanwhile, hold bonding electrons loosely. In an atom with a large atomic radius, the distance between the outermost electrons, used in bonding, and the central nucleus with a positive charge, is large. This increased distance means that the positively charged nucleus has little ability to attract new, bonding electrons toward it. In comparison, if the atomic radius is small, the force from the positively charged protons will have a stronger effect, because the distance through which they have to act is decreased. Atomic radius decreases when moving from left to right across periods in the periodic table (A). Atomic radius alone does not give enough information for one to ascertain the second ionization energy (B); it is significant to also consider the valence electron configuration. Finally, there is insufficient information for (D).

16. D

The effective nuclear charge refers to the strength with which the protons in the nucleus can "pull" additional electrons. The effective nuclear charge helps to explain electron affinity, electronegativity, and ionization energy. In Cl, the nonionized chlorine atom, the nuclear charge is balanced by the surrounding electrons, so without knowing the exact number, it is balanced: $17^+/17^-$. The chloride ion, in contrast, has a lower effective nuclear charge, because there are more electrons than protons: $17^+/18^-$. Next, elemental potassium also has a "balanced" effective nuclear charge: $19^+/19^-$. Finally, K^+, ionic potassium, has a higher effective nuclear charge than any of the other choices, because it has more protons than electrons: $19^+/18^-$. Thus, the potassium ion (D) is the correct answer.

17. D

Ionic bonds are bonds formed through unequal sharing of electrons. These bonds typically occur because the electron affinities of the two bonded atoms differ greatly. For example, the halogens have a high electron affinity because adding a single electron to their valence shell would create a full outer octet. In

contrast, the alkaline earth metals have a very low electron affinity and are more likely to be electron donors because the loss of one electron would leave them with a full outer octet. This marked difference in electron affinity is the best explanation for the formation of ionic bonds between these two different groups. Because the halogens have high electron affinity and the alkaline earth metals have low affinity, so (A) is incorrect, as is (B) because in ionic bonding electrons are not shared equally. Although (C) is correct because atomic radius decreases when moving to the right across a period, this is not the best explanation for formation of ionic bonds.

18. C

In the first period, all elements have only an s-orbital. Beginning in the second period, elements have a 2s- and a 2p-orbital. In the third period, there are 3s-, 3p-, and 3d-orbitals. However, the 3d-orbital is not filled until the fourth period of the table, in which one encounters the first set of transition elements. Despite the fact that it is unfilled in the third period, these elements still have a 3d-orbital, and some elements utilized unfilled spaces in this orbital for bonding.

19. D

Transition metals such as silver have the ability to form different types of complexes, including hydration complexes with water and complexes with other compounds. Formation of a complex with the transition metal ion will increase the ability of the solute to dissolve into solution. Because the AgBr does not dissolve readily in beaker A, it is unlikely that any complex is being formed. Even if a complex were being formed in that beaker, it has minimal, if any, effect on dissolving AgBr and thus does not explain the phenomenon observed. (A) is incorrect. However, because AgBr dissolves more quickly in beaker B, it is reasonable to consider that silver could form a complex with the solvent, ammonia

(D). Though there might be hydrogen bonding between water and bromide, (C), this would not explain why beaker A dissolves more slowly than B. (B) is irrelevant; the type of bond between Ag and Br would be the same in both beakers and would not explain the different rates of dissolution between the two beakers.

CHAPTER 3: BONDING AND CHEMICAL INTERACTIONS

1. B

Carbon monoxide, CO, has a double bond between carbon and oxygen, with the carbon retaining one lone pair, and oxygen retaining two lone pairs. The most important thing to know here is the definition of a polar covalent bond. This type of bond forms when the difference in electronegativity between two bonded atoms is great enough to cause electrons to move disproportionately toward the more electronegative atom, but not great enough to form an ionic bond. This is the case for CO. Oxygen is more electronegative than CO, and thus will cause a polarity of the bond, with the negative charge disproportionately carried on the oxygen, leaving the carbon atom slightly positive. The bond is not ionic, because this type of bond happens with large differences in electronegativity, typically between atoms in the first 1 or 2 columns of the periodic table when bonded to atoms like halogens. Nonpolar covalent bonds occur when there is no difference in electronegativity between the two bonded atoms, such as the carbon-carbon bond in CH_3–CH_3. Coordinate covalent bonding occurs when a Lewis acid and Lewis base bond through donation of a lone pair from Lewis base to Lewis acid.

2. B

Here you must understand the contribution of resonance structures to average formal charge.

In (B) CO_3^{2-}, there are three possible resonance structures. Each of the three oxygen atoms carries a formal charge of -1 in two out of the three structures. This averages to approximately $-2/3$ charge on each oxygen atom, which is more than that in any of the other answer choices. To prove this, we can estimate the formal charges on each oxygen atom in (A), (C), and (D). There are no formal charges in H_2O, which has no resonance structures. In ozone, O_3, there are two possible resonance structures. The central oxygen carries a positive charge in both structures, and each outer oxygen carries a negative charge in one of the two possible resonance structures. This leaves an average charge of $-1/2$ on the two outer oxygens, which is less than the $-2/3$ in CO_3^{2-}. Finally, CH_2O has no resonance structures and therefore no formal charge on oxygen.

3. C

The two most important contributing resonance structures are items I and II. Resonance structures are representations of how charges are shared across a molecule. In reality, the charge distribution is an average of contributing resonance structures. The most stable resonance structures are those that minimize charge on the atoms in the molecule; the more stable the structure, the more it will contribute to the overall charge distribution in the molecule. Both structures in I and II have one negative charge on one of the two oxygens, and one positive charge on the central nitrogen atom. Structure III would not be an important resonance structure because it distributes two negative charges, one on each oxygen atom, and two positive charges, both on the nitrogen atom. Due to this distribution of formal charges, it is a less stable configuration and thus not an important resonance structure for NO_2.

4. E

The key to answering this question is to understand the types of intermolecular forces that occur in each of these molecules. Kr (III) is a noble gas, so the only IMFs present are dispersion forces (also called London forces), which are the weakest type of IMFs. This means that these molecules are held together extremely loosely, and will be the easiest to transition from the organized liquid phase to the disorganized gaseous phase, because they are not held tightly together. Acetone (I) is a polar molecule, and as such it has the benefit of dipole-dipole forces, which are stronger than dispersion forces. In dipole-dipole forces, these polar molecules will be arranged such that the positive and negative ends of molecules associate with each other, holding these molecules more closely together than in nonpolar compounds. Next, the intermolecular forces present in isopropyl alcohol (IV) include hydrogen bonding. In hydrogen bonding, an electronegative atom (i.e., oxygen or nitrogen) is bound to hydrogen, and the highly electronegative atom strips hydrogen of its electrons, leaving hydrogen as a predominantly positive atom, allowing it to interact with nearby partial negative charges. These forces are even stronger than dipole-dipole interactions. Finally, the strongest interaction is a compound with an ionic bond, such as potassium chloride (II). In this compound, the intermolecular forces are so strong that they have formed an ionic bond between two atoms with disparate electronegativities; this type of molecule would have the highest boiling point.

5. C

First check each atom involved to be sure that it follows electron configurations as you would expect. Each of the fluorides should have a full octet, including three lone pairs on each fluoride, with one shared pair bonding the fluoride to the central chloride. All of these are correct. If the chloride did not have any lone pairs, it would have a formal charge of +3. Because chloride is in the third period, all elements in or beyond the third period have

d-orbitals, which can accommodate extra electrons. Thus, by adding two pairs of electrons as lone pairs on the central chloride, the central chloride will end up with: FC = 7 − ½(8) − 4 = −1, a formal charge of negative one, by following the equation:

Formal charge = V (valence electrons in the free atom) −½ $N_{bonding}$ (electrons shared in bonds) − $N_{nonbonding}$ (lone pairs/free electrons)

Because all the fluoride atoms have formal charges of zero, the entire molecule must have a charge of −1.

6. C

The central atom in CO_3, carbon, has no lone pairs. It has three resonance structures with each of its bonds to oxygen, thus carrying partial double-bond character, and it has no further orbitals used for bonding or use for carrying lone pairs. This makes CO_3's geometry trigonal planar. Alternatively, ClF_3 also has three bonds, one to each of three fluoride atoms. However, chloride still maintains two extra lone pairs (without which the formal charge on the central chloride atom is +4; with the two lone pairs it is zero, a more stable configuration). These lone pairs each inhabit one orbital, meaning that the central chloride must organize five items about itself: three bonds to fluorides and two lone pairs. The best configuration for maximizing the distance between all of these groups is trigonal bipyramidal. Although (A) and (B) are true, they do not account for the difference in geometry. (D) is incorrect; CO_3 has no lone pairs on its central atom, while ClF_3 has two lone pairs.

7. A

Try drawing the structure of each of these molecules and then considering the electronegativity of each bond as it might contribute to an overall dipole moment. HCN (A) is correct because it is linear in structure, and nitrogen is more electronegative than carbon, which is more electronegative than hydrogen. This would cause a strong dipole moment in the direction of the nitrogen, with the strongest delta-minus charge over the nitrogen atom. H_2O is bent, and oxygen is more electronegative than hydrogen, thus creating a dipole moment in the direction of the two oxygen atoms. However, due to the bent configuration, the dipole moment is of a smaller magnitude than that of HCN. Sulfur dioxide has a similar bent configuration, and has even less of a difference in electronegativity between sulfur and oxygen than that of the hydrogen and oxygen atoms in water. Thus, SO_2 (D) does not exceed the dipole moment of HCN. CCl_4 (C) has a tetrahedral geometry, so while each individual C–Cl bond is polarized, with the more electronegative chloride atom carrying the slightly negative charge, the orientation of these bonds causes the polarizations to cancel each other out, yielding no overall dipole moment.

8. D

Bond lengths decrease as the bond order increases, and they also decrease in a trend moving up the periodic table's columns or to the right across the rows. In this case, because both C_2H_2 and NCH have triple bonds, we cannot compare the bond lengths based upon bond order. We must rely on one of the other two periodic trends. Bond length decreases when moving to the right along rows because more electronegative atoms have shorter radii as a result of their increased electronegativity. The nitrogen in NCH is likely to hold its electrons closer, in a shorter radius, than the second carbon in C_2H_2. (A) is incorrect; a bond between similar atoms is longer than a bond between two different atoms. (B) is incorrect; there are no significant resonance structures contributing to the character of either triple bond. (C) is incorrect because although carbon is more electronegative than hydrogen, the C–H bond is not the triple bond and thus makes

little, if any, contribution to the length of the carbon-carbon triple bond.

9. C

When hydrogen bonds to a strongly electronegative atom such as nitrogen or oxygen, the electronegative atom disproportionately pulls the shared pair in the covalent bond toward itself. Because hydrogen has no lone pairs, the movement of the shared pair further away from the center of the hydrogen atom leaves the hydrogen atom with a partial positive character. This allows the hydrogen atom to have strong interactions—hydrogen bonds—with nearby negative or partial-negative charges. (A) is not true; hydrogen has little electronegativity and does not hold its valence electrons closely. (B) is true, and the fact that hydrogen has no lone pairs is somewhat relevant to the character of hydrogen bonding, though this doesn't explain as well as (C) the forces of hydrogen bonding. (D) is not correct; although these bonds are highly polarized, they are not ionic.

10. D

First you must recall that ammonium is NH_4^+, while ammonia (commonly confused) is NH_3. It helps to associate the suffix *-ium* with a charged form of the molecule. Once you remember that ammonium is NH_4^+, you can eliminate all of the answer choices that refer to three—not four—bonds (A) and (C). Next, it helps to recall that ammonium is formed by the association of NH_3 (uncharged, with a lone pair on the nitrogen) with a positively charge hydrogen cation (no lone pairs). In other words, NH_3 is a Lewis base, while H^+ is a Lewis acid. This type of bonding between Lewis acid and base is a coordinate covalent bond. Thus, we know that there is one coordinate covalent bond in this molecule, making (D) the answer. You can confirm this by knowing that there are three polar covalent bonds in NH_3, each between nitrogen and hydrogen, because nitrogen is more electronegative than hydrogen. (B) is incorrect because the final bond between N–H in NH_4^+ is a coordinate covalent bond, not a polar covalent bond.

11. D

All atoms in the third period and above in the periodic table have d-orbitals, which can hold extra electrons. They are not limited by the typical eight valence electrons of s- and p-orbitals, which hold two and six electrons, respectively. The octet rule can also be violated by having subvalent atoms, as with hydrogen or boron atoms, both of which are typically surrounded by fewer than eight electrons. (A) and (B) are irrelevant. (C) recognizes that an extra orbital can allow expansion, but the f-orbitals are not primarily responsible for expansion beyond the octet.

12. C

All of the listed types of forces dictate interactions among different types of molecules. However, noble gases are entirely uncharged, without polar covalent bonds, ionic bonds, or dipole moments. The only listed forces which could relate to noble gases could be (A) van der Waals or (C) dispersion. Of these two, van der Waals is a more general name for both dispersion and dipole-dipole interactions, whereas dispersion refers specifically to a type of interaction which occurs among all bonded atoms due to the unequal sharing of electrons at any given moment in the electron's orbit. Therefore, without even understanding how these forces relate to phase change, you should be able to appreciate that (C) is most likely correct. More specifically, dispersion forces result from the fact that spinning electrons at any given moment in time are shared unequally between the two atoms between which they form a bond. This unequal sharing allows for instantaneous partial positive and partial negative charges within the molecule, allowing some of the partial charges to provide attraction to their

opposite partial charges on nearby molecules. Without these interactions, although small, there would be no attraction at all between molecules of noble gases. Without any attraction, noble gases would be unable to liquefy. Thus, you have confirmed that (C) is in fact correct.

13. B

The key to this question is to understand the pattern of filling for s- and d-orbitals among the transition metals. The d-orbitals will fill first, with one electron in each of the 5 d-orbitals (one of each spin type). After there is one electron in each of the 5 d-orbitals, it takes less energy to put the next electron into the s-orbital than it would to add the same electron to one of the d-orbitals that is already inhabited. Thus, first the d-orbitals will fill for the first five electrons, followed by the sixth electron going into the higher-energy s-orbital, and then the filling of the d-orbitals will continue one at a time. For chromium, atomic number 24, the shorthand allows for designation of the preceding noble gas configuration for Argon (Ar – 18). The next orbitals to be filled for chromium, in the fourth row, are the 3 d-orbitals, up to its first five electrons, with the final electron going into the 4s1 position.

14. A

In this Lewis diagram, the PO_4^{3-} molecule has an overall formal charge of –3. The four oxygens each would be assigned a formal change of –1, based on the following formula:

formal charge = V (valence electrons in the free atom) $-\frac{1}{2}$ $N_{bonding}$ (electrons shared in bonds) $-$ $N_{nonbonding}$ (lone pairs/free electrons).

For each oxygen we calculate: FC = 6 $-\frac{1}{2}$ (2) $-$ 6 = –1. For the central phosphorus, we can assume that with a total formal charge of -3 and four oxygens with a charge of –1 each, the phosphorus must have a formal charge of +1. Alternatively, one could calculate its formal charge:

$$FC = 5 - \frac{1}{2}(8) - 0 = +1$$

Finally, this molecule is actually more complex than the drawn Lewis diagram; it has multiple resonance structures, in each of which the phosphorus forms a double bond with one oxygen, giving that oxygen atom and the central phosphorus each a formal charge of zero. There are four such resonance structures. Thus, the oxygens in fact have formal charges between –1 (in four out of the five structures) and zero (in the one favorable configuration in which it shares a double bond), while the phosphorus has a charge of zero in four out of five of the configurations and a change of +1 in one configuration. This further corroborates that the central phosphorus has the most positive formal charge. It is clear that the atoms do not share the charge equally (B), nor do the four oxygens share the highest charge (C) (they actually share the lowest (most negative) charge). The geometry of this molecule is not trigonal pyramidal, but rather tetrahedral (D).

15. D

Calcium chloride is a molecule formed by ionic bonding. Ionic bonding is a very strong type of bond, with strong intermolecular and electrostatic forces. As a result, ionic compounds have very high melting and boiling points due to the amount of energy required to break down these high-energy interactions. (A) is incorrect; covalent compounds would be more likely to have low boiling points. These electrostatic forces also cause liquid and aqueous states of ionic compounds to be good conductors of electricity, the opposite of (B) and (C). A covalent compound, alternatively, would not conduct electricity in the liquid or aqueous states. Finally, although ionic compounds can conduct electricity well in both the liquid and aqueous phases, they form strong crystal lattices in the

solid state, matching positive and negative charges on adjacent molecules, making them poor conductors of electricity in the solid state.

16. C

The reaction in this question shows a water molecule, which has two lone pairs of electrons on the central oxygen, combining with a free hydrogen ion, without any outer electrons. The resulting molecule, H_3O^+, has formed a new bond between H^+ and H_2O. This bond is formed by sharing one of the lone pairs on the oxygen with the free H^+ ion. This is essentially a donation of a shared pair of electrons from a Lewis base (H_2O) to a Lewis acid (H^+, electron acceptor). The charge in the resulting molecule is +1, and is mostly present on the central oxygen, which now only has one lone pair and three shared pairs in bonds, resulting in only five valence electrons. This type of bond, formed from a Lewis acid and Lewis base, is called a coordinate covalent bond. Although this bond is formed between a hydrogen atom and an oxygen atom, (D) is not as good a selection as (C).

17. B

NH_3 has three hydrogen atoms bonded to the central nitrogen, and one lone pair on the central nitrogen. These four groups—three atoms, one lone pair—lead NH_3 to be sp^3 hybridized. By hybridizing all three p-orbitals and the one s-orbital, four groups are arranged about the central atom, maximizing the distance between the groups to minimize the energy of the configuration. This property of NH_3's hybridization leads to its tetrahedral geometry. In contrast, BF_3 has three atoms, but no lone pairs, leading to sp^2 hybridization. This hybridization leads to a trigonal planar geometry. (A) is incorrect; although BF_3 has three bonded atoms and no lone pairs, its geometry is trigonal planar not pyramidal. Although NH_3 has one lone pair (C), that does not provide a strong explanation for the geometrical differences between the two molecules. Although (D) is true, the polarity of the molecules does not explain their geometry; rather, the molecules' different geometries contribute to the overall polarity of the molecules.

18. B

Beryllium is an unusual element in that it does not obey the octet rule. Most atoms require that they have eight outer electrons—the "octet rule." However, some atoms can have fewer than eight valence electrons (sub-octet) or more than eight outer electrons. Beryllium, like hydrogen, boron, and aluminum, can have fewer than eight outer electrons. As a result, when bonding with chloride, beryllium is likely to form only two bonds, using its own two outer valence electrons and one from each chloride to form $BeCl_2$, as drawn in (B). (A) completes the octet for beryllium with two lone pairs, which would be a much less likely configuration. Similarly, (C) and (D) complete beryllium's octet inappropriately. (D) is even less correct because there are too many electrons around each chloride—10 each, due to the double bonds— and chloride should not exceed the octet rule.

19. B

This question requires an understanding of the trends that cause higher or lower bond energies. Bonds of high energy are those that are difficult to break. These bonds tend to have more shared pairs of electrons, and thus cause a stronger attraction between the two atoms in the bonds, which is described in (B). This stronger attraction also means that the bond length of a high-energy, high-order bond (i.e., triple bond) is shorter than that of its lower-energy counterparts (i.e., single or double bonds). (A) is incorrect; bond energy increases with *decreasing* bond length. A high-energy bond, i.e., a triple bond, requires more energy to be broken; thus (C) is incorrect.

20. A

Polarity is dependent on the vector sum of dipole moments. Dipole moments describe the relationship of shared electrons between two bonded atoms. If there is a dipole moment between two atoms, then the electrons in their shared bond are preferentially centered on one atom (typically the more electronegative of the two). For example, in a carbon-nitrogen bond, the dipole moment would be in the direction of the nitrogen atom, indicating that it has a partial negative charge. The polarity of a molecule is then defined as the vector sum of these dipole moments in the molecule's three-dimensional configuration. For example, although individual carbon-chloride bonds have dipole moments with a partial negative charge on chloride, the molecule CCl_4 has a tetrahedral configuration and thus the three polarized bonds cancel each other out for no net dipole moment, creating a nonpolar molecule. (B) is incorrect since molecular geometry is an essential aspect of determining molecular polarity. It is possible for a molecule to contain at least one nonpolar bond and yet be a polar molecule (D). CH_3Cl, for example, has three non-polar bonds (C–H bonds) and one polar bond. In its tetrahedral arrangement, the one polar bond between C–Cl will have a dipole moment, creating a net polarity of the molecule in the direction of the chloride atom.

HIGH-YIELD SIMILAR QUESTIONS

Melting Points
1. Alkanes with even numbers of carbons.
2. Neopentane will melt higher, because of its greater symmetry.
3. Phenol will melt higher

Boiling Points
1. Eliminate the alcohol's ability to be a hydrogen bond donor by alkylating the oxygen to produce an ether.

2. Displace the chlorine with water or ammonia to give an alcohol or amine, respectively.

CHAPTER 4: COMPOUNDS AND STOICHIOMETRY

1. D

Ionic compounds are comprised of atoms held together by ionic bonds. Ionic bonds associate charged particles with very different electronegativities, for example, sodium (Na^+) with chloride (Cl^-). In ionic bonds, "shared" electrons are disproportionately located on the more electronegative atom. These bonds are different in character from covalent bonds, which result in an equal sharing of electrons between two atoms. As a result, ionic compounds are not formed from true molecules, as are covalent compounds. (A) and (B) describe covalent compounds; their smallest unit is a molecule, which is typically described in terms of molecular weight and moles. In contrast, ionic compounds are made of three-dimensional arrays of their charged particles, as indicated in (D). Ionic compounds do not share electrons equally (C); equal sharing occurs in covalent bonds.

2. A

Of the compounds listed, only (A) and (C) are ionic compounds, which are measured in "formula weight." (B) and (D) are covalent compounds and thus measured in "molecular weight." When estimating the formula weight for the above compounds, (A) is potassium (39.0983) plus chloride (35.453), which has a total weight of 74.551, which is correctly between 74 and 75. Although (B) is also between 74 and 75 (4 carbons: $4 \times 12.0107 = 48.028$ plus 10 hydrogens: $10 \times 1.00794 = 10.0794$ plus one oxygen (15.994) equals a total of 74.101), this is a covalent compound. Moreover, this would be its molecular weight, not its formula weight.

3. B

It is helpful to know the molecular weight of one mole of H_2SO_4, which is found by adding the molecular weight of the atoms that constitute the molecule: $2 \times$ (molecular weight of hydrogen) + $1 \times$ (molecular weight of sulfur) + $4 \times$ (molecular weight of oxygen) = $2 \times 1.00794 + 32.065 + 4 \times 15.9994 = 98.078$. Next, you must understand what "gram-equivalent weight" means. Gram equivalent weight is equal to the molar mass of a compound divided by the number of hydrogens used per molecule, which for H_2SO_4 is two hydrogens per molecule. Thus, the gram equivalent weight is simply 98.078 g/mole divided by two, or 49.039 g/mole.

4. C

An empirical formula is a formula that represents a molecule with the simplest ratio, in whole numbers, of the atoms/elements comprising the compounds. In this case, given the empirical formula CH, any molecule with carbon and hydrogen atoms in a 1:1 ratio would be accurately represented by this empirical formula. Benzene, C_6H_6 (A) and ethyne, C_2H_2 (B), and (D) with eight carbon atoms and eight hydrogen atoms, can all be expressed with CH. (C) is the only choice that cannot, since it has only three carbon atoms and four hydrogens. Both its molecular and empirical formulas would be C_3H_4, because that represents the smallest whole number ratio of its constituent elements.

5. A

This question is relatively simple if you understand to what percent composition refers. The percent composition of any given element within a molecule is equal to the molecular mass of that element in the molecule, divided by the formula or molecular weight of the compound, times 100 percent. In this case, it is clear acetone, C_3H_6O, has a total molecular weight of (12.0107 × 3 + 1.00794 × 6 + 15.994) 58.074 g/mol, of which 12.0107 × 3 = 36.0321 g/mol is from carbon. Thus, the percent composition of carbon is 63.132%. With this calculation serving as an example, you can calculate the percent composition for ethanol (C_2H_6O; MW = 41.023 g/mol) to be 58.556%; for C_3H_8 (MW = 44.096 g/mol) to be 81.713%; and for methanol (CH_4O; MW = 32.036 g/mol) to be 37.491%. Although both acetone (A) and ethanol (B) have percent compositions of carbon close to 63%, acetone is closer. You can estimate from their molecular formulas that the percent composition of carbon would be high in C_3H_8 and low in methanol (CH_3OH), making both of those unlikely solutions.

6. D

This question tests your ability to balance a double-displacement reaction. Calcium has a charge of 2^+, carbonate has a charge of 2^-, aluminum has a charge of 3^+, and finally nitrate has a charge of 1^-. First, it is clear that all of the answer choices undertake the same double-displacement reaction. Next, one must balance the equation so that there are the same number of equivalent moles of each element on both the left and right sides of the equation. In this case, recognizing that one of the products will be aluminum carbonate will combine an ion with a charge of 3^+ with one of a charge of 2^-. In order for this to work, there will have to be 2 aluminum atoms combining with 3 molecules of carbonate for the charge of this molecule to be balanced ($^+6$ and $^-6$ in total). (C) and (D) are the only choices where this is the case. The next step is to balance the reaction. In (D), there are three atoms of calcium on both sides, three molecules of carbonate, two of aluminum on both sides, and six of nitrate on both sizes. Thus, (D) has the correct products and is a balanced equation. (C) is unbalanced, with unequal numbers of multiple atoms/molecules on each side, and it does not have the correct $Ca(NO_3)_2$ product.

7. C

Single displacement reactions are reactions in which one atom/ion within a molecule is replaced by an atom/molecule of another element. Following is an example of a single displacement reaction, in which iron takes the place of copper in the molecule that combines with sulfate:

$$Fe(s) + CuSO_4(aq) \rightarrow FeSO_4(aq) + Cu(s)$$

Many single displacement reactions are in fact redox (reduction/oxidation reactions) reactions, of which the above reaction is one. Single displacement reactions typically change the oxidation states of the participating metals, as demonstrated above, which defines a redox reaction. Neither (A) nor (B) is correct because the number reactants and products is often equivalent in these reactions. Finally, single displacement reactions can have a combination solid and/or aqueous reactants and products (D); they need not have aqueous reactants and solid products.

8. B

This reaction is a classic example of a neutralization reaction, in which an acid and a base react to form water and a new aqueous compound. Although this reaction may also appear to fit the criteria for a double displacement reaction, in which two molecules essentially "exchange" with each other, neutralization reaction is a more specific description of the process. A single displacement reaction is typically a redox (reduction/oxidation) reaction in which one element is replaced in the molecules, making (A) and (D) incorrect.

9. B

You are first given the masses of both reactants used to start the reaction. In order to figure out what will be left over, you must determine which is the limiting reagent and which is present in excess.

First, determine the molecular weight of each of the reactants:

$$Na_2S = 78.05 \text{ g/mol}$$
$$AgNO_3 = 169.9 \text{ g/mol}$$

Thus, you are given 0.5 mol Na_2S for the reaction and 0.6669 mol $AgNO_3$. However, you need two molar equivalents of $AgNO_3$ for every mole of Na_2S, so $AgNO_3$ will be the limiting reagent (there must be two moles of it for every mole of the other reagent). Next, determine how much of the Na_2S will be left over by determining how much will be used if it reacts with all of the $AgNO_3$:

$$[(1 \text{ mol } Na_2S)/(2 \text{ mol } AgNO_3)] \times 0.6669 \text{ mol } AgNO_3 = 0.3334 \text{ mol } Na_2S$$

Then, subtract this amount of reagent used from the total available:

$$0.5 \text{ mol } Na_2S - 0.3334 \text{ mol } Na_2S = 0.1666 \text{ mol excess } Na_2S$$

Finally, determine the mass that this represents:

$$0.1666 \text{ mol excess } Na_2S \times 78.05 \text{ g/mol } Na_2S = 13 \text{ g } Na_2S$$

(A) and (D) are incorrect because there will be no remaining $AgNO_3$. One might incorrectly arrive at (A) if he did not convert to using two moles $AgNO_3$ per mole Na_2S.

10. A

Try to come up with your own answer before looking at the choices. First, begin with some give mass, of $KClO_3$, X grams. In order to convert that to a product, we must convert to moles. Thus far you would have:

$$(\text{grams } KClO_3 \text{ consumed}) \times \frac{\text{mol } KClO_3}{\text{g } KClO_3}$$
$$= \frac{(\text{grams } KClO_3 \text{ consumed})}{(\text{molar mass } KClO_3)}$$

This first step eliminates (C).

Next, we must convert the number of moles of $KClO_3$ to the number of moles of oxygen, according to the balanced equation presented in the question stem:

$$\text{mol } KClO_3 \times \frac{3 \text{ moles } O_2}{(2 \text{ moles } KClO_3)}$$

Putting both steps together, the equation thus far is:

$$\frac{(\text{grams } KClO_3 \text{ consumed})(3 \text{ moles } O_2)}{(\text{molar mass } KClO_3)(2 \text{ moles } KClO_3)}$$

This second step eliminates (B), because it does not use the correct molar ratio between $KClO_3$ and O_2. The final step is to convert the number of moles of oxygen to a mass, in grams of O_2. Because at this point in our equation the number of moles is in the numerator, and we want the number of grams of oxygen in the numerator, one can multiply, not divide, by the molar mass of oxygen.

11. C

In the reaction here, there is a single displacement (II), with the silver in silver oxide being replaced by the aluminum to form aluminum oxide. This single displacement reaction also necessitates a transfer of electrons in a reduction/oxidation reaction or "redox" reaction. Therefore, items II and III are correct. A double displacement reaction typically takes two compounds and causes two displacements, and only one occurs in the reaction given here. A combination reaction typically takes two atoms or molecules and combines them to form one product, usually with more reactants than products.

12. D

Begin by converting the grams of glucose reacted to moles of glucose:

$$\frac{10 \text{ grams glucose}}{(180.2 \text{ grams/mol glucose})} = 0.05549 \text{ moles glucose}$$

Next, convert the number of moles of glucose into the number of moles of water to be produced:

$$(0.05549 \text{ moles glucose}) \times \frac{(6 \text{ moles water}}{(1 \text{ mole glucose})}$$
$$= 0.333 \text{ moles water}$$

Next, convert the moles of water to the number of grams of water:

$$0.333 \text{ moles water} \times \frac{(18.02 \text{ g})}{(\text{mol water})}$$
$$= 6.001 \text{ grams water}$$

Finally, convert the number of grams of water into the number of milliliters by using the density of water. Don't get hung up with the exact density water would be at a given temperature, such as for a liquid at 4° Celsius, the density of water is 1 g/cm³. Even at a very high temperature, at 80° Celsius, the density is still close to 1, being 0.9718 g/cm³. So for the purposes of this question, estimating a density of 1 g/cm³ is most appropriate, which will yield about 6 milliliters of water.

13. A

The law of constant composition, (A), explains that any sample of any given compound will contain the same elements in the identical mass ratio as described by the compound's formula. In this question, although all of the water samples might be difference in phase or in source, they are all still samples of H_2O and as such will all have a 2:1 ratio of hydrogen atoms to oxygen atoms. Although H_2O, in addition to being the molecular formula for water, is also its empirical formula (B), this does not best explain why all three samples have the same composition. Although the percent composition of hydrogen and oxygen in all samples are the same, percent composition (C) is not as descriptive an answer as (A). Steady-state (D) is irrelevant.

14. C

Single displacement (or oxidation/reduction) and double displacement reactions typically have the same number of reactants and products. For example, single displacement reactions are often of the form (M = metal 1; M′ = metal 2; A = anion):

$$M + M'A \rightarrow M' + MA$$

M takes the place of M′ in combining with an anion. Typically, this is enabled by a process of oxidation and reduction of the involved metals. Double displacement reactions also tend to have the same number of reactants and products, represented by this type of reaction (C = cation 1; C′ = cation 2; A = anion 1; A′ = anion 2):

$$CA + C'A' \rightarrow C'A + CA'$$

The two compounds essentially "swap" anions/cations, beginning and ending with two compounds. Combination reactions typically have more reactants than products, represented by the reaction $A + B \rightarrow C$.

15. D

A net ionic equation represents each of the ions comprising the compounds in the reactants and products as individual ions, instead of combining them as molecules. (A) is not a net ionic reaction. Next, we want to find the simplest of the answer choices, which means that the correct answer does not include any spectator ions, ions that do not participate in reacting and remain the same on both the reactant and product sides of the equation. Here, nitrate, NO_3^-, serves as a spectator ion, and thus would not be included in the simplest net ionic reaction. The only answer choice that eliminates NO_3^- is (D). (B) is incorrect because it is not balanced properly, with only one nitrate in the reactants, and two nitrates in the products.

(C) is further incorrect because copper is not a spectator ion, rather it participates fully in the reaction; thus, it must be included in any net ionic equation, and it is not present in (C).

16. A

The theoretical yield is the amount of product synthesized if all of the reactant is used and goes to product. This question simply asks how much glucose is produced if the limiting reagent is 30 grams of water. First, calculate the number of moles of water represented by 30 grams by dividing by the molecular weight of water (18.01 g/mol), which yields 1.666 moles of water. Next, convert to the equivalent number of moles of glucose:

1.666 moles water × (1 mole glucose)/(6 moles water) = 0.2776 moles glucose

Finally, calculate the number of grams of glucose that are equal to 0.2776 moles by multiplying by the molecular weight of glucose (180.2 grams/mol glucose), which results in 50.02 grams of glucose produced. (B) would result from failing to convert via the 1:6 ratio of glucose:water. (C) would result from assuming 1 mole of water. (D) would result from multiplying by 6 instead of 1/6 when calculating the molar equivalents of glucose.

17. B

First, note that this is a net ionic equation, and that to answer this question one must work backward from the amount of product back to the reactant with its spectator ions. To do so, one must consider not just Fe^{3+}, which is shown in the net ionic equation, but actually iron sulfate, $Fe_2(SO_4)_3$, the original compound. The sulfate ion is not shown because it is a spectator ion; spectator ions are not included in net ionic equations. First, calculate the number of moles of $Fe_2(SO_4)_3$ per mole $FeSCN^{2+}$. The fully balanced equation would have two moles

of $FeSCN^{2+}$ per mole $Fe_2(SO_4)_3$, so all that needs to be calculated is how many grams of $Fe_2(SO_4)_3$ are in one mole, which is the same as its molecular weight:

(2 × iron) + (3 × sulfur) + (12 × oxygen) = (2 × 55.85 g/mol) + (3 × 32.06) + (12 × 15.999)

= (111.7 g/mol) + (96.18 g/mol) + (191.99 g/mol) = 399.9 grams/mole $Fe_2(SO_4)_3$

CHAPTER 5: CHEMICAL KINETICS AND EQUILIBRIUM

1. D

Based on the information provided, the rate is directly proportional to the concentration of the first reactant; when the concentration of the reactant doubles, the rate also doubles. Because the reaction is third-order, the sum of the exponents in the rate law must be equal to 3. Therefore, the rate law is defined as follows:

$$\text{Rate} = k \,[\text{reactant 1}]\,[\text{reactant 2}]^2$$

Reactant 1 has no exponent because its concentration is directly proportional to the rate. For this reason, the concentration of reactant 2 must be squared in order to write a rate law that represents a third-order reaction. When the concentration of reactant 2 is multiplied by ½, the rate will be multiplied by $(\frac{1}{2})^2 = \frac{1}{4}$.

2. A

First draw a potential energy diagram for the system:

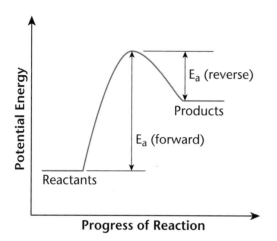

If the activation energy of the forward reaction is greater than the activation energy of the reverse reaction, then the products are higher up on the diagram than the reactants. The overall energy of the system is higher at the end than it was at the beginning, so the net enthalpy change is positive, signifying an endothermic system.

3. C

Recall the ideal gas law, $PV = nRT$, which states that volume is directly proportional to temperature and inversely proportional to pressure. If the volume of a gas is increased, the pressure will always decrease if the temperature decreases or is held constant; however, it is also possible for a small increase in temperature to be accompanied by a large decrease in pressure.

4. A

When the bottle opens, the volume of the container increases, which causes its pressure to decrease as well. You should have a solid understanding of Le Châtelier's principle, which implies that a decrease in pressure shifts the equilibrium so as to increase the number of moles of gas present; this particular reaction will shift to the left, thereby decreasing the amount of carbonic acid and increasing the amount of carbon dioxide and water. (C) and (D) are distortions; oxygen and nitrogen are not highly reactive and are unlikely to spontaneously combine with CO_2 or H_2CO_3.

5. D

ΔH is always positive for an endothermic reaction (item I is correct) and ΔG is always negative for a spontaneous reaction (item II is correct). Based on these two facts, ΔS can be determined by the free energy equation:

$\Delta G = \Delta H - T\Delta S$, which can be rewritten as:

$$T\Delta S = \Delta H - \Delta G$$

If ΔH is positive and ΔG is negative, $\Delta H - \Delta G$ must be positive. This means that $T\Delta S$ is positive. T (the temperature of the system in Kelvin) is always positive, so ΔS must also be positive. Item III is also correct.

6. C

The K_{sp} of a salt is equal to the product of the concentrations of each ion in the salt in saturated solution. This salt has three A^+ ions and one B^{3-} ion, so K_{sp} is equal to $[A^+][A^+][A^+][B^{3-}] = [A^+]^3[B^{3-}]$. The molar solubility of the salt is equal to the total number of moles of the salt in solution. The molar solubility of the salt is 10 M, thus the A^+ ion is present in a concentration of 30 M (3 A^+ ions per molecule) and the B^{3-} ion is present in a concentration of 10 M (one B^{3-} ion per molecule). These values can be substituted into the K_{sp} expression to yield $K_{sp} = [30$ M]^3[10 M] $= 3^3 \times 10^3 \times 10^1 = 27 \times 10^4 = 2.7 \times 10^5$.

7. B

Adding sodium acetate increases the number of acetate ions present. According to LeChâtelier's principle, this change will push this reaction to the left, resulting in a decrease in the number of H^+ ions and an increase in pH. This problem can also be solved with the K_a equation, $K_a = [CH_3COO^-][H^+]/[CH_3COOH]$. K_a remains constant at any given temperature and pressure, eliminating (C) and (D).

For K_a to remain unchanged while [CH₃COO⁻] increases, [H⁺] must decrease or [CH₃COOH] must increase. A decrease in products would require an increase in reactants, and vice versa, so the final effect would be both an increase in [CH₃COOH] and a decrease in [H⁺]. Again, removing hydrogen ions will increase the pH of the solution.

8. A

Only item I is correct. If the sum of the exponents on each concentration the rate law is equal to 2, then the reaction is second-order. Item I is correct because each of the exponents in this rate law is 1, so their sum is 2. Item II is incorrect because the exponents in the rate law are unrelated to stoichiometric coefficients, so NO_2 and Br_2 could be present in any ratio in the original reaction; this particular reaction actually consumes two moles of NO_2 for every mole of Br_2, which you can also guess based on the fact that NO_2 contains one unpaired electron and Br_2 contains two bromine atoms (each of which also has one unpaired electron). Item III is incorrect because the rate can be affected by a wide variety of compounds. A catalyst, for example, could increase the rate. Any compound that would preferentially react with NO_2 or Br_2 (including strong acids/bases and strong oxidizing/reducing agents) would decrease the concentration of reactants and decrease the rate.

9. C

In the first two trials, the concentration of XH_4 is held constant while the concentration of O_2 is multiplied by 4. Because the rate of the reaction is also increased by a factor of approximately 4, we can write the following equation:

Trial 1: $Rate_1 = 12.4 = k[XF_4 \text{ (trial 1)}]^x [O_2 \text{ (trial 1)}]^y$
$= k(1.00)^x (0.6)^y$

Trial 2: $Rate_2 = 49.9 = k[XF_4 \text{ (trial 2)}]^x [O_2 \text{ (trial 2)}]^y = k(1.00)^x (2.4)^y$

When you divide the bottom equation by the top equation, it simplifies to $4.02 = 4^y$, so y is approximately equal to 1. You can follow a similar procedure to calculate the exponent that goes along with [XF₄]. The rate increases by a factor of 4 when the concentration increases by a factor of 2, so the rate is proportional to the square of the concentration. Based on this, we can write the rate law, which is Rate = k [XF₄]² [O₂].

10. C

A higher K_a implies a stronger acid. Consider the following theoretical reaction, which defines the K_a of acid HA, HA ⇌ H⁺ + A⁻. In such a reaction, K_a = [H⁺][A⁻]/[HA]. A K_a near 1 therefore implies that there are enough hydrogen ions present to significantly affect the pH. Weak acids usually have a K_a that is several orders of magnitude below 1. A detailed understanding of K_a is not necessary to answer this question, however. According to the pH scale, which sets the K_a of water at 10^{-7} a compound with a K_a above 10^{-7} is acidic; even if the acid is very weak, it will still cause the pH to drop below 7.

11. D

The rate of a reaction is related to the concentration of reactants, but not to the overall volume of the vessel. If a sample of a certain concentration is increased in quantity, the reaction will not be affected. Adding heat will allow a reaction to reach its activation energy faster, while removal of heat will make it more difficult for the reaction to reach its activation energy, so (A) doesn't apply. Changing the activation energy (by adding a catalyst) is the most common way to significantly increase the rate of a reaction, so (D) does not apply, nor does (C) because almost all reactions have a rate law that includes the concentration of each reactant as a key variable.

12. A

Your first step here should be to write out the balanced equation for the reaction of H_2 and N_2 to produce NH_3 [$N_2 + 3H_2 \rightarrow 2NH_3$]. This means that K_{eq} is equal to $[NH_3]^2/([H_2]^3[N_2])$. Because the volume is 1 L, the value of the amount of each gas (in moles) is equal to the value of the concentration of each gas (in M). We can plug these concentrations back into the K_{eq} expression to get $K_{eq} = (.05)^2/([3]^3[1])$, which is equal to $(0.0025)/(27)$. This is approximately equal to 0.0001, and approximations are appropriate for the MCAT.

13. D

A system is exothermic if energy is released. For exothermic reactions, the net energy change is negative and the potential energy stored in the final products is lower than the potential energy stored in the initial reactants. Point E, which represents the energy of the final products, is lower on the energy diagram than point A, which represents the energy of initial reactants. Thus energy must have been released from the overall reaction in this case. While point A is useful for determining the energy of the overall reaction, point B represents the activation energy of the first transition state and point C suggests an intermediate. The difference between points D and E indicates the change in energy from the transition state of the second reaction step to the final products.

14. B

The activation energy of a reaction is equal to the distance on the y-axis from the energy of the reactants to the peak energy prior to formation of products. The activation energy of the first step of the forward reaction, for example, is equal to the distance along the y-axis from point A to point B. The largest energy increase on this graph occurs during the progress between points E and D, which represents the first step of the reverse reaction. The other answer choices are opposite.

15. B

This energy diagram presents a two-step system. The first reaction proceeds from point A to point C and the second reaction proceeds from point C to point E. This means the reactants predominate at point A, the intermediates predominate at point C, and the products predominate at point E. Point B, which is between points A and C, is the energy threshold at which most of the reactant starts to be converted into intermediate, so the reactant and the intermediate will both be present at this point. No product is produced until after point C, so it will not be present in the reaction mixture. Catalysts may be present in the mixture at any point, depending on the nature and the quantity of the catalyst.

16. C

Reaction 2 is simply the reverse of reaction 1. Because K_{eq} of reaction 1 is equal to [products]/[reactants], K_{eq} of reaction 2 must be equal to [reactants]/[products]. This means that K_{eq} for reaction 2 is the inverse of K_{eq} of reaction 1, so the answer is 1/0.1 = 10.

17. A

A negative ΔH value always signifies an exothermic reaction, so the forward reaction produces heat. This means that removing heat by decreasing the temperature is similar to removing any other product of the reaction. According to LeChâtelier's principle, decreasing the amount of a product will stimulate the reaction to produce more products; therefore, removing heat will cause the reaction to shift to the right, causing an increase in the concentrations of C and D as well as a decrease in the concentrations of A and B.

18. C

K_a is equal to the ratio of products to reactants in a dissociated acid. A compound with a K_a greater than 10^{-7} contains more H^+ ions than OH^- ions, which makes it a weak acid (unless K_a is several orders of magnitude higher than 1, which would indicate a strong acid). This means that the compound in the question is acidic and that it is likely to react with a compound that is basic. Of the four choices, NH_3 is the only base.

19. D

Recall that the slow step of a reaction is the rate-determining step. Therefore, the rate is always related to the concentrations of the reactants in the slow step, so NO_2 is the only compound that should be included in the correct answer. The concentration of NO_2 is squared in the rate law because, according to the question, the reaction obeys second-order kinetics.

20. D

The faster a reaction can reach its activation energy, the faster it will proceed to completion. Because this question states that all conditions are equal, the reaction with the lowest activation energy will have the fastest rate. (D) illustrates the smallest difference between the initial and peak potential energies, so that reaction can overcome its activation energy more easily than the other proposed scenarios on the energy diagram.

HIGH-YIELD SIMILAR QUESTIONS

Rate Law from Experimental Results
1. $k = 0.0149$ $M^{-1}s^{-1}$
2. Rate = $k[C_5H_5N][MeI]$; $k = 75$ $M^{-1}s^{-1}$; this is an S_N2 reaction, because it is second order overall.
3. Rate = $k[Ce^{4+}][Fe^{2+}]$; $k = 10^3$ $M^{-1}s^{-1}$.

Rate Law from Reaction Mechanisms
1. Rate = M s^{-1}, so k_{obs} will be in units of $M^{-3}s^{-1}$.
2. In solution, this should be a simple addition of HX to an alkene, so we would expect the rate law to be rate = $k[HCl][CH_3CHCH_2]$.

3. In the solution phase reaction, the key intermediate would be a carbocation, rather than an excited state of 2–chloropropane.

CHAPTER 6:
THERMOCHEMISTRY

1. A

The process is adiabatic. Adiabatic describes any thermodynamic transformation that does not involve a heat transfer (Q). An adiabatic process can be either reversible or irreversible, though for MCAT purposes, adiabatic expansions or contractions refer to volume changes in a closed system without experimentally significant losses or gains of heat. The internal energy of the system changes (U = –PΔV, where U = Q – W, W = PΔV, and Q = 0). An isobaric process (B) is conducted at constant pressure, but the curve is more severe. An isothermal process (C) requires a heat transfer at constant temperature, and there is no heat transfer along an adiabatic curve.

2. A

An adiabatic expansion does not involve a heat transfer, so pressure and volume data provide enough information to answer this question. That rules out (D). For ideal gases undergoing reversible adiabatic processes, PV^γ = constant. $\gamma = C_P/C_v$, the molar specific heats of the ideal gas at constant pressure and constant volume. (C) is out of scope. The problem does not provide an expansion constant for triatomic ideal gases, and you do not have to take into account the question of whether a triatomic gas could approximate "ideal" conditions. That leaves (A) and (B). For an ideal monatomic gas, $\gamma = 5/3$. For an ideal diatomic gas, $\gamma = 7/5$.

3. D

There is not enough information in the problem to determine whether the reaction is nonspontaneous.

(A), (B), and (C) are Distortions. Start with $\Delta G = \Delta H - T\Delta S$. Though the magnitudes of ΔH and ΔS might suggest a spontaneous reaction, the overall free energy is temperature-dependent. If the signs of enthalpy and entropy are the same, the reaction is temperature-dependent. If the signs of these terms are different, you can find the sign of the free energy independent of temperature. The most common thermochemistry questions on the MCAT test your ability to manipulate and interpret the $\Delta G = \Delta H - T\Delta S$ equation. Memorize it.

4. B

Sodium oxidizes easily at standard conditions. No calculation is necessary here. There is enough information to predict the equilibrium constant, eliminating (D). If $K_{eq} < 1$, the reverse reaction is favored, indicating that the forward reaction is non-spontaneous. If $K_{eq} = 1$, the reaction is at equilibrium. If $K_{eq} > 1$, the forward reaction proceeds spontaneously. The question states that the sample spontaneously combusts at room temperature, i.e. 25°C. The answer is (B), $K_{eq} > 1$.

5. C

Combustion involves the reaction of a hydrocarbon with oxygen to produce carbon dioxide and water. The longer the hydrocarbon chain, the more product is formed, and the more heat is released in the process of forming new bonds. (Though this question calls on your understanding of alkane structure, you are unlikely to see a quantitative question in the Biological Sciences section.) Exothermic is synonymous with the most negative overall enthalpy, here the heat of combustion. Isobutane combusts less easily than n-butane because of its branched structure.

6. A

This problem requires a quick calculation. The reaction, a Fischer esterification, is an MCAT favorite.

The hydroxyl group leaves acetic acid via nucleophilic attack of methanol on the carbonyl carbon of acetic acid. That means 1 O–H bond breaks (methanol), and 1 C–O bond breaks (hydroxyl on acetic acid to carbonyl carbon). One C–O bond reforms in the products, for the new ester, and 2 O–H bonds form (water). Enthalpy is a state function, meaning its value remains the same regardless of the reaction path, so you could calculate the same result in other ways. That allows us to calculate the overall enthalpy of a reaction with the heats of formation of each chemical involved, a calculation shortcut known as Hess's law. (An element's heat of formation is 0 by convention, as long as it is in its standard state.) The problem provides bond disassociation energies instead of heats of formation, meaning you subtract products from reactants, or for bonds broken minus bonds formed. (A) accounts for this error. (B) is opposite, while (C) and (D) are miscalculations.

7. C

Standard temperature and pressure indicates 0°C and 1 atm. Gibbs free energy is temperature-dependent. If a reaction is at equilibrium, $\Delta G = 0$. (C) is the answer. Note that there is no degree sign next to ΔG in this problem; this indicates a standard state reaction at 25° Celsius.

8. B

The correct answer is (B), using $K_{eq} = e^{-\Delta G^{\circ}/RT}$ from $\Delta G^{\circ} = -RT\ln(K_{eq})$. Use $e = 2.7$. R is the gas constant, 8.314 Jmol^{-1}K^{-1}, and T = 298 K, because of the standard-state sign. The answer in (A) would have omitted a negative sign; we know from the free energy that the reaction must be spontaneous, so the equilibrium constant should be greater than 1. (C) uses T = 273 K rather than 298 K. (D) substitutes a base-10 logarithm for the natural logarithm. With the base-10 log, use $\Delta G^{\circ} = -2.303RT\ln(K_{eq})$. Comfort with exponent and logarithm calculations is essential for success on Test Day.

9. D

There is not enough information to determine the energy of this reaction, only its entropy. While it appears that a reaction has taken place, we know only that the molecules have moved, not whether something has caused them to move into a new arrangement. Had the reaction been at equilibrium (C), there would not be this much reorganization between molecules.

10. A

This problem asks you to calculate the free energy of reaction at non-standard conditions, which you can do using the equation $\Delta G = \Delta G° + RT\ln(Q)$. (R is the gas constant, 8.314 $Jmol^{-1}K^{-1}$, and T = 298 K.) Though it's a good idea to memorize this equation for Test Day, you can set up the answer from information in the question stem. (A) is correct. (C) and (D) are distortions; with the base-10 logarithm, you must multiply by a conversion factor of 2.303. Often, the MCAT will test your ability to manipulate logarithms without the use of a calculator. Review this material well before Test Day.

11. C

There is not enough information to deduce anything about reaction temperature, which eliminates (B) and (D). Adiabatic and isothermal processes are necessarily opposite because adiabatic processes do not involve heat transfers. A reaction at constant pressure can be either adiabatic (no heat transfer to change volume) or isobaric (constant pressure, as the word roots imply). That means items I and III are correct.

12. A

This question requires interpreting the equation $\Delta G = \Delta H - T\Delta S$. Endergonic indicates a non-spontaneous reaction, and exergonic indicates a spontaneous one. In contrast, exothermic and endothermic suggest the sign of the enthalpy of the reaction. The problem does not provide enough information to determine the free energy of this temperature-dependent reaction. (A) is the correct answer. Endothermic reactions (B) have a positive enthalpy. (C) and (D) are distortions; the suffix –gonic indicates Gibbs free energy and is more commonly seen on the Biological Sciences section of the MCAT.

13. A

Disorder in the vessel increases over the course of the reaction. $\Delta S < 0$ (B) would indicate more molecular organization in the vessel after the reaction took place. (C) is faulty use of detail; S = 0 J/K at absolute zero, and compounds at any temperature above 0 K are dynamic. (D) is tricky. While we cannot make a quantitative determination of entropy from the picture, we can estimate the relative amount of disorder from the beginning to the end of the reaction in the vessel.

14. C

This is a definition question. A spontaneous reaction's free energy is negative by convention. Its equilibrium constant is greater than 1 because it is not at equilibrium and moves in the forward direction. (C) is the correct answer.

15. B

A calorimeter measures specific heat or heat capacity. Though calorimeters often incorporate thermometers, thermometers themselves (A) track only heat transfers, not the specific heat value. Barometers (C) measure change in pressure. Volumetric flasks (D) measure liquid quantities, not the heat capacity of the liquid.

16. C

Memorize the Laws of Thermodynamics; they may be stated in different forms on Test Day. Know the equation and how to rephrase it into a sentence or two. The First Law often confuses students—it refers to the overall energy of the universe, not to the enthalpy of the universe—even though enthalpy is usually substituted for this term in introductory college chemistry experiments. The Third Law (absolute zero) is not an equation.

17. A

Eliminate (C) and (D), which describe the free energy of reaction and cannot be determined from this graph. If the heat of formation of the products is greater than that of the reactants, the reaction is endothermic. We can determine this information by their relative magnitude on the graph; an exothermic graph would reflect products with a lower enthalpy than that of the reactants.

HIGH-YIELD SIMILAR QUESTIONS

Reaction Energy Profiles
1. [B]/[A] = 3.5
2. No, because a catalyst only lowers the activation energy (by lowering G†). It doesn't affect the energies of the reactants or products.
3.

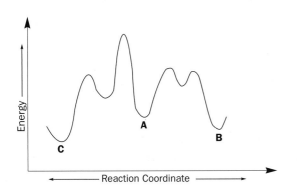

Thermodynamic Equilibrium
1. Reactants are favored
2. 8,688 J/mol; 52,373 J/mol; neither reaction is spontaneous; if $\Delta S > 0$ then $\Delta H > 0$.

3. The student should put flask A on the benchtop, flask E in the cold room, and flask P on the Bunsen burner.

Bond Enthalpy
1. 0.0021 kJ
2. 338.5 kJ/mol
3. 8.53 × 10^4 kJ/mol

Heat of Formation
1. ΔH_f for ethane
2. −1,255.4 kJ/mol
3. −359.9 kJ/mol

CHAPTER 7: THE GAS PHASE

1. A (D) $P_1 V_1 = P_2 V_2$ 1 atm · 22.4 L = .5 atm = 44.8

One mole of an ideal gas at STP is equal to 22.4 L. The extrapolation of the ammonia graph to zero pressure is extremely close to this value. The slope of the line does not indicate whether the gas is ideal or not, because all gases will deviate at their own rate with increases in pressure. The ammonia gas exhibits ideal behavior at zero pressure even though it deviates at higher pressures.

in other words slope = 0

2. A

The graph shows that gases deviate from ideal behavior at higher pressures, which force molecules closer together and create more intermolecular forces. Similarly, low temperatures cause less space to exist between molecules. Less space also makes the volume of the molecules more significant, causing the gas to lose characteristics of an ideal gas. At high temperatures molecules will move more quickly and exhibit random motion and elastic collisions, which is a property of ideal gases. In an ideal gas it is assumed that there are no intermolecular attractions between gas molecules. At low pressure gas molecules will have more space between them and thus any intermolecular attractions will become negligible.

3. D

Density equals mass divided by volume. The mass of 1 mole of neon gas equals 20.18 grams. At STP, 1 mole of neon occupies 22.4 L. Dividing the mass, 20.18 grams, by the volume, 22.4 L, gives an approximate density of 0.9009 g L^{-1}.

4. C

Graham's law of effusion states that the relative rates of effusion of two gases at the same temperature and pressure are given by the inverse ratio of the square roots of the masses of the gas particles. In equation form, Graham's law can be represented by:

$$\frac{\text{Rate}_1}{\text{Rate}_2} = \sqrt{\left(\frac{M_2}{M_1}\right)}$$

If a molecule has a higher molecular weight then it will leak at a slower rate than a molecule with a lower molecular weight. Both neon and oxygen gas will leak at slower rates than helium because they each have a greater mass than helium.

5. C

The difference between the atmospheric pressure and the pressure from the gas in the flask is equal to 117 mm of mercury. The atmospheric pressure can be seen exerting more force on the mercury compared to the gas in the flask. Therefore, the gas in the flask should have a pressure below 760 torr (760 mm Hg). The difference of 117 mm Hg must be subtracted from 760 mm Hg. So 760 – 117 equals 643 mm Hg, choice (C).

6. B

A hot-air balloon rises because the air inside the balloon is less dense than the surrounding air. We know the air inside is less dense because, according to Charles's law, temperature and volume are directly related. A greater volume creates less density, because D = mass/volume.

7. B

The pressure of the gas is calculated by subtracting the vapor pressure of water from the measured pressure during the experiment: 784 mm Hg – 24 mm Hg = 760 mm Hg, or 1 atm. The ideal gas law can be used to calculate the moles of hydrogen gas. The volume of the gas equals 0.1 L, the temperatures equals 298 K, and R = 0.0821 (L atm/mol K). Solving the equation PV = nRT for n gives 4.09 × 10^{-3} moles of hydrogen. (A) might result from using 784 mm Hg of the pressure instead of the pressure adjusted for water vapor. (C) and (D) would result from using a pressure in mm Hg instead of converting to atm while using the gas constant R = 0.0821 (L atm/mol K).

8. B

Ideal gases are said to have no attractive forces between molecules. They are considered to have point masses, which take up no volume. Items I and II are correct.

9. C

The first thing to do is balance the given chemical equation. The coefficients, from left to right, are 1, 1, 2. The mass of solid, 8.01 grams, can be converted to moles of gas product by dividing by the molar mass of $NH_4NO_{3(s)}$ (80.06 g) and multiplying by the molar ration of 3 moles of gas product to one mole of $NH_4NO_{3(s)}$. This gives approximately 0.300 moles of gas product. The ideal gas equation can be used to obtain the pressure in the flask. The values are as follows: R equals 0.0821 (L atm/mole K), the temperature in Kelvin is 500 K, and the volume is 10 L. Solving for P in the equation PV = nRT gives a pressure of about 1.23 atm. (B) is three times smaller than correct (C) and would be obtained if the gas moles conversion were not carried out. (D) would result from using 273 K instead of 500 K.

10. D

The partial pressure of each gas after the stopcocks are open can be calculated using $P_1V_1 = P_2V_2$. V_2 is the same for all three gases because the volume with open stopcocks equals 8 L in the system. For each gas, P_1 and V_1 are provided. We must then solve for P_2. The calculation for the various gases, will look like the following:

(2 L) (0.4 atm) = (8 L) (P_{Ne}), i.e. P_{Ne} = 0.1
(2 L) (0.1 atm) = (8 L) (P_{Ar}), i.e. P_{Ar} = 0.025
(4 L) (0.8 atm) = (8 L) (P_{He}), i.e. P_{He} = 0.4

11. A

The average kinetic energy is directly proportional to the temperature of a gas in Kelvin. The kinetic molecular theory states that collisions between molecules are elastic (B). Elastic collisions do not result in a loss of energy (C). The kinetic energy of each gas molecule is not the same (D); varies over a range of kinetic energies.

12. C

At STP, the difference between the distribution of velocities for helium and bromine gas is due to the difference in molar mass ($Rate_1/Rate_2 = \sqrt{(M_2/M_1)}$). Helium has a smaller molar mass than bromine. Particles with small masses travel faster than those with large masses, so the helium gas corresponds to curve B with higher velocities. (A) and (B) inaccurately identify each curve on the graph. (D) is incorrect because the average kinetic energies of the gases cannot be determined with the given information.

13. D

At STP the pressure inside the balloon equals 1 atm. The total number of moles in the balloon equals 0.2 moles plus 0.6 moles, or 0.8 moles. P_{O2} equals the mole fraction of oxygen (0.2/0.8) times

the total pressure, 1atm. The partial pressure of oxygen is 0.25 atm.

14. A

[handwritten annotations: "my bad", "wrong", "none are correct 2.6×10⁷", "correct"]

The ideal gas law can be modified to include density and determine the temperature of the sun. Solving for T, the equation looks like: $T = (P \times MW)/(R \times D)$. The density is given in g/cm^3 and must be converted to g/L so the units cancel in the above equation. Because $1 cm^3$ equals 1 mL and there are 1,000 mL in 1 L, the density can be multiplied by 1,000 to be converted to g/L.

15. C

Gases are compressible and can conduct electricity but do so very poorly. Because gas particles are far apart from each other and in rapid motion, they tend to take up the volume of their container. Gas particles can flow easily past one another because there is a great deal of space for movement between particles. *[handwritten: Really, all gases exist as X_2]*

16. B

We will use $V_1/T_1 = V_2/T_2$. First we must convert the temperature to Kelvin by adding 273 to get 300 K as the initial temperature. Plugging into the equation and solving for T_2 gives 450 K. Subtracting the initial temperature, 300 K, gives an increase of 150 K. This also corresponds to an increase of 150°C.

17. D

The reaction of two moles of gas, X and Y, to form one mole of gas, XY, will decrease the moles of gas. Because volume and moles of gas are directly related, the volume of gas will decrease and the pistons will move down. The piston does not move up (A) because the gas volume decreases due to less moles of gas that are present. Moreover, there is no way to know from the information given if there is energy given off during the reaction (B). (C) is incorrect because the piston will move down; the decrease in amount of gas in the space under the piston will cause the piston to move.

18. B

The partial pressure of each gas is found by multiplying the total pressure by the mole fraction of the gas. Because 80 percent of the molecules are nitrogen, the mole fraction of nitrogen gas is equal to 0.8. Similarly, for helium the mole fraction is 0.2 because 20 percent of the gas molecules are helium. To find the pressure exerted by nitrogen, multiply the total pressure (150 torr) by 0.8 to obtain 120 torr of nitrogen. To find the pressure exerted by helium, multiply the total pressure by 0.2 to get 30 torr of helium.

19. C

Heating a gas will increase the pressure, and cooling a gas will decrease the pressure at a constant volume. A decrease in volume will increase the pressure, and an increase in volume will decrease the pressure. Heating and increasing the volume will have opposite effects on the pressure of the gas. It is impossible to tell without quantifying if the end result is an increase or decrease in pressure. (C) is the correct choice.

CHAPTER 8: PHASES AND PHASE CHANGES

1. D

Water is the only substance with a negative slope of the solid/liquid equilibrium line shown in the figure. All of the other answer choices have a positive slope in the solid/liquid equilibrium line.

2. C

Solid water has a low density. This low density means that the same mass of water present in a living cell must expand at this lower temperature.

This process of increased volume destroys living cells upon freezing by disrupting membrane structures. (B) and (D) are factually incorrect. (A) is true but less relevant to the question about frostbite, which involves frozen water at 0°C.

3. D

The skater increases the pressure on the water molecules while not changing the temperature. This increased pressure causes a phase change from solid to liquid due to the negative slope of the solid/liquid equilibrium line. The other answer choices deal with processes not relevant to the question.

4. A

Intermolecular forces hold molecules closer to one another, which relates to the compound's phase. As the intermolecular forces increase, the amount of heat needed to change phase (such as in vaporization) increases as well, thus showing a proportional, positive relationship between molecular forces and the heat of vaporization.

5. B

This molecule is likely to have unequal sharing of electrons and thus polarity. Polarity often leads to increased bonding because of the positive-negative attractive forces between molecules. More bonding or stronger intermolecular forces both mean higher melting points because more heat is needed to break these interactions to change phase. (A) is nonpolar, making its intermolecular forces weaker than (B) or (C). (D) is only weakly polar, because the geometry of this molecule will make some of the polarized bonds cancel each other out. (C) will have some polarity, but less than in (B) because only one bond is polarized.

6. D

At low pressure there is less force holding the molecules in a more organized state—liquid or solid.

Because temperature is a measure of average kinetic energy of the molecules, an increase in the average kinetic energy increases molecules' movement and thus they move apart from each other, ultimately entering a gaseous state. Increasing pressure or decreasing the temperature (or kinetic energy) both favor more organized states of liquid or solid.

7. A

(A) shows that increased kinetic energy would be necessary to overcome the increased force of pressure holding the molecules within whatever state they're in. In order to maintain the same state at an increased pressure, the temperature must also increase, which would force the line graphing the increasing temperature and changing phase to move up.

8. C

Melting point depresses, making (A) and (B) incorrect. Added solute particles interfere with lattice formation, interrupting the intermolecular forces that would otherwise stabilize the lattice formation. Because these particles do not stabilize the lattice formation, (D) is also incorrect.

9. B

Viscosity implies stronger bonding/intermolecular forces, thus making it harder for molecules to move past one another and flow freely. Those interactions are associated with higher heats required to change phases, and in this question, vaporize. Fusion (C) and critical mass (D) are unrelated to viscosity.

10. D

Tar is the most viscous of the answer choices. With increased viscosity comes increased bonding interactions, which makes it most difficult to cause phase change in a highly viscous substance. As a result, the highest heat of vaporization to break

the stronger interactions is required for a highly viscous substance.

11. C

(C) shows movement from the solid to gas phase, which is by definition, sublimation.

12. A

With a positive slop for the solid/liquid equilibrium line, the phase change for solid under increased pressure and constant temperature is to remain solid. This phase change line would need to be negatively sloped, as seen with water, to skate on it. In that case, increased pressure from the skates would move the solid (ice) to a liquid phase (water). This liquid layer enables skating to be possible; otherwise it is like skating on a solid such as dirt.

13. A

In this final stage of the phase change, the particles are already in a gaseous state (the highest-energy phase), and with increasing temperature the particles retain increased kinetic energy. Temperature is the average kinetic energy of the molecules in a substance and so this answer addresses the change in energy shown by a slope in the line. (B) and (C) do not describe the gaseous phase indicated by X's location in the diagram, and (D) is simply incorrect.

14. D

Sweat causes a loss of heat when the high-energy, or hottest, molecules move from liquid to gas and leave the body surface. This evaporation process allows the loss of heat energy, thereby cooling the body (decreasing average kinetic energy). (A) and (B) refer to condensation, which is actually a warming process, instead of evaporation. (C) is incorrect chemically, Because evaporation does not lead to a gain of cooler/low-energy molecules.

15. C

Both items I and II are correct. Dissolved solutes break up the crystalline lattice bonds of a solid and in this phase equilibrium, solutes increase the equilibrium to favor liquid, in which they easily dissolved. As a result, a decreased amount of this solute would favor a solid state (I). Additionally, decreased temperature (II) is a decrease in the average kinetic energy of the molecules, making lower-energy phases (i.e., solid) more likely. Decreasing pressure (III) would actually favor higher-energy phase (i.e., liquid or gas) over solid. Neither (A) alone nor B alone captures all the important variables. (D) is incorrect, as described above, since less pressure means a less force keeping the molecules in the solid lattice-like phase.

III is correct at T near freezing/melting

16. A

Condensation occurs more on a humid day because there is a greater amount of water in the gaseous phase in the ambient air, which can interact with the human body and transfer heat from these high-energy molecules to the human body. Upon interaction, the initially gaseous water molecules change phase to a liquid (condensation) after losing their heat to the human body. On a dry day there would be few water molecules to cause this transfer of heat, making one feel less hot.

17. A

By definition, condensation is a move from water vapor (clouds) to liquid water (rain).

18. B

Ether (B) has the lowest heat required for vaporization, which by definition determines the boiling point or the lowest temperature required for phase change from liquid to gas. All of the other answer choices have higher heats of vaporization.

HIGH-YIELD SIMILAR QUESTIONS

Partial Pressures
1. P_{O_2} = 5 atm; P_{N_2} = 1.25 atm; P_{CO_2} = 3.75 atm
2. 8
3. 7.5 atm

CHAPTER 9: SOLUTIONS

1. A

The equation $\Delta T_b = k_b \times m_c$ can be used to solve this problem. The change in boiling point is found by subtracting the boiling point of water (the solvent), 100°C, from the elevated boiling point, 101.11°C. Using the given value for k_b we solve for the molality of the solution and get 2.17 moles/kg. Convert to grams by dividing by 1,000 and then multiplying by the volume of the solution, 100 g, to get the moles of solute. To obtain the molar mass, divide the mass of the solute, 70 g, by the number of moles, 0.217 moles, to get a molar mass of 322.58 g/mole. (C) and (D) would result from multiplying 1.11 by the k_b instead of dividing.

2. D

The phases in all three items can make a solution as long as the two components create a mixture that is of uniform appearance (homogenous). Hydrogen in platinum is an example of a gas in a solid. Air is an example of a homogenous mixture of a gas in a gas. Brass and steel are examples of homogeneous mixtures of solids.

3. B

Benzene and toluene are both organic liquids and have very similar properties. They are both nonpolar and are almost exactly the same size. Raoult's law states that ideal solution behavior is observed when solute-solute, solvent-solvent, and solute-solvent interactions are very similar. Therefore, benzene and toluene in solution will be predicted to behave as a nearly ideal solution. (A) states that the liquids would follow Raoult's law because they are different. It is true that the compounds are slightly different but the difference is negligible in terms of Raoult's law. (C) and (D) state that the solution would not obey Raoult's law.

4. A

If the membrane became permeable to water, water molecules would move to the side with the highest solute concentration, according to the principles of osmosis. The left side has a higher concentration of solute because NaCl is dissolved in water. Water will move to this side to attempt to equalize the concentration of solute on both sides. The level on the left will rise because of the excess water molecules and the level on the right will fall because it has lost water molecules. The level would stay the same (B) only if the number of particles dissolved on each side of the membrane were equal. (D) is not possible because it would add volume to the system.

5. D

Step 1 will most likely be endothermic because energy is required to break molecules apart. The strong ionic forces in the crystal must be overcome to separate individual molecules and ions. Step 2 is also endothermic because the intermolecular forces in the solvent must be overcome to allow incorporation of solute particles. Step 3 will most likely be exothermic because polar water molecules will interact with the dissolved ions and release energy.

6. C

CaS will cause the most negative ΔS°_{soln} because the Ca^{2+} and S^{2-} ions have the highest charge density compared to the other ions. All of the other ions have a charge with a value of 1, whereas Ca^{2+} and S^{2-} have charges with an absolute value of 2. When comparing ions with the same value of charge, the

size of the ions must be taken into account. Ions that are smaller will have a higher charge density. For example, LiK will have a higher charge density than KCl. It follows that the ΔS°_{soln} is more negative for LiK than for KCl.

7. D

A non-electrolyte solution will not dissociate into ions in solution. Its effective molarity in solution will be the same as the number of moles that were dissolved. On the other hand, an electrolyte like $Mg(NO_3)_2$ will dissociate into three ions (Mg and $2NO_3^-$). The effective molarity, which is important for colligative properties, will be three times the number of moles that were dissolved. Osmotic pressure is a colligative property and will therefore be three times larger for $Mg(NO_3)_2$ compared to a non-electrolyte. The molarity of $Mg(NO_3)_2$, 0.02 M, is also two times larger than the non-electrolyte solution (0.01 M). The osmotic pressure will have to be multiplied by three and then by two, which equals multiplication by six. 15 mm Hg × 6 equals 90 mm Hg.

8. A

Vitamin A is hydrophobic and is therefore fat-soluble. It will accumulate in fat for storage purposes and will be released when it is needed. Consuming too much of it will cause a large accumulation and thus hypervitaminosis. Unlike vitamin C, it will not be readily excreted in urine. Vitamin C is hydrophilic and will dissolve in the body's aqueous solutions, leading to regular excretion in the urine. It can be consumed regularly in large amounts and will not build up in the body. Though vitamin A is larger (B), its hydrophobicity is what accounts for its ability to be stored in body fat. Attached methyl groups on a compound are not toxic to a cell (C). Interactions with membrane lipids can occur but there is no evidence that this disrupts transport across the membrane (D).

9. B

The mass percent of a solute equals the mass of the solute divided by the mass of the total solution. To find the mass of the solution, we must find the mass of the solvent, water. Multiplying the volume of the solution by the density gives us a mass of 292.5 grams of water. Adding 3 grams of sugar yields a solution with a mass of 295.5 grams. Next, we divide 3 grams of sugar by 295.5 grams and multiply by 100 to get a percentage. (C) might result from dividing by the mass of the solvent rather the solution.

10. A

Mixtures that have a vapor pressure higher than predicted by Raoult's law have stronger solvent-solvent and solute-solute interactions than solvent-solute interactions. The particles do not want to stay in solution and evaporate more readily, causing a higher vapor pressure than an ideal solution. Two liquids that have different properties, like hexane (hydrophobic) and ethanol (hydrophilic, small), would not have many interactions with each other to cause positive deviation, so (A) is correct. Acetone and water (B) and isopropanol and methanol (C) would not show significant deviation from Raoult's law; due to their similar properties, the molecules are neither attracted to nor repelled from each other. Nitric acid and water (D) would interact well with each other and cause a negative deviation from Raoult's law. The liquids, when attracted to each other, would prefer to stay in liquid form and would have a lower vapor pressure than predicted by Raoult's law.

11. A

Dissolution is governed by enthalpy and entropy, which are related by the equation $\Delta G°_{soln} = \Delta H°_{soln} - T\Delta S°_{soln}$. The cooling of the solution indicates that there is a decrease in enthalpy. The only way the solid can dissolve is if the increase in entropy is great enough to overcome the decrease in enthalpy. It is stated in the question stem that KCl dissolves (B). $\Delta S°_{soln}$ must be positive in order for KCl to dissolve (C). (D) is irrelevant and also misstates boiling point depression instead of elevation.

12. D

The equation to determine the change in boiling point of a solution is as follows: $\Delta T_b = m_b(K_b)$. m_b is the molality of the solution and K_b is the boiling point elevation constant. In this case, the solvent is always water so K_b will be the same for each solution and the exact value of K_b is not needed to answer the question. Sucrose will produce the solution of highest molality (moles per kilograms solvent) of all four choices. Although (A) and (C) will dissociate into ionic species, the amount of moles dissolved in not large enough to yield as many particles in solution as sucrose. 0.1 mol of acetic acid, (B), is a very weak acid and only a few molecules will actually dissociate.

13. C

The solubility of gases in liquids is directly proportional to the atmospheric pressure. Therefore, we should expect a decrease in solubility with the decreased pressure in Denver. It must be known that at sea level the atmospheric pressure is equal to 1 atm, where the solubility is 1.25×10^{-3} M. We multiply this number by the new pressure over the old pressure (0.8/1) to get a solubility of 1×10^{-3} M. If you accidentally divided by the ration you would get the answer in (A), and if you just subtracted 0.02 from the solubility you would get (B).

14. C

30 ppb of Pb^{2+} is equivalent to 30 grams of Pb^{2+} in 10^9 grams of solution. We can divide by the molar mass of Pb^{2+}, 207 g/mole, to get moles of Pb^{2+} per

mass of solution. The density of water, 1,000 g/L, can be used to obtain the molarity of the Pb^{2+} in the water, 1.4×10^{-7} M. (B) might result from forgetting to multiply by the density of water.

15. C

All items but III are correct. An electrolyte is a molecule that dissociates into free ions and behaves as an electrically conductive medium. NaF (item I) is an electrolyte because it dissociates to form the ions Na^+ and F^-. Glucose (item II) is a nonelectrolyte because it is a ring structure which dissolves but does not dissociate. CH_3OH (item III) will not ionize in solution and so is not an electrolyte. Acetic acid (item IV) is a weak acid and also a weak electrolyte because it will partially ionize in solution.

16. D

A colligative property depends solely upon the number of molecules and disregards the identity of the molecules. (A), (B), and (C) are properties based on the composition of a solution determined by the number of molecules that are dissolved in the solution. The entropy of dissolution (D) will depend on the chemical properties of the substance, such as charge density and electron affinity. Therefore, the entropy of dissolution is not a colligative property.

17. A

The K_{sp} equation can be written as $[Ag^+][Br^-] = 7.7 \times 10^{-13}$. Because there is a 0.001 M solution of NaBr, the effective concentration of Br^- will be 0.001 M. Substituting this value for $[Br^-]$ in the K_{sp} equation and solving for $[Ag^+]$ gives a concentration of 7.7×10^{-10} M Ag^+. This value can be converted to g/L by multiplying by the molar mass of silver, 107.9 grams/mole. The solubility of Ag^+ is the same as the compound AgBr because there is one molecule of Ag^+ for every molecule of AgBr.

18. B

Formation of complex ions between silver ions and ammonia will cause more molecules of solid AgCl to dissociate. The equilibrium is driven toward dissociation because the Ag^+ ions are essentially being removed from solution when they complex with ammonia. This rationale is based upon Le Chatelier's principle, stating that when a chemical equilibrium experiences a change in concentration, the system will shift to counteract that change. (A) is incorrect because the complex ions may interact with AgCl but this is not the major reason for the increased solubility. (C) and (D) are incorrect because the solubility of AgCl will increase, not decrease.

19. D

Detergents contain a long hydrophobic chain with a polar functional group on one end. The long hydrophobic chains can surround grease and oil droplets, while the polar heads face outward and carry the particles in a solution of water. If a molecule ionizes into two parts, both parts will also be ionic, so (B) is incorrect. (C) is incorrect because, although multiple detergent molecules form a sphere-like shape with oil or grease droplets enclosed, the individual molecules themselves do not circularize.

HIGH-YIELD SIMILAR QUESTIONS

Normality and Molarity

1. 0.25 L of the 4 M solution; 1 L of the 4 N (with respect to H^-) solution

2. The product would be(±)–7–amino–2–heptanol. The reduction would require 0.375 L of th 2 M solution and 1.5 L of the 2 N (with respect to H^-) solution.

3. 1.2 L of the 2.5 M solution; 1.2 L of the 2.5 N (with respect to H^-) solution.

4. Additional question: With respect to H^+, is a 1 M solution of H_2SO_4 slightly greater than

1 N or slightly less than 1 N? What about with respect to HSO_4^-? Ans: Actually, $1\,M\,H_2SO_4 = 2\,N\,H_2SO_4$, and $1\,M\,HSO_4^- = 1\,N\,HSO_4^-$. Normality with respect to a particular species—in this case H^+—is calculated based on the maximum number of H^+'s the molecule could potentially donate, not how many it actually donates; thus, knowing an acid's strength is irrelevant to calculating its normality.

Molar Solubility

1. Shown in step 5
2. Solve for molar solubility as shown in step 5; substance with highest value is most soluble
3. Decreasing pH decreases sulfate ion concentration, leading to greater dissolution of the sulfate salt.

CHAPTER 10: ACIDS AND BASES

1. D
A Brønsted-Lowry base is defined as a proton acceptor. The other answer choices can accept a proton, while (D) cannot.

2. C
The equation for pH is $pH = -\log[H^+]$. If $[H^+] = 1 \times 10^{-2}$ M, as the question notes, pH equals 2.

3. A
(A) is correct. Acids ending in *-ic* are derivatives of anions ending in *-ate*, while acids ending in *-ous* are derivatives of anions ending in *-ite*. ClO_3^- is named chlorate because it has more oxygen than the other occurring ion, ClO_2^-, which is named chlorite.

4. C
Members of the IA and IIA columns on the periodic table combined with OH^- are always strong bases.

This means (A), (B), (D) are strong bases. (C) is the weakest of the choices.

5. B
The purpose of a buffer is to resist changes in the pH of a reaction. They will not affect the kinetics of a reaction. (D) is on the right path, but the wording is too strong because buffers work only to resist changes in pH over a small range, which is what (B) indicates.

6. C
The question is asking for pH, but because of the information given, we must first find the pOH and then subtract it from 14 to get the pH. The equation for pOH is:

$$pOH = pK_b + \log \frac{[\text{conjugate acid}]}{[\text{weak base}]}.$$

When the given values are substituted into this equation, and the Kaplan methods for estimating logarithms are used, we find that the pOH = 4.45, so the pH = 14 − 4.45 = 9.55.

7. A
The first pK_a in this curve can be estimated by eye. It is located between the starting point (when no base had been added yet) and the first equivalence point. This point is approximately at 7-8 mL added, which corresponds to a pH of approximately 1.9.

8. C
The second equivalence point is the midpoint of the second occurrence of a very quick increase in slope. This corresponds to approximately pH = 5.9.

9. B
The value of the second pK_a is notable because it is found in a slightly different way from the first pK_a. It is located at the midpoint between the first and second equivalence points. In this curve, that corresponds to pH = 4.1.

10. B

Gram equivalent weight is the weight (in grams) that would release one acid equivalent. Because H_3PO_4 contains three acid equivalents, we find the gram equivalent weight by dividing the mass of one mole of the species by 3. (B) is correct.

11. A

This question requires application of the following knowledge:

$$K_a = \frac{[H^+][X^-]}{HX}$$

We know that if HX is to dissociate, then $[H^+]$ = $[X^-]$. We can substitute y for both of these values and plug in K_a and $[HX]$; we then solve for y (representing $[H^+]$). When we do this, we find that $[H^+]$ is 8.0×10^{-3} M.

12. D

An amphoteric species is one that can act as an acid or a base depending on the environment, which means it can also act as an oxidizing or reducing agent depending on the environment, so (A) and (B) are true. (C) is true because, by definition, an amphoteric molecule must contain a proton. (D) is false, and thus the correct answer, because an amphoteric species can be polar or nonpolar in nature.

13. C

The solution to this question is found by using the equation pOH = $-\log[OH^-]$. We must use the Kaplan strategy for estimating logarithms to figure that the pOH is closer to 5 than it is to 4, so we know pOH = 4.5–5. We can then surmise that pH = 9.0–9.5, and because (C) is the only one within that range, it must be correct.

HIGH-YIELD SIMILAR QUESTIONS

pH and pKa

1. The pH would be about 8.85 if the concentration of acetate were halved; if it were doubled, 9.15. (You should be able to predict that the pH would have to go down if there were less acetate and up if there were more.)
2. pH = 13
3. The pH would be 2.87.

Titrations

1. The pH would be approximately 12.2.
2. The pH would be 12.9 (compare this to the pH of 4.72 at the half equivalence point!).
3. The pH would be about 4.4.

CHAPTER 11: REDOX REACTIONS AND ELECTROCHEMISTRY

1. C

In an electrolytic cell, an ionic compound is broken up into its constituents; the cations (positively charged ions) migrate toward the cathode and the anions (negatively charged ions) migrate toward the anode. Electrons are transported from the anode to the cathode in order to balance the charge, meaning that item III will be correct for all electrolytic cells. Because this cell is loaded with water, the ions involved are H^+ and O^{2-}. The cation, H^+, is transported to the cathode, so item I is also correct.

2. A

In a galvanic cell, oxidation occurs at the cathode and reduction occurs at the anode. In this example, Cu is being oxidized. Because the standard reduction potential is +0.52 V, the standard oxidation potential is –0.52 V. The potentials of the half-reactions in a feasible galvanic cell must add up to a value greater than 0, so we can answer this question by simply comparing the oxidation potential of copper to the reduction potentials of the other metals. Mercury has a reduction potential of 0.85 V, which is enough to outweigh the potential contributed by copper (–0.52 V). Zinc and aluminum both have negative reduction potentials, so the overall potential of the cell will be even lower than that of copper. Therefore, mercury is a viable option, while zinc and aluminum are not.

3. A

The oxidizing agent is the species that is reduced in any given equation. In this problem, the two H^+ ions from H_3N are reduced to one neutral H_2 atom. H_3N is not the reducing agent because the H^+ ions and the N^{3-} ions are independent of one another in solution.

4. B

First, we must calculate the oxidation state of chromium in $Cr_2O_7^{2-}$. Because oxygen always carries a –2 charge, the total charge from the O_7 is –14; this means that the Cr_2 contributes a total charge of +12. To reduce the +12 charge to a +4 charge (the charge from the two chromium atoms that are produced in the reaction), 8 electrons are required.

5. A

If a reaction represents a spontaneous process, then the overall potential must be positive. Both half-reactions currently describe a reduction process, so one of the two must be reversed to form an oxidation-reduction system. The only way to create a spontaneous oxidation-reduction system is to reverse the reaction involving O_2 to produce a positive net potential. To balance the reaction, the number of electrons must first be equivocated by doubling all of the quantities in reaction 2. The two reactions are then added together and duplicate

instances of H^+, e^-, and H_2O are eliminated from both sides. This yields the reaction in (A).

6. B

It is important to note here that the potential of a half-reaction remains constant even when the reaction is multiplied by a coefficient. $E°_{reaction1}$ is given as 1.23 and $E°_{reaction2}$ is –1.46 (because reaction 2 must be reversed in order to produce the system in question). $E°_{cell}$ is the sum of these individual $E°$ values, which is equal to –0.23.

7. D

In an electrolytic cell, electricity simply provides the energy to induce a reaction. The actual electrons come from within the molecule that is being electrolyzed. In this case, the positively charged sodium ion gains an electron from the negatively charged chloride ion, thereby creating two neutral atoms.

8. C

In the oxidation-reduction reaction of a metal with oxygen, the metal will be oxidized (donate electrons) and oxygen will be reduced (accept electrons). That means (B) and (D) can be eliminated. A species with a higher reduction potential is more likely to be reduced, and a species with a lower reduction potential is more likely to be oxidized. Based on the information here, iron is oxidized more readily than copper, which means that iron has a lower reduction potential.

9. A

To answer this question, you must know that a hydride ion is comprised of a hydrogen nucleus with two electrons, thereby giving it a negative charge and a considerable tendency to donate its extra electron. This means that $LiAlH_4$ is a strong reducing agent.

10. D

Even if you do not memorize the equation $\Delta G = -nFE^{\circ}_{cell}$, you should understand that Gibbs free energy can be calculated from E°_{cell} and the number of moles.

11. B

The salt bridge contains inert electrolytes. (A), (C), and (D) are all ionic electrolytes, but (B) is a covalent compound. This makes it unlikely for SO_3 to be found in a salt bridge.

12. ~~D~~ C +1

In NaClO (sodium hypochlorite), sodium carries its typical +1 charge and oxygen carries its typical –2 charge. This means that the chlorine atom must carry a +1 charge in order to balance the overall –1 charge; although this is atypical, it is not uncommon (NaClO, for instance, is the active ingredient in household bleach).

13. A

If an electrolytic cell is producing hydrogen and oxygen, it must be breaking up water or hydrogen peroxide. Hydrogen peroxide, however, does not maintain a pH of 7, so we can be sure that the cell is filled with water. Because a water molecule contains two hydrogen atoms for every oxygen atom, the cell will produce twice as much hydrogen as oxygen.

14. C

An increased current will mean that more electrons are transported from the anode to the cathode, thereby driving the electrolytic cell to produce more products. An increase in resistance (A) will decrease the number of electrons in the system, thereby producing the opposite of the desired effect. The amount of electrolyte (B) will affect only the amount of final product; it does not limit the rate. The pH (D) is relevant only to an electrolytic reaction if the reaction involves acids and bases.

15. D

A strong oxidizing agent will be easily reduced, meaning that it will have a tendency to gain electrons. Atoms usually gain electrons if they are one or two electrons away from filling up their valence shell. (A) has a full 4s orbital, meaning it can gain an electron only if it gains an entire p subshell. (B) has a half-full d orbital, so it is unlikely to gain electrons unless it can fill up the entire orbital. (C) has only a single electron in the outer shell, which will probably be lost upon ionization. (D) is the only answer choice that can fill up its outer shell by gaining just one electron.

HIGH-YIELD SIMILAR QUESTIONS

Balancing Redox Reactions

1. Zirconium is being reduced (Zr^{4+} to Zr^0), and therefore is the oxidizing agent. Sulfur is being oxidized (S^{4+} to S^{6+}) and is the reducing agent.

2. The balanced equation is:
   $2\ PbSO_4(s) + 2\ H_2O(\ell) \rightarrow$
   $\quad Pb(s) + PbO_2(s) + 2\ SO_4^{2-}(aq) + 4\ H^+(aq).$

3. The balanced equation is:
   $Zn(s) + 2\ H_2O(\ell) \rightarrow Zn^{2+}(aq) + H_2(g) + 2\ OH^-(aq).$
   The amalgam must be kept dry because on reacting with water in basic solution, hydrogen gas is generated. The expansion of the gas would potentially cause the tooth or crown to crack painfully and leave the dentist with one angry patient!

Electrochemical Cells

1. Placing a battery of greater than 2.25 V in the circuit (with the positive terminal connected to the cathode of the galvanic cell setup) would cause the current to flow the other way.

2. The cell potential would be about 2.24 V. Changing the amount of zinc metal wouldn't

affect this value (as long as some zinc metal is present), since as a solid it is not incorporated into the reaction quotient.

3. About 6.3 g of $KMnO_4$ would be necessary.

The Nernst Equation

1. $[Br^-] = 3.7 \times 10^{-13}$

2. $K_{eq} = e^{876}$. Clearly, permanganate is a very strong oxidizing agent!

3. The pK_a of acetic acid is approximately 4.74.

PRACTICE SECTIONS

PRACTICE SECTION 1

ANSWER KEY

1.	A	19.	C	37.	B
2.	C	20.	C	38.	A
3.	D	21.	A	39.	C
4.	A	22.	C	40.	D
5.	B	23.	D	41.	C
6.	D	24.	A	42.	B
7.	C	25.	C	43.	A
8.	C	26.	D	44.	A
9.	B	27.	B	45.	C
10.	B	28.	A	46.	B
11.	D	29.	B	47.	B
12.	B	30.	A	48.	C
13.	D	31.	B	49.	B
14.	A	32.	C	50.	A
15.	A	33.	D	51.	D
16.	B	34.	C	52.	C
17.	C	35.	A		
18.	B	36.	C		

PASSAGE I

1. A

There are two concepts involved here. The first is that both of these species are strong acids, so they will fully ionize in solution; the bivalent species has two H^+ ions for every one H^+ ion of the monovalent species, so it will produce a more acidic solution. Second is the idea that a more acidic solution will have a lower pK_a.

2. C

It is given in the passage that the pH of normal rain is 5.2, so this problem is simply asking you to convert pH = 5.2 into $[H^+]$. Using the Kaplan logarithm estimation procedure on the answers, it is clear that the only concentration that will produce a pH of 5.2 is (C).

3. D

It is important to know that every Arrhenius acid is also a Brønsted-Lowry acid, and that every Brønsted-Lowry acid is also a Lewis acid (the same idea applies for bases). This means that (B) and (C) can be eliminated. Sulfuric acid produces protons, so it is qualified as an Arrhenius acid, and we then know it can be called a Brønsted-Lowry or Lewis acid as well. All of the items are correct.

4. A

We are able to tell that HCO_3^- is a buffer because it can either donate or accept a proton. Being able to donate a its remaining H^+ allows it to act as an acid, while its overall negative charge allows it to act as a base and accept an H^+. (A) is correct because HCO_3^- will accept a proton from the acid introduced to the blood stream, and act as a buffer. (B) is incorrect because while it will act as a buffer, it will accept an H^+ ion, not donate an H^+ ion. (C) is incorrect because HCO_3^- does act as a buffer. (D) is incorrect because there is enough information.

5. B

Write down the steps as you go. First, we need to figure out what the original $[H^+]$ is in the rain. Because H_2SO_4 is bivalent, we double its concentration to find its contribution to the total $[H^+]$, which is 4.0×10^{-3} M. We then add this to 3.2×10^{-3} M to get $[H^+]_{rain} = 7.2 \times 10^{-3}$ M. If we divide this number by 4 (the factor by which the volume decreased, use $V_1C_1 = V_2C_2$), we get $[H^+]_{rain+pure} = 1.8 \times 10^{-3}$ M. Finally, we can use Kaplan's logarithm estimation strategy to find that the pH is just below 3, so 2.8 is the answer.

6. D

A conjugate base is an acid that loses a proton. (D) shows an acid and a molecule that has lost a molecule of H_2O, so it is not an acid/conjugate base pair. The other choices show an acid and conjugate base that has one less proton.

7. C

This question tests your ability to actively read the passage and synthesize the information presented. The student would likely agree with (A) because pollution is a major cause of acid rain, and industrialization over the past 150 years has greatly increased pollution levels. The student would likely agree with (B) because, as shown in the passage, radicals are integral in the formation of acid rain. The student would likely disagree with (C) because more acid content in water would increase the conductive capacity of water. The student would likely agree with (D) because while rain is naturally acidic, acid rain contains dangerous levels of acid.

8. C

The first pK_a in this curve can be estimated by eye. It is located between the starting point (when no base had been added yet), and the 1st equivalence point. This point is at pH of approximately 6.3. The value of the second pK_a is notable because it is found in a slightly different way than the first pK_a.

It is located at the midpoint between the first and second equivalence points. In this curve, that corresponds to pH = 10.3

9. B

Equivalence points are at the midpoint of the quickly escalating slope range. In this titration curve, the value of the first equivalence point is 7.8 and the value of the second is 12.0.

PASSAGE II

10. B

Many MCAT Physical Sciences questions include dimensional analysis calculations. If you do not know the specific heat of water from memory, you'll want to know this constant on Test Day! (It is reported in paragraph 1.) The correct answer is (B). (A) is tempting, as it has the same magnitude as the specific heat of water in $Jg^{-1}K^{-1}$. You will need to convert (A) from grams to moles using the molecular mass of pure water, 18 g/mol. (C) and (D) differ from (B) and (D) by factors of 1,000, a frequent source of error in thermochemistry problems (using kJ rather than J).

11. D

This is a discrete question which draws on information from the passage. The passage does not provide an explicit comparison of intensive and extensive physical properties. You can infer from paragraph 1, however, that intensive properties do not depend on the amount of substance present in the measurement, and that extensive properties do. While viscosity is irrelevant to this specific experiment, it is an intensive property of a liquid. Mass, heat, and enthalpy are all extensive properties. (Heat is an extensive property; temperature is an intensive property.) The correct answer is (D).

12. B

Use a calorimetry equation to determine the heat capacity of the calorimeter. This set-up requires referring to table 1, which describes how the student calibrated the instrument. The equation must account for all heat inputs and outputs in the closed system. In short, the heat lost by one part of the system must be gained by another part of the system. Here, the cold water heats up, and the hot water cools. That transition is summarized by the equation $m_{hot}C_{H20}(T_f - T_{i,\,hot}) = m_{cold}\,C_{H20}(T_f - T_{i,\,cold}) + K_{cal}(T_f - T_{i,\,cold})$. Use the density of pure liquid water, 1 g/mL, to convert the volumes of hot and cold water to mass quantities. (B) is the answer. (A) is the specific heat of water, not the heat capacity of the calorimeter. (C) results from reversing the sign of the hot water temperature change, which obtains a negative heat capacity value. (D) is off by a factor of 1,000, using water specific heat in kg.

13. D

While it is true that mercury is much more dense than alcohol, the thermometer content should not make a difference in the student's results within this temperature range (A) and (B). There is no information to suggest the relative precision of the instruments (C). (Had the question asked about a digital thermometer, this would be relevant.) (D) is correct. There should be negligible differences in the ΔT obtained by each respective thermometer, though initial and final temperature measurements may vary slightly for each instrument.

14. A

Styrofoam is an excellent, though imperfect, insulator. Calibration accounts for heat loss to the calorimeter. The amount of water is irrelevant in a specific heat measurement, and that the calibration is supposed to account for the properties of the styrofoam (B). Calibration (C) accounts for a heat transfer, not a temperature change. The water

temperature equilibrates in order to calibrate the thermometer, but that doesn't suggest anything about the reaction of other calorimeter contents inside (D).

15. A

The addition of salt ions to pure water disrupts hydrogen bonding between water molecules. When an aqueous solution is more disordered, there are weaker forces between component molecules. Compared to a highly stable hydrogen bond network like water, the salt water solution is disordered enough that its intermolecular bonding is much easier to break, lowering its specific heat.

16. B

Pressure must remain constant; paragraph 3 implies that bomb calorimeters are useful because they maintain constant pressure. Though specific heat is an intensive quantity, it is important to keep track of mass for the overall calorimetry calculation, which can involve different substances with different heat capacities. Heat should not enter or exit the system in a precise measurement. Items I and III are correct so the answer is (B).

17. C

Bomb calorimeters operate at high pressure, so they can accommodate temperature changes in a gas. Coffee cup calorimeters are no longer useful when the water boils. (A), (B), and (D) are distractors. Saltwater (A), as an aqueous ionic solution, is analogous to the fruit punch solution described in the passage. While ethanol (B) boils at a lower temperature than water, its structure is highly similar to that of pure water and it is relatively stable at room temperature. Coffee cup calorimeters can measure the specific heat of a metal like copper (D) if it is placed in water.

QUESTIONS 18–21

18. B

For every 2 mol of HCl 1 mol of hydrogen gas is produced (assuming excess magnesium). Multiplying both sides of the ratio by 1.5 means that 3 mol HCl under the same conditions should produce 1.5 mol hydrogen gas. At STP, 1 mol of a gas (assuming it to be ideal) occupies 22.4 L so 1.5 mol HCl should occupy 33.6 L.

19. C

Savvy test takers will note that (A) and (D) can be eliminated because the answer is internally inconsistent; favoring a reaction almost always means increasing its rate. To decide between (B) and (C), reason via Le Châtelier's principle. The stress is heat. An endothermic reaction requires heat and so is more likely to consume the heat (i.e., reduce the stress) than an exothermic reaction, which will add to the stress by producing heat.

20. C

By definition, gamma radiation is a stream of energy that in addition to creating the Hulk has neither mass nor charge. No such thing as delta radiation (D) has been defined. Alpha particles and beta particles have both charge and mass.

21. A

Rust, or corrosion, is the oxidation of a substance when it comes into contact with both water and oxygen. (B) can be eliminated because, if true, this would enhance the reactivity of Al or Zn. (C) can be eliminated because reducing agents are oxidized and so that would make Al or Zn more likely to rust. (D) is incorrect because, because Al, Zn still rust, they are oxidized and so function as reducing agents. Self-protective oxides (a common way of finding alkali metals as well) prevent further oxidation by complexing the atom with oxygen.

PASSAGE III

22. C

Compound C is shown to promote the reaction without affecting the overall yield of product. It is not consumed or produced in the net reaction, either. This is enough information to identify compound C as a catalyst, which decreases the activation energy of a reaction by definition. In this case, (C) is more likely than (D). Step 1 of the reaction is the fast step and step 2 is the rate-determining, slow step. Even though the catalyst may have an effect on the fast step, its primary purpose is to speed up the slow step. The bulk of the energy input in the overall reaction is in step 2. The catalyst decreases the activation energy, so it is likely to have its primary effect on the step that requires the greatest energy input.

23. D

To answer this question, you must apply Le Châtelier's principle, which states that adding a compound to a system will shift the system reaction such that less of that compound is produced. Adding compound A decreases the overall yield of the system. This change pushes the equilibrium in step 1 to the left to produce more of compound AB and less of compound A. Unbound compound B is not involved in any step of the reaction, so adding it will have no effect on any of the steps. Compound C is a catalyst; increasing the concentration of a catalyst may increase the rate of the reaction, but will not affect the equilibrium constant at any given temperature. The correct answer is (D), as compound D is present on the left side of step 2. Adding more of Compound D will push the reaction to the right, increasing the amount of product.

24. A

In terms of concentration, K_{eq} is equal to [products]/[reactants]. An increased concentration of products signifies an increased equilibrium constant, so K_{eq} of this reaction will increase along with the equilibrium concentration of BD. The data suggest that this concentration increases with increasing reaction temperature, but the concentration starts to stabilize after the temperature reaches approximately 100°C. Only (A) contains a graph demonstrating a K_{eq} which initially increases with temperature but starts to level off around 100°C. (B) shows a graph which follows the opposite of the correct path. (C) suggests that the equilibrium constant rises faster and faster as temperature increases, which is incorrect. (D) represents an equilibrium constant that does not change with temperature.

25. C

If a reaction is first-order with respect to each of the reactants, the overall rate is directly proportional to the concentration of each reactant. Doubling the concentration of compound A will double the rate of the reaction. In this new experiment, the concentration of compound A is twice as high as the concentration used in the first experiment, so the rate of formation is also twice as high.

26. D

The data in the two tables shows that the second experiment, which omitted the catalytic compound C, was significantly slower than the first at every temperature except 150°C. Recall that under normal circumstances, a catalyst will speed up a reaction by decreasing its activation energy, thereby allowing the reaction to reach its activation energy more easily. Consequently, increasing the amount of heat will also help the reaction achieve its activation energy. In this particular experiment, the catalyzed experiment was not much faster than the uncatalyzed experiment at 150°C. This suggests that the reaction reached its activation energy without the help of a catalyst at this temperature range.

27. B

Single-replacement reactions involve the direct replacement of one constituent of a molecule with another constituent molecule. In this case, compound C replaced compound A to turn AB into BC. Double replacement reactions, on the other hand, involve the replacement of two different species. An example of such a reaction is AB + CD → AC + BD. Combination reactions require two or more molecules to combine into one molecule, as in step 2. Decomposition reactions require one molecule to break down into two or more molecules, as in step 3.

28. A

Gases are highly compressible, while solids and liquids are not. For this reason, changes in pressure will not have a substantial effect on solids and liquids. An increase in pressure will push the reaction toward the side with less gas molecules, while a decrease in pressure will do the opposite. Becasue step 1 is the only part of the reaction mechanism that involves gases, it is also the only part that will be affected by a change in pressure.

29. B

This system starts out with two gases (AB and C) and one solution (D) and ends with one gas (A) and two solutions (BD and C). Gases have higher average kinetic energies than solutions do, so they are more disordered (i.e., they have a higher overall entropy, which is a thermochemical measure of the relative disorder in a system). The entropy of the products is lower than the entropy of the reactants, so ΔS for the overall reaction is negative. Based on the information given, it is impossible to determine whether ΔH is positive or negative. Although heat is added to stimulate the reaction, the passage does not specify how much heat is released at the end. ΔG is typically calculated from ΔH and ΔS. ΔH is not known, so ΔG is also impossible to determine.

PASSAGE IV

30. A

Newlands's table suggests that platinum is heavier than gold. According to the modern periodic table, gold is heavier than platinum. (B), (C), and (D) represent pairs of elements that were arranged correctly by Newland.

31. B

Periods 2 and 3 of the periodic table, which contain only elements in the s-block and the p-block, are the only periods that actually contain exactly eight elements. If most of the elements in the d-block and the f-block were discovered, it would become obvious that elements do not occur in matching octaves. (A) is incorrect because the discovery of all of the s-block and p-block elements would create more matching octaves (although the theory would have to be modified to accommodate the noble gases). (C) is incorrect because the law of octaves does not exclude the possibility of electrons, as long as the electrons are not organized as in Bohr's theory. (D) is incorrect for the same reason as (C).

32. C

Mendeleev's table was organized in terms of atomic mass rather than atomic number. Item I did require modification because it was subsequently discovered that an element is characterized by its number of protons (rather than its mass). Item II did not require direct modification of the table and the existing entries were left intact; the only change was the knowledge that future entries would be organized according to their outer orbitals. Item III only strengthened Mendeleev's original model, since the discovery of gallium fulfilled his prediction that two elements exist between zinc and arsenic. Items II and III did not require modification, so (C) is the answer.

33. D

The passage states that Newlands's table contains all of the elements that had been discovered at the time. Because his table contains no noble gases, we can assume that they had not been discovered. The table contains uranium, which is an f-block element (A), and several instances of halogens and metalloids (B) and (C) are evident throughout the table.

34. C

An element's first ionization energy, which is defined as the tendency of the element to donate an electron, decreases with increasing atomic number within a period. Because Mendeleev's predicted element had a higher atomic number than calcium, it is less likely to lose an electron. Atomic radius and ionic radius (A) and (B) both decrease with increasing atomic number. Electronegativity increases with increasing atomic number (D).

35. A

Atomic radius increases as an element gains energy levels and decreases as an element gains protons and electrons; you should know that the largest elements are those that have more energy levels and are found near the bottom of the periodic table. Uranium is the only element on Newlands's table that has seven energy levels, meaning it has the largest atomic radius.

36. C

If Mendeleev had created his table in response to Newlands's theory, then Mendeleev would clearly never have made his breakthrough without Newlands's contribution; if this were the case, it's reasonable to say that Mendeleev simply modified the law of octaves, which was eventually refined to produce the modern version. (A) is incorrect because it does not suggest that Newlands had any impact on the development of today's periodic table. (B) also makes it unlikely for Newlands to have made a direct contribution to the evolution of the system, because Mendeleev only learned about Newlands's work after he had already invented his own table. (D) clarifies the fact that Mendeleev was the first person to publish the modern periodic table and does not suggest that Newlands made any contribution to these findings.

PASSAGE V

37. B

This is a simple ideal gas law question. Using the equation PV = nRT, we are able to substitute: (1 atm)(V) = (1 mol)(R)(318 K), which simplifies to 318R. The answer does not need to be simplified past 318R (you are not allowed to use a calculator during the exam and multiplication by R takes too much time by hand).

38. A

This question tests your knowledge of the ideal gas law. The law shows that volume and temperature have a direct linear relationship (PV = nRT), meaning that as volume increases, so must T (assuming isobaric conditions). (B) shows an indirect linear relationship, (C) an exponential one, and (D) a logarithmic one.

39. C

In Experiment 2, we see that V_1 has been halved. So using the knowledge that temperature has been held constant, we know that the pressure must be double what it originally was to maintain the ideal gas law. So the right answer is 2 atm. The other choices all would violate the ideal gas law.

40. D

The "a" in the van der Waals equation accounts for the attractive forces between gas molecules. The "b" in the equation accounts for the actual volume that the molecules occupy (B). It isn't necessary

to memorize the van der Waals equation for Test Day, but do know what "a" and "b" correct for in the equation.

41. C

The key here is realizing that 64 g O_2 is 2 mol O_2. Substituting the values given into this law, we get: (2 atm)(3 L) = (2 mol)(R)(T). This simplifies to 3/R K.

42. B

Dalton's law of partial pressures says that a gas's molar fraction multiplied by the total pressure gives the partial pressure supplied by that specific gas. This question asks specifically about 1.5 mol of NO, out of a total of 3 mol, which means that NO has a molar fraction of X_{NO} = 0.5. Solve for P using the ideal gas law: (2 L)(P) = (3.0 mol)(R)(300 K), P = 450R atm. This value multiplied by X_{NO} comes to 225R atm.

43. A

This question simply tests your knowledge of the conditions under which the ideal gas law is most relevant. The reference to experiment 1 is included just to mislead you. It is necessary to know only that the gases act closest to ideal when they are at high temperatures and low pressures.

44. A

At first glance this question looks extremely simple, yet you must realize that if the center divider is receiving different pressures from each side, it will move until pressure from both sides is equal. When the experimenter reduced the molar concentration in V_2 by half, the pressure was reduced on the V_2 side of the divider, leading to the expansion of V_1. It is important to note that (B) and (D) are incorrect because the question explicitly states that the cylinder is allowed to re-equilibrate with the new molar concentrations.

PASSAGE VI

45. C

An oxidation-reduction reaction requires a transfer of electrons from one atom to another. This reaction simply involves the neutralization of a strong acid by a weak base; no electrons are transferred and all of the oxidation numbers stay constant throughout the reaction.

46. B

The conjugate base of a Brønsted-Lowry acid is the product that does NOT include the H^+ ion that came from the acid. Even if you did not know this definition, there is a hint to this answer in the passage; because the products in reaction 1 contain a salt and an acid, it is clear that the salt is not the conjugate acid in neutralization reactions. Based on this information, you should be able to determine that the conjugate base is $MgCl_2$. You can determine the percent composition of the cation (Mg^{2+}) in this salt by dividing the molecular weight of the cation (24.3 g/mol) by the molecular weight of the molecule (95.2 g/mol). It should be obvious that 24.3/95.2 is approximately equal to 25/100, which equals 25%.

47. B

The passage states that efficacy is equal to the number of moles of HCl that can be neutralized by one gram of antacid. This means that the most effective antacids are those with the maximum neutralization capacity per gram. Because CO_3^{2-} can neutralize two H^+ ions, $Al_2(CO_3)_3$ has the capacity to neutralize six HCl molecules. Similarly, each of the other answer choices can neutralize three HCl molecules. (C) and (D) can be eliminated because they have the same neutralization capacity as $Al(OH)_3$, but are significantly heavier molecules. To decide between (A) and (B), consider that $Al_2(CO_3)_3$ has a molecular weight of 234 g/mol, while $Al(OH)_3$ has a molecular weight of 78 g/mol. Because $Al_2(CO_3)_3$ can neutralize only twice as many molecules as

$Al(OH)_3$ but has nearly three times the weight, it is clear that $Al(OH)_3$ has the best per-weight efficacy.

48. C

The passage states that $NaHCO_3$ is an antacid, (A) is incorrect. The reaction suggested in (C) and (D), where $H_2CO_3(aq)$ decomposes to produce H_2O (l) and CO_2 (g), is a common reaction that recurs every time H_2CO_3 is present in aqueous solution. Because nearly all the CO_2 is in gas form, it does not significantly affect the pH of the solution; this means that there are no acids left to decrease the pH and, therefore, $NaHCO_3$ is an effective antacid.

49. B

The limiting reagent is the reactant that is completely used up during the reaction while the other reactant still remains. Antacids are alkaline, so if the pH is below 7, there must not have been enough antacid to neutralize all of the HCl. This means that the progress of the reaction was limited by the amount of antacid.

50. A

The passage states that the student initially tested 1 gram of antacid along with 100 mL of 0.1 M HCl. Magnesium hydroxide, $Mg(OH)_2$, has a molecular weight of about 58 g/mol; because the answer choices are all very rough approximations, we can estimate the weight as about 50 g/mol in order to make the calculations easier. At this molecular weight, 1 gram of antacid is approximately equal to (1g)/ (50g/mol) = 0.02 mol. 100 mL of 0.1 M HCl is equal to (0.1 L) × (0.1 mol/L) = 0.01 mol. Because each molecule of $Mg(OH)_2$ has two OH^- ions, only half a mole of $Mg(OH)_2$ is required to neutralize a mole of acid; therefore, only 0.005 moles of antacid is used up. The student started with 0.02 moles of antacid, so he is now left with 0.02 – 0.005 = 0.015 moles. To convert back to grams, we multiply 0.015 moles by 50 g/mol to get 0.75 g—which is equal to 750 mg.

51. D

A stronger antacid can neutralize the same amount of acid while using a smaller quantity of reactant. This means that more reactant will be left over after the neutralization is complete. Often, this leftover reactant will present itself in the precipitate (some antacids, however, will dissolve in the solution; this is why the student's logic was flawed). (A) is incorrect because the question states that the antacid is present as an excess reagent; increasing the amount of an excess reagent does not increase the amount of product unless more of the limiting reagent becomes available. (B) is incorrect for the same reason.

52. C

Sodium and potassium (and the rest of the alkali metals) form soluble salts, while aluminum, magnesium, and calcium do not; however, you do not need to know this fact in order to answer this question. The increased solubility of the compounds in group B caused the unreacted material to dissolve in solution, so the student was unable to detect any of the starting compound in the precipitate. The compounds in group A are sparingly soluble, so stronger antacids left a larger amount of unreacted solid. The alkalinity of the compound has no bearing on its ability to precipitate (A); also, you should know that strong bases containing sodium and potassium (i.e., NaOH and KOH) are just as alkaline as their counterparts which contain magnesium, calcium, and aluminum. (B) and (D) are accurate statements, but do not explain the student's results as well.

PRACTICE SECTION 2

ANSWER KEY

1.	B	19.	B	37.	A
2.	D	20.	A	38.	C
3.	A	21.	A	39.	B
4.	C	22.	C	40.	D
5.	B	23.	A	41.	B
6.	C	24.	B	42.	D
7.	D	25.	D	43.	A
8.	B	26.	C	44.	C
9.	B	27.	B	45.	C
10.	D	28.	D	46.	C
11.	A	29.	A	47.	A
12.	B	30.	C	48.	B
13.	A	31.	A	49.	A
14.	B	32.	A	50.	D
15.	C	33.	B	51.	C
16.	A	34.	A	52.	C
17.	C	35.	B		
18.	D	36.	D		

PASSAGE I

1. B

The dissociation reaction tells us that the coefficients for both products are equal to 1. We use this information to write the solubility equation. The solubility equation for the dissociation of $CaSO_4$ is the following:

$$4.93 \times 10^{-5} = [Ca^{2+}][SO_4^{2-}]$$

Because Ca^{2+} and SO_4^{2-} have a one-to-one ratio they can be replaced by the variable "x" to solve for their concentration. Solving the equation $4.93 \times 10^{-5} = (x)^2$, we obtain a concentration of 7.02×10^{-3} M for each ion. Because one mole of ion is equivalent to one mole of salt, this is the concentration of $CaSO_4$ needed to equal the K_{sp}, at which point the solution is saturated. The concentration of $CaSO_4$ ions,

7.02×10^{-3} M, can be multiplied by the volume, 3.75×10^5 L, to obtain a value of 2.63×10^3 moles. Converting moles of $CaSO_4$ to grams is accomplished by multiplying by the molar mass of $CaSO_4$, 136.14 grams/mole, to give a mass of 3.58×10^5 grams needed to reach saturation. (A) is the number of moles, not grams, of $CaSO_4$.

2. D

One way to solve this problem is to calculate the Ca^{2+} concentration for one mole of each compound using the K_{sp} and chemical equilibrium equation. Looking at the answer choices, (C) can be ruled out immediately because of the extremely small K_{sp}, which indicates that very few of the salt ions will dissolve. The other K_{sp} values are comparable for (A), (B), and (D). Remember to raise the ion to the power of its coefficient when setting up the equilibrium equation. For example, the equilibrium equation for the correct (D) would be $K_{sp} = 6.47 \times 10^{-6} = [Ca^{2+}][IO_3^-]^2$. The concentration of calcium for each of these answer choices, respectively, equals 6.93×10^{-5} M, 2.14×10^{-4} M, and 1.17×10^{-2} M. (D) has the highest concentration of Ca^{2+} at 1.17×10^{-2} M.

3. A

The concentration of a saturated solution of $CaSO_4$ is equal to approximately 0.015 M, according to the graph. This number was found by determining the corresponding concentration for a conductivity value of 2500 µS/cm. The concentration of $CaSO_4$ is equal to the concentration of both Ca^{2+} and SO_4^{2-} ions in solution according to equation 1 because the coefficients are all 1. Therefore, the $K_{sp} = [Ca^{2+}][SO_4^{2-}] = (.015 \text{ M})^2$, which equals 2.25×10^{-4} M^2. The concentration of $CaSO_4$ must be square to obtain the K_{sp}, so (B) is incorrect. (C) doubles, not squares, the concentration. (D) might be obtained if you had taken the square root, not squared, the concentration.

4. C

As temperature increases in a solution, movement of molecules and ions increase. This will increase the current between the electrodes in the probe and increase the value of conductivity. Temperature's effect on the solubility product constant cannot be determined without further information. Although many salts have a higher solubility with higher temperatures, not all salts share this property. The only sure way to determine the relationship is by experimentation. An increase in temperature would increase the conductivity, not decrease it, so (B) and (D) is incorrect. (A) is incorrect because it is impossible to determine the relationship between temperature and K_{sp}.

5. B

The common ion effect is when an ion is already present in the solution and affects the dissociation of a compound that contains the same ion. In this case, $Ca(OCl)_2$ contains calcium and will cause the reaction in equation 1 to shift to the left due to Le Châtelier's principle. If there is no $Ca(OCl)_2$ and therefore no extra Ca^{2+} present in solution, more $CaSO_4$ will dissociate. (C) is the opposite (A) is misleading because chlorine gas will not react with SO_4^{2-}. (D) is incorrect because changing from $Ca(OCl)_2$ to chlorine gas will remove the common ion effect and cause more dissociation of $CaSO_4$.

6. C

An increase in pH means that fewer H^+ ions are present in solution. Lowering the concentration of H^+ will shift the equilibrium in equation 2 to the right, and fewer HOCl molecules will be in solution. Because the HOCl molecules can oxidize harmful agents, the oxidizing power has been reduced as a result of the pH increase. An increase in pH will not break the HOCl compound (A), though over time it will break down. Although salts do act as buffers (B), it is still possible to change the pH of the pool. As for (D), an increase in pH will decrease [H$^+$] and thus result in fewer H$^+$ ions available to associate with OCl$^-$.

7. D

To make a supersaturated solution you must first heat the solution, which allows additional salt to dissolve. (While not all salts have a higher solubility at higher temperatures, this statement holds true for the majority of salts; an increase in temperature will generally increase the solubility of a collection of salts.) This occurs because at higher temperatures, the K$_{sp}$ generally increases. The solution can then be cooled and the salt will remain dissolved, creating a supersaturated solution.

8. B

Using the top equation we can write the following:

$$K_{a2} = \frac{([H^+][CO_3^{2-}])}{[HCO_3^-]}$$

We can manipulate the equation to solve for [H$^+$], where $[H^+] = \frac{(K_{a2}[HCO_3^-])}{[CO_3^{2-}]}$.

Using the bottom equation we can write the following: $K_{sp} = [Ca^{2+}][CO_3^{2-}]$

We can rearrange this equation to solve for [CO$_3$$^{2-}$], which can then be substituted into the top equation:

$$[CO_3^{2-}] = \frac{K_{sp}}{[Ca^{2+}]}$$

Substituting into the top equation gives:

$$[H^+] = \left(\frac{K_{a2}}{C_{sp}}\right) \times [Ca^{2+}][HCO_3^-]$$

The K$_a$ equation includes the reactant in the denominator because the reactant is aqueous (in contrast to the K$_{sp}$ equation which doesn't include the

reactant in the denominator). The K$_{sp}$ reactant is a salt in its solid form; solids are not included in equilibria equations.

9. B

The color change will occur slightly before the pK$_a$ of phenol red is reached. This is because the basic form, which is prevalent above the pK$_a$, has a higher absorptivity than the acidic form. This means that the basic form will absorb light more strongly than the acidic form. At the pK$_a$ the basic and acidic forms are equal (definition of pK$_a$), but because of the higher absorptivity of the basic form the color will begin to change when there still is more acidic than basic molecules of phenol red. (C) and (D) are above the pK$_a$ value, after the color change has occurred. (A) is under the pK$_a$ but is too low. At pH 4, acidic molecules heavily dominate the solution so the absorptivity difference between acidic and basic forms does not come into play.

PASSAGE II

10. D

Hydrogen is diatomic in its elemental state, i.e., H$_2$ (g). The passage refers to the fact that each gaseous hydrogen atoms has a single electron, for two total electrons in H$_2$, but the proper electron configuration of a diatomic substance requires using the bonding-antibonding model from molecular orbital theory. None of the choices are that specific, so they are not correct. (A) is a distortion; substances in their elemental state are presumed to keep their electrons in the ground state. (B) is a distortion. as well; hydrogen is diatomic in its elemental state, meaning two electrons.

11. A

(B) is opposite; light is absorbed when the electron moves away from the nucleus. While electrons make the energy transitions, the energy transitions result in light radiation, not the emission of the electron itself, so (C) and (D) are incorrect.

12. B

The Lyman series transitions occur in the UV range (λ = 200 – 400 nm). The Balmer series corresponds to four visible wavelengths (λ = 400 – 700 nm), though the Balmer constant itself is in the UV range. Both the infrared and x-ray ranges of the light spectrum (C) and (D) fall far outside the transitions which characterize these spectra. Infrared rays are low-energy and have higher wavelengths, while x-rays are high-energy and have very short wavelengths. It is not necessary to memorize the specific wavelengths in different kinds of radiation as long as you have a general sense of differences in magnitude.

13. A

If you ignore the digression about astronomy, the question is straightforward and does not require referring back to the passage. It simply asks what color of visible light corresponds to 656.3 nm. The visible light spectrum covers 400–700 nm. Using the ROYGBIV mnemonic and prior knowledge that infrared wavelengths are longer than visible wavelengths, you know that red is on the 700 nm end, and that violet is on the 400 nm end.

14. B

This image is an absorption spectrum, in contrast to the emission spectrum presented in the passage. Think of it as the inverse of the emission spectrum. We cannot tell from the passage what a Lyman or Bohr series looks like.

15. C

Deuterium is "heavy" hydrogen, with one neutron, one proton, and one electron. The Balmer series concerns only electron transitions, so there will be no change in the number of peaks. In other words,

there will be the same number of peaks, but with more splitting; the nucleus is heavier, which will slow down the transitions. This effect is visible at high resolutions.

16. A

A full explanation is out of the scope of the MCAT Physical Science section, but you should know from general physics that Bohr's model was incomplete because it didn't incorporate the theory of relativity. We know from the question stem and equation that the Balmer series works only for wavelengths related to the quantized energy levels (B). Though it is not stated explicitly in the passage, Bohr's quantitative model incorporates atomic number (C) (more detail is unnecessary for now; in short, it affects the atomic radius). Hydrogen atoms have only one electron (D), and we have no indication that other particles are involved.

17. C

According to Bohr's model, the energy differences between quantized energy levels become progressively smaller the further away the electron moves from the nucleus. Textbooks will sometimes describe this concept as if the energy levels themselves are "narrowing." (If energy levels are depicted as rings around a nucleus, they will appear to be closer together as you move further from the nucleus.) Read carefully. (B) describes a drawing like this one, but the graphical representation of this concept does not really explain the difference in energy. We do not have enough information in the passage to determine whether the energy levels themselves are a greater or smaller distance apart. (A) is the opposite of (B), intended to stump readers who might not read through to (C) and (D). Because (C) refers directly to energy differences between energy levels, it is more accurate. (Remember $E = hf = h \times$ [speed of light/wavelength].) (D) is its opposite.

QUESTIONS 18–22

18. D

Only (D) gives a response where both kinds of particles have a mass. Neither neutrons nor gamma rays have mass and so they are unchanged by the actions of a particle accelerator. The dependence on mass arises because a particle accelerator works by means of high-energy ideally elastic collisions. Also, if there is no mass, both kinetic energy and momentum are undefined.

19. B

A solution is available here which doesn't require an equation. Both the acid and base are monoprotic, thus there are no multiple dissociations. Notice that the acid is twice as concentrated as the base. Thus, double the amount of base will be needed to neutralize the acid or 2 × 15 mL = 30 mL. If you forgot this factor of 2, you might have chosen (A), and if you squared the 2 out of uncertainty (only in physics do you square things when in doubt) you might have chosen (D). C is the total volume of the solution, not the volume just of the base.

20. A

The ideal gas theory assumes that the particles have large interatomic distances and a relative absence of intermolecular forces. This is more true at lower pressures than at higher ones, thus eliminating (C) and (D). (B) implies that high pressure squishes the molecules. According to the kinetic theory of gases, individual atoms are treated as incompressible point properties. The main effect of the pressure is to reduce the interatomic distance, not the intra-atomic distance (i.e., the atomic radius).

21. A

Molecules can only be nonpolar if they have total symmetry around the central atom. Bent molecules lack this symmetry (think of a molecule of water with two lone pairs of electrons and two hydrogen atoms extending from the central oxygen atom) and so a dipole is created which causes polarity in the molecule. A diatomic covalent (B) molecule (such as H_2 or O_2) is perfectly symmetrical. (C) and (D) are incorrect because, although dipoles can exist in these configurations, symmetrical arrangements are also possible.

22. C

Isotopes of the same element have the same number of protons. Alpha decay results in the loss of two protons and two neutrons, while beta decay (β- decay) causes the gain of one proton. Thus, two beta decays must occur for each alpha decay to ensure that the number of protons in the daughter nucleus is equal to the number of protons in the parent nucleus. The answer is (C), 1:2.

PASSAGE III

23. A

In order to balance the equation, we must first combine the half-reactions. This requires writing all of the products and all of the reactants for both reactions in one equation:

$$LiCoO_2 + xLi^+ + xe^- + 6C \rightleftharpoons Li_{1-x}CoO_2 + xLi^+ + xe^- + Li_xC_6$$

If a certain compound/particle is on both the left and the right sides of the equation, then it is appearing as both a reactant and a product. Since there is no net change in that specific species, we can omit it from the net reaction; for this reason, we can eliminate the terms "xLi^+" and "xe^-" from both sides of this equation. This leaves us with (A) as the correct choice.

24. B

You should know that the overall potential of a galvanic cell ($E°_{cell}$) is equal to the sum of the potentials at the cathode and the anode. The overall potential of a discharging cell is always positive, but not necessarily greater than 1; for this reason, (B) is the only viable option. You can also arrive at this conclusion by realizing that the reaction in a battery is always spontaneous, since the battery must supply energy. Spontaneous reactions always have a negative ΔG, which you can plug into the free energy equation ($\Delta G = -nFE^\circ_{cell}$). To get a negative ΔG from the free energy equation, you must have a positive E°_{cell}.

25. D

The first thing to note here is that lithium acts as an electrolyte in this reaction, meaning that it is not oxidized or reduced; that rules out (A) and (B) immediately. By definition, reduction happens at the cathode and oxidation happens at the anode. However, because this is a reversible reaction (which you should know based on the fact that the reaction is at equilibrium), we cannot use these definitions to distinguish between the species that is oxidized and the species that is reduced. The easiest way to answer this question is by noting that the carbon in the anode is neutral on the left side of the forward reaction and is negatively charged on the right side. This means that carbon is reduced, allowing us to select (D) as the correct answer. You can verify this by checking the cathode side: Because the cathode is made of CoO_2^-, in which Co has a +3 charge (since oxygen almost always carries a –2 charge, two oxygen atoms add up to a –4 charge; to create an overall –1 charge, Co must be +3), Co^{3+} must be oxidized in the conversion of Li-CoO_2 to $Li_{1-x}CoO_2$. The product of this reaction, because it contains less +1 charge from lithium, must contain a more positive charge from cobalt (further confirming that the cobalt is reduced).

26. C

Because of the complexity of this question, the first step should be to eliminate as many choices as possible. There is no indication in the passage that E°_{cell} is positive for the forward reaction (A). The assumption about reaction kinetics in (B) is correct, but it's likely that the effect of a change in x will be different for each reaction. One reaction will shift to the left and the other will shift to the right, but the shifts will not be exactly identical to one another; therefore, K_{eq} will change and (B) is incorrect. A galvanic cell gradually discharges while transporting electrons from the anode, where oxidation occurs, to the cathode, where reduction occurs. In the forward reaction, oxidation occurs at the anode and reduction occurs at the cathode. This means that the forward reaction does not represent a discharging cell, so the reverse reaction must be favored when the battery is in use. Because the reverse reaction takes precedence over the forward reaction, K_{eq} is low when the cell is discharging.

27. B

$LiCoO_2$ is usually present in the battery since it is on the left side of the cathode reaction. The presence of the $Li(CoO_2)_2$ complex is more important for this question. It is clear that $Li(CoO_2)_2$ a form of the $Li(CoO_2)_{1/(1-x)}$ complex, so we can calculate x by writing the equation $1/(1-x) = 2$. Simple algebra yields the fact that ½ of the battery's initial energy is remaining. Because the initial energy was equal to 100 J, the current energy equals 50 J.

28. D

According to the passage, the system contains only lithium as a salt in a solvent. Because it is not part of the cathode or the anode, it always retains its +1 charge. All three items are correct.

29. A

When atoms or molecules are in close proximity for an extended period of time, there is a substantial probability that they will interact with one another. The reaction suggested in (A) would require reduction of Co^{3+} to Co^{2+}, which is not unlikely to occur in small quantities. Though the passage does not directly indicate that this was the mechanism of production of lithium oxide and cobalt(II) oxide, it is more likely than any of the other answer choices. It would be incorrect to dismiss the possibility of decomposition, but the reaction suggested in (B) ($LiCoO_2 \rightarrow Li_2O + CoO$) is stoichiometrically impossible. (C) is incorrect because interaction with environmental oxygen would affect cell 2 just as much as it would affect cell 1. (D) is incorrect because we have no evidence suggesting that any water is present in the system; the passage clarifies that organic solvents are used.

30. C

The scientist believes that battery deterioration is caused primarily by the formation of cobalt(II) oxide and lithium oxide in equal quantities. Therefore, increased amounts of cobalt(II) oxide suggest a decrease in battery capacity. (A) and (B) are incorrect because x is a ratio that is unaffected by the energy storage capacity of a cell. (D) is incorrect because, although a decrease in concentration of Li_xC_6 would suggest a decrease in cell capacity, most of the deterioration is caused by the conversion of $LiCoO_2$ to Li_2O and CoO_2.

PASSAGE IV

31. A

Ammonia's heat of vaporization is given in the data and described as low compared with that of water. Thus, its evaporation rate must also be high compared to that of water so life could not have evolved in a liquid ammonia environment as life on earth evolved in a liquid water environment. The phases in (B), (C), and (D) would matter less for life's evolution from a liquid environment; they are also incorrect applications of the data from the passage.

32. A

Solid water would have been most dense if it were like other substances, and thus sunk to the bottom of any liquid system. Liquid systems would have been frozen from the bottom up, and life could not have evolved in the liquid phase of a watery environment. (B), (C), and (D) do not address this "what-if" scenario.

33. B

It is the kinetic energy of the molecules that moves them further apart to allow a phase change from solid to gas, as described in the question. The same process would dictate a phase change from solid to liquid, or liquid to gas.

34. A

The electronegativities of the atoms comprising a molecule determine the polarity of that molecule. None of the other choices will make as significant a contribution. (C) is the next most logical but is less correct because forces emanate from the intrinsic nature of electronegativity within the water molecule, not between.

35. B

The crystalline lattice formed for a water-solid uniquely collapses under pressure to become a liquid. (A) is a true statement, though it doesn't directly address the question.

36. D

Both (A) and (B) are true. Water has a higher heat of vaporization than ammonia and therefore evaporates at a higher temperature. Temperature is a measurement of average kinetic energy, so high temperature means higher average kinetic energy; the molecules are also moving faster.

37. A

Ions dissolved in the lattice break existing inter-molecular attractive forces. This process interferes with the formation of a crystal lattice in ice, which explains why ice melts when salt is added.

PASSAGE V

38. C

Asking for the strongest reducing agent is equal to asking for the element with the highest electronegativity. Electronegativity increases as we move from the left to the right and from the bottom to the top of the periodic table. Therefore, you are looking for an element that is above and to the right of phosphorus. (C), oxygen, fits this description.

39. B

You're being asked which elements have a larger atomic radius than phosphorus. Atomic radius increases from right to left and from top to bottom of the periodic table. Therefore, you are looking for elements that are below and to the left of phosphorus. Both K and Pb fit this description, so B is the correct answer.

40. D

To answer this question, you must know that phosphorus is a nonmetal. The other answer choices describe properties of nonmetals. (D) describes a property of metals, so it is the correct answer.

41. B

(B) is the correct full electron configuration. (C) places the 3s-electrons in the 3p-orbital. (D) is incorrect because phosphorus does not have a 3d-orbital.

42. D

(A) and (B) are incorrect because alkaline earth elements are generally more dense than alkali metals. (C) is incorrect because alkali metals contain the same number of orbitals as the alkaline earth element in the corresponding row. (D) is a true statement.

43. A

Halogens can naturally exist in the gaseous, liquid, and solid states (iodine).

44. C

(A), (B), (D) are all true properties of transition elements, but they do not greatly contribute to the malleability shown by these elements. Their malleability can be attributed mostly to the loosely held d-electrons.

45. C

(A) is incorrect because phosphorus is not a metalloid. Metalloids do often behave as semiconductors (B) but it is not relevant here. (C) is correct because both arsenic and antimony are in the same group as phosphorus and they have similar properties.

PASSAGE VI

46. C

The reaction presented in the passage, beginning with acetic acid and forming methane and carbon dioxide, is a decomposition reaction. It begins with one reactant and ends with two products, which is typical of a decomposition reaction. A combination reaction (A) would have been the opposite: more reactants than products. A single displacement reaction (B) typically is an oxidation/reduction reaction, which is not demonstrated in this question. A combustion reaction (D) is catalyzed by oxygen and results in carbon dioxide and water as products.

47. A

First, calculate the molecular weight of acetic acid, CH_3COOH, which is 60.05 g/mol. Next, recognize that there is a 1:1 molar ratio between this reactant and the product, methane. By beginning with 120.0 grams of acetic acid and dividing by the molecular weight, this yields 1.998 moles of acetic acid and should produce the same number of moles of methane. The molecular weight of methane is 16.04 g/mol. By multiplying this molecular weight by the number of expected moles yield, 1.998, the theoretical yield expected if all of the acetic acid were decomposed would be 32.05 grams of methane product.

48. B

A key issue here in harnessing a gaseous product is its phase and transport, so (B) is correct. If compressible, then methane would take up significantly less volume and be easier to transport, making it more likely to be efficient as a common energy source. The passage states that this reaction typically takes place at a temperature well above room temperature. Even if (A) were true, it doesn't support an argument toward using methane gas as a major energy source. While (C) is true, the production of gas challenges, more than supports, the passage's argument of making clean energy. Finally, whether or not the reaction is exothermic, the energy source is the product, methane gas, so (D) presents an irrelevant piece of information.

49. A

To build the equation necessary to answer this question, begin with 88.02 grams of CO_2 in the numerator. Next, convert this to moles of CO_2 by dividing by grams per mole. This eliminates (D), since 88.02 grams is in the denominator and the molecular weight of CO_2 is in the numerator. (C) is also out with 88.02 grams in the denominator. Next, recognize that there is a 1:1 ratio of CO_2 to CH_3COOH, making it unnecessary to convert the number of moles. This eliminates (B), which incorrectly uses a 1:2 ratio. The only choice remaining is (A), which

correctly ends by multiplying by the molecular weight of acetic acid; this would yield the number of grams of acetic acid necessary for the proposed reaction.

50. D

The net ionic equation shows all aqueous ions that productively participate in the reaction, eliminating all spectator ions. The only true spectator ion in this equation is sodium, so it should not be present in a net ionic equation, which proves that (A) is incorrect. Next, $CH_3CH_2CH_2Cl$ has a covalent bond between the carbon and chloride atoms, meaning that it is unlikely to ionize in solution; chloride, thus, should not be represented as an ion on the reactant side of the equation, as it is in (A) and (B). Finally, (D) correctly keeps the reactant as one molecule and has the chloride ion written as a product.

51. C

The first step in this question requires you to consider the correctly balanced equation for converting CO_2 and H_2 to CH_4 and H_2O (the reactants and products specified in the passage and in the question stem):

$$CO_2 + 2 H_2 \rightarrow CH_4 + 2 H_2O$$

The correctly balanced equation uses the molar ratio of 1 CO_2 : 2 H_2 : 1 CH_4 : 2 H_2O. Next, recall that according to the ideal gas law, one mole of an ideal gas has a volume of 22.4 L at standard temperature and pressure (STP). From this, one can calculate that there are 0.134 moles of hydrogen gas and 0.0893 moles of carbon dioxide available as reactants. Then, calculate the molar equivalents of each, since 2 moles of hydrogen gas are required per mole of CO_2. Thus, there are 0.0670 molar equivalents available of hydrogen gas per 0.0893 moles CO_2, meaning that the hydrogen gas is the limiting reagent. Finally, because there is only one mole of methane produced per one mole of hydrogen gas used, there will be 0.0670 moles of methane produced. (A) does not correct for the 2:1 molar equivalency of H_2:CH_4. (B) uses carbon dioxide as the limiting reagent. (D) reverses the molar ratio of H_2:CH_4, thus multiplying 0.134 moles by 2 instead of dividing.

52. C

Begin by calculating the theoretical yield of methane, which is the amount (in either grams or moles) of methane expected to be produced if all the hydrogen were fully consumed by the following formula:

$$CO_2 + 2 H_2 \rightarrow CH_4 + 2 H_2O$$

Recall that at STP, one mole of gas has a volume of 22.4 liters, which allows one to calculate that there are 2.32 moles of hydrogen gas given to react. Next, use the balanced equation for converting CO_2 and H_2 to CH_4 and H_2O (the reactants and products specified in the passage and in the question stem). The correctly balanced equation uses the molar ratio of $1\ CO_2 : 2\ H_2 : 1\ CH_4 : 2\ H_2O$. Thus, with 2.32 moles of hydrogen gas, one would expect to form one mole of methane per two moles of hydrogen gas, or 1.16 moles of methane product. Finally, multiply by methane's molecular weight, 16.04, which results in 18.6 grams of methane; this is the theoretical yield. However, the question stem states that only 8.02 grams of methane were produced. Thus, the percent yield is calculated by dividing the actual yield (8.02 grams) by the theoretical yield (18.6 grams) and multiplying by 100 percent, which results in a percent yield of 43.1 percent.

PRACTICE SECTION 3

ANSWER KEY

1.	A	19.	A	37.	A
2.	B	20.	A	38.	C
3.	D	21.	D	39.	B
4.	D	22.	D	40.	B
5.	D	23.	A	41.	D
6.	A	24.	A	42.	C
7.	B	25.	B	43.	C
8.	C	26.	A	44.	B
9.	B	27.	A	45.	A
10.	B	28.	D	46.	D
11.	C	29.	C	47.	D
12.	B	30.	D	48.	A
13.	C	31.	C	49.	C
14.	A	32.	D	50.	D
15.	A	33.	A	51.	A
16.	C	34.	D	52.	B
17.	B	35.	D		
18.	C	36.	D		

PASSAGE I

1. A

For a molecule to pass from the systemic circulation to the central nervous system, it must pass between the tightly sealed endothelial cells or through the endothelial cells. Unless a medication has a transporter to cross the cell membrane twice, it is more likely to diffuse between endothelial cells, despite their tightly sealed spaces. Because cell membranes are composed primarily of nonpolar lipid molecules, it will be easiest for a lipophilic, or nonpolar compound to diffuse into the CSF. Although (B) does describe a method for delivering drugs to the CNS, a nonsystemic route would be inefficient for a process as routine as general anesthetic administration; (A) is a better option. (C) is incorrect, because nonpolar or lipophilic molecules will penetrate more effectively than will a polar molecule. (D) is irrelevant; furthermore, a slow-acting general anesthetic would be impractical when physicians are aiming to minimize time under anesthesia and maximize patient comfort.

2. B

The key to understanding the blood-brain barrier is that the endothelial cells are tightly sealed, prohibiting free passage of molecules, unlike the leaky capillary systems of the peripheral circulation. The molecules that are most likely to still move between these cells and enter the CSF are those that are uncharged and not repelled by the hydrophilic cell membranes. Even though charged particles might associate closely with one another (A), this doesn't affect their passage through the blood-brain barrier. (D) is incorrect because the passage relates no information about the differential solubilities of charged molecules in the bloodstream versus CSF.

3. D

The blood-brain barrier, as described in the passage, provides a tight seal between the systemic circulation and the more sensitive central nervous system. As a result, this barrier can serve to protect the central nervous system from potentially damaging substances that can more readily enter the systemic circulation, and then be filtered before entering the CNS. (A) is incorrect because the blood-brain barrier's adaptive seal is not designed for maximizing nutrient transport; in fact, it limits transport/transfer between two systems. (B) is incorrect because this barrier necessarily means that many molecules and particles cannot pass between the CNS and systemic compartments, thus making these two micro-environments different. (C) is incorrect because the blood-brain barrier's main role is not to limit movement of particles or agents from CSF to the systemic circulation, but rather to limit flow in the other direction because the systemic circulation is more readily contaminated.

4. D

According to the passage, molecules most likely to cross the blood-brain barrier are hydrophobic or nonpolar. Thus, ion-dipole and dipole-dipole interactions (A) and (B) are unlikely to be the most important forces governing intermolecular interactions among these molecules (because they require charge and/or polarity). Although hydrogen bonding (C) might have a role in these molecules, hydrogen bonds, because they occur between atoms in otherwise polarized bonds (a hydrogen with a partial negative charge and a lone pair or otherwise electronegative atom with a negative charge), would be unlikely to facilitate transport in a hydrophobic environment. Dispersion forces (D) refer to the unequal sharing of electrons that occurs among nonpolar molecules as the result of rapid polarization and counterpolarization; these are likely to be the prevailing intermolecular forces affecting molecules that move easily through the blood-brain barrier.

5. D

All three items are false. A polar molecule can still have a formal charge of zero, because the molecule's formal charge is the sum of the formal charges of the individual atoms. Each atom could individually still have a positive or negative formal charge, calculate by the formula:

FC = Valence electrons − ½ bonding electrons − nonbonding electrons

Thus, a molecule with a formal charge of zero could have multiple polarized bonds and/or multiple atoms with positive/negative formal charges, making it unlikely to permeate through the nonpolar blood-brain barrier. Similarly, having a negative formal charge on the molecule overall would be unfavorable to move through a nonpolar barrier. Finally, two molecules, both with formal charges of zero, could have very different characteristics, making them more or less likely to permeate the blood-brain barrier. For example, one compound could be comprised entirely of nonpolar bonds, with all atoms of formal charge of zero, both of which would make it favorable to pass through the blood-brain barrier. Size also plays a key role, as large molecules do not readily pass through the barrier. A separate molecule with a formal charge of zero could, as described above, contain positive or negative formal charges on different atoms and/or have polar bonds, making it pass through the barrier less readily.

6. A

In cisplatin, a molecule with square planar geometry, two chloride atoms and two ammonia molecules each are bonded directly to the central platinum, without any remaining lone pairs on the central platinum. The NH_3 groups bond to the central platinum by donating a lone pair of electrons into an unfilled orbital of the platinum atom. As such, NH_3 is acting as a Lewis base, and platinum is acting as a Lewis acid, and they form a coordinate covalent bond. A polar covalent bond (B) is not formed from this type of donation of a lone pair; an example of a polar covalent bond would be the N–H bonds in the NH_3 group, with partial negative charge on the nitrogen and partial positive charge on the hydrogen. In (C) and (D), the Pt–N bond is formed by a Lewis acid/base relationship, which is not the case for a nonpolar covalent bond or ionic bond.

7. B

Although the geometry of this carbon atom is likely to be changed somewhat by the ring strain on the adjacent ring structures, it is still most likely to approximate a tetrahedral geometry. This carbon is bonded to four groups: the two phenol groups, a nitrogen, and the additional carbon atom in the adjacent carboxyl group. The tetrahedral geometry

(B) maximizes the space among these four groups. Octahedral geometry (D) typically refers to a central atom surrounded by six groups, not four.

8. C

Resonance structures serve to spread out formal charge. The most important resonance structures minimize or eliminate the formal charge on individual atoms. As a result, polarity in any single bond might be minimized. (A) is essentially the opposite of this argument. (B) is incorrect; it is possible for molecules with or without resonance to be polar, and this is too broad of a generalization to be true. (D) is incorrect because polar bonds will intrinsically place a partial negative charge on the more electronegative atom. Important resonance structures would likely further accentuate this inclination, placing extra electrons on more electronegative atoms. Counteracting this effect and essentially "removing" electrons from highly electronegative atoms to counterbalance the natural polarity of the bond would form an extremely high-energy, unfavorable, and thus unimportant, resonance structure.

PASSAGE II

9. B

The order of this reaction can be determined by the equation $r = k[A]_x [B]_y$. You must divide r_3 by r_1 to get: $\frac{8.09}{2.04} = \frac{k(4.00)^x(1.00)^y}{k(1.00)^x(1.00)^y}$. This simplifies to $4 = 4^x$, so $x = 1$. This means that H^+ is a first-order reactant.

10. B

The equation for the rate of a reaction is:

$$\text{Rate} = k[\text{reactant}_1]^{\text{order1}}[\text{reactant}_2]^{\text{order2}}$$

Using the equation for determining order of a reactant detailed in the explanation for the answer to question 9, we find that O_2 is second order. Substituting the information into the equation for the rate of a reaction leads to:

$$\text{Rate} = (0.5)[2.0 \text{ M}]^1[2.0 \text{ M}]^2$$

Simplifying this equation allows us to determine that the rate is 4 M/sec.

11. C

(A) is incorrect because it describes a reactant, and Fe^{2+} – SOD is not a reactant. (B) is incorrect because it describes a product, and Fe^{2+} – SOD is not a product. (C) is correct because it describes a catalyst, which is exactly the role Fe^{2+} – SOD plays. (D) describes a transition state, and is incorrect because transition states are temporary states of highest energy of the conversion of reactant to product.

12. B

(A) is true because particles must collide to react, and thus the rate of reaction is both dependent on and proportional to the number of particles colliding. (B) is not true (making it the correct answer) because all the colliding particles must have enough kinetic energy to exceed activation energy if a collision is to be effective. (C) is the accurate definition of a transition state. (D) is true because "activated complex" is another name for "transition state," which by definition has greater energy than both reactants and products.

13. C

Section C shows the energy that must be put into the reaction to drive it in a forward direction. Section A in the diagram represents the change in enthalpy; it shows the difference between the starting and the final energy values. Section B does not represent any specific energy value. Section D represents the reverse activation energy. It is much greater than the forward activation energy because the reactant is starting at a much lower level of energy, yet must still reach the same amount of total energy to proceed with the reaction.

14. A

Section A is correct because it shows the difference between the starting and the final energy values.

15. A

The equation to determine the equilibrium constant for a reaction aA + bB = cC + dD is $K_c = ([C]^c[D]^d)/([A]^a[B]^b)$. For this reaction, $K_c = ([2]^1[1]^1)/([3]^2[1]^2) = 2/9 = 0.22$. When the corresponding values are plugged into the equation, $K_c = 2/9$, or 0.22.

16. C

(C) is correct because an increase in pressure will cause an equilibrium to shift toward the side of the reaction with fewer moles of gas, which in this case is the right side of the equation. An increase in volume (A) would have no effect or would cause a decrease in pressure, shifting the equilibrium to the left. An addition of product (B) would also cause a shift to the left. A temperature decrease (D) would most likely cause a shift to the left due to fewer numbers of collisions between particles, assuming kinetic energy is proportional to temperature.

QUESTIONS 17–21

17. B

The question says that latent heat flux is caused by evaporation. Therefore, simply identify which value of ΔH is related to this phase change. Vaporization is another way of saying evaporation, so (B) is correct. Fusion (A) refers to the change from a solid to a liquid, and sublimation (C) refers to the change from a solid to a gas. Ionization (D) is unrelated to a phase change.

18. C

The centripetal acceleration is equivalent to the tangential velocity squared divided by the radius or [(10 m/s)^2 divided by 10 m = 10 m/s^2]. Because the tangential acceleration vector is parallel to the tangential velocity vector, and the centripetal acceleration is perpendicular to the direction of velocity, the vector sum will provide the angle between the velocity and acceleration vectors. Because the tangential acceleration is equivalent to the centripetal acceleration, the velocity and acceleration vectors are 45° apart.

19. A

The question requires you to know the solubility rules. Because an electrolyte must dissociate into its component ions in water, look for the substance that will not dissolve. The answer is (A), silver chloride (AgCl), which is insoluble in water. All of the other compounds will readily dissociate into their constituent ions.

20. A

(A) is correct. Because aluminum oxide is alkaline, immersion in an acidic solution would readily strip away the protective coating and allow the acid to oxidize the metal below.

21. D

How can you relate the average velocities of gases at the same temperature? Two gases at the same temperature will have the same average molecular kinetic energy. Because two gases at the same temperature will have the same average molecular kinetic energy, $(1/2)m_A v_A^2 = (1/2)m_B v_B^2$, which gives $m_B/m_A = (v_A/v_B)^2$. Since $v_A/v_B = 2$, we have $m_B/m_A = 4$. Only (D) lists two gases with a mass ratio around 4:1 (krypton 83.3g/mol and neon 20.2 g/mol).

PASSAGE III

22. D

The solid block becomes smaller in the experiment and so must move from the solid phase to the gaseous phase, sublimation. The other answer choices require a liquid phase, which is not valid because the experimental results demonstrate that no liquid was detected when the solid shrunk in size.

23. A

The solid/liquid equilibrium line is sloped positively and so the phase change from liquid to solid at a constant temperature is the only correct possible phase change. (B) is wrong because the gas phase is not possible as pressure increases; the liquid would change to gas, however, if the temperature were increased while maintaining constant pressure. (C) and (D) are illogical because kinetic energy is equivalent to temperature. Because temperature is constant according to the question stem, there is no kinetic energy change.

24. A

You must deduce from both the experimental results and the chemical equation that the volume does not change. The volume does not change because it is described as a rigid container, and no change in volume is described in the experimental results. As a result, the dry ice must absorb energy from its surrounding (the air in the container) in order to change phase. Because the total energy must remain constant, the air initially present in the container must lose an equivalent amount of kinetic energy.

25. B

The chemical equation shows that the dry ice absorbs heat from its environment to change into a gas, requiring it to overcome the intermolecular forces that organize it in the solid form. (C) and (D) refer to hydrogen bonds, which are not present in carbon dioxide.

26. A

The chemical equation shows that the heat of room temperature ambient air must be absorbed to change the carbon dioxide from solid to gas. This use of heat defines an endothermic reaction, which must therefore characterize the reaction occurring in the container. (C) and (D) refer to an exothermic reaction, which would release heat. (B) is incorrect since an endothermic reaction absorbs/uses heat, which increases the energy of some of the molecules in the reaction; thus, the potential energy should not decrease.

27. A

The air gains dry ice molecules and these exert a pressure on the container, according to the equation PV = nRT, where n represents the number of moles of gas. (B) is the opposite; its volume would increase, according to the same equation if possible. However this experiment takes place in a rigid container, preventing any change in volume. (C) is incorrect because the question clearly states that the solid changes phase. Air temperature decreases with this endothermic reaction, absorbing heat to change from a solid to gas carbon dioxide (D).

28. D

None of the choices shows a substance moving from the solid directly to the gas phase in the process of sublimation. (A) and (B) show fusion and evaporation, respectively, but not sublimation. (C) indicates the heating of a gas; in the experiment, the carbon dioxide solid is increased in its kinetic energy; the gas is not being heated.

29. C

(C) indicates change from a solid to a gas as described in the passage for dry ice, which is called sublimation.

QUESTIONS 30-36

30. D

Because $\Delta G = \Delta H - T\Delta S$ can be used to relate free energy to enthalpy and entropy, and T is always positive, a negative ΔH (enthalpy) and a positive ΔS (entropy) will always give a negative ΔG value; that is, the reaction will occur spontaneously. (D) is correct.

31. C

Moving from left to right across the periodic table, atomic radii will decrease. Because calcium is on the left side of the table and gallium is on the right, in the same period, gallium should have a smaller atomic radius. As stated in (C), this is due to the greater number of protons in the nucleus holding the electrons more tightly.

32. D

The major forces that cause gases to deviate from ideal behavior are intermolecular attractions and the volume of the gas molecules. These factors are minimized when gas molecules are far apart and moving quickly, which occurs at low pressures and high temperatures, (D).

33. A

The question says that this gas is ideal, so use PV = nRT. The ideal gas law shows that P is directly proportional to T. So with volume held constant, if pressure is reduced by a factor of 2, temperature will also be reduced by a factor of 2. (A) is correct.

34. D

Though this question begins by telling you about greenhouse gases, it ultimately asks you to identify similarities between CO_2 and H_2O which N_2 and O_2 lack. CO_2 is not a polar molecule; its linear geometry allows the opposing dipole moments to cancel out, so (A) is incorrect. Because its dipole moments cancel, (B) is incorrect. Furthermore, it lacks hydrogen atoms and is therefore incapable of hydrogen bonding, so (C) is incorrect. However, both CO_2 and H_2O have polar bonds, while N_2 and O_2 both have diatomic, nonpolar covalent bonds between two atoms of the same element.

35. D

Fluorine (A) is not a transition metal, so its ionized counterparts will have an valence octet of electrons implying no unpaired electrons. (B), (C), (D) are all transition metals; however (B) and (C), commonly oxidize to the 2 and 3 positive states, respectively, which fill their d subshells. Iron (D) commonly oxidizes to the 2 positive state, which gives one extra s-subshell electron. This unpaired electron helps to give iron its magnetic properties and explains why iron in the body is further oxidized to the 3 positive state (to avoid inductive currents that could damage protein structure).

36. D

Chromium is an exception to the general rule that the 3d-subshell is filled completely before the 4s-subshell. The 3d-subshell partially fills, then the 4s-subshell fills completely and finally the 3d-subshell finishes filling. (B) is incorrect because the nearest noble gas to Cr is Ar not Kr.

PASSAGE IV

37. A

Henry's law states that the amount of gas dissolved in a liquid is directly proportional to the partial pressure of the gas in equilibrium with the liquid. Therefore, Henry's law can be used to calculate the concentration of oxygen in water using the partial pressure of oxygen in air. Boyle's law (B) deals with the relationship between the pressure and volume of gases but does not address concentration of gases in water. Raoult's law (C) pertains to the vapor pressure of a mixture of liquids, not a gas

dissolved in a liquid. Le Châtelier's principle (D) addresses changes to an equilibrium state and cannot stand alone to explain the equilibrium between a gas in air and in solution.

38. C

We can use the solubility constant for nitrogen provided in the passage, 8.42×10^{-7} M/torr, to solve this question. Because the units in the constant are in torr, we first convert 0.634 atm to torr by multiplying by 760 torr/1 atm. The partial pressure of nitrogen equals 481.8 torr. Multiplying the pressure by the constant 8.42×10^{-7} M/torr gives us 4.06×10^{-4} M nitrogen. The units for the answer are in g/L, so we multiply by the molar mass of nitrogen, 28 g/mole, to get our answer of 1.14×10^{-2} g/L.

39. B

The solubility constants provided in the passage can be used to determine that helium is the least soluble gas. A soluble gas is not desired because we want to minimize gas bubbles in the body. Moreover, helium is an inert gas, meaning it does readily react with other gases. Whether helium is diatomic (A) has no bearing on its use in scuba tanks. Many gases are present in trace amounts in the water (D), so this fact alone could not account for the use of helium in scuba tanks.

40. B

This is a classic ideal gas law problem using PV = nRT. You are given the volume, then must convert the temperature to degrees Kelvin to obtain a useable temperature and must convert the mass of oxygen to moles to find n. P equals 2.80 L. T equals 273.15 + 13.0 = 286.15 K. The mass, 0.320 kg, equals 320 grams. We divide the mass by the molar mass of oxygen, 32 g/mole, to obtain the moles of oxygen, 10 moles. R equals 0.0821 L atm/(mole K). Plugging in these numbers to the equation, PV = nRT. Solving for P gives a pressure of 83.9 atm.

41. D

Immediate isolation in a hyperbaric chamber is the most effective and common treatment for those suffering from severe decompression sickness. The chamber recreates a high-pressure environment to allow gas bubbles to dissolve back into body fluids and tissues. The chamber can be brought back to normal pressure slowly in order to allow the body to adjust to the decreased pressure. Helium gas administration (A) or gas and air mixture (B) would not rid the body of excess gas bubbles. In fact, it might increase the gases bubbles and make symptoms worse. A hypobaric chamber (C) would certainly make symptoms worse because it decreases the pressure below 1 atm.

42. C

The solubility of gas in liquids decreases with an increase in liquid temperature. The warming of oceans has resulted in less dissolved oxygen and many oxygen-depleted "dead zones." It is true that carbon dioxide has increased ocean acidity (A), but acidity alone cannot account for decreased oxygen levels. A predator shark may explain why certain fish are dying off (B), but it would not explain the decrease in oxygen. If rainfall did increase water levels in the ocean (D), the oxygen levels would equilibrate (as per Henry's law) between the ocean and atmosphere to allow more dissolved oxygen in the oceans.

43. C

This is a PV = nRT problem. Find the moles of oxygen by converting 0.38 kg to grams and dividing by the molar mass of oxygen, 32.g/mole. The number of moles equals 11.875. STP indicates a temperature of 273.15 K and a pressure of 1 atm. R equals 0.0821 (L atm/mole K). Plugging these numbers into PV = nRT and solving for V gives a volume of 266 L.

44. B

Multiplying the amount of nitrogen gas in the air by the solubility constant of nitrogen will give the amount of nitrogen that is dissolved in the diver's blood. The solubility constant for nitrogen can be obtained by dividing the solubility of nitrogen, 6.2×10^{-4} M, by 1 atm to get 6.2×10^{-4} M/atm. The amount of nitrogen in the air can be obtained by finding the partial pressure of nitrogen. The total pressure, 3 atm, is multiplied by the percentage of nitrogen in the air, 78 percent, to get a partial pressure of nitrogen equal to 2.3 atm. Finally, we multiply 2.3 atm of nitrogen by the solubility constant to obtain a value of 1.4×10^{-3} M for the concentration of nitrogen in the diver's blood.

45. A

The root mean square velocity (v_{rms}) can be calculated by taking the square root of ($3RT/M_m$). This equation tells us that the v_{rms} increases when molar mass decreases. Tank 2 contains a mixture of helium and oxygen; the helium will lower the average molar mass of the gas molecules because it has a lower molar mass compared to oxygen. The v_{rms} of tank 2 will therefore be higher. Tank 1, which contains only oxygen, will have a higher molar mass and a lower v_{rms} value.

PASSAGE V

46. D

F- is related to less acid production and reduces the risk of dental caries, choice (D). The fluoride ion is related to acid production and reduces the risk of dental caries, according to the passage. Fluoride has not been proven to directly cause or even be related to bacterial death (B, D), nor has it directly been proven to stop bacteria from forming dental caries (A). However, fluoride is related to/correlated with acidity reduction and dental caries reduction. The other choices imply relationships and causations not inferred from the passage.

47. D

The high electronegativity of fluorine means that it is inclined to hold onto or pull electrons. (C) is the opposite of this atomic property because fluorine would not easily give off electrons. While the passage discusses fissures as a cause of caries (A) and (B), it does not infer that fluoride is involved directly with its filling or repair.

48. A

You must deduce from the definition of electronegativity that in order for the nucleus to pull on the orbital electrons, it should be closer to the electrons; therefore, a smaller radius is desirable. (B), (C), and (D) all contribute to a decrease in electronegativity because the distractors either favor a larger size of the atom with more electron shells or a smaller positive core of the protons that are responsible for the electronegative attraction in the first place.

49. C

The fluoride ion has the atomic structure of the element fluorine, which would be $1s^2 2s^2 2p^5$, with an additional electron to make it an anion with a charge of negative one. Using [He] at the beginning of the notation accurately reflects the fact that F⁻ has the same structure as helium, but with the additional shells as noted. (A) is incorrect because this is the notation for the element fluoride, not the ion. (B) is the structure for oxygen. (D) is incorrect because when using the notation [Ne], one implies that the atom has the structure of that noble gas, with additional shells. [Ne] comes after fluorine in the periodic table, and it would not be correct to add a level 2 shell after completing that shell in [Ne].

50. D

(D) is correct because Heisenberg's uncertainty principle states that the momentum (m and v) cannot be determined exactly and quantitatively if the location of an electron in an atom is known

and conversely, the location cannot be known if the momentum is known. One could get a qualitative measurement of momentum, since the measurement is still possible, but simple becomes less accurate as the accuracy of the measurement of position increases. (A), (B) and (C) all violate this principle, as the location is stated to be known in the stem of the item.

51. A

The effective nuclear charge is calculated by the following equation: $Z_{eff} = Z - S$, where Z is the atomic number (the number of protons in the nucleus), and S is the average number of electrons between the nucleus and the electron in question. Because fluorine's atomic number is 9 and there are 9 electrons in this element, the outermost electron in fluorine (not an ion), would have a Z_{eff} of the following: $Z_{eff} = 9 - 8 = +1$. However, in the fluoride anion, an additional electron has been added, so the $Z_{eff} = 9 - 9 = 0$. (B) would require an additional electron between the nucleus and the outermost electron, and (D) is impossible because no protons/electrons would allow a calculation of ½ of a unit of charge.

52. B

(B) is correct because the highest electron shells, or orbitals, are most loosely held by the nucleons and thus are most available for bonding. 3s is higher than any other level (A), but it is unoccupied in the fluoride ion. (C) and (D) are lower energy levels/orbitals than 2p.

INDEX